Iris Murdoch
and the
Moral Imagination

Iris Murdoch and the Moral Imagination

Essays

Edited by M.F. Simone Roberts *and* Alison Scott-Baumann

McFarland & Company, Inc., Publishers
Jefferson, North Carolina, and London

Acknowledgments of Permissions to Reprint

From *Metaphysics as a Guide to Morals* by Iris Murdoch, copyright © 1993 by Iris Murdoch. Used by permission of Penguin, a division of Penguin Group (USA) Inc.

From *Existentialists and Mystics* by Iris Murdoch, copyright © 1950–52, © 1956–59, 1961–62, 1966, 1969–70, 1972, 1977, 1978, 1986, 1997 by Iris Murdoch. Used by permission of Penguin, a division of Penguin Group (USA) Inc.

From *Metaphysics and a Guide to Morals* by Iris Murdoch © 1992, published by Chatto & Windus. Reprinted by permission of the Random House Group Ltd.

From *Existentialists and Mystics* by Iris Murdoch © 1997, published by Chatto & Windus. Reprinted by permission of the Random House Group Ltd.

From *The Sea, the Sea* by Iris Murdoch, published by Chatto & Windus. Reprinted by permission of the Random House Group Ltd.

From *Sartre: Romantic Rationalist* by Iris Murdoch, published by Chatto & Windus. Reprinted by permission of the Random House Group Ltd.

Jacob Wrestling with the Angel (1659) by Rembrandt, reproduced with permission of BPK / Gemäldegalerie, Staatliche Museen zu Berlin. Photograph: Jörg P. Anders.

"Enchantment, Transformation, and Rebirth in the Green Knight" by Sharon R. Wilson, copyright © 2008, Palgrave, reproduced with permission of Palgrave Macmillan.

Sections of "Morality, the Visual Arts, and Rembrandt, in Iris Murdoch's *Under the Net* and Zadie Smith's *On Beauty*" from *Iris Murdoch and the Visual Arts* by Anne Rowe, copyright © 2002 Edwin Mellen Press, reprinted by permission of the Edwin Mellen Press.

LIBRARY OF CONGRESS CATALOGUING-IN-PUBLICATION DATA

Iris Murdoch and the moral imagination : essays / edited by M.F. Simone Roberts and Alison Scott-Baumann.
    p.   cm.
Includes bibliographical references and index.

ISBN 978-0-7864-4026-9
softcover : 50# alkaline paper ∞

1. Murdoch, Iris—Criticism and interpretation. 2. Murdoch, Iris—Philosophy. 3. Postmodernism (Literature) I. Roberts, M.F. Simone, 1968– II. Scott-Baumann, Alison.
PR6063.U7Z7135   2010
823'.914—dc22   2010016696

British Library cataloguing data are available

©2010 M.F. Simone Roberts and Alison Scott-Baumann. All rights reserved

No part of this book may be reproduced or transmitted in any form or by any means, electronic or mechanical, including photocopying or recording, or by any information storage and retrieval system, without permission in writing from the publisher.

Front cover: Rembrandt, *Jacob Wrestling with the Angel*, oil on canvas, 54" × 45⅝", 1659.

Manufactured in the United States of America

McFarland & Company, Inc., Publishers
  Box 611, Jefferson, North Carolina 28640
    www.mcfarlandpub.com

Table of Contents

Introduction: *A Cheerful and Encouraging Element in a Confusing Scene*
    M.F. SIMONE ROBERTS *and* ALISON SCOTT-BAUMANN   1

1 — Two Women in Dark Times
    FRANCES WHITE   13

2 — A Third Sense of Ethics Between Fiction and Philosophy
    AMY SMITH   34

3 — Narrative and Symbolic Layering in *The Unicorn*
    JUDIT VARGA   53

4 — Morality, Visual Arts, and Rembrandt in Iris Murdoch's *Under the Net* and Zadie Smith's *On Beauty*
    ANNE ROWE   74

5 — Enchantment, Transformation, and Rebirth in *The Green Knight*
    SHARON R. WILSON   92

6 — Messy Is Flourishing Is Sublime
    M.F. SIMONE ROBERTS   107

7 — Domination, Resistance, and Anglo-Irish Landlordism in *The Servants and the Snow*
    WEI H. KAO   127

8 — Nausea Under the Net
    ALISON SCOTT-BAUMANN   147

9 — Suffering and Contentment
    TONY MILLIGAN   168

10 — A Subterranean Dialogue with Nietzsche on the Demonic and Divine in *The Sea, the Sea*
    PETER MATHEWS   190

11 — Naturalism and the Good
    JOHN HACKER-WRIGHT   203
12 — Morality in a World Without God
    MILES LEESON   221

Conclusion: A Meditation in Swerves
    LUISA MURARO   237
Bibliography   251
About the Contributors   261
Index   263

Introduction: A Cheerful and Encouraging Element in a Confusing Scene[1]

M.F. SIMONE ROBERTS *and*
ALISON SCOTT-BAUMANN

The book in your hands, reader, was conceived several years ago when we met at the annual conference of the Modern Language Association. Our panel on Murdoch was one of those Sunday at 8 P.M. panels at the exhausted end of the conference. We two decided, basically because we took an instant liking to each other, to send out a call for papers and see what happened next. We got lucky. We have assembled for you a group of authors who reflect the cosmopolitan nature of Murdoch's vision. We believe that Dame Iris Murdoch — writer of some twenty-six novels, winner of the Booker Prize for *The Sea, the Sea*, and author of two collections of philosophical essays and a monograph on Sartre — deserves more attention as a philosopher and novelist who understood both Europe and America and was a truly European thinker. Her characters are firmly rooted in England, occasionally in Ireland, and her thinking was very strongly influenced by that of Continental Europe. Her relationship with America was weaker. On several occasions in her books she exiled characters to America, and she herself found it hard to gain entry to America as a result of past membership of the Communist Party, which perhaps lends a touch of gentle irony to her comment that "Henry James' characters very often regard Europe as a wicked, dark place whereas America is a place of innocence and clarity and moral goodness."[2]

She regarded Ludwig Leferrier, the American in *An Accidental Man*, as a redemptive character; he reverses his self-imposed exile from America as a draft dodger of the Vietnam war, and returns because it is morally right to face his fate. She admitted that she only "shadowily touched America in one or two of the books," and Conradi reports a distinct ambivalence on her part towards America.[3] Yet it is clear from the work of Bove, Antonaccio, Schweiker and others that Murdoch creates literature and philosophy that resonates strongly with Americans and Britons. Murdoch's reputation is moving onto a global stage with the Italian translation of *Existentialists and Mystics,* with conferences in Turkey and Portugal, as well as with some reportedly troubled engagements in Romania that seem to be a matter of difficulties in translation.[4] It would seem that careful translation would be the next stage in Murdoch studies and would likely inaugurate a host of rich conversations between cultural others.

This collection enters a growing and robust scene. New about this collection is its coherent analysis that shows how Murdoch developed a moral imagination that was indelibly imprinted with modern European thought (including her uneasy relationship with her own Irish heritage) and yet communicates her vision fluently to her primary audiences in America and Britain. Moreover, many of our authors distance themselves from previous orthodoxies in Murdoch criticism and open new vistas for reading her work in both disciplines.

This collection focuses on moral imaginations: not only where Murdoch's thinking comes from, or what we can say about it in relation to the traditions and disciplines she engages, but also where our engagements with her work take us. In ways both overt and subtle, the essays collected here want more than to investigate problems, but to creep or run toward imagining responses to them. Such gestures are necessarily partial, polyvalent, contingent, and tentative, but for all that the authors here vigorously propose their readings of this imagination. Like Murdoch's "messy reality," a fully engaged, moral and critical imagination is open to the future and thus must accept the partiality of its efforts. Murdoch tirelessly revealed the egoistic fantasy of the solitary subject, the tightly structured circle of the philosophical ideal that is closed to the future, to reality, to the other. Each of these essays engages imagination in the strong sense we have in mind: they trace Murdoch's imaginative processes, or suggest implications of her work for our own imaginations, or enact and engage those implications for themselves. In each case, the authors assembled here want us to see Murdoch in reality, and through that process to see our realities more clearly. We include in the concept of imagination here the kind of reason that seeks not only its own establishment, but the terms on which it may engage with others, the ways in which our egos must imagine their own well-being to continue through attention to the other. We take these intellectual and ethical gestures to have some structural kinship. Several of these essays address that kinship directly, the rest in degrees of obliqueness. On questions of aesthetic, philosophical, and historical imagination, these essays reach both backward and forward in time, through critical and imaginative gestures, to suggest harmonies that ethical becoming calls us to create. They are as interdisciplinary as Murdoch's own work, reaching for new combinations of tools, even the invention of new tools, for engaging with the dilemmas of human being.

For readers new to Murdoch's work, some contextualization is in order.

She trained in philosophy at Oxford alongside philosophers of the ordinary language and also the analytical school. Her education and career coincided with most of the major developments in the European century's thought, and Murdoch insisted on cutting her own path in it. Admiring analytical philosophy for its insistence on clarity, and phenomenology (with Husserl, for instance) for its insistence on complexity, Murdoch set herself the task of a philosophy adequate to being human that valued both clarity and complexity. In accordance with these dual commitments and her advice to us to learn to see clearly realities outside of our own being and desire, Murdoch engaged philosophers from Kant and Hegel to Sartre and Heidegger with an eye to retaining the elements of their thought that contribute to that ability. We believe that she deserves renewed attention as a European thinker. Mary Midgley, a friend of Iris and also a formidable philosopher, comments upon Murdoch's discussion of existentialism as being rooted in a much wider European tradition than Sartre alone:

> Under the term "existentialism" she includes, of course, a wide tradition stretching from Dostoevsky, Kierkegaard and Nietzsche to Heidegger and Sartre, a tradition that is less mentioned to-day than it used to be simply because its cruder elements are by now accepted and taken for granted. They are also echoed in a different accent by American libertarians.[5]

It is one of the emergent themes of this book that Murdoch's combinatory path and her sometimes unfashionable independence of thought make a good model for interdependence in both literary and philosophical studies, and this needs to be seen in the context of continental European thought as well as within the Anglo-American tradition of modern literature.

Readers familiar with Murdoch and recent trends such as the ethical turn in philosophical and literary studies will find it only sensible that interest in Murdoch has picked up since the late 1990s because Murdoch is precisely interested in questions of ethics (as understanding, representing, and enacting progress in openness to the other) in and *of* both philosophy and literature. The new Centre for Murdoch Studies at Kingston University, England, and its three anthologies and online bibliography go a long way toward reinforcing this interest, under the impressive leadership of Anne Rowe. Our book hopes to further both discussions of ethics in these disciplines and of Murdoch's work generally.

In our attempt to keep faith with Murdoch's work, we collected essays addressing three broad areas: aesthetic, philosophical, and historical imagination. For readers familiar with Murdoch's own themes and questions, this will be no surprise. Her breadth and depth of thinking rivals that of most writer-philosophers, and surpasses some. Almost all of these essays deliberately seek to open new spaces for thinking with and about Murdoch, spaces in both philosophy and literature. Several of the essays are comparative, of the Murdoch and Insert-Philosopher variety. We chose to use those essays as connections between the "sections," as they made a good introduction or conclusion to a cluster of essays.

We open with a comparative piece, Frances White's "Two Women in Dark Times." White considers the parallels between the lives and work of Iris Murdoch and Hannah Arendt, and the biographical element of this essay recommended it as the opening gesture on behalf of readers new to Murdoch studies. To those more familiar, the parallels and perpendiculars between Murdoch and Arendt will be arresting in themselves. White's essay also performs one of the common gestures across this collection, that of opening new ground for other writers and critics, in this case by describing "deep and abiding connections between the lives and thoughts of these two women." Rather than concentrating solely on the biographical particulars and scandals of these women's lives (both had their share), White presents Arendt's relationship with Heidegger and Murdoch's relationship with Canetti in terms of the women's intellectual development — development not to be dismissed as Arendt was the first woman to present a Gifford Lecture at Oxford in 1972–74, and Murdoch the second in 1981–82. Arendt was Heidegger's student, and Murdoch engaged deeply, though incompletely, with Heidegger's work in her unpublished manuscript, *Heidegger: The Pursuit of Being*. It is here that the philosophers' paths track and cross each other. Both concern themselves with questions of good and evil and of moral philosophy, both consciously in shadow of the Holocaust's irredeemable human violence and unmooring of the West's sense of itself as a civilization. While the two think for the same goal: love and respect between persons and societies, the security of the right of people to exist as humans, White details for us the vast differences in their paths and conclusions. Arendt finds that "it is not private personal virtue which will provide the means of protection for vulnerable persons, but public political strength." Murdoch, on the other hand, holds that no political system can make people good, but that "it is only by striving after absolute goodness that individuals will be enabled to resist the kind of evil which results in persecution, concentration camps and genocide. Political well-being and personal virtue go hand in hand: the former cannot be created or sustained in the absence of the latter."

The particular fascination of White's essay is that she reads the differences between these thinkers with her own moral imagination, sees their thought as part of their lives, and vice versa — takes these women and work for the complicated wholes that they are — and sets them in a carefully detailed, respectful but cooperative relationship to each other for the sake of all of us.

In her contribution, "A Third Sense of Ethics Between Fiction and Philosophy," Amy Smith argues that by reading the "inconsistencies" between the moral pronouncements in favor of reality's difficulty and the sometimes archetypal characters Murdoch draws, a reader will find a third or fuller ethical position emerging. Readers are engaged in a paradox (Murdoch says to do *this*, yet her fictions do *that*); however, the position is not systematic, but experiential.

In her philosophy she is highly critical of form, or the closed circle of philosophical thought and the illusions both rhetorical and logical of a radical freedom, rationality, and autonomy; while at the same time, her novels seem almost too artfully formed or "overly plotted," especially for a philosopher who wants us to recognize, live, and learn to think in life's contingent and surprising mess. That mess, Smith argues, is an overwhelming and unmanageable situation on a par with the sublime making on us rather similar ethical demands. In her ethics, Murdoch insists on realism and reality, the messy, contingent, disobedient world and the people in it. In her fiction, however, her characters often closely follow the mythic types and stories on which they are based: Dionysus, the Great Mother, Medusa, for example. Smith finds that the non-realism of Murdoch's fiction is itself a kind of realism, but of the way people see each other through myths and roles, and the conflicts generated by the friction between these fantasies of others, their fantasies of us, and our independent realities. The whole of Murdoch's ethics is not in her philosophy and failed by her fiction, but lies rather in the completion of each by the other.

An essay on the fiction that places itself squarely in the uses Murdoch makes of paradox is Judit Varga's "Narrative and Symbolic Layering in *The Unicorn*." Her interest is in inscrutability, the difficulty this novel performs concerning even the most sincere efforts at living with the reality of others. The nexus of this exploration is Hannah Crean-Smith: "As each plot characterizes Hannah according to its own context, she comes to act as a decorporealized mirror image that reflects the meanings projected on her by *The Unicorn*'s different narrative discourses." One of the problems for both readers and characters in the novel is that the imposition of our meaning, our narratives, onto Hannah participates in her own voluntary "death" while the novel argues (against the symbol of the unicorn, a creature that is only narrative) that to be in the narrative flow is to be alive. Varga finds that buried in the layers of intersecting gothic and romance plots, under the unicorn and Lilith and the Ate, there may be no Hannah after all; that like a Baudrillardian simulacrum, Hannah has been made and made of herself a pure image, a person without a reality to report. She can be gazed upon, but not seen. This condition only serves to point up the postmodernity of the novel. Characters do not develop their own plots or narratives (live, that is, in the terms of a novel) but move from one narrative motif to another, one type to another: innocent to initiated, hero to villain, from the legend of the unicorn to the legend of the Fisher King, and so forth. After reading Varga's essay, one finds that in *The Unicorn*, while one may want to capture plot, what one cannot capture is the other — she or he will often disappear into illusion and puzzlement before rendering up their reality, whether that illusion is chosen or imposed.

Another facet of Murdoch's making of meaning is her work with the visual arts, especially that of Rembrandt. In "Morality, Visual Arts, and Rembrandt in Iris Murdoch's *Under the Net* and Zadie Smith's *On Beauty*," Anne

Rowe considers the relations of both novelists to the visual arts and attempts to locate Smith as an heir to Murdoch. For both, the arts and the novel provide a space in which to consider our relations to our own becoming and that of others. Murdoch wants us "seeing the world in all its unutterable particularity and reflecting that truth in art, [so] the novelist performs a moral function by moving the reader emotionally in a sublime moment of experience that is both exhilarating and painful, and makes the 'otherness' of others breathtakingly evident." Smith too understands the novel as a moral laboratory, and is frustrated at "the contemporary embarrassment about the affective response to literature that Murdoch could expound on unapologetically decades before ('I would include the rousing of emotions in the *definition* of art')." To this end, both novelists call on the visual arts to constitute a texture in both the narrative and tone of their works. Focusing on engagements with Rembrandt, whom both find a paragon of moral attention to human particularity, Rowe demonstrates how the authors read paintings into their novels, and how the novels read paintings. Both authors accomplish this dialogue through encounters and discussions by characters and with the use of paintings as symbolic sources of the narratives in which the characters chart their courses, learning or failing to learn their lessons.

Closing our section on aesthetics, Sharon R. Wilson's essay, "Enchantment, Transformation, and Rebirth in *The Green Knight*," picks up on Varga's exploration of narrative layering by tracing the astonishingly rich intertextuality at work in *The Green Knight*. It is possible that in an era of literary study concerned with the postmodern novel, *The Green Knight*'s embroidery of fairytale and myth into its plots, characterizations, and motifs may have distracted critics from the richly postmodern uses to which these allusions and intertexts are put. Wilson brings us a Murdoch who is more postmodern than has often been noted, and whose sense of literary intertext should frustrate philosophers who wish to read her characters as mouthing Murdoch's philosophical positions, which is more difficult to do once the "unreliability and irony of [her] third person centers-of-consciousness" are recognized. Following on these insights, Wilson challenges the prevailing view of Murdoch's fiction as realist and attempting to refer to objective reality by explicating the intertextual gestures in *The Green Knight* that help to create the nearly mythic *mise en scène* in which characters, like so many in Murdoch's oeuvre, "feel enchanted, under a magic spell, and either awaiting rescue or salvation or assuming that they are able to rescue" another. Often Murdoch's characters can be accused of treating each other as characters in their own rebirth myths, and this sense of enchantment is one that many characters use to excuse their lack of ethical attention, or of love, to the realities of other people.

Between aesthetics and politics, Simone Roberts's "Messy Is Flourishing Is Sublime" seeks to open a dialogue between readers of two utterly divergent women philosophers. Iris Murdoch was no fan of what she called "the deconstructionists," and Luce Irigaray would have squarely qualified as one in Murdoch's view. More, Murdoch writes in a very wide humanist vein, thinking about persons general in her philosophy, where Irigaray begins her philosophical work arguing that to do so is necessarily to miss half the story of persons general: women. Murdoch's concern that we all "unself" and open our stubborn, defensive egos to the being of the other in the midst of life's contingent and ever shifting mess, however, finds a friend in Irigaray's gendered sense of philosophy. Roberts outlines how Irigaray's attempt to describe a world of "being two" cooperates, unexpectedly, with Murdoch's insistence that to be loving and ethical we must get out of our own way. In their ways, both philosophers want philosophy (and its attendant cultures) to move into the mess, where flourishing can happen, where the sublime can be found between selves, especially gendered and positively valued particular selves.

While Roberts thinks about gender and Murdoch's thought, Wei H. Kao considers one of Murdoch's few direct engagements with class and Irishness. Though her novels are filled with characters from various class backgrounds, her central characters are usually middle class and educated, but not in the play Kao considers in "Domination, Resistance, and Anglo-Irish Landlordism in *The Servants and the Snow."* Kao reads the play as examining a combination of the Hegelian Master-slave dialectic and Freudian theory of sadomasochism to demonstrate the complexities of oppression: the curious way that parties involved can come to need, and find satisfying, even as they resist, a system damaging to them. Through a series of interactions both political and erotic, Basil's attempts to liberalize (though not liberate) his servants fail utterly. As the newly arrived master, he must negotiate traditions that include various bodily disciplines and the sexual exploitation of his servants (established by a tyrannical father whose practices Basil seeks to revise), and finds that his position as landlord is nearly unrecognizable to the servants without these practices. Though the most socially marginalized character in the play, the traveler Patrice is the only person able to meet the Hegelian requirement for freedom from this dialectic, staking his life. Kao finds that the near sexual pleasure the servants take at the opportunity to punish Patrice for an infraction reinforces the interweaving of political and sexual structures Murdoch explores, and in this case, finds tragically insurmountable. The play depicts the effort and failure of moral imagination.

Alison Scott-Baumann offers our third reading of Murdoch alongside another philosopher. Her essay, "Nausea Under the Net," considers Murdoch's view of Sartre, examining Murdoch's work through her engagement with him as a moral philosopher. Particularly, Scott-Baumann focuses on Murdoch's critique of negativity, denial, lack, loss and nothingness — and the neurosis that can accompany them — in light of Murdoch's analysis of Sartre's practice as a novelist and responses to him in her fiction. After placing Murdoch in the context of twentieth century philosophy the author argues that Murdoch admired

Sartre's failed attempt to resolve the perhaps too rigid antinomies of Kant and the perhaps too unifying force of Hegel's dialectic. But, at the same time, Murdoch is highly critical of the moral implications of the "sense of absolutism that pervades Sartre's writings, together with revulsion towards other people for their unpredictability, their bodily presence and the sheer otherness with which their flesh endows them. This is balanced by self-loathing: self-knowledge is negative and destructive." To do this, Murdoch examines Sartre's fiction alongside his philosophy and finds, for instance, that characters like Roquentin, "[experience] many nightmare moments of trying to achieve [an] Hegelian totalization, a sense of control of the world and its negative pull." This impossibility can trigger both narcissism and neurosis. Murdoch demonstrates Sartre's unethical use of stylistic exaggeration when he challenges "the accuracy of our perceptions by telling us we are deceived and he can therefore tell us what to think." Rather than simply write fiction that rejects Sartre's existentialism, or simply ignores his practice as a novelist, Scott-Baumann finds that Murdoch "takes Sartre's negativity and populates his 'void at the centre' with characters that play out the tension between *his* negativity and *her* love of life."

In "Suffering and Contentment," Tony Milligan considers the suspicion in much of moral philosophy of the participation of happiness/contentment in a life dedicated to the good and Murdoch's negotiations with this problem. Milligan argues that Murdoch's sense of unselfing—making room in the self for the reality of the other—has a dual nature: a movement into or welcome of various discomforts and toward a "vulnerable contentment." He admits that Murdoch leaves the discovery of these contentments to us and our experience. After all, on pain of hypocrisy, she cannot tell us how to live our realities. The ego in its narcissism is a stubborn thing, and Murdoch acknowledges this by calling its suffering "real deathly" and an "absolutely deathly pain." However, this pain is, like other experiences, temporary and rather unglamorous. The trouble is, Milligan points out, that the tone and feeling of Murdoch's philosophical essays leads readers to feel that she is concerned for our happiness, even if Murdoch's is the explicit goal of "being good *for nothing*." Experiencing contentment beyond the self-absorption of the ego comes in the process of moral courage expressed in our every day lives, in our every day ways of "holding the demands of the self at bay," even as we some times fail to do so. That failure returns us to the need for our courage, our ability to leave room for the reality of others, which can lead to various contentments. It is, after all, possible that to have the fortitude of this courage, one would require some consolations and contentments in order to be available to others' realities.

Peter Matthews takes the Booker Prize winning novel *The Sea, the Sea* and moves away from discussions of Shakespeare's *The Tempest* and Zen Buddhism as its influences to examine how Murdoch is working out a relationship to Nietzsche's thought. "A Subterranean Dialogue with Nietzsche on the Demonic and Divine in *The Sea, the Sea*" argues that "Murdoch is not straightforwardly opposed to Nietzsche's project ... but seeks instead to complement the 'demonic' force of his thought by evoking a 'divine' vitality that simultaneously purifies and revalues the object of its critique." Surprising similarities arise between Murdoch and Nietzsche, such as their "common dilemma: the insidious paradoxes that arise when critical thought turns, demonically, against itself." Matthew's example here is Zarathustra's fear that in liberating members of the herd he must only liberate those "would follow me because they want to follow themselves," for as Matthews observes, "To instruct others to leave the herd opens a dangerous contradiction, for people who obey such a command blindly merely exchange one herd for another. Within the pages of *The Sea, the Sea*, it is James, Arrowby's cousin, who masters the subtleties of this philosophical distinction."

Nietzsche's idea of star friendship, "Let us then *believe* in our star friendship even if we should be compelled to be earth enemies," bases itself on a possibility that matters (who we are to each other) might be otherwise. Once Matthews makes this connection, it seems more than right. If to love another is to struggle against the ego's mythology in order to recognize the reality of that other, the kind of friendship required is one that leaves the other the whole world in which to roam and live. Balancing, as Matthews argues, the demons of chaos and critique with the divine of love and redemption, Murdoch comes to a rather Nietzschean accord with the process of unselfing in the character of Arrowby.

One problem for some contemporary readers of Murdoch's philosophy is that she does not wholly accept the primacy of empiricist or "objective/scientific" descriptions as the limit of thought, philosophy or human being. Rather than wholly rejecting empiricism, John Hacker-Wright argues in "Naturalism and the Good" that Murdoch shows how natural scientific descriptions of the world do not address the whole of the matter. For those committed to empirical positions, Murdoch's assertion of the "existence of the Good" seems metaphysically suspect because she so deliberately maintains the Good as a transcendent source of meaning and object of contemplation. Hacker-Wright describes Murdoch's working out of a "more adequate naturalism," inclusive of the troubling role of perceptual interpretation of these more or less found facts. Murdoch posits a contingent and unpredictable (but not entirely hostile) world confronted by a self often too bound up in its own fantasies to actually perceive that world with any accuracy. For Murdoch then, empiricism is a gradually increased result of "overcoming our attachment to ourselves and directing our attention to the world as it is independently of those selfish attachments." The more we shed our illusions, even of empiricism, the more moral and aligned with the Good our view of and engagement with the world becomes. Stated in one of its strongest forms, Murdoch claims that "morality ... is a form of realism." By tracing Murdoch's arguments concerning the failures of scientific naturalism and detailing Murdoch's arguments for a Good which exists necessarily, Hacker-Wright explicates what he calls a position of "ethical naturalism (a view that grounds ethics in a substantive picture of human nature)" that deserves further attention in contemporary philosophy.

In the last of our essays pairing Murdoch with another thinker, Miles Leeson addresses contested territory in Murdoch studies in his essay "Morality in a World without God." Murdoch spent a great deal of time reading for and writing her manuscript on Heidegger only to esteem it a failure and refuse to allow its publication. Reading both the available portions of "Heidegger: The Pursuit of Being" and the novel *The Time of the Angels*, Leeson describes Murdoch's engagement with Heidegger's *Being and Time* and suggests that further study of her manuscript might illuminate her life-long engagements with existentialism because "for Murdoch the 'trinity' of Plato, G.E. Moore and Simone Weil were counter-balanced throughout her career by Kant, Sartre and Heidegger (and, to an extent Nietzsche): opposing forces from which her best fiction seemed to emanate." She finds that these philosophers seek to wrest free "the self ... from any concept of the transcendent other," whether God or Good (vertical) or another person (horizontal) and filling that void with a will devoted primarily to a delusional self-protection. With its focus on "the development of world secularization in relation to an enclosed community (of sorts) as well as the abuse of power and sexual domination," *The Time of the Angels* asks "Can one be a theist without succumbing to the lure of a false idol or simplistic consolation within religious belief?" Here Leeson reads Murdoch as using the novel to expose deep reservations about Heidegger's thought as she does with Sartre in *Under the Net*. Though Leeson ultimately finds Murdoch's work on Heidegger troubled and incomplete, he argues that we might read it, in the light of her other accomplishments, with a forgiving eye interested in a more fully real understanding of Murdoch's own philosophy.

Our conclusion is Luisa Muraro's "A Meditation in Swerves." Muraro, a major philosopher in her own right, wrote the introduction for the 2006 translation of *Existentialists and Mystics* into Italian. Although the author muses that most of her essays on Murdoch feel like introductions, we have placed this essay as a conclusion because her main concern is with the style of Murdoch's thought and writing. Muraro is keen to trace the swerves between philosophy and fiction that Murdoch performs, as well as swerves within the philosophy. If there is a Murdochian quality, it is

> the typical mobility of her thought that prevents her mind from remaining stably on one point of focus, prevents her reasoning from moving along a single trajectory, and prevents her discourse from developing on the same level. There is no shortage of post-modern thinkers who theorise this mobility without practising it; she does not theorise it but she practises it, and we, reading her, feel "caught off guard," as they say.

Muraro observes that Murdoch juxtaposes those aspects of Kant or Hegel, of analytical or existential philosophy, which mitigate against the honest difficulty of attending to each other's being in a contingent world in which we are both free and a bit overwhelmed — neither subjects without agency, nor agents without (real) obligations. Rather than a lack of philosophical acumen, this level of swerve is a formal sign of Murdoch's concern for the particular, the details of real lived life, and of reading other modes of philosophy with an eye to their moral implications. This shapeless form of Murdoch's follows her content, in Muraro's estimation. This is to "pay attention to her effort to say something that commonly exists but is weighed down by a sort of incredulity and indefensibility that pushes it towards illusion," whether the illusions of insecure narcissism or of ideal systematic perfection. Correspondingly, Muraro's essay swerves from examinations of Murdoch's anti-method to reflections on her own engagement with Murdoch, to Murdoch's arrival at a "thirdness without synthesis" that pushes philosophy a good bit beyond its accustomed tidiness.

Murdoch's essential thought was that, hard as it can be, people ought to grow up and recognize each others' realities as reality, a place we create together in both conscious and unconscious ways. In that spirit, we the editors thank the authors for your generous work. You have written these essays as much for the sake of your own thinking as for the creation of new opportunities for others. You make your case and deliberately leave ample room for your readers' own thinking. You deepened and refined your thinking in conversation with us, and in that process brought us editors to a much richer knowledge of Murdoch's work, and of the possibilities of collaboration. It is not every day that editors get so lucky in their partnerships with authors. This project was born out of chance and sometimes survived on luck; your dedication and engagement was a great source of its realization. With you as partners, contingency turns out not to be a bad thing at all. Thank you.

To you, reader, we wish pleasure in the reading of this book.

Notes

1. Midgley, 2005, 86.
2. Conradi, 2001, 246–7; Dooley, 2003, 175.
3. Dooley, 2003, 40; Conradi, 2001, 246–7.
4. For Italy, the notes in Luisa Muraro's essay in this collection indicate responses to Murdoch's thought in philosophy and political science. In Ankara, Turkey, the 16th Annual British Novelists Seminar was devoted to "Iris Murdoch and Her Work," hosted by the Department of Foreign Language Education at the Middle East Technical University in August 2008. The 10th Annual International Conference on Iris Murdoch, "Philosopher Meets Novelist," was hosted by the Instituto de Literatura Comparada and the Facudad de Letras de Universidade do Porto in February 2009. An article by Marinela Cojocariu, "The Reception of Iris Murdoch by the Romanian Literary Criticism," argues that due to faults in translation, several Romanian critics misunderstand Murdoch's work in crucial ways (2008, *Studies of Science and Culture* [*Studii de Stiinta si Cultura*], 13: 57–62).
5. Midgley, 2005, 128; libertarian views, through the influence of Locke, are seen in, for example, the American thinker Nozick.

1

Two Women in Dark Times

Frances White

In Iris Murdoch's last novel *Jackson's Dilemma*, Benet, who is working on a study of Heidegger, asks, "What had Heidegger said to Hannah Arendt after it was all over?"[1] Later he muses, "And did dear good Célan, they say, visit him in his mountain hut — and Hannah Arendt forgive him...?"[2] And in *Metaphysics as a Guide to Morals*, Murdoch remarks parenthetically, "(Compare Hannah Arendt's much quoted remark about the banality of evil.)."[3] These are the only three references to Arendt made by Murdoch,[4] and Murdoch is never (I believe) referred to by Arendt. What justification can be offered, therefore, for yoking together these two writers? An *apologia* for so doing can be found in Arendt's Preface to her collection of biographical essays entitled *Men in Dark Times*.[5] She explains that she is here "primarily concerned with persons — how they lived their lives, how they moved in the world, and how they were affected by historical time," and she amplifies her sense of their connectedness:

> The people assembled here could hardly be more unlike each other, and it is not difficult to imagine how they might have protested, had they been given a voice in the matter, against being gathered together into a common room, as it were. For they have in common neither gifts nor convictions, neither profession nor milieu.... But they were contemporaries.... Thus they share with each other the age in which their life span fell, the world during the first half of the twentieth century with its political catastrophes [and] its moral disasters....[6]

Arendt and Murdoch were indeed twentieth century contemporaries, Arendt living from 1906 to 1975 and Murdoch from 1919 to 1999, but these two women likewise might have demurred at "being gathered together into a common room" as the differences between them are manifest. Arendt, a German Jew by birth, was educated in the German philosophical tradition at Marburg, Freiburg and Heidelberg universities. She fled Europe for the United States in 1941 and became an American citizen in 1951. Her work focuses on political theory and the philosophy of politics. Murdoch, an Irish Protestant Christian by birth, was educated in the English philosophical tradition at Oxford and Cambridge universities. She was debarred from studying in the United States because of her brief membership of the Communist Party and spent her whole life in Oxford and London. Her work was divided between moral philosophy and fiction, and she is best known for her twenty-six novels. If all that they held in common was happening to overlap by slightly over half a century, with half the world between them geographically, then any sense of connection would indeed be tenuous. In this essay I want to suggest that there are deep and abiding connections between the lives and thoughts of these two women, and to raise some questions about such connections which could fruitfully be pursued by readers and critics of either of them.[7]

Immediate biographical points of comparison between Arendt and Murdoch are that both were only children who proved to be exceptionally able, were educated by men whom they revered, and became women working as philosophers in a predominantly male environment. Both felt a sense of unbelonging in the worlds they inhabited; Arendt as an actual refugee from the Third Reich, exiled from her homeland and cut off from her roots, and Murdoch always aware of being an Irish woman in England. Both had affairs of deep consequence for their personal and intellectual lives; Arendt with Martin Heidegger, and Murdoch with Elias Canetti.[8] Both married other men and had long, fulfilled childless marriages.[9]

It is, however, in the connections between their philosophical careers and their thinking that possible significance lies. Arendt and Murdoch are two of the most influential women philosophers of their generation in their disparate fields. Recognition of this is evinced by the Gifford Lectures. Hannah Arendt was the first woman ever to be invited to give these prestigious lectures.[10] In 1972–74 she gave two series of lectures, "The Life of the Mind: Thinking" and "The Life of the Mind: Willing."[11] The next woman to be appointed Gifford Lecturer was Iris Murdoch, who in 1981–82, gave the lectures on "Metaphysics as a Guide to Morals" which were to be published by that title in 1992.[12] This is an indicator of the esteem in which both women were held by the academic world. Furthermore, both Arendt and Murdoch took very particular interest in the philosophy of Martin Heidegger. Arendt's early thinking was formed by him as her teacher and she continued to grapple with his work throughout her own writing; in her last work, *The Life of the Mind: Willing*, she analyzes Heidegger's concept of the will-not-to-will. Murdoch likewise engaged with Heidegger over three decades and her last (unpublished) work was an analysis of his thought. Both women ultimately find Heidegger wanting, both as a moral figure and as a thinker, despite their sense of his immense significance in the development of philosophy during the twentieth century.

In her Preface to *Men in Dark Times*, Arendt identified telling aspects of early twentieth century history which impacted strongly on individual lives: "political catastrophes" and "moral disasters." Both women reflected deeply and wrote about these things; Arendt as a political theorist and journalist, Murdoch as a moral philosopher and novelist. The most obvious events which shaped their lives and thought were the Second World War and, within that, the Holocaust. Arendt, being Jewish, was forced to flee for her life. She then worked in Paris, helping to rescue Jewish children, before having to leave France too, for America. Murdoch, "safe" in England during the war, lost close friends who died fighting, and in 1944–46 became a Relief Worker for UNRRA in Belgium and Austria, experiencing the sufferings of refugees at second hand. For both women, these years were personally traumatic and intellectually formative. "It is hardly an exaggeration to say that [Arendt's] political and philosophical work developed in the course of sustained reflection on the life in Nazi Germany and the horrors of concentration camps," says Bhikhu Parekh,[13] and all of Murdoch's writing, philosophical and fictional, is likewise a sustained reflection on what she calls "our Hitler and after age."[14] I will return to these "sustained reflections," but before that more needs to be said about their earlier lives.

There has been increasing knowledge of, and interest in, the private lives of these two women; sadly more so than in their work. However, the secretive[15] relationships which Arendt had with Heidegger, and Murdoch with Canetti, had such major influence on their work as well as their lives that these relationships take on importance in understanding their writing. Both Heidegger (1889–1976) and Canetti (1905–94) were married men, considerably older than Arendt and Murdoch.[16] Arendt's father died when she was seven, and although Murdoch didn't lose her father until she was an adult, both women sought father-figures.[17] Although these relationships were sexual, the primary dynamics which drove them were concerned with power and with the teacher-pupil, or master-apprentice, relationships. Murdoch's novels show a preoccupation with such relationships; Arendt's affair with Heidegger seems like life mirroring Murdoch's art.[18] Indeed, Arendt herself described their later relationship as "the continuation of this novel."[19] There is a flavor of *hetaerae*[20] in the erotic-intellectual mix, but at this stage in the history of women's education it was just becoming possible for women to separate from the men who dominated them intellectually and strike out a path for themselves, as both Arendt and Murdoch did. Each became as well known and respected for her work as Heidegger and Canetti, neither of whom were well pleased by this independence and fame. Arendt's escape from Heidegger's dominance was ironically facilitated by the terrible events of her dark time. In America she lived an academic life out from under Heidegger's shadow, although his influence on her thinking remained strong. Murdoch's escape from Canetti's puppeteering came from an "improbable rescuer," John Bayley, in marriage with whom she was to find the space and security in which she could develop her art and her thinking in peace, although again Canetti's lasting influence on both can be traced.[21]

That such intelligent women with strong personalities of their own were both able to be held in thrall by older, married, men is a matter of bewilderment and fascination to biographers, and has given rise to attempts at analysis. The essence of the matter appears to lie in the erotic attraction of the intellectual mastery already mentioned. Arendt and Murdoch were attractively *clever* as well as physically personable young women, and were themselves attracted by high intelligence. These were affairs of minds as much as of bodies. Biographers have variously tried to account for Arendt's subordination to Heidegger. When Arendt became his student, Heidegger was known as the "little magician from Messkirch," and by 1923 he "was beginning to be regarded as the secret king of philosophy."[22] His personal charisma had created around him an image which had an erotic as well as intellectual authority. It was, at least in part, to this image that Arendt became enslaved. Her student, friend, and biographer, Elisabeth Young-Bruehl, describes the situation that developed between them thus:

> Hannah Arendt was just turning eighteen when she met Heidegger and developed for him what she called ... a *starre Hingegebeneit an ein Einziges*, an "unbending devotion to a single one" ... [Heidegger] let the romance flourish; but he did not let it change the course of his life. By the summer of 1925 Hannah Arendt had realised that he was to remain a stranger, no matter how deeply tied they were.... She felt caught in the dilemma of an illicit and impossible love [and] deeply saddened.... Hannah Arendt had been isolated and estranged in her secret love for Heidegger.[23]

Elzbieta Ettinger views the formal academic relationship between Heidegger and Arendt as a central dynamic in the relationship:

> Arendt did not resist but rather welcomed her role as Heidegger's apprentice. Her obedience or even passivity cannot be judged by today's standards but by the prevailing norms of behaviour, which dictated that students treat a professor like a master. Yet to deal with a lover and a professor in one person could not but deepen Arendt's confusion. The professor-student relationship at a German university presupposed not a mentor-disciple attitude so much as a master-apprentice one.[24]

Vivian Gornick's interpretation lays stress on mutuality:

> Heidegger did all the controlling, Hannah did all the worshipping—naturally, how could it have been otherwise—but the dynamic between them was something of an equalizer. He needed her intelligent adoration as much as she needed to give it. They both approached his talent for thinking with reverence, each believing he was a vessel of containment for something large, something to be served, protected, and responded to always. This intensity between them, as it turned out, proved a bond stronger than either love or world history.[25]

However differently weighted individual readings of the affair between Arendt and Heidegger may be, the mix of eros and pedagogy cannot be gainsaid, and it appears that the pedagogical relationship in itself generates the erotic attraction.[26]

Canetti's sway over Murdoch may have had a similar basis. She had previously been held in thrall by "two immensely influential male tutors" at

Oxford, Donald MacKinnon and Eduard Fraenkel.[27] The latter was notorious for his behavior with female students, which some found alarming. But Murdoch "had no objection to difficult men," and "was moreover to make of the relations between eros and intelligence a whole philosophy."[28] Bayley stresses the predominance of the mental aspect of such relationships over the physical as far as Murdoch was concerned:

> ... Iris had several lovers, often apparently at the same time. I ... intuited ... that she usually gave her favours out of admiration and respect: for, so to speak, the godlike rather than the conventionally attractive or sexual attributes in the men who pursued her. Men who were like gods for her were also for her erotic beings, but sex was something she regarded as rather marginal, not an end in itself.[29]

Canetti was chief among these "godlike" beings in Murdoch's life. Bayley refers to him as the *Dichter*, and says that "Iris was very much under his sway."[30] They met in 1952, and from January 1953 to late in 1955, they had a three-year affair. Murdoch had known of Canetti previously from the mutual friend who introduced them, Franz Steiner, whom she loved deeply, and Steiner's early death in November 1952 may have made her easy "prey" for Canetti. Be that as it may, she was soon "obsessively in love."[31] Canetti possessed fascination for many women, but some were more wary of his manipulative charm. Murdoch, however, willingly played a role in his sado-masochistic fantasies, which complemented her own.[32] She revered his intellectual ability, and was also enchanted by Canetti's exotic multi-cultural background, his linguistic abilities, his connection with great European figures of the age, and by his charismatic "svengali-like power."[33] She took him at his own estimation, and fell in love with her image of him.[34] Conradi's stress on this aspect of Canetti and Murdoch's relationship has, however, recently been challenged by Elaine Morley, who argues for a less eroticized influence grounded in "shared intellectual interests: focussing on the particular problem of the post–Kantian autonomous individual."[35]

For both women the influence of their early master-figures remained strong. Heidegger's lasting legacy to Arendt is evident in the radio talk she gave to mark his eightieth birthday,[36] and in letters Arendt acknowledges his rare intellectual gifts and his pedagogical gift in imparting his insights to his pupils.[37] However, she discerningly described him as "the last (we hope) romantic," and recognized that he was not "the moral example ... cosmopolitan[... and] model of the public philosopher" that she perceived in her other old friend and mentor Karl Jaspers.[38] In *The Life of the Mind*, Arendt presents her views of the strengths and weaknesses of Heidegger's philosophy,[39] and she makes the comment that "in Heidegger's understanding, the will to rule and to dominate is a kind of original sin, of which he found himself guilty when he tried to come to terms with his brief part in the Nazi movement."[40]

In this way Arendt obliquely attempts to explain from a philosophical position, the actions and attitudes of Heidegger which puzzle her (and others) from a biographical stance. She achieves a precarious balance between gratitude and judgment. The legacy which Murdoch took from her relationship with Canetti is very different from Arendt's ambiguous inheritance from Heidegger. Although he had "a massive polymath intelligence and an original mind" Murdoch's debt to Canetti has less to do with her intellectual development than with her development as a novelist.[41] "Through Canetti Iris discovered something about the workings of power, and her own complicity in this," suggests Peter Conradi.[42] Eros and power are two strong and complex themes in Murdoch's fiction. She creates powerfully erotic/erotically powerful characters, and "[a]ll her power-figures somewhere echo Canetti."[43] His influence on her art long outlived their personal closeness, and as Conradi observes, "Where *he* can be felt behind a novel of hers, the sense of danger is unavoidable, disturbing."[44] John Bayley comments percipiently on the metamorphosis of Murdoch's lovers in her art. Having initially felt threatened by them he came to realize that "was Iris's own imagination which had in a sense created them, and continued to create and nurture them as the strange and unique characters of her wonderful novels" [which were] "distilled from the alembic of those original obsessions and enchantments."[45]

Her relationships in life fed the art into which she transmuted them; they were not, as it were, that "real" to her in themselves: "Falling in love with people who represented for her spiritual authority, wisdom, beneficence, even a force that might seem darkly ambiguous and enigmatic, was an adventure in the soul's progress and experience; she craved it, needed it, but she was far too sensible ever to become enslaved."[46]

Murdoch created characters whose intensely passionate and tormented relationships mirror that which existed between Arendt and Heidegger: in her own life she preserved a self-protective distancing from such extremes.

Both Murdoch's fiction and her philosophy are dominated by contemplation of the nature of good and evil, in which the Holocaust is a focal point: "the fate of the Jews under Hitler ... has become a symbol of the capacity and strength of human wickedness."[47] Behavior in concentration camps also became for her a moral indicator.[48] Her last, and unpublished, philosophical treatise is *Heidegger: The Pursuit of Being*.[49] Murdoch was fascinated by Heidegger, both from a philosophical perspective as a thinker of rare genius, and from a novelist's perspective as a figure of charismatic (and erotic) power.[50] But she had major problems with him from a moral perspective, asking similar questions to those of George Steiner:

> What, if any, are the connections between the doctrines and idiom of *Sein und Zeit* and those of National Socialism? And what explanation can be offered to account for Heidegger's total refusal, *after* 1945, to say anything candid or even intelligible either about his personal record under Nazism or even about the general holocaust?[51]

Such questions are consciously set aside in her philosophical writings but emerge in the musings of Benet in *Jackson's Dilemma*.[52] Here she asks, through his voice, the question: "What had Heidegger said to Hannah Arendt after it was all over?"[53]

The short answer is, a great deal. Some 120 letters between them are extant, and they conversed on many occasions when Arendt visited Germany. But it is in a letter of May 6, 1950,[54] that one may, reading between the lines, glimpse a proper answer to that question. Heidegger writes of a "shift in 1937/1938 when Germany's catastrophe became clear to me" and says that "this burden became a pressure that enabled me to think through the issue"; he refers to "the memory of one's own mistakes"; and then he writes, "Hannah, reconciliation is rich, but apparently we must wait for a turning point, when the world changes and overcomes the spirit of revenge." Oblique words indeed, hardly constituting either an apology or an *apologia* for his past actions. Yet Arendt seized on reconciliation immediately, despite the deeply personal nature of the injury done to her by Heidegger. This was not merely because she valued this individual man as a friend: Arendt's philosophy has much to say about forgiveness being a vital element in human society and she practiced what she preached.

In her analysis *The Human Condition*, Arendt discusses "Irreversibility and the Power to Forgive," grasping the nettle of such problems as were posed by her own dark times: "The possible redemption from the predicament of irreversibility — of being unable to undo what one has done *though one did not, and could not, have known what he was doing*—is the faculty of forgiving."[55]

The words I have italicized may be an echo of Christ's words from the cross, "Father, forgive them, for they know not what they do"; Arendt considers Jesus of Nazareth to be "the discoverer of the role of forgiveness in the realm of human affairs."[56] She was lead to think deeply about this predicament because of her own suffering as a Jew in the Third Reich, and specifically because she herself had to find an answer to the particular problem posed by Heidegger. Is it of him that she was thinking when she wrote those italicized words? Be that as it may, Arendt shows forgiveness to be the key element in allowing human society to continue after periods of darkness. This can be true of individuals and of whole societies: "Without being forgiven, released from the consequences of what we have done, our capacity to act would, as it were, be confined to one single deed from which we could never recover; we would remain the victims of its consequences forever."[57]

As an individual Jew, Arendt had the largeness of spirit to forgive: as a political philosopher, she built the notion of forgiveness into her picture of a workable human society.

For Murdoch, as for many others, such forgiveness is problematical. This may be because the concept of forgiving is commonly confused with the concept of forgetting, and it is rightly felt that the victims of the Holocaust (and other atrocities) should not be forgotten. As Jean Baudrillard has crisply remarked: "Forgetting the extermination is part of the extermination itself."[58] The other factor which militates against the acceptability of forgiveness is the concept of judgment — a sense that justice requires that evil-doers should not be released from the consequences of what they have done. Arendt offers insight into this apparent *impasse* in her essay on Bertolt Brecht:

> Every judgment is open to forgiveness, every act of judging can change into an act of forgiveness; to judge and to forgive are but two sides of the same coin. But the two sides follow different rules. The ... law demands that we be equal — that only our acts count, and not the person who committed them. The act of forgiving, on the contrary, takes the person into account; no pardon pardons murder or theft but only the murderer or the thief. We always forgive *somebody*, never *something*....[59]

This complex interrelationship between forgiveness, justice, and judgment continues to exercise philosophers, theologians, and artists.[60]

Murdoch was apparently antipathetical to Arendt. John Bayley says, "Iris never met Hannah Arendt and seemed cool to her image ... perhaps as a result of talking about her with Isaiah Berlin."[61] It is a pity that Murdoch found Arendt's forgiveness of Heidegger unforgivable as both women grapple with similar philosophical and moral problems and many of their chief concerns overlap.[62] I want to suggest that, malgré Murdoch's mistrust, there are strong points of potential convergence in Arendt's and Murdoch's thinking, study of which could prove fruitfully reflexive. Arendt's texts could hermeneutically challenge Murdoch's philosophy, and vice versa, and further, Murdoch's fiction might help to supply the lack, which Arendt perceived in philosophy, of ways to tell the story of the Holocaust.

Murdoch is famously philo–Semitic. This characteristic originated from the influence of Beatrice Mary Baker, Headmistress of Badminton, Murdoch's school, who took in Jewish refugee children in 1936; by 1945 Murdoch wrote to David Hicks, "I find my pro–Semitism becoming more and more fanatical with the years."[63] Pro-Semitic influences on Murdoch continued the more she encountered Jewish intellectuals: she described Frederic Sampson as "the latest of my Jewish teachers, of whom the first was Fraenkel and the most beloved Franz [Steiner]."[64] Years later, she even claimed, "I am practically a Jew myself."[65] But of course, Murdoch was *not* Jewish; she neither owned the riches of that cultural identity, nor suffered the persecutory consequences of it. An inclination to romanticize the Jewish people and history is evident in Murdoch's writing (as is also the case with regard to Poland and Ireland).

Arendt, as a Jew who experienced persecution, takes an unromanticized, intellectually dispassionate approach to her identity and her people. In *Antisemitism*, she offers an impartial historical view of Jewish-Gentile relations through the centuries and points out "an optical illusion" suffered by both Jewish and non-Jewish historians:

> Historiography "has until now dealt more with the Christian dissociation from the Jews than with the reverse," thus obliterating the ... fact that Jewish dissociation from the Gentile world ... specifically from the Christian environment,

has been of greater relevance for Jewish history than the reverse [because] the very survival of the people as an identifiable entity depended upon such voluntary separation and not, as was currently assumed, upon the hostility of Christians and non-Jews."⁶⁶

She wrote this book because it seemed to her obvious that "the unprecedented crime of genocide in the midst of Occidental civilization ... called not only for lamentation and denunciation but for comprehension," and she defines comprehension as "the unpremeditated, attentive facing up to, and resisting of, reality—whatever it may be or have been."⁶⁷ Not everyone appreciates such hard-headed "facing up to ... reality." The furor caused by her report of the Eichmann trial for the *New Yorker* in 1963, which came before the public eye with a force that her earlier writings on the subject did not, was evidence of this. Misrepresented as having declared the Jews responsible for their own extermination, Arendt was anathematized.⁶⁸ Murdoch, identifying intensely with the Jews, and not given to cool historicized thinking, unsurprisingly, if unfairly, took against Arendt.

Murdoch was not, however, blind to the complexity of the Jewish situation. Her identification with the suffering of the Jews made her feel, it would appear, inadequate, even guilty, for *not* being Jewish. Conradi suggests that "she came to see that the Jewish expatriates whom she loved, ... who had undergone the worst their century had to offer, carried within themselves ... an understanding that she and other British people lacked." He observes that "Jews in her novels are sometimes idealised; and the notable Jew who is not—Julius King in *A Fairly Honourable Defeat*—is demonised instead."⁶⁹ Closer to the observations of Arendt, however, is Willy Kost in *The Nice and the Good*, whose unbearable remorse is for having betrayed two fellow Jews in Dachau, out of fear.⁷⁰ Perception of the complex dynamic between bullies and victims complicates Murdoch's response to Canetti, as depicted in *The Flight from the Enchanter*, in which "those who are enslaved to Mischa Fox/Canetti are enslaved voluntarily."⁷¹ Murdoch's ability to see other aspects of the situation than the simplistically pro–Jewish were also evident in 1977 when she and John Bayley visited Israel: she "wanted the Palestinian case advocated in the group's final press statement [and was] furious when this was first diluted, then ignored."⁷²

Despite Murdoch's antipathy toward Arendt, their mutual focus on the Holocaust, and their diverse attempts to penetrate the mysteries of suffering and evil which it poses, link their concerns. For both these writers the dark time caused by Hitler was a crucible for concentrated ethical thinking. The creation of a "mass" of people (Jewish, homosexual, Gypsy, and so on) who can be disposed of, and a corresponding "mass" of people who will act (or passively *not* act), made possible the unthinkable. The loss of the individual within such masses is of paramount importance to both women. How this could have come about exercises their minds throughout their writings; philosophical, political and fictional. They approach the problem, however, from characteristically different perspectives: Arendt from an "external" historical, politicized angle, Murdoch from an "internal" ethical, even at points mystical, angle. These differences of approach derive from their very distinct, but potentially complementary, philosophical starting places.

Arendt is above all fascinated by man as a *political* animal, man in society, in public, in interaction. Murdoch, by contrast, is more preoccupied with man as a *spiritual* (as distinct from *religious*) animal, man as individual soul, in private, in introspection. Both, from these variant perspectives, are concerned with reality, with attention, with apprehension of the other. Loss of these vital human insights leads to the kind of evil both had witnessed in their own lives. Politically, both Arendt and Murdoch refuse to fit neatly into any category. In her essay on Rosa Luxemburg, Arendt says of her: "What mattered most in her view was reality, in all its wonderful and all its frightful aspects, even more than revolution itself. Her unorthodoxy was innocent, non-polemical." This description would equally fit either Arendt herself, or indeed Murdoch.[73]

Arendt's doctoral dissertation was on "The Concept of Love in St Augustine,"[74] and she then began working on a biography of Rachel Varnhagen which was not to be published for another thirty years,[75] during which she turned her attention to political matters, first as a journalist and then as an academic. The war and the Holocaust had forced her to look back and think about the nature of totalitarianism, of anti–Semitism, of revolution: looking forward, she sought to analyze and describe a workable *polis*, which takes account of the reality of human nature and of political interaction. In her best known work, *The Human Condition*, she considers forgiving and promising as key concepts in political as well as personal life. She thought in large general concepts, but was never drawn to party politics and has been praised and vilified by both Right and Left on different grounds. "Hannah Arendt's writings have always had a maverick, marginal and even experimental tinge to them," Eleanor Honig Skoller comments in her study of Arendt.[76] Skoller observes that as "her writings work along the borders of several disciplines"; Arendt's work is "difficult to categorise ... consistent with her stance in the world," which is "not systematized" and refuses to be "pigeonholed into a political position or type."[77] Arendt shares Murdoch's mistrust of systems and theories, which are always inclined to lead away from the particular details of individual situations.

Murdoch once claimed to have been a communist by the time she was thirteen,[78] and she did indeed belong briefly to the Communist Party (c. 1938–42). Her membership was, however, more in the nature of a "gesture of solidarity with sufferers," and a bonding with contemporaries at Oxford, than a thoroughly thought-out political decision.[79] She moved from Communism to a broad sympathy with the Left for being "on the side of the dispossessed, the underprivileged," to disenchantment with it over education, and hence, although she continued to believe theoretically in Socialism, to the Right.[80] She voted Conservative in 1983 and 1987.[81] This rather stereotypical movement across the English political spectrum supports the impression that Murdoch's early political allegiance was as romantically inspired as was her identification with the Jews. In fact, Murdoch "took almost no day-to-day interest in politics": politics were, she accurately saw, "not in her blood." She felt "ordinary private things close, politics not."[82] It is this predisposition which drives Murdoch's philosophical stress inwards to the private person, in contradistinction to Arendt's outward, public philosophical orientation.

Murdoch's recognition of the unavoidable part played by the political in human life, and the interaction between the political and the personal is evident in her novels. The almost caricatured Lefty Todd, a proselytizing Socialist in her debut novel, *Under the Net*, refuses to allow Jake to wriggle out of political concern: "If you can care at all you can care absolutely. What other moral problem is there in this age?" Lefty challenges him.[83] But Murdoch rapidly realized that she could not write convincingly about politics in her fiction.[84] Patricia Duncker's introduction to *The Flight from the Enchanter*, speaks of "the ghost of political commitment which haunts the novel."[85] This phrase could equally be applied to later novels such as *Nuns and Soldiers*. Despite making Mor in *The Sandcastle* an aspiring Labour candidate; despite constructing the plot of *The Red and the Green* around the 1916 "Easter Rising"; despite the Vietnam War theme running throughout *An Accidental Man*; and despite the fact that the "book" in *The Book and the Brotherhood* is a critique of Marxism and a program for a radically new political understanding, politics in Murdoch's fiction always diminishes to background, against which her exposure of the pains and pleasures of the human heart is played out in comic drama. She is no more a "political novelist" than a "philosophical novelist." Yet when, in her fiction, she illuminates "the human condition,"[86] with regard to the vital concepts of the individual, attention, love, remorse, goodness, and evil, her work cannot but manifest a political dimension at a level beyond specific parties and policies. Her concern with human nature and with relationships between people, based on attention and love, or on egoism and power, inescapably has political implications. Murdoch attempts to give voice to these in her philosophical work.

The twelfth chapter of *Metaphysics as a Guide to Morals* is entitled "Morals and Politics." In over forty pages of richly illustrated argument, Murdoch encompasses Liberalism and Marxism, Kant and Adorno. Detailed analysis, beyond the scope of this preludial essay, of Murdoch's treatise in the light of Arendt's thought, and vice versa is requisite. The crux of the matter for present purposes is Murdoch's insistence on the absolute value of the individual and the moral necessity for all political thinking to hold this firmly in focus. It is the concept of "the individual, the person who is in innumerable ways special, unique, different from his neighbour" for which people fight tyrants.[87] And, philosophically, for which "Kierkegaard fought Hegel": intellectual ideas affect actual lives. Murdoch is adamant that "[h]uman beings are valuable, not because they are created by God or because they are rational beings or good citizens, but because they are human beings," and she resists their reduction in any guise: "The individual is contingent, full of private stuff and accidental rubble, and must be accepted as such, not thought of as an embryonic rational agent, or in terms of some sort of social theory."[88] Her anxiety about all forms of political theories or parties is how they cause the individual to be (mis)/understood and (de)/valued. She wants to distinguish between political philosophy and moral philosophy, but knows that the latter always exists in a politicized context. Not content to settle for pragmatism, although she acknowledges the necessity for it in everyday political existence, Murdoch desiderates perfection. (For Murdoch, *axioms* form the appropriate basis for political pragmatism.) This higher requirement of perfection evokes the mystical which she describes as "an ever-present moral ideal, that of extending ordinary decent morals indefinitely in the direction of perfect goodness."[89] It is only by striving after absolute goodness that individuals will be enabled to resist the kind of evil which results in persecution, concentration camps and genocide. Political well-being and personal virtue go hand in hand: the former cannot be created or sustained in the absence of the latter. Therefore, for Murdoch, the onus of responsibility, and the locus of improvement, is always the individual human heart. This is made strikingly clear in her earlier work, *The Sovereignty of Good*, and it remains true that in Murdoch's view no political system can elicit goodness. Bad ones, however, militate against it.

Arendt, while valuing the unique individual equally with Murdoch, reads the means to safeguard individuals very differently. For Arendt it is not private personal virtue which will provide the means of protection for vulnerable persons, but public political strength. She argued, "The harsh fact ... was that [human rights] depended not on "the abstract nakedness of being nothing but human," but on political communities strong enough to enforce them."[90] Both philosophers share the same goal: their insights on the way to achieve that goal diverge. But this does not have to present an either/or situation of adjudicating between Murdoch and Arendt. Rather it can be viewed as a both/and situation, in which each reciprocally augments the other. Without the full realization of the reality of the other brought about by the attention which Murdoch sees as love, and which it requires moral effort against solipsism to achieve, as she demonstrates in both her philosophy and her novels, there would be no incentive to cherish and protect the individual. But without the full realization of the need for action which Arendt understands as shared significant undertakings, which requires cooperative public engagement, goodness by itself will be impotent to withstand attacks on the individual, as the deaths of Jewish sympathizers testify.[91] Both Arendt and Murdoch can be right in their assessment of the human condition: each may supply what the thinking of the other may be lacking.

The disciplines within which Arendt and Murdoch chose to write, historical-political analysis and fiction, may likewise be perceived as augmentative. "Arendt compared the concentration camps to a 'hell' in which 'radical evil' makes its appearance.... For the camps had confounded humanity's very notions of innocence and guilt."[92] This confusion was in operation with regard to both victims and oppressors: "Just as no one, whatever he or she had done, could deserve to be a camp inmate, so no punishment for those who created and operated the camp system could be commensurate with the acts they had perpetrated."[93]

The Jewish people (and others) were persecuted and exterminated simply for being who they were: innocence and guilt did not enter into this Kafkaesque world. But also, after the war, how were guilt and (relative) innocence to be apportioned amongst the German people, from Hitler at the top of the pyramid of evil-doing to those citizens who simply closed their eyes to what was happening without having any personal involvement in it? Arendt embarked on an analysis of evil, which later — influenced by her experience of listening to Eichmann during his trial — she came to categorize as "banal" in preference to "radical." By "banal" (arguably an infelicitous choice of word), Arendt meant commonplace, not merely as in "insignificant, trivial or petty," but commonplace also as in "open to the use of all the community"[94] (that is, recognizably human). (Etymological comparison may be made with the French *banaliser*, to make public or open to all, and the German *Alltäglichkeit*, banality, ordinariness, everydayness, commonplaceness.) "The trouble with Eichmann," Arendt wrote, "was precisely that so many were like him, and the many were neither perverted nor sadistic [but] terribly and terrifyingly normal."[95] Eichmann, it appeared to her, was not a monster, but a very ordinary, unthinking, unimaginative man. She explains her perception thus:

> ... when I speak of the banality of evil, I do so only on the strictly factual level, pointing to a phenomenon which stared one in the face at the trial. Eichmann was not Iago and not Macbeth, and nothing would have been further from his mind than to determine with Richard III to "prove a villain." Except for an extraordinary diligence in looking out for his personal advancement, he had no motives at all.... He *merely*, to put the matter colloquially, *never realized what he was doing*.... It was sheer thoughtlessness— something by no means identical with stupidity — that predisposed him to become one of the greatest criminals of that period.[96]

The lesson that Arendt took from her experience in Jerusalem was that "such remoteness from reality and such thoughtlessness can wreak more havoc than all the evil instincts put together which, perhaps, are inherent in man."[97] The evil intents of a purposefully destructive Iago or Hitler can only be put into action on a huge scale, as it was in the Holocaust, by the self-serving refusal to think and to accept personal responsibility, of those around them. To the extent that these qualities were manifested in the many people further down the line of management than Eichmann, the same could be said of them. It is common to humankind to (not) think and to behave like this. It is truly "banal."

In her novel of 1968, *The Nice and the Good*, Murdoch explores the nature of evil, setting two unpleasant characters against the figure of John Ducane, a man who sees himself and is seen by others, as good and decent. One is a sinister dabbler in black magic, Joseph Radeechy, who has committed suicide; the other is a violent womanizer and adulterer, Richard Biranne. Ducane is placed in the position of being required to investigate and judge the dealings of these men. Visiting the cellar full of dead pigeons where Radeechy practiced his dark rites, Ducane thinks: "It's the dreariness of it ... that stupefies. This evil is dreary, it's something shut in and small." He realizes that "the great evil, the real evil, is inside myself."[98] Then later in the story when Ducane is close to death by drowning, he realizes that the gap which separates him from Radeechy and Biranne is not as wide as he had imagined:

> I wonder if this is the end, thought Ducane, and if so what it will all have amounted to. How tawdry and small it has all been. He saw himself now as a little rat, a busy little scurrying rat seeking out its own little advantages and comforts. To live easily, to have cosy familiar pleasures, to be well thought of.... He thought, if I ever get out of here I will be no man's judge. Nothing is worth doing except to kill the little rat....[99]

Evil as tawdry, as arising from within each individual through egoistic concern, seems close to the perception of evil as banal, as commonplace, as existing in every ordinary human being. Eichmann was guiltier than others on a scale of degree, not in essence. None are good. Arendt and Murdoch are close in their insights into the human condition here.

Of the Holocaust, Arendt said: "Human history has known no more difficult story to tell."[100] Indeed some have wished to claim that art is (or should be) silenced by it: "It is barbarous to write a poem after Auschwitz," said Adorno in 1949.[101] Yet attempts to tell the story are on-going; in history, in philosophy, in published diaries of the dead and memoirs of the survivors, in reflections on those diaries and memoirs, in poetry, drama, film and novels. A whole discipline of Holocaust Theory has grown up in the half century since it occurred, and Arendt was one of the unwitting founders of this new discipline—most works still cite her.[102] The question of whether the story of the Holocaust can/should be told, can further be refined according to the writer telling it: sufferers must be allowed to tell their own story, but have those not directly involved the right to tell stories of, or on behalf of, the sufferers? Murdoch shows concern over this issue, saying in *Metaphysics as a Guide to Morals*: "There are stories which we hesitate to repeat lest we seem to be gloating over horrors or trying to gratify unworthy emotions in ourselves or our hearers."[103] This unease recurs in her fiction. Tuan, a Jewish man in *Jackson's Dilemma*, tells a particular family story from the Holocaust to his fiancée, and then regrets it:

> He ought not to have told that hideous story to Rosalind.... Even to tell it to anybody was a sin, why this one little story, when the w*hole thing* was so eternally hideously immense.... His having told it to *anybody* made it a thousand times more vivid, more violent. His father must have known that *he* should not tell that tale to his son, and he must have regretted it afterwards. Perhaps telling it had seemed some great necessary duty, some gruesome *detail* picked out of the black mountain. But what good had it done?—it had damaged Tuan and now Tuan had damaged Rosalind.[104]

But the alternative case is put by the rabbi, Daniel Most, in *The Message to the Planet*. He feels that the story must be told, and by everyone:

> We've all got to do it, *we*, I mean perhaps everybody, weave the past into the present, work at it, like endlessly imagining, not just falling into it like into a pit, but surrounding it, I don't mean in a theoretical way, like discussing whether it was unique or exactly what caused it and so on, but connecting it, a sort of Midrash, like people in the camps telling the stories of their lives....[105]

Murdoch is ambivalent about her own story-telling activities in relation to the Holocaust, but her practice indicates that she found in favor of the second position—the stories must be told by everyone. Countless details from "the black mountain" as Tuan describes it in the quotation above, are picked out in her novels, such as for example, Stuart Cuno meditating on the girls' plaits in *The Good Apprentice*[106]; indeed *The Message to the Planet* is a sustained reflection on the experience and meaning (or lack thereof) of the Holocaust. She did indeed "work at it, endlessly imagining" in her own books as Rabbi Most enjoins. Murdoch's mistrust of theory makes her prefer this method of "surrounding it" through art to Arendt's method of "discussing whether it was unique" and "exactly what caused it" through historical analysis.

Arendt herself valued story; Isak Dinesen is one of her "men" in dark times, and she is interested in her *as* a story-teller. Arendt quotes Dinesen: "All sorrows can be borne if you put them into a story or tell a story about them." This is because for Arendt, "[t]he story reveals the meaning of what otherwise would remain an unbearable sequence of sheer happenings."[107] Murdoch's novels reveal meaning in and through such unbearability: art *shows* what philosophy can only *say*. Yet Arendt's own writings have affinities with fictional narratives although they are always concerned with fact. Skoller describes it as "a tone of the liveliest and most passionate kind—the ... Arendt style (her story-telling)."[108] It seems less helpful to judge between disciplines than to see them as diverse forms of narrative, all contributing to the Midrash which simultaneously laments, denounces, and seeks to comprehend the Holocaust, facing up to, and resisting, its reality. The forms employed by different writers supplement one another, the *sine qua non* being that "narrative matters," as Richard Kearney puts it. "Whether as story or history or a mixture of both ... the power of narrative makes a crucial difference to our lives."[109] Arendt and Murdoch would both concur with that.

Narrative is always necessarily written from a particular stance: black/white, Jewish/Gentile, male/female. That there is no neutral place from which things can be viewed is now strongly argued, but Arendt and Murdoch both believed in such a locus of neutrality. Thus another point of agreement *between* these two women is their attitude to *being* women. Despite doing pioneering work in political and moral philosophy, fields dominated by men, neither Murdoch nor Arendt favored feminist thinking. It could be argued that Arendt's key concept of "natality" springs from a female apprehension of the human condition, and that Murdoch's use of homely, "ordinary and everyday" examples, such as her much discussed "M and D" scenario in *The Sovereignty of Good*, is likewise a female perspective on morality.[110] But each would have pooh-poohed the suggestion. Arendt "saw her gender, like her Jewishness, as a fact of life; she did not claim an epistemological privilege for women."[111] Skoller enlarges on this anti-feminist perspective:

> [Arendt] would not engage the woman's question from as early on as the thirties, because she would not entertain the separation of women's issues from the larger range of political concerns, just as she was against the divorce of Jewish issues from national and international ones. As a singular and controversial female figure in philosophy and political theory, she could have been useful to the movement. But she was unreceptive to the publicity that goes along with paving the way for others ... because of her distaste for exceptionism — whether of women, Jews, or blacks.[112]

At a conference on her work in Caen in 1978, Murdoch expressed a strikingly similar position:

> The point of liberation is not, and this is to differ with certain views of women's lib, to say we're better, or we're special, or we're wonderful, but just to be equal, to be ordinary, to join the human race, to be people, just people like everybody else ... I disapprove of "separatism" as a mode of liberation: women's studies, black studies, and nonsense of that sort. The point is to join the great main stream of thought and art from which we have been excluded.[113]

Such firmly expressed attitudes raise problems for feminist approaches to the work of either woman. Consequently "literary feminists have virtually left Arendt unread," and there have been few and tentative efforts to read Murdoch from a feminist perspective.[114] There is however a growing body of feminist Arendt criticism[115]: some Murdoch critics have likewise begun to read her work against the grain of her own anti-feminist perspective.[116]

This is but one of several areas for future study indicated by this preliminary essay on the putative links between the lives and work of Arendt and Murdoch. Others which suggest themselves are comparative study of their conceptions of happiness, freedom, evil, the past, judgment, and solipsism; their respective interpretations of Kant; their understandings of the use of metaphysics and the threat posed by an anarchy of values; and the importance to both philosophers of the very concept and practice of *thinking* itself. Because of the dark times through which these women lived, questions of politics and ethics have a cutting edge of urgency. They are not academic matters-of-interest to be indulged in by intellectuals, but the tools with which humanity must forge a better world to live together in. Arendt and Murdoch are both deeply serious. They are concerned with the improvement of the human condition, and with the role of philosophy in furthering it. In her Preface to *Men in Dark Times*, Arendt says:

> That even in the darkest of times we have the right to expect some illumination, and that such illumination may well come less from theories and concepts than from the uncertain, flickering, and often weak light that some men and women, in their lives and their works, will kindle under almost all circumstances and shed over the time span that was given them on earth — this conviction is the inarticulate background against which these profiles were drawn.[117]

In their own time span on earth, Hannah Arendt and Iris Murdoch were such women; and that their lives and works kindle such light, is the conviction underlying this profile of two exceptional, innovatory thinkers and writers.

NOTES

1. Murdoch, 1995, 14.
2. *Ibid.*, 47.
3. Murdoch, 1992, 103.
4. These are the only references in Murdoch's published work: Murdoch refutes Arendt's connection of Heidegger and Plato with regard to tyrants on p. 39 of her unpublished manuscript, *Heidegger: The Pursuit of Being*. This is held in the Iris Murdoch Archive at Kingston University Library Special Collections, currently catalogued as KUAS/6 Peter Conradi Research Collection.
5. Arendt, 1968. This essay cites the 1973 Pelican edition. It is noteworthy that among the men Arendt includes are Rosa Luxemberg and Isak Dinesen, just as Murdoch is herself included in Bryan Magee's *Men of Ideas* (London: BBC, 1978).
6. Arendt, 1973, 7.
7. The work of Arendt and Murdoch is frequently studied adjacently, as recent anthologies and conferences indicate. See for example: Adamson, et al., *Renegotiating Ethics in Literature, Philosophy and Theory* and Touglas and Ebenreek, *Presenting Women Philosophers*. My contention is that instead of being read in parallel with one another, the texts of Arendt and Murdoch should be read dialectically. This may be beginning to happen in Scandinavia where the work of both writers is receiving much attention: interestingly a course at Uppsala University links them with Simone Weil in "Skirting the Subject: 3 Woman Philosophers," which addresses the question of whether "there is some specifically female way of philosophizing to which these thinkers give voice." Uppsala Universitet: http://www.selma.uu.se/publik/main? [Editor's Note: The course is no longer on the university website.]
8. Accounts of the relationship between Arendt and Heidegger include: Young-Bruehl, *For Love of the World*; Young-Bruehl, *Why Arendt Matters* ; Ettinger, *Hannah Arendt and Martin Heidegger*; Safranski, *Martin Heidegger: Between Good and Evil*; Gornick, "Hannah Arendt and Martin Heidegger"; and Ludz, *Letters 1925–1975: Hannah Arendt and Martin Heidegger*. Accounts of the relationship between Murdoch and Canetti are to be found in Conradi, *Iris Murdoch: A Life* and Wilson, *Iris Murdoch as I Knew Her*.
9. Arendt was briefly married to Günther Stern (1929–37) but her marriage to Heinrich Blücher in 1940 which lasted until his death in 1970 was source of deep happiness to her, see *Letters*, No.127.

Murdoch was married to John Bayley from 1956 until she died in 1999. Announcing her death, the BBC News quoted an interview from 1994 in which she said: "But above all else, the most important thing in my life is my husband. To have had a happy marriage is a very good thing" (Holt, 1999).

10. Arendt was also the first woman at Princeton with the rank of full professor in 1959; the first woman to give the Frankfurt Peace Prize address, when Karl Jaspers was awarded it in 1958; and the first woman to receive the Danish government's Sonning Prize for Contributions to European Civilization, in 1975 (Young-Bruehl, 2004, 272, 310 & 460).

11. Edited by Mary McCarthy and posthumously published as *Hannah Arendt, The Life of the Mind: Volume One, Thinking* and *The Life of the Mind: Volume Two, Willing*.

12. Since the mould was thus broken by Arendt and Murdoch, the inclusion of women as Gifford Lecturers has snowballed.

13. Parekh, 1981, ix. Cf. Canovan, 1974, vii.

14. Murdoch, 1992, 120.

15. Arendt, Heidegger, and Heidegger's wife were all discreet during their lifetimes. It was not until 1982 when Elisabeth Young-Bruehl published the biography *Hannah Arendt: For Love of the World* that she "first revealed what she had learned for the most part from oral sources: beyond their pupil-teacher relationship and their intellectual relationship, Arendt and Heidegger had had an intimate relationship" (Ludz, 2004, ix). Murdoch likewise held her own counsel, and it was with surprise and some shock that her readers learned from John Bayley's memoir *Iris* and Conradi's biography in 2001 of the extent of Murdoch's sexual involvement with Canetti, amongst others.

16. Heidegger's traditionally "hausfrau" wife, Elfride, seems not to have known about the affair at the time, but by the time Heidgger and Arendt resumed their friendship platonically in 1950 she "knows about everything" (Ludz, 2004, 57) and appears to have accepted Arendt as a family friend, even turning to her for help with selling manuscripts (Ludz, 2004, Nos. 46, 47, 108 & 109). Canetti's wife, Venetiana, "Veza," colluded with her husband's affairs (Conradi, 2001, 348).

17. The importance of Heidegger as a father-figure to Arendt is stressed by Gornick, building on Ettinger's presentation of their relationship, but this interpretation is repudiated by Young-Bruehl.

Conradi refers to "Iris's beloved father-figures: Fraenkel [...] Michael Oakeshott [...] Thomas Balogh and Canetti [...] Arnoldo Momigliano and Franz Steiner" (Conradi, 2001, 522).

18. See for example: Annette and Mischa in *The Flight from the Enchanter*; Morgan and Julius in *A Fairly Honourable Defeat*; Julian and Bradley in *The Black Prince*; and Aleph/Sefton and Lucas in *The Green Knight*.

19. Young-Bruehl, 2004, 247.

20. In Ancient Greece an [intellectual] female companion or paramour, a mistress, a concubine, OED.

21. Conradi, 2001, 374.

22. Safranski, 1998, 100, 121.

23. Young-Bruehl, 2004, 53, 54 & 59.

24. Ettinger, 1995, 23.

25. Gornick, 1999, 106.

26. In *Why Arendt Matters*, Young-Bruehl vehemently opposes Ettinger's version, calling it "a fantasy [...] bearing little relation to reality" (Young-Bruehl, 2006, 21). While it is true that Ettinger's somewhat sensationalist book fails to do justice to the mature judgments on Heidegger made by Arendt, Young-Bruehl's own biography gives insufficient weight to, and fails to account for, the passion that connected Arendt with Heidegger. It is this strong sense of eros which Murdoch captures in the teacher-pupil relationships in her novels.

27. Conradi, 2001, 114. Fraenkel, who came to Oxford from Freiburg, brought with him the German tradition of the *Seminar*, new to Oxford (Conradi, 2001, 115), and possibly also the German Master-pupil concept, defined by Ettinger. It is significant that it was he who inflicted erotic attention on female pupils: "Iris recalled Isobel Henderson saying briskly in the first year, 'Go to Fraenkel's classes—I expect he'll paw you about a bit, but never mind.' [...] This was before the days when such demonstrativeness was deemed gross moral turpitude" (Conradi, 115). See also John Bayley, 1998, 49.

Furthermore, in the context of this essay, there is a certain irony inherent in the fact that Heidegger was instrumental in forcing Fraenkel to leave Germany: see Sheehan, 1998, 38–47.

28. *Ibid.*, 115.
29. Bayley, 1998, 46.
30. *Ibid.*, 54.
31. Conradi, 2001, 346.
32. *Ibid.*, 357–8.
33. Conradi, 2001, 353. Loyalty seems to have clouded her public judgment on him, however. See an incisive article by Luprecht, "A Most Uncritical Critique: Looking at Murdoch's Textual Notes for Elias Canetti's *Crowds and Power.*"
34. Canetti was "the king," yet Iris saw little of him, having to "live on a myth in intervals of seeing the flesh & blood man" (Conradi, 2001, 386).
35. In a paper presented to the 4th International Iris Murdoch Conference at Kingston University, September 2008, "The Monster and the Maiden — An Unfinished Portrait? Towards a Reassessment of Murdoch's and Canetti's Relationship," Elaine Morley makes a strong case for rethinking Murdoch's engagement with Canetti.
36. Reproduced as "Martin Heidegger at Eighty" in Murray, 1978, 293–303.
37. In working through a book by Schelling she tells him, "I felt as I did almost fifty years ago, when I learned to read with you. [...] No one reads or has ever read like you" (Ludz, 2004, No. 146).
38. Young-Bruehl, 2004, 218, 301.
39. Like Murdoch, Arendt sees late Heideggerian philosophy as very different from and of less value than the early work: both women are wary of his later concepts of Being and the Will.
40. Arendt, 1978, 173.
41. Conradi, 2001, 353.
42. *Ibid.*, 350.
43. *Ibid.*, 449. Specifically traceable to his inspiration are Mischa Fox in *The Flight from the Enchanter*, her suggestively entitled second novel which she dedicated "To Elias Canetti"; Julius King, in *A Fairly Honourable Defeat*; and Charles Arrowby in her Booker Prize winning novel, *The Sea, the Sea.*
44. *Ibid.*, 585.
45. Bayley, 1998, 48.
46. *Ibid.*, 66.
47. Murdoch, 1992, 94.
48. Murdoch, 1970, 57, 73.
49. See note 3 for details of the manuscript.
50. There are traces of Heidegger behind John Robert Rosanov in *The Philosopher's Pupil* and Marcus Vallar in *The Message to the Planet.*
51. Steiner, 1978, 19.
52. See Frances White, "*Jackson's Dilemma* and 'The Responsible Life of the Imagination'" in *Iris Murdoch and Morality*, edited by Anne Rowe and Avril Horner, 2010.
53. Murdoch, 1995, 14.
54. Ludz, 2004, No. 62.
55. Arendt, 1958, 237.
56. *Ibid.*, 238.
57. *Ibid.*, 237. This need for release from becoming a victim of consequences and from confinement to a single irreparable deed, is well explored by Murdoch at the level of the individual in *The Good Apprentice.* She seems, however, to have been unable or unwilling to extend the insights she shows here to Heidegger's situation, perhaps because his failure to express remorse stuck in her craw.
58. Quoted in Young, 1993, 1.
59. Arendt, 1955, 245.
60. The theme of just judgment is enigmatically presented in Murdoch's penultimate novel, *The Green Knight*, in which the second section is entitled "Justice."
61. Letter to the author, February 2005. Berlin's biographer, Michael Ignatieff, who also won the Hannah Arendt Prize in 2003, analyzes the animosity felt by Berlin towards Arendt: "He felt [...] that she lacked pity, and that her standards of responsibility were guilty of arrogance and cruelty." But Ignatieff defends her, for having "the tenacity to make the German catastrophe the cen-

ter of her life's work," and for being "the first to ask the unanswerable questions." Michael Ignatieff, "Arendt's Example," Acceptance speech at Hannah Arendt Prize Ceremony in Bremen, Germany, November 28, 2003, PDF, p. 9.

62. In the Murdoch Archive there is an unannotated copy of Derwent May's short Introduction to Hannah Arendt's life and work, *Lives of Modern Women Series* (Harmondsworth: Penguin, 1986) (IML/508), and Arendt's essay "Martin Heidegger at Eighty" is underlined and annotated by Murdoch in her copy of *Heidegger and Modern Philosophy* (Iris Murdoch Library IML/965). But there is no copy of any text by Arendt. While it is possible that Murdoch could have read copies belonging to libraries or friends, it seems unlikely in the light of two facts: first, she did own many books by writers in whom she was interested, and second, she does not refer to Arendt's thinking in her own work. The sole reference is the parenthetical "(Compare Hannah Arendt's much quoted remark about the banality of evil.)" (Murdoch, 1992, 103), which suggests that Murdoch has adopted this remark out of context from the heated discussion of Arendt's controversial *Eichmann in Jerusalem* which went on at the time of its publication. Hannah Arendt, *Eichmann in Jerusalem: A Report on the Banality of Evil*.

63. Conradi, 2001, 100. Other friends were "non-plussed" when Murdoch suggested that "any worthwhile person ought to have at least *some* Jewish blood" (*Ibid.*, 308). Jewishness was a significant element in her reactions to Canetti and to Simone Weil, and she gives a partially Jewish background to innumerable characters in her novels.

64. *Ibid.*, 325.
65. *Ibid.*, 437.
66. Arendt, 1951, ix.
67. *Ibid.*, x. Within the text of *Antisemitism*, Arendt rejects both the "scapegoat" theory and the "eternal antisemitism" theory as explanations for the Holocaust, and seeks for more rooted historical causes.
68. Murdoch, and her biographer, swallow this unexamined version of Arendt's views unquestioningly: "The provocative idea of victim-guilt was topical in 1963, the year of Hannah Arendt's *Eichmann in Jerusalem*, with its scandalous implication of Arendt's fellow-Jews in their own sufferings" (Conradi, 2001, 455).
69. Conradi, 2001, 371.
70. Murdoch, 1968, 342.
71. Conradi, 2001, 371.
72. *Ibid.*, 538.
73. Arendt, 1968, 44. Murdoch shares Arendt's interest in this revolutionary heroine and martyr; Rosa Keepe in *The Flight from the Enchanter* is reputedly named after her, and she is mentioned again in *Nuns and Soldiers*, 2001, p. 7.
74. Originally published in 1929: posthumously edited by Scott and Stark, 1996, and published as *Love and St Augustine*.
75. Arendt, 1958.
76. Skoller, 1993, 97.
77. *Ibid.*
78. Interview with Susan Hill, *Bookshelf*, BBC Radio 4, 30 April 1982.
79. Conradi, 2001, 275. It did have life-changing consequences, however, as it was because she refused to lie about it that Murdoch was denied access to America to study in 1946 (*Ibid.*, 246). Had this not been so, Murdoch might conceivably have become a colleague of Arendt, and the history of women philosophers might be very different.
80. Wilson, 2003, 35.
81. Conradi, 2001, 499.
82. Wilson, 2003, 100–01; Conradi, 2001, 499.
83. Murdoch, 1954, 109.
84. See de Pue, 2008, 10.
85. Dunker, 2000, xiii.
86. This Arendtian phrase was used of Murdoch's work by the BBC when announcing her death: "Dame Iris Murdoch's works were intricate studies of the human condition which never bowed to literary fads" (Holt, 1999).
87. Murdoch, 1992, 349. Murdoch selects as representative "heroes of our time" the dissidents Wallenberg, Bukovsky, and Scharansky, in *Metaphysics as a Guide to Morals*, p. 354. This is a polit-

ical concept which she explores in her novels, notably *An Accidental Man* and her radio play, *The One Alone* (1995).
88. Murdoch, 1992, 349, 365, 368.
89. *Ibid.*, 355.
90. Baehr, 2000, xiv.
91. See the stories of Propst Heinrich Grüber and Dompropst Bernard Lichtenberg which Arendt recounts in *Eichmann in Jerusalem*. Excerpts in Baehr, 2000, 358–9.
92. Baehr, 2000, xix.
93. *Ibid.*
94. Oxford English Dictionary.
95. Baehr, 2000, 373.
96. *Ibid.*, 379.
97. *Ibid.*
98. Murdoch, 1968, 214.
99. *Ibid.*, 304–5.
100. Baehr, 2000, xix.
101. Variously translated as "writing poetry after Auschwitz is barbaric," this much quoted phrase is from Adorno, 1967, 34.
102. See for example: Levi and Rothberg, *The Holocaust: Theoretical Readings*; Hartman, *The Longest Shadow: In the Aftermath of Holocaust*; LaCapra, *Writing History: Writing Trauma*; Clendinnen, *Reading the Holocaust*; Milchman and Rosenberg, *Postmodernism and the Holocaust*; and Brenner, *Writing as Resistance: Four Women Confronting the Holocaust*.
103. Murdoch, 1992, 95.
104. Murdoch, 1995, 172.
105. Murdoch, 1989, 429–30.
106. Murdoch, 1985, 160, 267, 561.
107. Arendt, 1955, 106. In this (as in so many other things) Arendt was prophetically ahead of her time. Her understanding of the importance of story has made its way into Narrative Theory, see for example: Kearney, *On Stories*; Wood, *On Paul Ricoeur: Narrative and Interpretation*; and King, *Memory, Narrative, Identity: Remembering the Self*.
108. Skoller, 1993, 116.
109. Kearney, 2002, 14.
110. Murdoch, 1970, 17.
111. Baehr, 2000, xxxv.
112. Skoller, 1993, 12.
112. Chevalier, 2003, 83.
114. Skoller, 1993, 10.
115. See for example: Honig, *Feminist Interpretations of Hannah Arendt*.
116. See for example: Johnson, *Iris Murdoch*; Grimshaw, "Plato, Foucault and Beyond: Ethics, Beauty and Bisexuality in *The Good Apprentice*;" and Altorf, "Reassessing Iris Murdoch in the Light of Feminist Philosophy: Michèle Le Doeuff and the Philosophical Imaginary."
117. Arendt, 1968, 9.

2

A Third Sense of Ethics Between Philosophy and Fiction

AMY SMITH

In her nonfiction Iris Murdoch presents an ethics that emphasizes the uniqueness of the individual and the importance of recognizing the messiness of reality, which exceeds our attempts to fix it in a form. Given Murdoch's commitments to realistic vision of the world and other people, in other words, to recognizing the sublimity of reality, what are we to make of her treatment of character in her fiction, which often draws on literary convention and form? While in her philosophical writings she generally displays a critical attitude toward form — toward the consolatory attempt to simplify and reduce reality's overwhelming flux — some critics have called her novels "overly plotted" and her characters often recall mythic archetypes and motifs, sometimes coming across as schematic rather than the "realistic" characters she advocates for literature.

There is an obvious area for investigation here, and it has not escaped the attention of critics of Murdoch's fiction. Some critics have seen this feature of her work as demonstrating her limitations as a writer. Bran Nicol paraphrases this kind of criticism thus: "She claims to be against rigid patterning and for 'free' individual character, the argument goes, but she takes an obvious delight in plotting and presents little more than variations on the same set of characterological archetypes."[1] Other critics, such as Barbara Stevens Heusel, Elizabeth Dipple, and Bran Nicol, have been more sympathetic to the author's style. In *Iris Murdoch: The Retrospective Fiction*, Nicol argues that the inconsistencies between Murdoch's theory and practice are due to her historical location; that the crisis of representation permeating the post-war period demands a new kind of realism which must be evaluated according to its own standards. Heusel, in her study of Murdoch's fiction of the 1970s and 80s, understands Murdoch's troubled relationship to form in terms of her neo–Platonism: "Being an unorthodox neo–Platonist, Murdoch instinctively struggles with form, knowing how easily she creates form and fearing, as does Plato, its consolations."[2]

This essay focuses on the status of form in Murdoch's philosophy and fiction of the 1960s. Particularly, I examine Murdoch's allusions to Greek myth in her characters in the context of the tension between her philosophical statements and her literary practice. Rather than accepting Murdoch's statements in interviews that her novels are not connected with philosophy or considering the gulf between the two as a sign of her failure as a novelist, I propose that the apparent contradiction between her theoretical position and her fictional practice is not a contradiction at all. Rather, when we read the fiction and nonfiction in dialogue and explore the inconsistencies between them, we see that a more complex understanding of form and a richer ethical position regarding form emerge. Murdoch can sometimes come across as rigid and extreme when she discusses form and myth in her philosophical writings, displaying a negative attitude toward them; the different treatment of form and myth we see in her fiction corrects some of this harshness. That is, she presents form and reality as opposed in her nonfiction while in her fiction form is granted a more integrated role in the portrayal of reality. In addition to this difference between the two disciplines, whereby the fiction augments the nonfiction, her use of form in the fiction supports some of her philosophical commitments, particularly concerning her critique of rationalism, and thus we can detect an underlying logic that connects her fiction and nonfiction.

We should think of Murdoch's use of myth in the context of her understanding of reality, and especially the human personality, as sublime and resistant to the mappings of reason. While Murdoch wants fiction to portray sublime reality, and conceives reality as unformed, fiction is art and requires form of some sort. The nature of myth, its multiplicity, inconsistency, locality, and paradox — in short, the fact that it is not a totalizing system — make it the kind of form most suited to represent unrepresentable, sublime reality. It is the kind of form that most closely approaches Murdoch's vision of reality.

The Status of Form in Murdoch's Thought

In her 1961 essay, "Against Dryness," Murdoch critiques the picture of human personality that was common in contemporary Anglo-Saxon and French philosophy and questions the way this picture of the human is reflected in literature. She characterizes the Anglo-Saxon notion of human personality, exemplified by Hume, Russell, the "Tractatus" Wittgenstein, Hobbes, Bentham and Mill, and influenced by Kant, as only taking the externally verifiable actions of a person into consideration and envisioning the individual as a free rational will. The French philosophical position, by which Murdoch means Sartre, similarly pictures the individual as solitary and free. Murdoch argues that these assumptions of rationality and freedom, coupled with a misplaced faith in science that is evident in the emphasis on the externally verifiable as the essential qualities of the individual, are both inaccurate and *bad for us*.

Murdoch conceives of human personality in a radically different way. As she puts it, "We are not isolated, free choosers, monarchs of all we survey, but benighted creatures sunk in a reality whose nature we are constantly and overwhelmingly tempted to deform by fantasy."[3] In her 1964 essay, "The Idea of Perfection," which is based on a 1962 lecture and takes up some of the same issues addressed in "Against Dryness," she provides a more developed portrayal of this human personality. She suggests that "we have to accept a darker, less fully conscious, less steadily rational image of the dynamics of the human personality."[4] Rather than seeing human beings as free, rational agents, she argues that we are more historically conditioned and less clearly conscious than the Anglo-Saxon view would claim.[5]

While Murdoch's view of the human being is not strictly Freudian there are clear similarities between her picture of human personality and the psychoanalytic model of the psyche.[6] The most striking of these are her insistence that we are less clearly conscious than we would like to imagine and her concomitant rejection of rational materialist views of the self. In "Against Dryness" she emphasizes the need for a renewed sense of the opacity of persons. This emphasis on opacity, which is complemented by her characterization of reality as dense, is an important element in Murdoch's philosophy. The language of density and opacity connects to Murdoch's definition of the human being as sublime, a notion Murdoch adapts from Kant. In "The Sublime and the Beautiful Revisited" Murdoch characterizes the Kantian sublime as "an emotional experience resulting from the defeated yet invigorating attempt of reason to compass the boundlessness and formlessness of nature."[7] For the boundlessness and formlessness of nature in this equation Murdoch substitutes "a vast and varied reality outside ourselves ... our surroundings as consisting of other individual men."[8] For Murdoch, the individual faced with sublimity has a somewhat different experience than one who faces the Kantian sublime. When faced with the Kantian sublime, the dignity of one's rationality is reinforced. In contrast, Murdoch writes that "the man I have in mind, faced by the manifold of humanity, may feel, as well as terror, delight, but not, if he really sees what is before him, superiority. He will suffer that undramatic, because un–self-centred, agnosticism which goes with tolerance."[9]

Murdoch's characterization of the human being as sublime, dense and opaque has important implications for the status of form in her thought. She opposes reality to form, and associates form with the fantasies created by the self to avoid the sublimity of reality. Part of Murdoch's definition of the human being is that we are "benighted creatures sunk in a reality whose nature we are constantly and overwhelmingly tempted to deform by fantasy."[10] The nature of this reality—which we continually attempt to escape because we feel we cannot bear very much of it—is contingent, boundless, unpredictable and unknowable.

In "Against Dryness" she describes form as "an aspect of our desire for consolation ... a danger to our sense of reality as a rich receding background."[11] This notion of reality does not appear to leave room for an understanding of form as an organically occurring phenomenon. Rather, here she defines form as externally imposed upon reality after the fact by the human mind, as the creation of false unities and wholes, as something that distorts reality rather than as an integral part of reality. Whereas objects in reality do not fit together like puzzle pieces to form a coherent pattern, but are rather unique aspects of a jumbled, messy universe, form attempts to press these phenomena into a mold. Form, the creation of false unities, is a distortion of reality created by the ego in an effort to console itself in the face of the terror and decentering it experiences in the encounter with the sublime, incomprehensible and contingent world around it.

In Murdoch's philosophical writings form takes on a decidedly negative connotation. It is associated with fantasy, consolation, and egoism. These phenomena are roughly equivalent to the shadows on the wall of Plato's cave and her moral imperative demands that we leave behind these inherently false forms in order to live in reality and respect the particularities of this world, especially of the human personality.

In contrast, Murdoch is aware of the need for form in literature; she acknowledges that artists are pattern-makers. In fact, she writes in "On 'God' and 'Good'" that "[t]he claims of form and the question of 'how much form' to elicit constitutes one of the chief problems of art."[12] However, while she acknowledges its inevitability her reservations about it lead her to be wary about literature that employs it too copiously and rigidly. Her criticisms of twentieth-century literature—specifically what she terms journalistic literature, which she sees exemplified in some of the novels of Sartre and De Beauvoir, and crystalline literature, exemplified by Camus—center on her sense that much contemporary literature leans too far in the direction of form and as a result neglects the presentation of reality. In "The Sublime and the Beautiful Revisited" she writes:

> Form is the temptation of love and its peril, whether in art or life: to round off a situation, to sum up a character. But the difference is that art has got to have form, whereas life need not. And any artist both dreads and longs for the approach of necessity, the moment at which form irrevocably crystallises. There is a temptation for any novelist, and one to which if I am right modern novelists yield too readily, to imagine that the problem of the novel is solved and the difficulties overcome as soon as a form in the sense of a satisfactory myth has been evolved. But that is only the beginning. There is then the much more difficult battle to prevent that form from becoming rigid, by the free expansion against it of the individual characters. Here above all the contingency of the char-

> acters must be respected. Contingency must be defended for it is the essence of personality.... A novel must be a house fit for free characters to live in; and to combine form with a respect for reality with all its odd contingent ways is the highest art of prose.[13]

Murdoch's literary heroes are writers of the nineteenth century and throughout her essays she praises nineteenth-century realism for its presentation of real people. She feels that, in contrast to the fiction of her day, nineteenth-century novels contain "a plurality of real persons more or less naturalistically presented in a large social scene, and representing mutually independent centers of significance which are those of real individuals."[14] The negative view she takes of the twentieth-century tendency to "too readily employ form" is evident in another passage in which she describes this literary practice as a *symptom* of the inaccurate—because overly optimistic and simplistic—view of human personality put forth by contemporary Anglo-Saxon and French philosophy.[15]

Maria Antonaccio highlights the parallel between Murdoch's critique of pictures of human personality that ignore the reality of other people (including Romantic descendents of Hegel on the one hand and Anglo-Saxon descendents of Kant's liberalism on the other hand) and her theory of literary realism. The bridge, for Antonaccio, is Murdoch's reading of John Stuart Mill. Mill exemplifies for Murdoch a liberalism that both corrects the problems of the Kantian liberal tradition, principally its exclusion of particularity and its overemphasis on rationality, and corrects the problems of the Romantic or Hegelian view, which tends to subsume particularity into a larger unity. Mill turns our attention to the fact that other people exist, as Murdoch explains in "Against Dryness," and this movement should remind us of what Murdoch believes is so good about the nineteenth-century novel. Antonaccio suggests that "the nineteenth-century novel represents a kind of literary analogue to Mill's liberalism"; both liberal moral theory and the novel require the same kind of agnosticism that comes with tolerance.[16]

In line with her criticism of contemporary novelists, Murdoch sets out to produce art that moves towards what Bran Nicol has termed an aesthetic of the sublime, an aesthetic that would faithfully represent the contingency and irrationality of reality and human personality. Nicol identifies "the return to a proper realist form of characterization" as the most important part of developing an aesthetic of the sublime.[17] Murdoch explicitly pits this aim in literature against form, championing naturalistic characterization in language in a way that suggests it is a righteous weapon against the evils of form: "Against the consolations of form, the clean crystalline work, the simplified fantasy-myth, we must *pit* the *destructive power* of the now so unfashionable naturalistic idea of character."[18] Thus, while she acknowledges that form is necessary in literature, and therefore allows it more room in literature than she does in life, she still thinks of it as something to be avoided as much as possible.

One of the difficulties in the treatment of form as anathema and the attempt to write in a way that would faithfully represent the formlessness of reality is that literature is inherently a formed object. Critics such as David Gordon and Bernard Bergonzi have discussed the impossibility of aesthetic contingency in the novel.[19] However, Nicol responds to their criticisms of Murdoch's aesthetic of the sublime by acknowledging the limits of her project: "The contradictory nature of suggesting the contingent in a form which, by definition, always precludes the unplanned, means that a 'willed idea of contingency' is the best one can aim for. If Murdoch's sublime aesthetic is ultimately a defeat, it is at least a fairly honorable one."[20]

We might ask at this point why form is necessarily associated with fantasy and the distortion of reality? If reality is dense, opaque and sublime, does it necessarily follow that it is therefore devoid of form? In Murdoch's philosophy form is defined as rigid, unified, unchanging, and as an artificial fixing of contingency. But isn't it possible to conceive of form as something other than a totalizing force? What about a notion of form that does not round things off and sum them up, tying up all the loose ends and flattening the rich receding background of reality into a pattern, but rather is an organic component of reality? While such a notion of form as flexible, multiple and part of the manifold of reality may not be found in Murdoch's early writings on literature and philosophy, it can be found in some of her fiction of the same period, and it is this understanding of form, I argue, that explains the disjunction between her disapproval of form in philosophical writings and her use of form in fiction.

It is not, as some critics have suggested, that her philosophy is superior to her fiction and that in her fiction she is incapable of escaping the traps of form that she describes so eloquently in her nonfiction. Rather, I would suggest that we need not necessarily think of Murdoch's philosophy and fiction in opposition or choose one or the other as the place to look for her "real" meaning. Instead, I believe that it is only when we examine both disciplines in relation to each other that the full development of her understanding of form emerges. When we look only at her philosophy, her treatment of form in her fiction does not make sense; when we look at her fiction without the context of her philosophy, the significance of the status of form in her fiction is not clear.

Why should we care about Murdoch's treatment of form? Form has a central position in Murdoch's theory of the nature of reality and human personality as well as in her ethical thought and her ideas about how art and literature shape morality. Her moral imperative is that we resist the tendency to impose form on reality. One of the most important influences on her moral philosophy is Simone Weil, from whom Murdoch borrows the idea of attention. In "The Idea of Perfection" Murdoch describes the relationship between attention and fantasy thus: "Psychic energy flows, and more readily flows, into building up convincingly coherent but false pictures of the world, complete with systematic vocabulary.... Attention is the effort to counteract such states of illusion."[21] Murdoch's notion of form as false unity imposed on sublime reality comes through in her description of coherent yet false pictures of the world against which attention is directed.

The most crucial ethical direction of attention for Murdoch is our fellow human beings whom we have a moral imperative to see as unique individuals. The reality of our treatment of each other is very different than this, of course. Our unwillingness to recognize the singularity of others is a favorite topic for Murdoch. In *The Black Prince* Bradley Pearson explains to Julian, "The unconscious delights in identifying people with each other. It has only a few characters to play with."[22] In *A Fairly Honourable Defeat* Murdoch repeats the lesson when Julius says that for human beings, "[a]nyone will do to play the roles. They never really see each other at all."[23] Our usual vision of one another and of ourselves is inaccurate and follows patterns; whereas each person is unique and changeable, human beings are not able to see this unless they develop the capacity of attention. Attention is ethically important because our vision of the world determines our choices and actions in the world: "I can only choose within the world I can *see*, in the moral sense of 'see' which implies that clear vision is a result of moral imagination and moral effort.... One is often compelled almost automatically by what one *can* see."[24] In "The Sublime and the Good" Murdoch describes proper attention to the other as love: "Love is the perception of individuals. Love is the extremely difficult realisation that something other than oneself is real."[25]

Myth in the Fiction

Since our way of imagining others is so central to her ethics let us examine Murdoch's use of form in her fiction with particular attention to the way she writes characters. If we are familiar with Murdoch's philosophical position regarding attention to individuality and her advocacy of realism, particularly concerning character, Murdoch's fiction can be puzzling to read because she seems to violate her own rules for the treatment of character. Her characters often come across as unrealistic to the reader and can seem schematic or archetypal. In addition to this, she makes frequent allusions to literary models such as figures from Greek myth. These mythic allusions, and her "formed" characters in general, are of two kinds. First, characters see other characters as types; that is, they project mythic or psychic content onto other characters thus perceiving them in an unrealistic way. This corresponds to Bradley's description of humans in *The Black Prince* as identifying people with roles. Second, some characters are presented as mythic types within the narrative itself.

We can see both of these practices in *A Severed Head*, a novel with very strong mythic overtones. The character of Palmer Anderson resembles Dionysus in several ways including, of course, his name with its allusions to the trickster figure and deception (palming), as well as his effects on Antonia and Martin, over whom he exerts psychological control. Palmer, as a psychoanalyst, is a professional liberator who is referred to by the narrator, Martin, as a modern magician. As Martin says about Palmer, "Anyone who is good at setting people free is also good at enslaving them."[26] This description links him to Dionysus, who simultaneously binds and liberates the human worshiper. Georgie accuses Martin of being carried away by Palmer, and he literally takes Antonia and Georgie away from Martin; likewise, Dionysus is the god who carries one away from oneself and from one's home and identity. Similarly, Honor is identified (though not identical) with Medusa; this identification is explicitly mentioned in the blurb on the back of the Penguin edition. The blurb reads in part, "[Martin] attempts to behave beautifully and sensibly. Then he meets a woman whose demonic splendour at first repels him and later arouses a consuming and monstrous passion. As his Medusa informs him, 'this is nothing to do with happiness.'" In letters to Roly Colchrane from the 1980s, Murdoch revealed that she composed the blurbs for her novels.[27] This intentional and very conscious portrayal by Murdoch of characters as participating in mythic models is prevalent in the novels.

On another level, within the story itself, characters view each other through the lens of mythological figures and archetypal situations. One example is Martin and Antonia's vision of each other as mother and child. We also see this pattern in the way Martin views Georgie. He repeatedly describes her as primitive, barbaric, uncivilized, chaotic, animal-like, and thinks of her as a "river goddess" and a "child of nature." His categorization of Georgie and Antonia as two different sides of the feminine, as the Classical, civilized woman versus the primitive, uncivilized woman renders him unable to see the reality of either woman. The result is that he is blind-sided when they exceed his preconceptions of their possible behavior and feelings. Martin's subsequent reassessment of Georgie and Antonia, among the other characters he has to reassess, including himself, is an education for him. He makes an ethical change when he comes to see the complexity of the other characters in the novel more completely and accurately, when he sees the ways in which they do not conform to his preconceptions of them. These two fictional practices are not completely distinct from one another, especially in a first-person novel like *A Severed Head* in which it is sometimes hard to draw the line between Martin's sense of people and what they are really like. For example, the Oedipal relationship between Martin and Antonia occurs on the level of Martin's perceptions of Antonia but is also verified by others who have mistaken Antonia for Martin's mother and by other characters who characterize the marriage as a mother-child relationship.

Let us examine more closely the first use Murdoch makes of myth in building her characters: having characters view each other as abstract types or parts in their psychological dramas. This use of form does not present a challenge to Murdoch's philosophical commitments because by showing characters' distorted views of each other and the destructive consequences of this inattention she provides a literary demonstration of her philosophical argument that we are constantly tempted to deform the nature of reality by fantasy and an example of the ethical pitfalls of continuing to do so.

Peter Conradi writes, "Myth opposes particularity, history and contingency because it digests all of them, bullying the plural into the singular.... You can service it with any amount of disparate material or information, but it is encoded only to deliver the same timeless, neurotic answer."[28] This mechanistic treatment of the disparate data of experience is certainly characteristic of the way characters in *A Severed Head* view and treat each other. When Martin relates to Antonia through the lens of his Oedipal framework he fails to see her particularity, just as he fails to see the particularity of Georgie. The latter failure of attention leads to Georgie's suicide attempt. But Murdoch uses this aspect of myth—that our vision of the real, formless world is distorted by our willful projection of mythic patterns onto ourselves and other people—to the advantage of her moral imperative that we ought to try and see reality more accurately. She uses the abstracting, generalizing form of myth, representing characters in a less realistic way, in order to show us how people *really* view one another. That is, she is using myth to reveal to the reader the ways in which myth conceals reality; our myth-distorted vision hides from us the formlessness and contingent sublimity of reality. Myth (and therefore form) is capable of both revealing and concealing reality. Murdoch employs its schematizing and generalizing tendencies to reveal the ways in which we are constantly living in myth. Thus, in this instance, rather than undermining the realism of her fiction, Murdoch uses form, and particularly myth, *to realist ends*. This practice also corresponds to Murdoch's belief that art does important ethical work when it shows us reality. By holding up a mirror to our unethical vision and treatment of one another Murdoch's novels provide a warning of the dangers of such behavior.

However, this reasoning does not account for characters in Murdoch's fiction that are represented on the level of the narration such that they resemble mythic figures, and this other practice demands its own examination. These characters, who often come across as archetypal, seem to contradict Murdoch's arguments in her nonfiction that what is needed in fiction is free characters, and it is this practice that has given critics such pause. It must be noted that there is not a direct one-to-one correspondence between these characters and the mythic figures that are alluded to in them. For example, Honor Klein is explicitly identified with Medusa by Murdoch, as is Palmer Anderson with Dionysus, but the novel complicates these identifications by not supporting a reading of Honor simply as Medusa or Palmer simply as Dionysus. Perhaps the most we can say about these characters is that Palmer is Dionysian and Honor Medusan. In fact, most of Murdoch's "mythic" characters are written such that they resemble the mythic model, or multiple mythic models, but are not simply contemporary copies of these mythic figures. Nevertheless, these characters in Murdoch's fiction pose a challenge to her literary critical argument that what fiction ought to do is present free, realistic characters, not types.

An example of one of these character types is the figure of the distant yet mysteriously powerful female. This type of character is usually not at the center of the novel and is more or less removed from the other characters, yet exerts an almost magnetic power over them. Rather than exerting direct control over other characters or the plot, these women operate indirectly. It is as if other characters engage in action, which moves the plot forward and produces changes in themselves and others, for the sake of these separate figures. These figures are similar to the male characters David Gordon has described as satanic or demonic: "In earlier novels, like *The Flight from the Enchanter* and *A Severed Head*, the demonic source is a charismatic figure somewhat removed from the foregrounded characters, who are themselves stirred by the demon into a complicity that is the moralist's particular target."[29] Gordon goes on to discuss other ways power works in Murdoch's later fiction but this introductory remark is interesting for our purposes since the female figures function in a similar way to these demonic characters. I would not call the female figures demonic, however, because they more closely resemble another group of figures from Greek myth. Since Greek myth figures so prominently in her fiction an exploration of the possible Greek sources is helpful.

This type is at least partly recognizable to us because it echoes the Fates: feminine figures that remain outside the action of the world yet control it in an unknowable, mysterious way. They also bring to mind another mythic type that is related to the Fates: feminine figures such as the Sirens or the Sphinx that remain outside the action of a play or story yet control it indirectly because the mythic protagonist is either inescapably drawn by them or consciously or unconsciously undertakes action for their sake or through their direction.

One such figure from Murdoch's early fiction is Anthea Barlow in *The Time of the Angels*. Mrs. Barlow, as she is called throughout much of the novel, is so minor in the plot as to be almost unnoticeable until the end when the reader learns of her significance. During the majority of the novel she appears as merely an annoying woman who frequently calls on Carel Fischer, the new rector, a man who refuses to entertain visitors despite having recently moved to town to start a new post.

The plot of the novel turns on secret family relationships and incest. Carel Fischer shares with his brother Marcus custody of their niece Elizabeth, who is the daughter of their dead brother Julian. Mrs. Barlow seems to have nothing to do with anything that goes on in the house, apparently not knowing any of the family and not ever gaining entrance. It is only at the end of the novel, after the incest between Carel and Elizabeth has been exposed and Carel has committed suicide, that we discover Anthea Barlow's significance.

Early in the novel Marcus tells a friend of the event that ruptured the closeness of the three brothers:

> "We were all very happy together when we were boys," Marcus mumbled, his mouth full of warm buttery scone and greengage.
> "Well, it looks as if something came unstuck."
> "I suppose it was just growing up. And then there was a girl. And, oh, various things."
> "What did the girl do?"
> "Oh, just made trouble. She was an ecstatic type, sort of in love with all three of us, and we were sort of in love with her. I escaped by rushing off to the U.S.A. Carel and Julian were already married then."[30]

When Carel's daughter tells his mistress Pattie of Carel's incestuous relationship with his niece Elizabeth, Pattie shares that Elizabeth is in fact Carel's daughter by Julian's wife. When they were young Carel and Julian had both fallen in love with the same girl and Julian had left his wife for her. Carel had seduced Julian's wife out of spite; when Julian found out that his wife was pregnant (with Elizabeth) he killed himself. Later in the novel we discover that this girl who "made trouble" is in fact the same Mrs. Barlow who has haunted the edges of the narrative.

Indirectly, Anthea Barlow determines much of the plot. She is the object of desire who inspires acts that create the underlying situation of the narrative. By "falling in love" with the three brothers she draws Julian away from his wife. Because of his jealousy in losing Anthea to Julian, Carel seduces Julian's wife, with whom he begets Elizabeth, who will later be his lover and "niece."

In a much more direct and overt way Carel Fischer is the cause of the action in the novel and he acknowledges and revels in his power to direct the course of events. He wants to control others, telling his daughter Muriel that she will do as he wants her to, not allowing Marcus access to his ward Elizabeth, and keeping Pattie in a kind of prison situation in which she feels owned by him. In some ways he fits David Gordon's description of a demonic character. But by the end of the novel Carel has lost his control of the situation and this is most clearly demonstrated by his suicide (although this act itself could be read as a perverse form of control).

The fact that Carel and other characters are responsible for their actions, including Carel's incestuous relation with his daughter/niece, his suicide, and going back as far as the brothers' original "sins" of adultery and seduction, does not overshadow Anthea's involvement, though her involvement is subterranean in relation to the narrative action. Her influence is similar to the way Lola Lola causes the suicide of Professor Immanuel Rath in *The Blue Angel*, not through any act per se but simply through the nature of her being.[31]

The parallel suicides of the two brothers suggest that they have both met the same fate at the hidden hands of Anthea Barlow, and that her power, while unseen, continues to shape their destinies. This likelihood is strengthened by the strange meeting of Anthea and Marcus, the only remaining brother from the original *ménage à quatre*. His status as the last survivor of the triad of brothers is emphasized in the moment before he meets Anthea:

> Now Carel was gone too and seemed already to recede so fast, as if he were in haste to find his way back to Julian in some distant land of youth. Only Marcus remained, heavy with these deaths, these lives. Only within him did all that was singular of them upon this earth live and grow now. There was a sound behind him and he turned sharply.[32]

The sound Marcus hears at this moment, when he realizes that he is the last vestige of their singularity, is Anthea. Her appearance at this moment is significant because it interrupts his awareness of his survival, suggesting that she is a deadly figure. Anthea appears to Marcus out of the blue and he remarks, "Wherever did you spring from? ... But where have you been all these years? And whatever in the world are you doing here?"[33] These questions are appropriate from Marcus's position but as readers we know that Anthea Barlow has been in the background during the entire narrative unbeknownst to the other characters. This split is acknowledged in this scene with Anthea explaining that she is now Mrs. Barlow and that Marcus must have heard of that person. There is an uncanny quality to Anthea Barlow's reappearance in the lives of Marcus and his family. Since she has actually been there the whole time yet was never recognized, she is like an invisible and ever-present force that operates on the lives of men without their awareness, laying in wait for her influence to unfold. Similarly, his thoughts that he alone of his brothers has survived and that once he is dead their singularity will be eradicated foreshadow his vulnerability to death. When Anthea and Marcus part he insists that she come to dinner at his house. He is entering her web, the last of the brothers, and we wonder if he will join them in their fate.

Anthea's name underscores her feminine natural danger. The name Anthea means "flowerlike." It is derived from the Greek word *anthos*, which means "flower blossom" and was an epithet of the goddesses Hera and Aphrodite. Persephone, or Kore as she is sometimes called, is the Greek goddess who first comes to mind in connection with flowers since she is picking flowers when she is abducted and is described in several sources as having a flowerlike existence. Significantly, Persephone represents both the beautiful young girl, which is how Anthea first appeared to the three brothers, and the cold queen of the dead. Jean-Pierre Vernant tells us that flowers were more broadly a trope for female sexuality for the Greeks, and here we find a connection to the Sirens as well. The Sirens are identified with the paradoxical and deceptive location in which they are permanently fixed — a flowering meadow "encircled by a heaped-up mass of whitened bones and putrefied corpses with desiccated skins."[34] This flowering meadow is tied to their seduction of men, such as Odysseus, to whom they promise release from the suffering of life. These feminine figures combine fertility, or the promise of fertility and life, with death; death through feminine sexuality represented as flowers.

Marcus's encounter with Anthea brings together these themes as well. He thinks of the reappearance of Anthea as a healthy movement back into life after the suffering he and his loved ones have undergone throughout the novel. He thinks concerning their meeting, "There was a kind of silly innocence about it all, a kind of thoroughly cheerful innocence.... With her the ordinary world seemed to resume its power, the world where human beings made simple claims on one another and where things were small and odd and touching and funny."[35] But there is an eerie feeling in this meeting and this passage has more than a touch of irony. Marcus imagines that the world Anthea ushers in is one in which people make simple claims on one another and that her appearance signifies innocence, but given Anthea's subterranean, indirect role in the deaths of Julian and Carel and the incestuous relationship between Carel and Elizabeth, we know that the claims made on people in Anthea's world are far from simple and innocent. While Marcus's comments suggest that he thinks of Anthea's presence as breaking a spell, it is more likely that this is a sign of his enchantment by her, as the sailors who listen to the Siren's song are enchanted to their deaths.

Anthea Barlow recalls a complex of feminine figures in Greek religion that includes Hera, Persephone and Aphrodite as well as the Fates and the Sirens. The Cambridge anthropologist Jane Harrison, who may have been a source of inspiration for Honor Klein in *A Severed Head*, argued that many Greek goddesses and mythic figures derived from a single ancient figure.[36] While Harrison's theories have since fallen out of fashion they are still helpful in understanding these interrelated figures and Murdoch was surely familiar with at least some of Harrison's work, given her interest in Classics and her work at Cambridge.

In *Mythology*, Harrison traces Artemis, Hera, Athena, Aphrodite, Demeter and Kore, Medusa, and the Eumenides back to a single figure called the Mistress of Wild Beasts, Earth-Mother or Mountain Mother of Cretan religion. Other anthropologists, psychologists and classicists have called this figure the Mother Goddess or Great Mother. While in this book Harrison does not identify the Fates and the Sirens as belonging to this group, based on their symbolism they belong to the same period of Greek religion in which figures were not yet clearly delineated from one another. Elsewhere, Harrison presents several figures, including the Sirens, the Sphinx, the Fates, the Gorgons and the Mistress of Wild Beasts as interrelated in this prehistoric period. They all represent the terrifying, mysterious and overwhelming power of the world, which is semi-anthropomorphized as female, over the individual. We might say that Anthea Barlow is a modern representation of such a figure; a shadowy, inchoate feminine presence that exerts a deadly and mysterious influence over other characters.

Reconciling the Contradictions, Recognizing the Logic

To return to our question about this type of character, variations of which are also found in *An Unofficial Rose* and *A Severed Head*, how do we reconcile characters in the fiction that are strongly formed, and particularly characters that resemble a mythic model, with Murdoch's philosophical and literary critical advocacy of realism and the uniqueness of individuals?[37] Why does Murdoch use mythic forms in her fiction while at the same time using the word myth so negatively in her nonfiction? This use of form would seem to pose a much stronger challenge to Murdoch's philosophical arguments than characters that view other characters as conforming to a type. I suggest that Murdoch's use of myth in the novels has several important implications for the ethical aims and metaphysical views she makes explicit in her philosophical writings.

One of the ethical consequences of Murdoch's allusion to mythic models in her characters lies in the jarring effect these characters have on the reader; it is clear to us as readers that they are not realistic characters and this experience can produce discomfort. Murdoch's practice creates an opportunity for readers to become aware of the extent to which reading participates in the dissemination of types and erases individuality by drawing attention to readers' tendency to search for patterns in characters. In this, there is a Brechtian quality to Murdoch's fiction; she makes us uncomfortably conscious that we are reading a work of fiction by highlighting the non-realist aspects of the form. Because Murdoch often inserts into her fiction her ethical imperative that we view others realistically, by having a character either communicate directly or live through the ethical consequences of not seeing other people with loving attention, readers may therefore be made aware on some level, though not necessarily consciously, of their own ethical position as readers.

In addition to creating this "*Verfremdungseffekt*" (alienation effect) with its lessons for ethics, attention and sublimity, Murdoch's use of myth lies at the heart of a bridge between her fiction and nonfiction, and goes a long way toward helping us understand why the apparent inconsistency between her treatment of form in each is not necessarily an actual discrepancy. Myth is particularly suited to Murdoch's project of offering an alternative to the prevailing pictures of human personality that she critiques in her nonfiction and her project of representing reality as sublime. Despite Conradi's description of myth as "oppos[ing] particularity, history and contingency because it digests all of them, bullying the plural into the singular" I argue that myth, and myth as Murdoch deploys it in her fiction, is characterized by multiplicity, localism, overlap and inconsistency.[38] It is the opposite of a totalizing system.[39] Myth may be the type of form that both corresponds most closely to Murdoch's vision of reality as messy and occupies a position that is outside of the Anglo-Saxon rationalist picture of the human being.

To explore this aspect of Murdoch's use of myth we should return to her practice of writing characters that view each other as types. The latter practice allows her to demonstrate the way human beings relate to one another, the extent to which, as Conradi puts it, "[t]he unenlightened psyche, or unenlightened level within the psyche, coerces others because it sees them playing roles within an Oedipal romance whose terms were laid down in childhood."[40] To Conradi's formulation I would add that this practice includes more mythic patterns than the Oedipal romance, as is evident in Murdoch's many examples of characters thinking of each other as Medusas and demons. Characters that are written by Murdoch as "formed," so that they participate in mythic models, may be an extension of characters that are viewed as types by other characters within the novel. The inscription of a portrait of human beings as participating in culturally shared forms *within the narrative* lends the portrait a greater validity than when it is painted through the eyes of a character we may not trust, as it is in *A Severed Head*. Thus, one way this practice can be read in relation to her philosophical commitments to realism is that by presenting characters as types she is again demonstrating that myth is an integral part of how we see ourselves and live. That is, by presenting mythic characters she may be practicing realism, since as she puts it, we live in myth all the time, rather than failing at realism, of which some critics have accused her.

This position has interesting implications for human nature and the place of form in human nature. What is implied here is that form is endemic to human psychology on a deep level, and that we are in fact formed beings in ways that extend beyond others' perceptions of us. This possibility does not preclude Murdoch's Platonic belief that we can move beyond form and out of the cave of images, but merely assumes that some characters do not do so. However, it does suggest a different and more central status for form than her philosophical presentation of it as something imposed on formless reality after the fact. Rather, in her fiction form appears as something that is part of the fabric of reality in a substantial way, and this shift requires attention.

We may find help if we turn again to Murdoch's philosophy, specifically to her critique of the over-reliance on rationalism in modern philosophy, which conceives of form as a closed, complete circle. Nicol writes that

> to look back at it from a postmodern perspective, her philosophy amounts to a sustained critique of the Enlightenment project. She is keen throughout her philosophical writings to temper what she sees as a growing emphasis on the transcendent power of the rational mind and will by reminding us of the spiritual and irrational dimensions of human experience.[41]

This insistence that human beings are much less rational than we would like to think and that mysterious forces (some of which she thinks of as inner machinery) restrict our freedom can be detected throughout her early philosophical writings and fiction. This commitment to creating a picture of the human personality that allows for and emphasizes the irrational parts of the soul may explain her use of mythic forms on such a wide scale. The nature and the kind of myth she incorporates make it particularly suited to the anti-rationalist aspect of Murdoch's project as it is highlighted in Nicol's quotation.

Since the nineteenth century, myth has occupied a position of irrationality in relation to modernity, a position shared by pre-modern culture generally and primitive thought more particularly. Some of the mythic figures that predominate in Murdoch's fiction belong to what Harrison terms chthonic religion. For instance, the feminine figures alluded to in the character of Anthea Barlow, as well as Medusa and Dionysus, are considered pre–Olympian deities and, by some critics, figures of irrationality. Even when Murdoch uses a figure that has served as the poster boy of Greek rationalism, Apollo, she interprets the figure in such a way as to emphasize its irrational aspects.[42]

As well as emphasizing the irrationality of myth Murdoch employs it in a particular way that furthers her aim of creating a portrait of the personality that resists rationalism. Her use of myth is not simplistic; there is usually not a direct, one-to-one relationship between a character and a mythic figure, as we have seen in *A Severed Head* and *The Time of the Angels*. Perhaps because of this quality Lorna Sage has characterized Murdoch's use of myth as *provisional*: She uses pieces from myth temporarily as she needs them and then gives them up in favor of other pieces.[43] While I agree that this is an important aspect of Murdoch's practice, I would suggest that her use of myth is *combinatory*, that she weaves together allusions to multiple myths and figures in a way that reflects the nature of myth as described above (overlapping, inconsistent). The borders between figures are not discrete and contradictions between and within figures coexist in myth and in Murdoch's mythic allusions. This structure allows Murdoch a way of approximating the complexity and messiness of the human personality; the extent to which it is multi-faceted and multi-dimensional and does not conform to order. This quality of myth and of Murdoch's use of myth allows her the opportunity to slip out of the bounds of the kinds of rational approaches to the human psyche that she criticizes in the Anglo-Saxon and French portraits of the human. Myth is more suited to this task than straightforward psychology since that science aims at systematically mapping the human personality whereas myth more fluidly presents the complexities and inconsistencies of the psyche. Thus, the way in which she uses myth allows Murdoch's fiction to more accurately represent the complexity and internal contradictions of sublime reality. It allows her to tackle a task that seems all but impossible, creating in her fiction what I would like to term a *mimesis of sublimity*, a representation of that which defies conceptual grasp, the endless complexity and unknowability of the human psyche.

Murdoch has said that myth is not merely decorative in her fiction. Rather, by allowing her flexibility in the representation of sublime reality, it performs work that is essential to Murdoch's ethical project. If reason is not capable of making the sublime human personality wholly transparent to ourselves and each other, if it cannot reveal the whole truth of human reality, then something else outside the realm of the merely rational is required. If myth can be said to have a function it is that it reveals something that cannot be revealed in other ways, something in flux and ungraspable to the rational mind. That this reality is in flux and cannot be grasped by reason, that it is sublimely unknowable in its essence, does not mean that it is formless, however, only that it does not hold to rigid, unchanging form. By creating characters that feel constructed or artificial, rather than writing more "realistic" characters as some of her contemporaries do, and as she advocates in her literary criticism, Murdoch refuses to erase the unknowable and unrepresentable quality of the human personality, thus emphasizing its sublimity. This sublime mimesis emphasizes the extent to which representations of the human that we can create in literature are just that, representation not presentation.

Bran Nicol says with regard to her plotting, which he characterizes as sublime, that Murdoch uses form to suggest formlessness.[44] With regard to her mythic characters, I suggest that it is not so much formlessness that is presented through the use of form but a more subtle understanding of form as fluid and contradictory, and that myth is precisely the medium for such a presentation. While form and myth are both generally treated negatively in her nonfiction as forces that strip reality of its complexity, a different notion of them emerges in her fiction and this inconsistency has caught the attention of many critics. But rather than this inconsistency signaling a weakness in her fiction, or a lack of relation between her philosophy and her fiction, it signals a modification and augmentation of some of the arguments she works out in her nonfiction regarding form. Nicol writes of a tension in Murdoch's thought between two kinds of language:

> Like Wittgenstein, Plato was deeply concerned with the relationship between language and reality. For Plato, transcendent concepts exist *beyond* representation, in the realm of ideal forms, and are only properly accessible via *anamnesis*— extralinguistically, in other words. While words enable us to reproduce the shape of reality (its forms and ideas) they can just as easily lead us *away* from it. Language can produce its own forms, and therefore its own truth. Murdoch's work often centres on the difficult task of negotiating both kinds of language: one that is faithful to truth, one that is unfaithful.[45]

A similar movement between two notions of form, one that reveals and is part of sublime reality and one that is imposed on and distorts reality's complexity, underlies the tension between her fiction and nonfiction. The more positive function form serves in her fiction does not nullify the definition of form she presents in her nonfiction. Rather, these two understandings of form coexist in her work. Moreover, aspects of her uses of form, and specifically myth, in her treatment of character point to an underlying logic: her definition of human beings as sublime and her critique of rationalist pictures of humans that stretches between her philosophy and her fiction rendering the contradiction only an apparent one.

NOTES

1. Nicol, 2004, 10.
2. Heusel, 1995, 212.
3. Murdoch, 1997, Penguin, 293.
4. Murdoch, 1989, 43–44.
5. *Ibid.*, 37.
6. For discussions of Murdoch's relation to Freud see Bran Nicol, *Iris Murdoch: The Retrospective Fiction*, David Gordon, *Iris Murdoch's Fables of Unselfing* and Maria Antonaccio, *Picturing the Human: The Moral Thought of Iris Murdoch.*
7. Murdoch, 1997, Penguin, 263.
8. *Ibid.*, 282.
9. *Ibid.*, 283.
10. *Ibid.*, 293.
11. *Ibid.*, 294.
12. Murdoch, 1989, 65.
13. Murdoch, 1977, Penguin, 285–86.
14. *Ibid.*, 271.
15. *Ibid.*, 294.
16. *Ibid.*, 110.
17. Nicol, 2004, 6.
18. Murdoch, 1997, Penguin, 294.
19. Bernard Bergonzi, *The Situation of the Novel* (London: Macmillan, 1970); David J. Gordon, *Iris Murdoch's Fables of Unselfing.*
20. Nicol, 2004, 10.
21. Murdoch, 1989, 37.
22. Murdoch, 1973, *The Black Prince*, 95.
23. Murdoch, 1970, *A Fairly Honourable Defeat*, 104.
24. Murdoch, 1989, 37.
25. Murdoch, 1997, Penguin, 215.
26. Murdoch, 1976, 7.
27. Conradi, 2006, 29–32.
28. Conradi, 2001, 104.
29. Gordon, 1995, 62.
30. Murdoch, 1966, 31.
31. Feminine figures of this type are often characterized as monsters (e.g., Medusa, the Sirens) because of their death-dealing powers. The horror and danger of these feminine monsters is different than the danger of masculine monsters; it is a peculiar feature of feminine monsters that their monstrosity takes the form of passivity. Since passivity is traditionally associated with femininity, we may ask if they are cast as monsters by virtue of their femininity. Lola Lola is a particularly good modern example of the femme fatale whose femininity is a danger to men who are seduced by it. In this, Lola Lola brings to mind Charybdis in *The Odyssey*, which sucks men down to their deaths with an inescapable power. As with Charybdis and other figures in *The Odyssey*, Lola Lola and Anthea Barlow do not kill men in an active way, but rather *naturally* bring them to their deaths.
32. Murdoch, 1966, 246.
33. *Ibid.*
34. Vernant, 1991, 104.
35. Murdoch, 1966, 248–49.
36. Harrison, 1963.

37. Miranda Peronett, the little girl in *An Unofficial Rose*, and Elizabeth Fischer in *The Time of the Angels* are variations on this type. Honor Klein is another one, although since *A Severed Head* is a first-person narrative, it is hard to distinguish between the objective presentation of character in the narrative and the view of a character through the eyes of the protagonist/narrator. To come back to the issues of feminine figures of death and of Murdoch's relation to Freud, we note that Martin's choice of Honor among the three women in the novel may be a comment on Freud's essay "The Theme of the Three Caskets."

38. Conradi, 2001, 104.

39. This understanding of myth is widespread in twentieth-century theories of myth. See, for example, the writings of Marcel Detienne, Jean-Pierre Vernant, Karl Kerenyi and Erich Neumann.

40. Conradi, 2001, 101.
41. Nicol, 2004, 15.
42. See Murdoch's portrayal of Loxias in *The Black Prince*.
43. Sage, 1977, 57–87.
44. Nicol, 2004, 9.
45. *Ibid.*, 15.

3

Narrative and Symbolic Layering in *The Unicorn*

JUDIT VARGA

This essay focuses on the process of meaning production through the layering of several plot structures in Iris Murdoch's *The Unicorn*. Through investigating the relation of the narrative structure to the novel's main characters, my aim is to suggest a further way of thinking about the mysteriousness and puzzlement in the Murdoch scholarship with regard to its meaning.[1] I look at *The Unicorn* as a narrative made up of several coexisting symbolic patterns, which come about as a result of the characters' attempts at making sense of Hannah Crean-Smith. The patterns evolve around characters and create several parallel story lines that produce the novel's coexisting points of view on Hannah. These multiple perspectives proliferate the meaning of actions and events. Drawing on Bran Nicol, I want to claim that the excessive generation of possible meanings deliberately renders the novel difficult to perceive and interpret.[2] Furthermore, I want to argue that despite being in the focus of all the narratives, the pivotal source of mystery in the novel is Hannah, the lady imprisoned in Gaze Castle. I want to investigate the narratives for ways in which they prefigure characters like Marian, Effingham and Gerald, and for the ways in which they insert Hannah into their formulaic structures. "There is much story in *The Unicorn*," observes Robert Scholes in *Fabulation and Metafiction*; however, he mentions only two of them: the Gothic and the *Legend of the Unicorn*.[3] In addition to these two, I will explore the Chivalric romance and the Platonic narrative of *ascesis* as paradigmatic plot structures that contribute to the shaping of the novel's meaning. I will argue that the Gothic and the Romance that frame the figure of Marian and Effingham, respectively, coincide and intersect at crucial events and over the figure of Hannah, and claim that the multiplication and dispersion of signification originates in these instances. The genealogy of the figure of the unicorn will be explored briefly to suggest an alternative unicorn narrative that might complement the currently prevalent *Legend of the Unicorn* and introduce metafictionality as a viable aspect in the critical discourse on the novel. The Platonic plot will be investigated for its faculty to reveal, through its interpretation of Hannah, the true meaning of *The Unicorn*.

Compared to the complexity of meanings on the level of plot, the story line of *The Unicorn* appears to be relatively straightforward. Marian Taylor, a governess arrives in Gaze Castle, where Hannah Crean-Smith is imprisoned. Marian attempts to set Hannah free with the help of Effingham Cooper from Riders Castle, whose proprietor is Max Lejour, the Plato scholar. Marian and Effie's attempt does not prevail and instead, it brings more blight to the land and its inhabitants. The male characters, including Pip Lejour (Max's son), Effingham, and Gerald all fall in love with Hannah. Hannah later kills Gerald Scottow, her gaoler, at which moment Denis Nolan, Hannah's valet, admits to have murdered Peter, the imprisoned lady's husband. The novel ends with Marian and Effingham's departure from Gaze following Hannah's suicide and Max's inheriting of her Castle.

As in *A Severed Head*,[4] recurring events in *The Unicorn* imply the function of the story as a "replay" of events that happened *before* the novel's time and that might be seen to double the narrative's semantic strata. As events like the attempted kidnap, Effingham and Gerald's falling in love with Hannah, Denis' murder of Peter and the meeting of the sea and the river in a destructive flood all turn out to be repetitions, they start to figure as the perceptible shapes of an evanescent content that has previously escaped signification.

By repeatedly eluding the narratives that attempt to shape her figure into a meaningful form, Hannah Crean-Smith symbolizes of the novel's attempts at figuring an evasive meaning. I want to argue that the multiple meanings of her figure contribute to the hermeneutic difficulty regarding the novel's meaning. Characters in and the readers of the novel are both caught up in attempts to make sense of Hannah, as the discovery of Hannah and the meaning of her narrative is expected to dissolve the mystery of Gaze Castle and the mystery of *The Unicorn*. Robert Scholes also reflects the difficulty in attaining to Hannah's meaning when he claims that "she is the center of the story yet most remote from us."[5] Hannah's palindromic first name, Han/nah, might be though to allude to the delusive function of her figure.[6]

As she resides in the focus of characters' attention, Hannah is posited as the fulcrum of the narratives in *The Unicorn*. She appears at once as the fetish and then the guilty woman of fantasy narratives. Characters conceive of her as a Gothic heroine, a unicorn, the lady of Chivalric Romances, the *femme fatale*, Lilith, and *Até* of Greek mythology. She contemporaneously appears as the protagonist of several narratives and her meaning becomes that which these narratives prefigure for her. Hannah therefore might be seen as a reflection of roles and meanings, a reflection that stands in the place of the ungraspable meaning of Hannah *as Hannah*. The meaning of Hannah's figure is caught up in the process of inscription and erasure as characters, in *The Unicorn*, in their attempts at pinning down her meaning, subject Hannah to their particular discourses.

I will demonstrate in this essay that inscrutability is inherent in Hannah as Hannah and that it might be seen as one of the causes of the mysteriousness of *The Unicorn*.

The way in which Marian describes Hannah underscores the mirror-like quality of the imprisoned lady: "[Hannah] rose and began to glide about the room. She was much given to looking at herself in mirrors. She moved now from glass to glass."[7] Her palindromic name also suggests insubstantiality; Hannah is pronounced as if it were an effortless sigh.[8] During its phonetic production, the word "hannah" runs a cycle from *h* to *h*, and parallels the closed, mirror-like structure of her figure. Hannah's room contains all the elements that are associated with her figure: it is always brightly lit and it is full of mirrors. Gold and yellow become Hannah's leitmotifs in the narrative: "She had reddish gold hair and eyes of almost the same colour.... She was dressed in a flowing robe of embroidered yellow silk...."[9] These characteristics and the fact that she never appears in the dark imply that Hannah is like a mirror reflection which is emphasized by her association with light and the sun. The link between her figure and light is especially evident in relation to the rest of Gaze Castle, which is presented, in contrast, in marked darkness. Hannah's brightly lit room, therefore, appears to enclose an ill-fitted space in the Castle:

> The room was brilliantly lit with a great many lamps and the curtains were always drawn although it was still bright outside. Marian was dazzled by the soft flooding light and by fear.... A small turf fire was burning in a big grate and there was fine china on the black marble mantelpiece. There were a great many mirrors, some of them pretty but no pictures and few attempts at orderly embellishment.[10]

Beyond linking her figure to the ideas of reflection, light, the drawn curtains and the "great many mirrors" associate Hannah with an uncanny sameness. When present, Hannah often brings the narrative to a halt. She explicitly refuses the attempts of her "audience" at knowing or *seeing* her when she says: "Ah, but nobody can be with me on the inside. Nobody can see."[11] That she claims to be metaphorically dead, underscores the idea of sameness in her figure: "We have run out of life, at least I have. I'm doing something quite different."[12] When this strange idea of sameness and motionlessness is accompanied by insensibility, "Oh, I don't *feel* much any more.... I have felt frightened, guilty, many things—but not now," we might claim that Hannah appears inanimate. Her figure seems to be suspended in the illusion of sameness, which is emphasized by the unreal atmosphere of her room.[13]

Although she brings the narrative to a halt in scenes where she is present, each character is caught up in the quest of finding her meaning when she is "off-stage." Characters conceive of her in terms of narratives when they call her the lady of Chivalric Romances, the *femme fatale*, *Lilith*, and *Até*. By receding to stillness, sameness and motionlessness, Hannah appears as the image or the role that the narratives in *The Unicorn* prefigure for her, while Hannah, herself, remains invisible. Although she is "much given to looking at herself in mirrors," neither the characters nor the reader are shown that which Hannah sees.[14] That her own mirror reflection remains hidden might be thought to imply that Hannah fails to appear *as Hannah*. She is also always presented in the company of other characters and never on her own, which might underscore the claim that she personifies other characters' *vision* of her.

In Gaze Castle, Hannah resides at a magical space created by mirrors. That her room "was brilliantly lit" with the "great many mirrors" indicates the intersection of reflected light rays where Hannah is implicitly figured as a play of light, a virtual image.[15] When Marian and Effie try to kidnap and take her away from Gaze, they destroy Hannah on a metaphorical level: they shatter the identical, timeless and plotless presence of her existence by introducing a structure that might shape her illusive figure into meaning. "To go somewhere else would have too much significance now, it would make me *be* something," claims Hannah, implying that in Gaze Castle her meaning is ungraspable.[16] Similarly to a mirror image that disappears when no one looks in the mirror, Hannah vanishes when she steps outside the specular world of Gaze Castle.[17] While Hannah is present, the aim of the characters in *The Unicorn*, as remarked explicitly by Marian, Effingham and Max, is to find out who Hannah is and what her story is.[18] Marian imagines her in terms of the Gothic, Effingham sees her as the lady of the Chivalric Romance and Max, the Plato scholar, interprets her in the context of the Platonic narrative of suffering. These conceptions of Hannah and her story run contemporaneously in *The Unicorn* and they devise coexisting roles and meanings for her. To suggest a further way of thinking about *The Unicorn*'s mysteriousness, I propose to investigate the ways in which Hannah's meaning alternates and proliferates in the plot structures.

Drawing on Peter Brooks, I consider the narrative threads in *The Unicorn* spatial formations that simultaneously generate and populate the novel's narrative space.[19] Due to the coexistence of several plot structures, a vertical axis complements the novel's horizontal story line that is constructed by the linearly unfolding events. The proliferation of allegorical and symbolic meanings in *The Unicorn* is due to the multiplicity of angles on the meaning of certain events and characters, but most significantly on Hannah. Although tropes might render a narrative more visible poetically, they might be also argued to reduce the transparency of its meaning by calling attention to its constructed-ness.[20] That the multiplicity of tropical meanings in *The Unicorn* appears to "suffocate" the literal level of the plot might be argued to result in the evident uncertainty with regard to its meaning. In this context, we might think of *The Unicorn*'s transition from a literal to a figurative meaning production[21] as a process that turns the narrative less and less discernable behind the halo of figures and conceive of *The Unicorn* as a metafictional narrative of concealment and disappearance.[22] I want to suggest that hermeneutic uncertainty is an inherent characteristic of the novel's meaning, and that it might be explained in relation to *The Unicorn*'s complex narrative structure.

In the first section of this essay, I show how these layered narratives result in a complex proliferation of the novel's meaning/s. In the first chapter, the figure of the unicorn will be shown to denote another narrative in addition to the currently prevalent *Hunt of the Unicorn*. The figure of the unicorn devises meaning production as a self-reflexive process and suggests that it introduces metafictional discourse into our explorations of meaning creation. The second section is devoted to thinking about the role of the Gothic and the Romance plots in the shifting of the meaning of events and characters. The simultaneous deployment of the two fantasy genres affects characters' meaning depending on the narrative they belong to rather than on an essential difference between the characters themselves. The third section proposes that the phenomenon of repetition in *The Unicorn* suggests the existence of an inconspicuous legend in Gaze. I will examine this narrative for the ways in which it introduces the idea of concealment into our investigations. In the fourth section, I demonstrate how the narrative of Platonic *ascesis* as a meaning for Hannah's story turns out, similarly to the Gothic and the Romance, to be a self-centered fantasy plot. I want to challenge the authenticity of the Platonic narrative in the context of Murdoch's allegory of unselfing, and suggest that it turns out to be the solipsistic fantasy of Max Lejour.[23] Finally, I will argue that the critical puzzlement with regard to the novel's meaning results from the fact that critics attempt to identify an element of Murdoch's philosophy or an idea suggested by one of the plots as an essential message. Considering *The Unicorn* as a metafictional narrative, however, might enable us to look at the lack of a well-defined message as constitutive of the novel's meaning.

Capturing Sight—The Unicorn Plot

The critical confusion about the image of the unicorn might be argued to have contributed to the puzzlement about *The Unicorn*'s meaning. That the mythical creature in the title of Murdoch's novel denotes a character in a tapestry that was possibly embroidered in the 15th or 16th century is suggested by Iris Murdoch in Cheryl K. Bove's monograph, *Understanding Iris Murdoch*. "The idea of this novel was brought about by a 16th century French tapestry exhibited in the Musée de Cluny," claims Iris Murdoch, yet the novel's critics unequivocally consider the meaning of the unicorn in terms of the *Hunt of the Unicorn* tapestries.[24] This series, however, is exhibited in The Cloisters, a branch of the Metropolitan Museum of Art in New York and not in Cluny. The focus of critical attention on this narrative has created a paradoxical situation in so far as the other tapestry sequence that features the unicorn has been largely neglected by academics but recognized in the novel's commercial production. The panels entitled "Sight" and "Touch" of the Cluny Tapestries were selected as cover illustrations to various Vintage Classics (1999, 2001) and Penguin (1987) editions of the novel, thus implying a connection between the narrative and *The Lady and the Unicorn*. The five panels of this tapestry series are exhibited in the Musée de Cluny in Paris, and besides the biographical reference in Bove's monograph, the subject of the piece entitled "Sight" also pertains to Murdoch's novel. I would like to suggest that the still, golden, tapestry-like scenes and the colors that accompany Hannah in the novel[25] do not only originate in the *Legend of the Unicorn* but also in the Cluny tapestries. *The Unicorn*, therefore, might be read in relation to both allegorical tapestry sequences. *The Hunt of the Unicorn* tapestry tells the story of how the mysterious creature was captured, while the Cluny tapestries (supposedly) form a series of allegorical representations of the senses.[26] On the basis of Bove's reference and the tapestry's relevance in subject matter to the novel, I want to suggest that the allegory of sight from *The Lady and the Unicorn* might be conceived as the origin of Murdoch's *The Unicorn*.[27]

As this essay's interest lies in the nature of interpretation and meaning creation, the pivotal detail of the piece "Sight" appears to be the looking glass held by the lady, which draws attention to the notion of self-reflexivity. The little hand mirror bears the unicorn's reflection, even though the unicorn is not looking towards it. Since the tapestry shows the unicorn as it is contemplating *the lady*, we might claim that as the mirror reproduces that which is in front of it, the reflection shows the act of *looking*. That the lady, who is the object of the unicorn's gaze, does not appear in the mirror surface tends to emphasize this claim. "Sight," therefore addresses the paradox that seeing is always the *sight of something*, and attempts to display vision *as vision*, as an act that is devoid of the object seen. This instance about the self-reflexivity of representation in the tapestry calls attention to self-reflexivity with regard to the representation of Hannah. *The Unicorn* problematizes the process of representation through the figure of the imprisoned lady. That Hannah is represented *as something* might be conceived of is one of the novel's main concerns. As characters and readers seek to find or determine Hannah's meaning, they are repeatedly faced with the problem that in order to tell Hannah's narrative, she has to be represented. Hannah's representations as the unicorn, the lady of Chivalric Romances, the *femme fatale, Lilith,* or *Até,* however, all prove to be the projection of other characters' fantasies. Hannah *as Hannah* therefore appears to elude both readers and characters.

The scholarship on *The Lady and the Unicorn* agrees that the series is an allegorical representation[28] and I want to argue that in terms of the tapestry's self-referential mirror image we might think of "Sight" as an allegory. I suggest, however, that "Sight" is about the *unreadability* of allegory as opposed to the embodiment of an abstract meaning. The tapestry stages interpretation as a self-reverting process.[29] Read as a twofold trope that draws its meaning both from the *Hunt of the Unicorn* and the *Lady and the Unicorn*, the unicorn relates to sight as an act of capturing and imprisoning the viewing self rather than explicating the object seen. With regard to this essay's interest in interpretation and meaning creation, "Sight" might be argued to conceive of vision as a metafictional process. By being about the act of looking and not about what is seen, *Sight* introduces metafictional discourse into *The Unicorn*. We might suggest, in this context, that Murdoch's novel also discusses the *process of meaning creation* in addition to the quest for Hannah's meaning. The unicorn tapestries, therefore, not only generate a multiplicity of narratives but also initiate the discourse of self-reflexivity and metafictionality which, as I shall demonstrate, might be employed to think further about the critical puzzlement about the novel's meaning.

Layers of Gothic and Romance

Turning from the Unicorn plot, without forgetting it, I examine here the way in which the intersections between two types of Gothic and between the Gothic and their layering into the Chivalric romance multiply the meaning of events and characters. I shall look at events that do not seem to make sense in the Gothic but might appear as an integral detail in the chivalric romance. Because they belong to several plots, these events and characters mark points where multiple meanings are created.

Following Victor Sage and Jacqueline Howard's explanation in *The Gothic Novel* and *Reading Gothic Fiction*, respectively, I suggest that the romance and the Gothic plot in *The Unicorn* are two variations of the same material, and conceive of the Gothic as the female version of romance, denounced as its "underside" or "dangerous form."[30] Both structures are fantasy genres with very formulaic and repetitive plot structures and culminate in a wedding that is considered a happy ending, typical of romance. The hero of the romance goes through adventure and always wins, and the heroine of the Gothic experiences ordeal after ordeal, but gains the hand of a gentleman in the end.[31] Neither of the two narratives reach conclusion in *The Unicorn*, but the novel's structure asserts that the main difference between the Gothic and the Chivalric Romance follows from the fact that the protagonist in the Chivalric Romance is traditionally a male character, while the Gothic is understood as the female genre *par excellence*. The Gothic Gaze Castle employs women as protagonists while Riders is symbolic of the male principle. According to the gender specific distribution of narrative roles, Hannah appears as the lady of Chivalric romances. The character of the chivalric knight is played by Effingham Cooper, Hannah's Platonic lover and a former student of Max Lejour, the master of Riders. Following the teaching of Max, Effingham reads Hannah spiritually and projects onto her the idealized *princess lointaine* image of romances.

Iris Murdoch's critics pay a great deal of attention to her use of the Gothic, and classify *The Unicorn* as one of the finest examples of the genre. They claim that this novel has the characteristics of a Gothic novel in its setting, incident, magical signs and theme[32] or that it is an "elegantly wrought, significantly artificial Gothic novel with a tight end-game closure which skims the surface of tragedy."[33] According to Peter Conradi, the novel "deliberately makes use of the stage props and scenery of the romantic sublime," and Robert Scholes calls *The Unicorn* a "Gothic allegory."[34]

The Gothic in *The Unicorn* is present not only in setting and incidents; it is present as a "thread of design, the organizing line" that lends itself as the pattern of events.[35] Gaze Castle emerges as an archetypal Gothic topos, and the characters automatically assume the stereotypical roles the Gothic machinery offers. *The Unicorn*'s Gothic plot sets off with the arrival of Marian, the new governess at Gaze, who acts as the shy and innocent heroine. Hannah's husband, Peter Crean-Smith, is the villain from whom all the evil magic comes, and the hero's role is taken by Gerald Scottow:

> "Are you Marian Taylor?" With a relieved sense of regaining her identity she took the hand and reassuring grip of the tall man who stepped out of the car.
> "Yes, I'm so sorry. However did you know I was here?"
> "...I thought you should not prove hard to identify!" He gave a smile with this which made the remark complimentary.[36]

It is Gerald, therefore, who should be destined to rescue Marian, the maiden, and symbolically reintroduce her into social order by marrying her. Jacqueline Howard claims that initiation Gothic is a "puberty rite for young women" in which female anxieties and desires are displayed, to be overcome by the hero in the end.[37] In this sense, the horror of the Gothic is perceived as being in opposition to the familiarity of marriage. Nevertheless, Maggie Kilgour argues that "Gothic itself is not a ratification but an exposé of domesticity and family," and she claims that marital Gothic enables us to realize that home is actually a prison for the woman, where she is subjected to the authority of the husband.[38] Analyzing the notion of repetition in both types of the Gothic, Michelle A. Massé observes that the "structural and thematic repetition of the novel's [Ann Radcliffe's *The Mysteries of Udolpho*] body moves beyond the pleasure principle and leads to the recognition and not relish of the incredible and unspeakable that happened."[39] In the Gothic, she argues, it is the frame that is dangerous, because it suggests that the danger is *over*. As it closes, the heroine is lulled into repeating the omission of anxiety. For Massé, the horror of the Gothic lies in that the story tries to pass for a dream or a fantasy, while it is about *reality*; it is the trauma of culture's gender expectations: "The Gothic plot is not an escape from the real world but a repetition and exploration of the traumatic denial of identity found there."[40]

Both the marital and the initiation Gothic are present in Gaze Castle. Marian Taylor plays the role of the maiden in the initiation Gothic, whereas Hannah Crean-Smith, the lady imprisoned in Gaze, acts as the heroine of the marital Gothic. When Gerald Scottow seduces Hannah, he metamorphoses into Peter and "marriage's heterosexual geniality" that is the apotheosis of the initiation Gothic, is turned into the continuation of Gothic nightmare under the guise of reality.[41] The transformation of the hero into the villain marks that point where Marian's Gothic initiation plot coincides with the marital Gothic. Gerald's falling into the role of the villain is contemporaneously the sign and result of the momentary intersection of the two patterns and causes the dissolution of boundaries between Gothic fantasy and the social reality of the ordinary world: "Gerald is Peter now. He has Peter's place, he is possessed by Peter, he even looks like Peter. He is no longer what keeps Peter away from her [Hannah]. Nothing keeps him off her now."[42]

The same time as Gerald becomes the villain in Marian's Gothic by taking Peter's role, Hannah's marital Gothic turns him into the hero when he announces to rescue Hannah from her prison upon the news of Peter's arrival. Gerald's next change of roles happens when he seduces Hannah and takes Peter's role as the villain of the marital Gothic: "As Gerald passed him by, moving in the direction of his own room, as the silk sleeve brushed lightly in passing, as the lamplight for a moment illumined her, Effingham saw Hannah's head resting quietly against Gerald's shoulder, her eyes wide open."[43] The symbolic ritual of the husband carrying his new wife over the threshold of their home marks the moment of the transformation of the hero into the villainous husband. Gerald's transgressive act of seduction also rearranges the structure of Hannah's marital Gothic plot. Through Gerald's change of character, Hannah is placed into the role of the heroine from being a wife, which transforms her narrative into an initiation Gothic and makes her assume the role of the maiden, the same as Marian. We might claim, therefore, that the characters' changes of role seem to be the result of the content of *The Unicorn*'s plots rather than the essential difference between the roles themselves.

Gerald's unexpected announcement of taking Hannah away might be seen as an intersection between the Gothic and the Chivalric romance:

> "Marian, will you please go and pack Hannah's things."
> There was a silence. Then Marian said, thickly and heavily, "Why?"
> "Because I am going to take her away."
> There was silence again. The scene seemed to shift and shimmer in the dim greyish bluish light. The little crowd below huddled together, aware of their insubstantial faces raised to the stairhead.[44]

This turn of events fails to make sense in either version of the Gothic, but fits the Chivalric romance. As the rescuing of the imprisoned lady is a typical stage in the course of events in knightly romances, this moment might be understood to mark a point in the narrative where the perspective of the Chivalric romance coincides with the Gothic. Gerald's chivalrous act gains a duplicitous overtone, however, when subsequent actions reveal that it may be the context of the legend of Gaze that originated his action. That Gerald is shot and thus punished for transgressing Peter's taboo on Hannah suggests the presence of a further, more mysterious narrative in Gaze.

The Legend of Gaze

> "Isn't there a village in Gaze?" Marian asked, her heart sinking a little.
> "Not now. Or scarcely. There used to be some fishermen's cottages and a sort of inn.... But the place was killed by a storm some years ago. The fishing-boats were all lost and the lake came flooding down the valley. It was quite a famous disaster, you might have read about it." [45]

According to Gerald, the events that brought about the narratives of *The Unicorn* originate in a further narrative that was told in a newspaper. Hannah calls this mysterious narrative a "fairy tale" and Marian refers to it as a "spell," a "legend," and a "ghastly tale." That the events at Gaze appear to have "happened, somewhat like this, many times before" underscores the uncanny nature of the legend. The flood, the drowning of people in a car and the man lost in the bog are all revealed as the repetitions of the events during the "famous disaster."[46]

The Unicorn begins with a paradigmatically Gothic scene, the arrival in Gaze of Marian Taylor, an innocent looking new governess. The beginning of the novel, however, coincides with the end of mysterious events of the inconspicuous legend of Gaze:

> "She [Hannah] is a legend in this part of the country. They believe that if she comes outside the garden she will die."
> "They think she is really under a curse?"
> "Yes. And they think that at the end of seven years something will happen to her."
> "Why seven years? Just because that's the time things go on for in fairy tales? But it is the end of seven years now!"
> "Yes. But nothing is going to happen."
> "Something has happened. I have come."[47]

This conversation situates the novel on the borderline between the mysteries of the past events in Gaze and the present narrative of *The Unicorn* that is setting off. That the termination of the legend marks the commencement of the novel defines the novel as an endplay. In this sense, *The Unicorn* might be seen as the enactment of the *dénouement* of the enigmatic legend of Gaze.

According to the local legend, which is full of Todorovian marvelous details,[48] the origin of the situation in Gaze Castle is a terrible event: Hannah was imprisoned seven years ago by Peter because she had allegedly pushed him over the cliffs into the sea. Peter miraculously survived the accident but was terribly wounded, and punished his wife by confining her to captivity in Gaze. That the Castle is revealed as a prison does not elevate the uncanny atmosphere that surrounds it. Gaze remains a sick place even after Marian and Effingham's romantic attempt at rescuing the imprisoned lady, as their endeavor does not bring a consoling resolution to the narrative. Something that acts as the source of the land's calamity inflicts deprivation on Gaze. As the Arthurian Fisher King legend suggests, the land cannot be cured in the absence of the master of the castle. That Peter's mysterious injury and subsequent departure from Gaze Castle was succeeded by the "famous disaster" that destroyed the land implies that Peter acts as a Fisher King figure.[49] The king's self, according to the Arthurian legend, is sympathetically bound up with his land and if he falls ill, the kingdom suffers a permanent blight as well. To heal the king and save the kingdom, the origin of the king's wound has to be asked. According to the paradigm of the Fisher King legend, disclosing the origin of Peter's wound will resolve the mystery of Gaze. By revealing the truth about what happened on the cliff seven years ago and revealing the way in which Peter was wounded, Hannah's narrative might be shaped into a meaningful form. However, when Effingham, the chivalric knight, asks the Percevalian question "What had really happened to Peter when he fell over the cliff? In what way was Peter maimed or disfigured?" the answer never comes.[50] The secret of Peter's wound and the meaning of Hannah remain hidden under the white shroud that covers Peter's dead body:

> There was a smell of sea-water in the room and the carpet at his feet was damp and darkened. He [Effingham] felt a stirring of his hand, a desire to whisk off the sheet and see what lay beneath. But again he could not. Perhaps he feared to see, not some terrible disfigured face, but laid thereupon, like a hideous mask, the likeness of his own features.[51]

Instead of receiving the answer to his Percevalian question, Effingham has a terrible vision. The appearance of his own features in the place of Peter's marks the departure of Effie's narrative from the Arthurian legend and the Chivalric romance. Seeing his own face as a death mask on Peter not only identifies Effingham with Peter but also implies his metaphorical death. Furthermore, due to the association between the two characters, we might claim that similarly to Peter, Effingham also imprisoned Hannah. While Peter physically confined her to captivity seven years ago, Effie metaphorically locks her into the role of the *princess lointaine*. What the scene reveals therefore, beyond the "not-seeing," and "not-knowing" of the origin of the wound is that the Chivalric romance is *secretly* a prison and that it is *secretly* about Effingham. Although it is *disguised* as providing a meaning for Hannah, the Chivalric romance might be thought of as a pattern that defines, in the role of the Chivalric knight, Effingham's place in The Unicorn.[52] While the Chivalric romance is revealed to be about Effingham, Hannah herself continues to elude meaning and remains hidden from our eyes like the mysterious wound of the Fisher King.

The Bedrock of the Platonic Plot

Coursing through the myth of the unicorn, the gothic and chivalric narratives, the Platonic myth of *ascesis* acts as another complicating narrative for the novel's meaning. The topography of *The Unicorn* suggests a bipolarly constructed narrative, a contrast between states of being. That the land is divided by a river and the two houses are situated on opposite river banks emphasize the antinomy of Gaze and its neighbor, Riders Castle. That Riders physically overlooks Gaze might be argued to foreshadow the metaphorical superiority suggested both by its architecture and the novel's topography:

> A turn in the road suddenly revealed in the distance a big handsome house. Its appearance was startling in the midst of the naked scene and had, in the sunny mist, something of the air of a mirage. It stood high up on the seaward side, on a promontory of the cliffs, a long grey three-storey eighteenth century house.[53]

Riders appears as a Georgian house with classical elegance, while Gaze Castle seems to be its inverse both in architectural and topographic terms:

> As the car began to descend, Marian made out on the opposite hillside a big grey forbidding house with a crenulated facade and tall thin windows which glittered now with light from the sea. The house had been built of the local limestone and reared itself out of the landscape, rather like the dolmen, belonging yet not belonging.[54]

The image of the lowering road comes to imply a metaphorical descent towards Gaze when Gerald remarks: "'Not a thing of beauty, I'm afraid,' said Scottow. 'Nineteenth century, of course.'"[55] From the outside, Gaze seems strangely ungraspable due to the way in which it simultaneously differs from and conforms to the landscape. That it appears frighteningly alive inside highlights the castle's Gothic flavor: "The floors were mostly uncarpeted, tilting, creaking, echoing, but there were soft hangings above her head, curtains on archways and vague cobwebby textiles which hung down at doors and corners and tugged her passing sleeve."[56] These clichéd phrases describe Gaze as the archetypical setting of Gothic narratives; the remote, derelict castle. Although both buildings appear monumental, Marian characterizes Riders as "handsome" and calls Gaze "forbidding." That Marian and Gerald both identify Gaze in negative terms implies its opposition to Riders. The bipolarity of topography, therefore, appears to foreshadow the binary structure of the fourth major pattern that shapes the unfolding of the plot of *The Unicorn*, the Platonic narrative.[57]

Similarly to topography, the imagery of light and sunshine seems to divide the narrative along positive and negative values. Riders appears startling in the "sunny mist," while the tall windows of Gaze *reflect* "the light from the sea."[58] That the light comes from the sea and not from the sun might be argued to carry sinister implications, as the sea in *The Unicorn* is predominantly associated with violence and danger.[59] In addition, the phenomenon of reflection implies that light fails to enter the Castle and therefore associates it with darkness. Riders, however, is positively immersed in sunlight: "The windows were twinkling orange in the western sun."[60] Its inhabitants appear to emphasize the association of the house with the sun: the name Lejour (*le jour*) is the French word for "day" and "daylight." Through Max Lejour, his son Pip and Effingham's constant watching and theorizing Gaze, Riders might be thought of as a big eye that emits beams of visual rays in the direction of its neighbor.[61] According to Plato's "Simile of the Sun" in *The Republic*, it is the sight of the Sun and the Good that enables the mind to achieve true knowledge.[62] He explains that the journey towards the upper sphere of existence involves the soul's discarding of deceptive forms and shadows that blur its vision. Through its association with the sun, knowledge and spirituality, Riders is conceived of as the metaphorical destination of the soul's narrative of ascension. Gaze Castle, the binary opponent of Riders, might be thought of as the dwelling place of untruthful forms, fantasy narratives and precarious substitutes of hidden truths.

The name of Riders, as we have seen, gains its allegorical meaning from Plato's philosophy. In *Phaedrus*, Plato compares the soul to the carriage of a winged charioteer drawn by two horses. He explains that the wings symbolize the soul's rising to the sphere of intellectual vision and knowledge. Plato devises a vertically divided world: the upper world of the idea of absolute truth and reality is opposed to the lower, physical world of the deceptive forms of sensual perception. He breaks up the soul into three elements: the charioteer, a white and a black horse. The white horse symbolizes modesty and restraint, while the black one stands for lust and unbridled desire. The task of the charioteer is to control the horses and drive the carriage to the upper world. In the world of sensuality it is only beauty and love that remind the soul of the truth and wisdom of the upper world.[63] Plato explains how unselfish love offers a way for the soul to raise, provided the charioteer controls its lustful desires.[64] The strange dark-haired maids, the pervasive darkness, the precarious space and the love triangles identify Gaze with the black horse of Plato's allegory. Effie's chivalric love and Max's engagement in philosophy (he is writing a book on Plato) associate Riders with the white horse. Riders and Gaze in this context symbolize a soul torn apart, which might be seen as a starting point for a potential narrative of unification through unselfish love followed by the elevation of the soul from its sensual existence. That Max the charioteer occupies Gaze Castle after Hannah's death might be understood as the allegorical merging of the two houses, and the unification, therefore, of the torn apart soul. However, the subsequent *ascesis* and the revelation of the truth about Hannah appear to be deferred.

I want to suggest thinking about the Platonic narrative as the pattern that conceives of Gaze Castle as a site of untruthful narratives and fantasy plots. According to the logic of binary opposition, by imagining Gaze as dark, solipsistic and sensual, the Platonic journey defines itself as that which enlightens, elevates the soul and reveals the truth, which should reside in Riders. Since it appears as the narrative in possession of the truth, Platonic *ascesis* might be though of as the pattern that provides meaning to Hannah's story and becomes, therefore, the authentic narrative of *The Unicorn*. However, the phrase in which Marian associates Riders with sunshine ends in comparing it to a *mirage*: "Its [Riders'] appearance was startling in the midst of the naked scene and had, in the sunny mist, something of the air of a mirage."[65] Riders as a "mirage," a *play* on vision implies deceit, it implies illusion and fantasy. I would like to argue therefore, that conceiving it in terms of an optical delusion foreshadows the house's *illusory* Platonism.

The Challenge of Platonism

As we have seen, the inhabitants of Riders appear as bearers of Platonic attributes: Max Lejour, "a curious recluse," is a Plato scholar and his daughter Alice is involved in a Platonic love affair with Effingham Cooper, her father's former student.[66] Effingham and Alice's love stories associate Riders with Plato's Eros the capability to recall the soul's forgotten knowledge of the true forms and elevate it from the world of experience.

As suggested by the act of his watching Hannah from the Platonic Riders, Max interprets her legend as a spiritual story of suffering. He links it both to the Christian tradition and the Greek myth of Até[67]: "Hannah is beautiful and her story is as you say, somehow beautiful.... And it is in the good that Até is finally quenched, when it encounters a pure being who only suffers and does not attempt to pass the suffering on."[68] That Max reads beauty and goodness into Hannah's suffering associates his interpretation with Platonism and prefigures, her narrative as the allegory of the soul's *ascesis*. However, Effingham's remark about Max watching his own mirror image when he contemplates Gaze challenges the legacy of the Platonic narrative: "It then occurred to him that in some curious way Max might derive consolation from the spectacle, over there in the other house, of another captivity, a distorted mirror image of his own.[69] Max's self-reflexive remark that "perhaps Hannah is my experiment! I've always had a great theoretical knowledge of morals, but practically speaking I've never done a hand's turn" highlights the claim that Max's spiritual interpretation of Hannah is the projection of his fantasy.[70] The strange relation of mutual resemblance between Hannah and the Plato scholar further emphasizes the correlation of their narratives. Although they never meet, they both know about each other: Hannah leaves a will in favor of Max that makes him the proprietor of her house, her story and her death, and Max discusses Hannah with Effingham.[71] Both act very little and the trajectory of their narratives is determined by legends telling about the moment of the end of their lives. Alice believes that Max will die when he finishes his book on Plato: "And when he finishes it [the book]—I think he'll suddenly get much older. It's been with him such a long time. It will be like the end of his life."[72] As related by Denis, the local people consider Hannah a legend and think that at the end of seven years something will happen to her: "They believe that if she comes outside the garden she will die."[73] In the context of the correspondence between the figure of Hannah and Max it might be argued, therefore, that the Platonic conception of Hannah is also about Max and that the narrative of *ascesis* provides the projection of the Platonic scholar's fantasies rather than the reflection of Hannah's true meaning.

When Max occupies Hannah's room after she has left Gaze and, as foretold by the legend, died mysteriously, Max undergoes a strange metamorphosis: "'Open the windows, would you,' said Max. He spoke with his usual authority but very wearily, letting his big head, yellow and hollowed like some Chinese object, fall heavily back against the cushions. He looked like death itself usurping Hannah's place."[74] As Max *impersonates* death, he also becomes like death: "Effingham stared at the old man, the great hollow mask, the crumpled dangling body. He said, 'So Jamesie was right. You are the owner of her [Hannah's] death and she was waiting for you. You *are* her death and she loved you.'"[75] The image of the "great hollow mask" echoes the scene of Effingham's metaphorical death where Effingham's Chivalric narrative, similarly to Max's *ascesis*, was revealed as the projection of a solipsistic fantasy, and Hannah was subsequently reduced to a character enacting a prefigured role. Max's metaphorical transformation into death might be argued to imply Murdoch's conception of the self in the process of elevation as a result of its purged the solipsistic fantasies. The "hollow mask" in the place of Max's face implies the lack of meanings, an empty self, which, in the context of Murdoch's "unselfing" enables it to perceive the "reality of the surrounding world in its otherness from the self."[76] The revelation of Hannah's meaning unshaped by the fantasies of other characters, however, is again postponed. During Max and Effingham's discussion of the meaning of Hannah's narrative, Max himself suggests that the narrative of spiritual suffering might be his own fantasy: "It may all be to meet some need of my own. I've meant all my life to go on a spiritual pilgrimage.... Perhaps Hannah is my experiment."[77] The image of Hannah as the suffering woman expiating a crime, therefore, appears to be a product of Max's imagination. The way in which the narrative of *ascesis* discloses itself as an illusory reflection of Max's fantasies and thus problematizes the process of meaning creation, evokes *Sight* in the *Lady and the Unicorn* tapestries. As the little mirror in the lady's hand reflects the act of looking, the process of representation itself, the tapestry's self-reflexive strategy echoes in *The Unicorn*. Instead of revealing her meaning, narratives in *The Unicorn* display the process of their *elusion* of Hannah, and through this self-reverting process, Hannah remains un-narrated.

When Max has entered Gaze Castle sunshine floods the room, the house and the landscape and the only colors in the novel are "yellow," "saffron" and "gold." That the blackness that signifies Gaze Castle merges with the light of Riders might be understood to prefigure the *ascesis* of the soul from the darkness of self-engulfing fantasies toward the truth that is enlightened by Plato's sun. Max's occupation of Gaze and the engulfing of the landscape with sunshine might be thought to be succeeded by the revelation of the truth about the novel's meaning. Yet the *revelation* of its meaning appears to be deferred and *The Unicorn*, like the *Legend of the Fisher King*, ends in further questions rather than the uncovering of answers:

> On the golden yellow hillside a little figure had appeared, climbing up the path toward the bog. Marian watched it recede. It was the last flicker, the last pinprick that showed the light through from that other world which she had so briefly and so uncomprehendingly inhabited.... [And] she did not know whether the world in which she had been living was a world of good or of evil, a world of significant suffering or a devil's shadow-play, a mere nightmare of violence.[78]

Marian's confusion is similar to the puzzlement of the criticism. It allegorizes the reader's not-knowing and inability to give a meaning to *The Unicorn*, and the frustration of Platonic ascesis as a layer of the confounding plot. The scene calls attention to the inscrutability of the novel to suggest that the Platonic narrative in *The Unicorn*, like the small hand mirror in *Sight*, exhibits meaning creation as a self-reverting, metafictional process. In this context hesitation, puzzlement and the quality of mysteriousness *constitute* the meaning of *The Unicorn*.

Hannah's Death and the Mystery of The Unicorn

As foretold by the local people, if she leaves Gaze Castle, Hannah will die. Her death marks the termination of the enigmatic legend of Gaze that started seven years prior to the events of *The Unicorn*. When she walks out of the castle she disappears from the novel into the mysterious legend: "All the clocks seemed to have stopped. Hannah had been found almost at once. A fisherman had seen it happen, and her body had been recovered without much difficulty from where it lay among the rocks."[79] That her death was only witnessed by a strange fisherman associates it with Gaze Castle *before* the time of the novel. Fishermen in *The Unicorn* evoke the legendary time of the great storm that destroyed the land seven years ago, the same time as Hannah's supposed attempt at killing Peter happened. Through her death, therefore, Hannah returns to the legend of Gaze.

By the time Hannah dies, a magic transformation has evolved between Hannah and Denis Nolan, a local man who once worked at Riders, but now works at Gaze. Hannah acts as an unattainable taboo throughout the narrative but during a hair cutting ritual Denis is allowed to touch her hair: "He [Denis] picked up the comb and scissors and began to handle the plentiful mass of red-golden hair.... Once he had started, his face softened into a dignified intentness as he flicked the silky stuff this way and that."[80] According to the laws of contagion, Hannah and Denis will continue to have an effect on each other after the ritual: "Things which have once been in contact with each other continue to act on each other at a distance after the physical contact has been severed."[81] The magical correlation of Hannah and Denis becomes explicit after Marian and Effie's attempt at kidnap and her seduction by Gerald. Hannah's voice starts to resemble Denis': "Her eloquent voice was suddenly almost like Denis's voice."[82] The coincidence of moment that Denis utters the phrase "Whether one must not in the end fight evil with evil," with Hannah's shooting Gerald, "a great deafening noise rang thunderously through the house" emphasizes the intertwining of the two characters' narratives.[83] I would like to argue that the culmination of the magical transformation is the moment that Denis takes over Hannah's guilt by committing the same crime. Denis' drowning of Peter might be seen as the repetition of Hannah's act of shooting Gerald and her supposed attempt at killing Peter. By being involved in the same crime Denis might be argued to have *become* Hannah: "I let myself be driven mad by jealousy, by *her* [Hannah's] *actions*, and I was faithless to her and so became mad. I am the most guilty. The guilt passes to me. That is why I must go away by myself" (262, italics added). As Denis inhabits Hannah's role and recreates the suffering and the expiating crime, he enters the narrative of *The Unicorn* into the cycle of repetition:

> And with Denis's words she [Marian] had an eerie sense of it all beginning again, the whole tangled business: the violence, the prison house, the guilt. It all still existed. Yet Denis was taking it away with him. He had wound it all inside himself and was taking it away.[84]

Having assumed Hannah's guilt, Denis appears to carry the story of *The Unicorn* away. Drawing on the logic of repetition, we might think of the "whole tangled business" to be repeated, similarly to the way in which the "Mysterious Legend of Gaze" is repeated in *The Unicorn*, in the narrative that will unfold around Denis' figure.[85]

It might be argued that the narratives of *The Unicorn* are generated by Hannah's enigmatic guilt and the mysteries of her suffering. Dennis' taking it away, therefore might be thought to imply the "release" of the imprisoned lady from the confinement of the narratives. As *The Unicorn* does not end in an *aletheia* or the "revelation of truth" but reveals concealment, hesitation and repetition, its meaning continues to be elusive. Similarly to the tapestries and Effie's Parcevalian question, *aletheia* in *The Unicorn* does not appear to have an essential object and therefore it becomes a self-reflexive comment on meaning creation. Narratives, in relation to Hannah reveal that mysteriousness and the feeling of hesitation are inherent in her figure. *The Unicorn* tells a repetitive, elusive and metafictional narrative and that it irrecoverably remains beyond our reach is allegorically emphasized by the way in which "Denis was taking it [the whole tangled business] away with him. He had wound it all inside himself and was taking it away."[86]

Notes

1. The reception of *The Unicorn* splits between two contradicting interpretive stances. Guy Backus (1986, 121), Elizabeth Dipple (1982, 266) and Robert Scholes (1979, 72) note the deliberately puzzling quality of *The Unicorn*, while Richard C. Kane reads the novel as a didactic allegory (1988, 49), and claims the existence of a straightforward moral lesson in *The Unicorn*.
2. The phenomenon of refusing to provide one underlying mythical structure that includes all the details is understood by Bran Nicol as one of Murdoch's ways of "using form to reflect contingency"(1999, 8).
3. Scholes, 1979, 87.
4. Examining the relationship of repetition and the textual uncanny in *A Severed Head*, Bran Nicol observes, "The story is full of repetitions on the level of events and paralleled by the repetition of the story" (1999, 113), that is how text comes to function as a replay, "providing a way of signifying what initially escapes signification" (120).
5. Scholes, 1979, 64.
6. Richard Kane, in his discussion of the role of mirrors in *The Unicorn*, reads Hannah's palindromic name as "a symbol of self-containment" (1988, 47), and connects, in the context of Murdoch's Platonic perception on sight, the demonic enchantment of Gaze to a distortion of vision.
7. Murdoch, 1966, 43.
8. The muscles are relaxed during the phonetic production of *Hannah*: the air, flowing from the lungs, is stopped by the tongue as it touches the hard palate to turn the sound nasal from oral, and then retreat to its original position and let the name die out silently.
9. Murdoch, 1966, 23.
10. *Ibid.*, 23–24.
11. *Ibid.*, 92.
12. *Ibid.*, 91.
13. *Ibid.*, 92.
14. *Ibid.*, 46.
15. *Ibid.*, 23.
16. *Ibid.*, 288.
17. In a different context, we might think of Hannah's death upon leaving Gaze Castle as the result of her leaving the space where narratives shape her figure into a meaningless form.
18. See, for example, pages 46, 58–60 for Marian's devotion to find out about Hannah. Chapter 12 relates Max and Effie's discussion of Hannah (Murdoch, 1966).
19. Brooks, 1992, 5.
20. Shklovsky explains, in his *Theory of Prose*, that the function of art is to make the world look strange: "The technique of art is to make objects 'unfamiliar,' to make forms difficult, to increase the difficulty and length of perception because the process of perception is an aesthetic end in itself and must be prolonged. Art is a way of experiencing the artfulness of an object: the object is not important" (1990, 6). Engulfing *The Unicorn* with allegories and symbols turns the readers' attention to the defamiliarizing nature of its tropes. The characters' attempts at interpreting Hannah mirror the process of reading, and thus suggest a potentially rewarding metafictional reading of *The Unicorn* as a narrative about the unreadability of allegories.
21. Analysing the Gothic pattern in *The Unicorn* in his *Fabulation and Metafiction*, Robert

Scholes notes a shift from the fictional to the ideational; from Gothic action to Gothic allegory, and claims that "Iris Murdoch is teaching us how to read allegorically" as we follow the path "from Gothic action to Gothic allegory in this tale"(1979, 60).

22. Scholes calls *The Unicorn* a "modern allegory" precisely because of its lack of final explanations and answers (1979, 67). Elizabeth Dipple claims that Max is an "undeveloped character" (1982, 268) and that the novel is a "deliberately puzzling book" (266). In my view, its inscrutability serves to connote the futility of attempts at revealing the truth about Hannah by means of allegorization.

23. In *The Sovereignty of Good* Murdoch emphasizes the indefinability of "Good" due to the fact that it is seen through the boundaries of the self. Drawing on Plato she understands "Good" as a transcendental concept, the source and condition of true knowledge. Murdoch explains that the experience of the true good in human beings is both the condition and the result of an unselfish relationship to the world, a transcending of the self's boundaries through the process of "unselfing," by means of which it discards self-centred fantasies to be able to perceive the reality of the surrounding world in its otherness from the self (2003, 94–101).

24. Bove, 1993, 172.

25. See, for example, the following scene as an example for the famous golden tapestry-like scenes of *The Unicorn*: "An unclouded sun, very soon to be quenched in a level golden sea, had turned everything on the land to a brilliant saffron yellow. Marian felt as if she and Hannah were on a stage, so violent and unusual was the lighting. Their hands and faces were gilded" (1966, 50).

26. A short plot description of the Hunt of the Unicorn goes as follows: The unicorn is a ferocious, solitary animal that has a horse's body, a stag's or goat's head, a sow's tail and, as an indication of its strangeness, a horn on its forehead. It lives in the mountains or in the forest and nobody and nothing can overcome it. It can only be captured by a young, innocent maiden, who, stepping in the animal's path, tames him and the unicorn falls asleep on her lap. The knights in companion of the maiden catch it afterwards. The unicorn being an extremely prolific image (it appears in Greek, Indian and Persian legends), its symbolic associations are endless. The most generic understanding of the legend of the unicorn in the West followed the Christian paradigm, where the unicorn appears as the symbol of Christ. The legend of the unicorn's hunt became a source of courtly symbolism in the Middle Ages, with the unicorn as the symbol of the lover captured by his lady and its falling asleep was associated with the death of the lover's desire at the moment of satisfaction.

27. Many speculations enshroud the iconography of the *Lady and the Unicorn* series. Its revelator was George Sand who saw the tapestries for the first time at the Château of Boussac in the Creuse in central France, and mentioned it in one of her novels. She gave the first public meaning to the series, connecting it to a marvellous legend of the Orient "an evocation of the love of Prince Zezim for a young person from whom he was separated in his exile, or for a niece of Pierre d'Aubuson, whose prisoner he was" (Erlande-Brandenburg, 1997, 67). Being a writer of romanticism, her thinking and interpretation are obviously marked by the spirit and philosophy of the era. Sand's explanation of the series was challenged by others, of which the most widely known is the identification of the unicorn as the image of Christ, the lady as the Virgin. This reading is based on the interpretation drawn from the *Bestiaires du Moyen Age*. The most likely and most widely accepted hypothesis is that the tapestries are allegorical representations of the five senses. Alain Erlande-Brandenburg initiates the tapestries into a Platonic narrative of morals by claiming that the lady seen on the last of the series is not taking but replacing a necklace: "The cast-off necklace symbolises the renunciation of the passions aroused by the senses when they are not under control" (1997, 68). Therefore, the lady's gesture is the illustration of the inscription on the tent a *mon seul desir* meaning "at my own will" and the tapestries of T*he Lady and the Unicorn* reveal a narrative of deep moral significance.

28. Gottfried Büttner, Margaret B. Freeman, John Williamson and Alain Erlande-Brandenburg all interpret the tapestries as allegorical representations.

29. The panel associated with Iris Murdoch's novel is considered to represent the allegory of sight. As Margaret B. Freeman observes, "Sight" is the only tapestry in the series where the unicorn does not appear in a heraldic role, he is represented to be engaged in viewing the lady. Situations showing the interrelated glances of figures are repeated throughout the whole tapestry; the small animals are all looking either at each other or towards the tapestry's potential viewer. The panel's focal scene is situated on an island against the flowery background, and shows the unicorn

and the lady contemplating each other. The lady, who occupies the center of the composition, is holding a mirror in her right hand, where appears the considerably minimised image of the unicorn with its gaze directed towards herself. Not reflecting the unicorn itself, so much as the act of gazing at the lady, the mirror image foregrounds the process of viewing as the central theme of the tapestry, rather than providing a replica of the viewer's self. The alternative space of the mirror in this sense includes a *myse-en-abyme* that, in my view, repeats the subject matter of the tapestry by turning it into a display of the act of viewing rather than an allegorical representation.

30. Howard, 1994, 62; Sage, 1990, 2.
31. Frye, 1976, 67; Massé, 1992, 13.
32. Bove, 1993, 172.
33. Dipple, 1982, 265.
34. Conradi, 1986, 121; Scholes, 1979, 59–60.
35. Brooks, 1992, 4.
36. Murdoch, 1966, 8.
37. Howard, 1994, 59.
38. Kilgour, 1995, 9.
39. Massé, 1992, 12.
40. *Ibid.*, 18.
41. *Ibid.*, 15.
42. Murdoch, 1966, 229.
43. *Ibid.*, 184.
44. *Ibid.*, 188.
45. *Ibid.*, 9.
46. *Ibid.*, 214, 141, 65, 41, 9.
47. *Ibid.*, 64.
48. Todorov, 1975, 46.
49. Murdoch, 1966, 9.
50. *Ibid.*, 256.
51. *Ibid.*
52. Following Hannah's death and the collapse of the novel's "crystalline structure," Effingham retrospectively rewrites his own narrative. He attempts to reinvent his relationship with Hannah in Freudian terms.
53. Murdoch, 1966, 13.
54. *Ibid.*, 15.
55. *Ibid.*
56. *Ibid.*, 17.
57. If Gaze is identified as the mortal world of the body and Riders the superior world of spirituality, then the implied allegorical narrative of *The Unicorn* can be expected to depict the arch of the soul's ascending journey from the dark fantasy world of Gaze to the spiritual Riders.
58. Murdoch, 1966, 13, 15.
59. The sea in *The Unicorn* is a dangerous element — it kills people who try to swim in it, it is ice cold and "inky black" with violent waves that have a "grinding roar" (Murdoch, 1966, 32).
60. *Ibid.*, 142.
61. Riders' association with watchfulness and light and its implication as an eye turned towards Gaze Castle coincides with the ways in which Plato imagined that functioning of vision. As a follower of the theory of emission he explains that the sensation of seeing occurs in the soul as a result of the emission of light rays from the eye. These rays coalesce with daylight and form a single homogeneous body between the eye and the visible object. When this intermediary body of daylight and ocular light comes into contact with an emanation from the object, the motion is transmitted to the soul where it creates visual sensation (Lindberg, 1976, 5).
62. Plato, 2003, 232–35.
63. Plato, 1973, 62–64.
64. For the Platonist Murdoch, love and the perception of beauty are two occasions to reveal truth and goodness for the soul. Perception of the "reality" of our love object as "it is" engenders unselfish love through the dissolution of the soul's egoistic fantasies, and the Murdochian Eros brings the soul into contact with transcendental goodness. The practices of aesthetic perception have a similar effect on the soul: Murdoch's moral self becomes other-oriented as the result of ego

3. *Narrative and Symbolic Layering in* The Unicorn *(Varga)*

"unselfing." Murdoch contends that through this process, the moral self effaces the self-centered, falsifying fantasies that conceal from it the world and the reality of other people (2003, 91).
    65. Murdoch, 1966, 13.
    66. *Ibid.*
    67. The myth of Até, first mentioned in Book XIX of Homer's *Iliad*, tells how Até, the daughter of Zeus, influences him and brings destruction to men through manipulating them. Até in Greek means "ruin" and "delusion," whose allegorical impersonation is the goddess herself (Homer, 1973, XIX, 90–101).
    68. Murdoch, 1966, 97–99.
    69. *Ibid.*, 97.
    70. *Ibid.*, 101.
    71. See Chapter Twelve for Max and Effie's discussion of Hannah.
    72. Murdoch, 1966, 77.
    73. *Ibid.*, 64.
    74. *Ibid.*, 251.
    75. *Ibid.*, 254.
    76. Murdoch, 2003, 101.
    77. Murdoch, 1966, 100–101.
    78. *Ibid.*, 263.
    79. *Ibid.*, 245.
    80. *Ibid.*, 41.
    81. Frazer, 1957, 48.
    82. Murdoch, 1966, 218.
    83. *Ibid.*, 244.
    84. *Ibid.*, 262.
    85. *Ibid.*
    86. *Ibid.*

4

Morality, the Visual Arts, and Rembrandt in Iris Murdoch's *Under the Net* and Zadie Smith's *On Beauty*

ANNE ROWE

Iris Murdoch was acutely aware of the necessity for innovation in the novel form so that writers could more accurately represent the unobservable inner experience of characters, and she frequently acknowledges her own experimentation with it. Rather confusingly, though, she also aligns herself with the English Realist tradition that encompasses Jane Austen, Charles Dickens and George Eliot, those writers who demonstrate the "truthfulness of great art" and "overcome egoism and fantasy."[1] Like all these writers, Murdoch's novels incorporate a strong moral dimension which often employs analogues from painting to illustrate it. However, Murdoch's use of the visual arts not only reinforces her moral perspective and intensifies the aesthetic and emotional appeal of her novels but also, more in the manner of Henry James, is central to her experimentation with the novel form.[2] This essay attempts to illustrate ways in which the acclaimed British novelist, Zadie Smith is a literary heir to Iris Murdoch, perpetuating and developing the "Novel of Ideas" in similar moral and aesthetic ways.[3] Smith cites E.M. Forster as a role model because his "chaotic, irrational characters" demand an unashamedly affective (moral) response, and the "infamous muddle" of his narrative style has moral value in its truth to life.[4] Moreover, Smith's third novel, *On Beauty*, also incorporates painterly analogies to endorse this moral position and intensify its emotional appeal. A comparison between the careers, ambitions, literary theories and the aesthetic devices in the writing of Iris Murdoch and Zadie Smith not only illuminates these strong parallels, but also reveals some telling idiosyncrasies in each writer's work, as Murdoch's restrained representations of women pale by comparison with Smith's full-blown generosity to them, and Smith's faithfulness to Realism appears prosaic when studied alongside Murdoch's sophisticated experimentation with form.

The two women's careers display marked similarities: both were high-flying students (Murdoch reading Greats at Somerville College, Oxford; Smith reading English at King's College, Cambridge), both are celebrity prize-winners (Murdoch a Booker Prize winner and Smith an Orange Prize winner, and both won the James Tait Black Memorial Prize)[5]; both have been academics and teachers (Murdoch at St Anne's College, Oxford, and the Royal College of Art in London; Smith at Harvard as Radcliffe Institute Fellow), and Smith intends to continue an academic career alongside writing fiction, hoping that her study *Fail Better: The Morality of the Novel* might earn her a PhD.[6]

It seems likely that these similarities will intensify as in interviews, lectures and essays, Smith expresses views on the novel that closely echo Murdoch's.[7] Both express alarm about the ubiquitous imposition of theories that replaced the affective response to literature in the mid to late twentieth century, and both advocate the reinstating of unfashionable ways of writing and reading the novel that redirect critical attention to its moral status, which was marginalized by postmodernism and high-theory.[8] Murdoch thought that "any theory which cuts people off from the great literature of the past deprives them of a historical and moral education and a great deal of pleasure," and Smith echoes this sentiment when she suggests that "along with [the] bathwater, we threw out the baby."[9] Murdoch talks of her own "absolute horror" of putting theory into her work and feels that "critics are better off without any close-knit systematic background theory, scientific, or philosophical."[10] She wants critics to approach novels with an open-minded manner which does not exclude "treating a tale as 'a window into another world,' reacting to characters as if they were real people, making value judgements about them and about how their creator creates them."[11] In hindsight, Smith thinks that in early career she subscribed too readily to theorized responses to texts; once if anyone had discussed her characters as if they existed she would have though it "ridiculous": characters were a "collection of sentences, and I couldn't engage at all with the idea that they were in any way real people."[12] However, about *On Beauty*, she says, she feels differently.

Smith now suggests fiction "as a way of doing moral philosophy" and agrees with Aristotle's contention that the novel is "a place to imagine what you would do in this, that, or the other situation."[13] Although Murdoch frequently minimizes the connection between the two disciplines in her own work, she also admits that "certain philosophical ideas *must* somehow find expression in my novels,"[14] and Murdochian criticism has inevitably been defined by analogies between her philosophy and fiction. What is interesting is how far the central tenet of Smith's "moral philosophy," as she has so far developed it, mirrors Murdoch's. Each writer revolves her thinking on truthfulness, morality and character around the concept of "Love." For Murdoch, by seeing the world in all its unutterable particularity and reflecting that truth in art, the novelist performs a moral function by moving the reader emotionally in a sublime moment of experience that is both exhilarating and painful, and makes the "otherness" of others breathtakingly evident. Smith does not yet express her ideas in any formal philosophical discourse, but she does articulate concern at the contemporary embarrassment about the affective response to literature that Murdoch could expound on unapologetically decades before ("I would include the rousing of emotions in the *definition* of art").[15] And Smith understands that with the loss of the affective response came the loss of the moral impact of the novel: "Our interest became analytical not ethical."[16] Murdoch takes the argument further:

> Art and morals are, with certain provisos ... one. Their essence is the same. The essence of both of them is love. Love is the perception of individuals. Love is the extremely difficult realization that something other than oneself is real. Love, and so art and morals, is the discovery of reality.[17]

Smith heads in the same direction when she says that the novel "engages your feelings for certain characters and situations over others, it compels particular hermeneutic procedures.... Fiction always applies for that same 'fine awareness,' which Henry James recognised we must employ in order to fully inhabit our ethical lives; to become, as he put it 'richly responsible.'"[18] Both argue that writers should be aware of their ethical responsibilities because, whether they intend a moral or not, the fact that characters make choices and readers draw meaning from them illustrates that the novel *is* a moral medium: "Life is soaked in the moral, literature is soaked in the moral," says Murdoch, and Smith suggests that "every variety of literary style attempts to enact in us a way of seeing, of reading, and this is never less than an ethical strategy."[19] "English fiction was something I loved growing up and it changed my life," she says, and "if the novel relates to the lives of readers it *can* change those lives."[20] As Murdoch had to brave her critics, so Smith is careful to acknowledge the quirkiness of her position, understanding that morality is "considered to be a bit old hat these days," but she says she "wanted to prove to [herself] that an old-fashioned type of novel could be written that would be able to do things that were modern."[21]

Of course, writing decades apart and from dissimilar cultural backgrounds, their novels are inevitably different: while Murdoch confines her settings to the milieu of the upper-middle "chattering classes," Smith is associated with "deconstructing Western mythologies of racial stereotypes" and "the ethics of science and multiculturalism," and she has been linked with writers such as Salman Rushdie and Martin Amis.[22] Her style too has often been linked to these writers, so her relation to Forster, less noted until the publication of *On Beauty*, is in part a reconsideration of her use of form. In fact, critics may have been over-zealous in confining Smith too rigidly as a writer of race: "it isn't really the race thing I'm interested in" she says, "I'm just interested in the difference thing."²³ Perhaps like Murdoch, who has said that "one can only write about the world one understands,"²⁴ Smith began her concern with differentiation from a racial perspective because she was brought up in a biracial family, but if the work of each writer is stripped of its cultural specificity, their thematic concerns are remarkably similar: both are interested in the search for identity, the egocentric desires of their male characters; the need for connection between the sexes; obsession and the desire for truth; the centrality of love in the moral life and, most significantly, the idea that morality resides at the point of vision rather than choice. The two novels discussed in this essay, Murdoch's first published novel, *Under the Net*, and Zadie Smith's third novel, *On Beauty*, illustrate such concerns, and focus in particular on how the cultural stereotyping of women damages relationships. Both novels reference paintings by Rembrandt as an antidote to such ways of seeing and as a vehicle for soaking their novels with moral significance. Like Murdoch, Smith chooses Rembrandt not only as an ideal standard by which to judge the way her characters respond to the world, but also as an ideal against which she judges herself as a writer.

Under the Net and *On Beauty* are both self-reflexive novels which debate how art should be constructed and responded to. Both novels share a moral perspective which is rooted in aesthetics and vision and offer Rembrandt as a paradigm for seeing the world with a clarity and truthfulness that induces rational, benign and loving judgment. Although Smith is reluctant to provide an intellectual rationale for her use of Rembrandt and says that he is in the novel simply because she loves his work and thinks him a "genius,"²⁵ *On Beauty* suggests that she is close to Murdoch's understanding that this genius is generated by attentive, objective looking which is moral because it illustrates a sustained effort to *see* what is outside the self. The great painter, focusing intently on the other, Murdoch suggests, is emptied of self, sees truth, and reveals it in art. As an example of this objective, moral looking she quotes Rilke, who says of Cezanne, "He did not paint 'I like it,' he painted 'There it is.'"²⁶ The spectator of such an impersonal work of art shares in this clarity of perception and experiences truth by proxy. Murdoch suggests a hierarchy of art in an early novel, *The Sandcastle*, when the art master, Bledyard, discusses three paintings: Hals' *Laughing Cavalier* which, he suggests, portrays only what the sitter wants to see; an abstract mosaic in Ravenna of the Emperor Theodoric, which is merely a portrait of power and munificence, and the self-portraits of Rembrandt which cut through personal fantasy and explore the spiritual and physical reality of the sitter by means of intense realism and expressionistic use of form.²⁷ Bledyard thus articulates Murdoch's aesthetic paradigm and, by proxy Smith's, who loves Rembrandt because "he tries to give you a human being ... his work is so full of love."²⁸

Under the Net makes explicit and implicit references to painters and paintings and allusions to schools of art theory to explore how inner fantasies distort perception of the world and how popular cultural images endorse such fantasies. *On Beauty* is also peppered with meaningful allusions to paintings that illustrate how aesthetics and morality are linked. The process of seeing, transforming and misreading, forms the pattern of both novels, which are littered with descriptions of eyes or faces, and which remind readers that it is vision, rather than choice, that generates morality. Like many of Murdoch's middle-aged, well-educated protagonists (Martin-Lynch Gibbon in *A Severed Head*, Bradley Pearson in *The Black Prince*, Charles Arrowby in *The Sea, the Sea*) Smith's protagonist, Howard Belsey, Empson Lecturer in Aesthetics at the fictional Wellington college in New England, superimposes celebrated images from Western art onto the world. When he meets his wife, Kiki, and his daughter, Zora, on a stairway, their pose, as one stands above the other, reminds him of Picasso's chubby water-carriers.[29] The habit of superimposing painterly images over reality suitably anesthetizes any moral requirement to see people as they are (in this instance hurt and perplexed by his disloyalty) and sidesteps their humanity. Howard does the same when he meets Carl, the black rap singer who is befriended by his son, Levi: he misses the reality of a vulnerable, young, black teenager, and sees only one of the faces from Rubens's *Four African Heads*.[30] Such reductiveness is insulting; Howard's intellectualism is an excuse for rudeness and insensitivity. By contrast, the reverse transformation that both writers attempt in these novels is to use aesthetics to intensify reality for readers rather than distance it, encouraging a deeper more penetrative vision that generates morality.

The central male protagonist of each novel is a writer and theorist and is constructed to critique the over-theorization that corrupts the moral perception of practitioners and readers alike. Murdoch's narrator is the aspiring novelist, Jake Donaghue, who is living a bohemian life as a translator and indulging in a complex love life while he learns to become a good writer. In the Platonic dialogues that take place in the cold-cure center between Jake and his mentor, Hugo Belfounder, Murdoch sets up a contest between the man who wants to theorize and the man who wants to particularize. Jake relinquishes himself to the necessity for theories as organizing principles and the need for language despite its falsehoods. Hugo renounces language for silence and resists any general theories; all theorizing, he insists, is flight, and for the artist, theory is death. Only by paying attention to what is "unutterably particular," he insists, can one come close to the truth. Both Jake's and Hugo's views are only partially Murdoch's own, but it is Hugo's ideas about particularity, not Jake's views about theory, that represent the direction in which art must move so that it illuminates truth and not obscures it. In many ways, Smith's protagonist, Howard Belsey, is the delusional man Jake could have become had Hugo (and art) not educated him. Howard applies radical Marxist theories to Rembrandt's paintings in his book, *Against Rembrandt: Interrogating a Master,* which contests Rembrandt's reputation as a genius in representing the human soul and interprets his work as part of the Western myth with which we "console ourselves and make ourselves."[31] Howard replaces the humanist view of Rembrandt with the idea of the painter as merely a competent artisan who paints what his wealthy patrons request. His book ridicules any belief in the redemptive capacity of art and such distorted perception of art is linked to a distorted perception of human beings.

Both Jake's and Howard's theorizing wreaks havoc in their relationships. Each novel carries a comic vignette that illustrates how immersion in theory leads them to construct themselves as texts. When Jake visits the Wallace Collection in London because he needs a quiet place to think, Murdoch situates him alongside Frans Hals' *The Laughing Cavalier*, the painting that Bledyard in *The Sandcastle* describes as "only what the sitter wants to see."[32] The swashbuckling cavalier is a comical image of the man Jake believes himself to be, the man of Kant, Hegel and Sartre who thinks he has total knowledge of his situation and clear conceptualizations of all possibilities. The parallel illuminates Jake's over-inflated will, his deluded perception of the world and the transformative power of the ego.[33] The painting fuels this inflated self-image as Jake imagines the cavalier would applaud his misguided theories. Murdoch sets Jake up as the paradigm of the man who can only see art as a "symbol of his own internal drama [so that] the self [remains] locked within the self," and Jake and the painting become synonymous as he appears as much a product of a theory and the indulging of fantasy as the cavalier himself.[34] For Murdoch, Jake and the cavalier remain figures of good humored fun, but Smith's representation of Howard's embodiment of the theories he espouses is more scathing. When the relationship between Howard and his wife, Kiki (who has become aware of his infidelity with a colleague, Claire Malcolm) is at its worst, he admits that he needs to "explain my narrative in a way that's comprehensible ... and achieve an ... explanation ... in terms of motivation." Kiki replies, "Don't worry, I comprehend your narrative, Howard ... are you able to talk to me in a way that means anything?"[35]

In both novels such distancing from reality generates misogyny that is intensified by the cultural influences of popular visual art. Jake's and Howard's perceptions of females are so stereotyped that the reality of women is invisible. Jake's craving for Anna Quentin, a singer whose voice triggers a reservoir of preconceptions about women, is evoked by Murdoch's linking of her to the mermaids of Botticelli, "rising out of a motley coloured sea"[36] or, with voluptuous silks at hip and breast, to Renoir's sumptuous portraits of women as objects of yearning.[37] Jake finds Anna "deep" and "unfathomable" and her face is "tenderly moulded" and "constantly lit from within. It is a face full of yearning, yet poised upon itself without any trace of discontent."[38] The allusion here is to Walter Pater's famous account of Leonardo's *La Gioconda*[39]; "hers is the head upon which 'all the ends of the world are come' and the eyelids are a little weary. It is a beauty wrought out from within upon the flesh."[40] Both *La*

Gioconda and Anna have the serenity of the dead and both appear close to water. By linking Jake's perception of Anna with the *Mona Lisa*, and its repute as an emblem of every man's ideal of femininity, Murdoch indicates powerful negative connotations within visual culture that seep from generation to generation: "The presence that rose thus so strangely beside the waters is expressive of what in the ways of a thousand years men had come to desire ... she is older than the rocks among which she sits; like the vampire she has been dead many times, and learned the secrets of the grave."[41] When a woman fails to conform to a man's expectations, Murdoch frequently employs the metaphor of her having "broken through a screen upon which she had been painted."[42] Murdoch does not confine criticism to her male protagonists; many of her female characters pander willingly to such preconceptions (Lizzie Shearer in *The Sea, the Sea*, Georgie Hands in *A Severed Head*, Rosa Keepe in *The Flight from the Enchanter*, and there are many others).

Smith's representation of cultural influences is more damning. Howard despises all artistic representations of human beings and imposes a ban on them in his home where only conceptual art is on display. Like Murdoch, Smith does not shy away from suggesting a hierarchy in the visual arts and Howard's immorality is directly aligned with his tastes in art. She, too, constructs a dramatic scene overshadowed by a work of art which silently but comically mirrors and comments on the foolhardiness of her character (and interrogates the art with which she associates him). Howard and Kiki, arguing, pause in front of a piece of conceptual art. Its

> main feature was a piece of thick white plaster, made to look like linen, crumpled up like a rag someone had thrown away. This action of throwing had been caught, by the artist, in mid flight with the "linen" frozen in space, framed by a white wooden box that thrust out from the wall.[43]

The wooden box is a toy, devoid of any human relevance other than that which the spectator ascribes to it. Its minimalism suits Howard's aesthetic and moral purposes perfectly; it eradicates the mess and muddle that would compromise its aesthetic beauty and intimate moral accountability. In a painful and funny moment Kiki berates Howard for choosing to have an affair with a woman who weighs less than one of her legs: "'You married a big black bitch and you ran off with a fucking leprechaun,'" she wails. "I didn't," replies Howard. "I married a slim black woman.... It's true that men — they respond to beauty.'"[44] The row ends in a simultaneous door-slamming and the floating, crumpled linen falls crashing to the floor, a metaphor for Howard's careless destruction of his marriage. But he is blind even to this obvious analogy between art and life. Both writers suggest that mediocre art is morally culpable by linking it with immoral behavior. Murdoch suggests that "we can see in mediocre art, where perhaps it is more clearly seen in mediocre conduct, the intrusion of fantasy, the assertion of self, the diminishing of any reflection of the real world."[45] Smith makes similar value judgments when she reveals how, in a debate on Modern

British Art at the ICA, she was accused of "aesthetic fascism" for suggesting there was more value in *King Lear* than the text on the back of a cornflake packet. Once, she says, she would have been on the side of her accusers; now she no longer finds it impossible to speak of "value in art."[46]

On Beauty and *Under the Net* both offer Rembrandt as an antidote to the corruptive influence of mediocre art. Smith gives Rembrandt's acute and loving vision to the sixteen-year-old student, Katie Armstrong, who has to overcome her nerves just to enter Howard's lectures because she feels he speaks a different language to her. When Howard discusses Rembrandt's *Seated Nude* (an etching from 1631), depicting a naked woman with a hugely distended stomach, which moves Katie to tears, Howard merely "interrogate[s] ... the mytheme of the artist as autonomous individual with privileged insight into the human." Katie looks at the *detail*: "The crenellated marks of absent stockings on her legs, the muscles in her arms suggestive of manual labor. [The] loose belly [that] has known many babies" and can see herself. It is, she thinks,

> as if Rembrandt were saying to her, and to all women — "For you are of the earth, as my nude is, and you will come to this point, too, and be blessed if you feel as little shame, as much joy as she." ... And all this from cross-hatching ... intimations of mortality from an inkpot![47]

If Howard could see Rembrandt with the penetrative vision of Katie, he could see Kiki's inner beauty and save his marriage.

Such a direct example of the attentive, loving appreciation of art that induces moral perception is missing from *Under the Net*. Murdoch's first person narrative means that Jake's limited perspective governs the novel and all the female characters are perceived reductively though his eyes, and necessarily diminished by it. There are, in fact, only two women in Murdoch's fiction who respond morally to a painting, Dora Greenfield in *The Bell* (1958) and Paula Biranne in *The Nice and The Good* (1968). Dora's response to Gainsborough's portrait of his two young daughters, *The Painter's Daughters Chasing a Butterfly* is sentimental and has no intellectual rationale, and Paula's reaction to Bronzino's *An Allegory of Venus, Folly and Time*,[48] although intended as an example of deep attentive looking that occasions love, is compromised because readers find it difficult to like her, and critics difficult to interpret her.[49] Both incidents have effective moral outcomes, but neither woman commands the emotional response from readers that Smith creates so effortlessly with Katie Armstrong.

Both writers are at pains to suggest the redemptive power of good art and both novels illustrate how Jake's and Howard's perception is altered by it without their conscious knowledge or complicity. Jake searches for Anna in Paris and thinks he glimpses her face, "like a saint's face in a picture," on the banks of the Seine.[50] After an erotically charged pursuit he reaches the *Fontaine de Médicis* in the Luxembourg Gardens. It is an Ottin statue of the lovers, Acis and Galathée watched over by Polyphemus and is mysteriously shaded by trees and reflected in its own pool.[51] Jake is "held by the spirit of the place," while the sound of the fountain triggers a mystical state: "The hearing of an unheard sound. A gentle refutation of Berkeley."[52] The irrefutable *presence* of the statue defies Berkeley's notion that whatever we perceive by the senses cannot exist unperceived, and alerts Jake momentarily to what lies outside his own obsession.[53] He pauses, arrested by the statue's beauty, and *looks* at the Ottin lovers, noticing that the male cups the female's head in his arm with a look "too concerned to be sensual."[54] Jake meditates

> on the curve of her thigh; how her right leg is drawn under her, and her naked left leg out-stretched in that pure undulation which can lift contemplation and desire almost together to the highest point of awareness, the curve of a reclining woman's thigh.[55]

The lovers' pose echoes Jake's and Anna's, as he had earlier held her in a Judo hold and similarly cradled her head in his arm at the mime theatre in Hammersmith. Then the living curve of Anna's thigh induced raging sexual desire in Jake; now he notes that the detached, attentive, bronze lover desires without possessiveness. At some unconscious level Jake learns from looking; his ability to see the bronze woman intently but dispassionately induces a more just perception of Anna, and Jake consequently moves a step closer to the quality of consciousness necessary to the creation of good art, but this is only evident to the reader, not to Jake. By suggesting the moral impact of the statue, Murdoch refutes Kant's claim that art and morality are separate and illustrates her own contention that "art and morality are one."[56]

Smith's comparable illustration of the subliminal moral effect of art comes when Howard shows his students Rembrandt's *Dr. Nicolaes Tulp Demonstrating the Anatomy of the Arm* (1632), which depicts a group of scientists gathered around Dr. Tulp who is dissecting the arm of a corpse and whose left hand, according to Howard, is "raised in explicit imitation of the benefactions of Christ."[57] Howard interprets the painting as an apotheosis of science that anticipates the Enlightenment. The narrative voice notes that he had seen this painting so often he could no longer see it at all. But something has changed and now, for the first time, "the rigorous scientific pursuance of the dictum *Nosce te ipsium*, 'know thyself'" takes on new meaning and Howard is "caught in the painting's orbit. He could see himself laid out on that very table."[58] As the *Fontaine de Medici* had triggered buried self-knowledge for Jake, so does *Dr. Tulp* for Howard. Now he has lost Kiki, the painting demands to know if he is a living or a dead man, and he begins to see that he has failed in that task which makes us most alive and most human: to love. He may also begin to understand that he has failed to see that the truth of this painting lies beyond a rigidly historical exposition of the "clarion call of the enlightenment."[59] As Howard turns away he glimpses Zora through a window and, engulfed with love, wishes a better moral life for her than he has displayed himself: "Don't live in a way that makes you feel dead and don't betray anybody or yourself and take care of what matters."[60]

While Murdoch is content to allow her allusions to rest in suggestion and innuendo, leaving her readers to complete the *gestalt* process that begins but is not completed by the novel, Smith's more expansive narrative is reluctant to leave such a large gap between authorial intention and reader reception. Later, yet another Rembrandt painting, *The Sampling Officials of the Draper's Guild* (*The Staalmeesters*, 1662) makes the unconscious, redemptive power of art even more explicit.[61] The painting depicts six shareholders of a similar age to Howard, seated at a table and looking directly at someone in the audience who has asked a question. The six faces depict six different reactions to this question which traditional art history suggests represent "considered, rational, benign, judgment."[62] (Unsurprisingly, Howard considers this view nonsensical and sentimental.) The same process of seeing, unconscious assimilation and subsequent change in perception is repeated as Howard now reads this painting as he did when he was fourteen, and his art master had suggested that the Staalmeesters were judging *him*.[63] Howard wonders, "What would be their judgment now?" and his discomforted gaze refocuses on the patterned rug in the painting to avoid the Staalmeesters' gaze; but they have made their point.[64] Such chaotic detail (suggesting perhaps Smith's homage to Forster) epitomizes a vital difference in style between the two writers. Murdoch identifies two types of twentieth century novels, the "journalistic" ("a large shapeless quasi-documentary object not concerned with the human condition but with real various individuals struggling in society") and the "crystalline" ("a small quasi allegorical object portraying the human condition and not containing characters in the nineteenth century sense").[65] Surprisingly, despite her desire to emulate nineteenth century Realists, she believes the crystalline ones to be better, but nonetheless dislikes them because they attempt to console by myth. She vacillates between these "open-journalistic" and "closed-crystalline" novels throughout her *oeuvre*, depending on whether her characters are more accidental, separate and free, or whether her own obsessions inevitably govern their construction.[66] Murdoch, aware of the difficulty of reconciling these two styles, did not want to oscillate between the two, and her best novels (*Under the Net* is one) are those where she manages to marry the two competing styles most successfully. To date, Smith's novels tend toward the "journalistic," probably as a result of her unashamed admiration for Forster's "muddled, impulsive, meandering, irrational narrative structures" which she acknowledges allow his books "to get bent out of shape."[67] She justifies Forster's and her own position by suggesting that learning to read through the muddle of narrative helps readers to understand difference and otherness as the moral purposes of the novel. For Murdoch, the *aesthetic* pleasure of the novel participates most crucially in arresting the attention that generates moral understanding; her aesthetic paradigm is Rembrandt not only because his paintings illustrate truth to reality but also because of his "expressionistic" use of form. For Murdoch, creating a beautiful form is part of her literary manifesto and has to do with Plato, who understands that beauty is a visible and accessible part of the good. She not only commands love for her characters by asking readers to empathize with them, but seduces her readers into loving them by forcing them to re-experience the world as they do. Thus in *Under the Net* Jake's deluded perception is suggested by language which borrows from Impressionism (he describes Paris "with quais that look as soft and deep as icing sugar"), and from Surrealism (in his depression when he hides in Dave Gellman's flat and the wall of the hospital outside the window is imbued with a blank white light and is "revealed with abnormal clarity" which triggers nightmares.[68]

Murdoch and Smith join company as Murdoch saves her apotheosis of the visual arts in *Under the Net* for Rembrandt. Murdoch, however, manipulates the novel form itself to illustrate her point as she attempts to recreate the act of painting so that readers see as Jake sees. When Hugo and Jake meet finally in the hospital where Hugo lies injured, he reveals that it is he whom Anna loves, not Jake. The result is a realigning of perception that resembles the reformation of an image in a kaleidoscope: "I could feel my very memory images altering.... I no longer had any picture of Anna, she faded like a sorcerer's apparition, and yet somehow her presence remained to me more substantial than ever before. Anna really existed now as a separate being and not part of myself. To experience this was really painful."[69] Hugo reminds Jake that "God is a task, God is detail. It all lies close to your hand," and Jake now not only sees Anna for the first time but also Hugo, with a loving curiosity about particulars that is implicitly likened to the perceptiveness of Rembrandt, as Murdoch encloses the scene in the verbal equivalent of a Rembrandt self-portrait.[70] Her description of Hugo, with a white bandage on his head and the hint of a red blanket, calls to mind the late Rembrandt self-portrait of 1665, depicting him in the act of painting.[71] Their meeting is presented as if framed by the small rectangular window of about eighteen inches square in the hospital door. Murdoch's writing mimics the act of painting and she becomes a colorist, using subtle contrasts of darkness and light, broken only by the red splash of the blanket:

> The light from the door [which] glinted on the tumbler seemed to find an echoing flash in Hugo's eyes ... [and] as he looked up at me anxiously from underneath the bandage, his face, wrinkled and intent, looked like Rembrandt.[72]

The brief allusion to Rembrandt is the only hint at the larger analogy, and only indirectly suggests a change in Jake's perception and its associated moral benefit. This communication of unobserved inner experience is achieved by stimulation of vision and physical sensation, and readers respond emotionally to Jake, who is clearly fallible, but touching. The rendering of character by means of such unspecified allusions allows Jake to remain elusive, not wholly comprehensible, and the mystery of the human has not been compromised. The exercise itself is part of Murdoch's dialogue with Wittgenstein and her attempt to take the novel, by means of allusions to the visual arts, "under the net" of language which confines it.

Smith's final dialogue with Rembrandt is characteristically more explicit but suggests the same renewed capacity to *see*. Howard's move towards refined perception is illustrated at his Faculty lecture, for which he has compiled an electronic Power Point file. Arriving flustered because of delays, he realizes he has forgotten his notes. For once devoid of theories he is rendered speechless (echoing Hugo's attempt at conveying meaning without language in the Mime Theatre at Hammersmith). A series of Rembrandt's paintings passes silently across the screen, and the final frame is of *Hendrickje Bathing* (1654) portraying a woman wading up to her calves in water; she has bare shoulders and a scarlet ribbon in her plait.[73] Howard usually describes this picture as "a confirmation of the ideality of the vulgar [as] it is already inscribed in the idea of a specifically gendered class debasement."[74] Now, however, Howard has no theories, no contexts, only silence. He looks as in a tennis match between the painting and Kiki in whose face he now sees "his life."[75] As Murdoch had echoed Jake and Anna's pose in the *Fontaine de Médici*, Smith echoes Hendrickje's pose by describing Kiki looking coyly into her lap. Like Hendrickje, she is also considering "whether to wade in deeper" and take Howard back. As Howard's gaze passes from Henrdrickje to Kiki and back again, he finally understands the relevance of art to life. He enlarges the picture so that he can see in Hendrickje's hands "the underlying blue of her veins and the ever present hint of yellow, intimation of what is to come."[76] This is the intimation of mortality that all theorizing camouflages; Howard and the reader understand that all art is to do with the human and is inherently about love, loss, fragility and death.

Rembrandt's *Jacob Wrestling with the Angels* (1659), which features in *On Beauty*, can provide a closing metaphor for how both writers understand the relationship between art and humanity.[77] The painting depicts Jacob and the angel in a pose that is something between an intimate embrace and a struggle. Katie Armstrong finds the relevant passage in the Bible to add to her notes:

> And Jacob was left alone: and there wrestled a man with him until the break of day.... And he said, "Let me go for the day breaketh." And the angel said, "I will not let thee go, except thou bless me."[78]

Katie intuits that this painting is not really about a battle for faith, "the struggle isn't really there," but she cannot make out what it means.[79] Jacob and the Angel are perhaps symbolic of humanity and art respectively. Art looks down on humanity's struggling form with love, while humanity resists its truth by constructing self-protective devices to shield itself from the terrifying intimations of mortality that are crucial to the redemptive power of art.

There are other Murdochian presences in *On Beauty* and Murdoch even makes three guest appearances there. A philosophical cross-fertilization emerges

Jacob Wrestling with the Angel (1659) by Rembrandt, reproduced with permission of BPK/Gemäldegalerie, Staatliche Museen zu Berlin (Photograph: Jörg P. Anders).

as Kiki resembles the quintessential Murdochian "Good Man." When she suffers deeply at Howard's betrayal, she understands that justice and vision are inseparable because "she saw differently now [and] it was certainly stark, revelatory. She saw every fold and tremble of [Howard's] fading prettiness."[80] Yet Kiki knows that this vision of Howard is no more real than her earlier idealization of him, and so can prevent suffering from destroying love. She has always been able to *see* Howard with this degree of clarity and will, in all likelihood, take him back. Smith's narrative provides more room to give her female characters depth, and she constructs a "good woman" who has none of the self-consciousness and angst of Murdoch's male moral pilgrims. Smith gives Kiki a religious significance when Claire Malcolm remembers her as a nursing student with a beauty that was "natural, powerful, unmediated ... a goddess of the everyday.... [Proof] that a new kind of woman had come into the world as promised."[81] When in *Under the Net* Murdoch gives Anna a similar religious significance as Jake sees "a saint's face in a picture" it merely links her to male constructed stereotypes of virgin and whore.[82] Smith's expansive and loving representation of Kiki puts Murdoch's representation of her female characters into stark relief. By employing an exclusively male first person narrative (as she does in six of her novels), Murdoch excludes any significant female perspective from *Under the Net*. The women who have featured in Jake's life remain ghostly, and never find a concrete presence in the reader's imagination. None emerge well: although Murdoch intends Jake to be judged rather than the women, Madge is complicit in subscribing to the fantasy men construct around her; Anna is not very bright; and although Sadie is designated intelligent by Jake, that quality is not fully demonstrated to the reader. Murdoch finds it difficult to ascribe Kiki's magnificence to her female characters either in this or any other novel. She celebrates the abstract quality of love more than the physicality of the women who embody it, who frequently demonstrate a cloying subservience, so that their love must redeem them as much as the men on whom they bestow it.

Of Murdoch's three guest appearances in *On Beauty*, two are associated with Howard and Kiki's son, Jerome, a religious seeker with no sense of ego who undergoes "a blissful unselfing" that identifies him too as a type of Murdochian Good Man. In London he walks through Hyde Park, one of Murdoch's favorite haunts, and his dog is called Murdoch. When Claire Malcolm gives an over-effusive humanist response to Rembrandt's *The Shipbuilder and his Wife* her husband points out that Howard's position is contrary to this view, at which point Murdoch, the dog, yaps furiously. Murdoch the novelist would have applauded the joke. Dogs in her fiction are the apotheosis of instinctive loving obedience to the Good. The famous dog, Mister Mars, provides Jake with his first experience of selfless love in *Under the Net* and Jake absorbs the dog's instinctive trust when they sleep on a bench together on the Embankment. At the end of the novel, the good holy fool Hugo, who has the depth of vision most closely aligned with Rembrandt, exits the hospital ward on all fours, dribbling, with his boots in his mouth and his rear in the air. Murdoch makes her second appearance in Jerome's journal: "'*It is easy to mistake a woman for a philosophy,*" he writes, "the mistake is to be attached to the world at all. It will not thank you for your attachments. Love is the extremely difficult realization.'"[83]

This sentence is a direct quotation from "The Sublime and the Good" and could be completed by glancing back to the opening of this essay: "that something other than oneself is real. Love, and so art and morals, is the discovery of reality."[84]

The third reference initially seems erroneous, for when the Belsey family visits London, Zora says she wants to see Iris Murdoch's grave at Highgate Cemetery. Murdoch's ashes were, in fact, scattered in Oxford.[85] Murdoch herself always distinguished between actual and imaginative truth and suggested that the "truth" of a work of art need not lie in its verisimilitude. Perhaps Smith has similarly constructed a metaphorical truth, hinting that Murdoch's creative legacy lies in her own home of North London. If so, Murdoch would feel the novel to be in safe hands. Smith has "lent her nervous voice" to Martha Nussbaum's Aristotelian demands that literature must once again be taken seriously as a mode of ethical enquiry, and Iris Murdoch is being positioned at the forefront of this return to ethics.[86] Aligning morality and the novel is no longer the anomaly it was, and Smith clearly shares Murdoch's dedication to the moral seriousness of the novel and her affiliated interest in aesthetics. She surely surpasses Murdoch in a glorious celebration of femininity from which Murdoch shrinks, perhaps because she was too much a product of her class, and too bound by her profession as philosopher, her time, and even her bisexuality. Smith may not yet have the philosophical maturity of Murdoch, or the sophistication of her manipulation of form, but her capacious narratives demonstrate the same respect for truth and love and the same belief in the redemptive power of art to work toward the greater good of humanity.

Notes

1. Murdoch, with Jeffrey Meyers (Dooley, 2003, 226).
2. "The only person who I know who has influenced me is Henry James," Murdoch has said (interview with Rose, Dooley, 28). For a more detailed discussion of Murdoch's borrowing from art theory in her experimentation with form see Rowe, 2002, 27–56.
3. Murdoch's legacy can also be found in the work of other contemporary British writers including Ian McEwan. See Rowe 2006, 136–47.
4. See Smith, 1 November 2003, 4–6.
5. Murdoch won the Booker Prize for *The Sea, the Sea* in 1978; Smith won the Orange Prize for *On Beauty* in 2006. The James Tait Black Memorial Prizes were for Murdoch's *The Black Prince* in 1973 and for Smith's *White Teeth* in 2000.
6. Smith, 2009.
7. See Murdoch, "Literature and Philosophy: A Conversation with Brian Magee"; "Art is the Imitation of Nature" and "Against Dryness" in Murdoch, 1997. See also Smith, 2009.
8. Murdoch's relationship with literary theory is ambivalent, and several critics illustrate how she advocates divisions between theory and practice that she cannot sustain in her own work (see Ramanathan and Nicol in Rowe, ed., 2007, and Nicol 2007). However, Murdoch persisted in articulating her fear that highly theorized responses to literature would come to be seen as the only truths that literature has to tell, that literary criticism would become reductive and the moral impact of literature destroyed. Her quest was always that texts should be understood to have a multiplicity of perspectives, but primarily a moral one. While Murdoch's position was in part a reac-

tion to what she saw as excesses in the theories of Barthes and Derrida, Smith's can be read as a reaction to the excessive theorizing of Postcolonial literature.

9. Murdoch, 1997, Chatto, 25; Smith, 2003, 5.
10. Murdoch 1997, Chatto, 19.
11. *Ibid.*, 19.
12. Smith, 2008.
13. *Ibid.*
14. Dooley, 2003, 36.
15. Murdoch, 1997, Chatto, 10.
16. Smith , 2008, 4.
17. Murdoch, 1997, Chatto, 215.
18. Smith 2008, 5.
19. Murdoch, 1997, Chatto, 27; Smith, 2003, 5.
20. Smith, 2008.
21. Smith says that *On Beauty* is an "*hommage*" to Forster and the opening lines, "One may as well begin with Jerome's e-mails to his father," almost exactly echo the opening lines of *Howard's End*. See Smith, 2008.
22. Ellam, 2007.
23. Smith, 2008.
24. Murdoch, interview with Stephen Glover (Dooley, 2003, 40).
25. Smith, like Murdoch, is careful about suggesting too much significance in the inclusion of painters and paintings in her work. Smith says she "didn't want to do anything more than the lightest touch" (2008), and Murdoch would occasionally deter critics from inferring too much from such details, probably because such theorizing over–intellectualized her novels and intruded into the affective response she sought. The same may be true of Smith.
26. Murdoch, 1997, Chatto, 348.
27. Murdoch, 2003 (1957), 250.
28. Smith, 2008.
29. Bradley Pearson, in Murdoch's *The Black Prince* (1973, 33), also experiences a fleeting moment of aestheticized perception as he looks down at faces on a stairway. Bradley feels a strange foreboding when he meets Arnold Baffin and Francis Marloe on the stairs after he leaves the bedroom where Arnold's wife Priscilla lies weeping after having been struck by her husband. Bradley observes that two men resemble "two faces in a crucifixion crowd who represent the painter and his friend." Both writers construct moments where a character superimposes an image from a painting to distance reality and anaesthetize the moral responsibility of having to respond to an actual situation.
30. Smith, 2005, 77.
31. *Ibid.*, 155.
32. Frans Hals, 1624, *The Laughing Cavalier* (held by the Wallace Collection, London).
33. This discussion of the appearance of *The Laughing Cavalier* in *Under the Net* and the discussion that follows on Jake's perception of Anna Quentin and Hugo Belfounder have been adapted from Chapter Two, "Literature, Painting and Form" and Chapter Three, "A Complete and Powerful Picture of the Soul" in Rowe 2002. Later discussions of *The Fontaine des Medicis* and the allusion to the Rembrandt self-portrait of 1665 also appear there in more detail. Thanks are due to the Edwin Mellen Press for kindly agreeing to my using and adapting material from these chapters for this essay.
34. Murdoch, 1997, Chatto, 264.
35. Smith, 2005, 204.
36. Murdoch, 2002 (1954), 44.
37. *Ibid.*, 47.
38. *Ibid.*, 31.
39. Leonardo Da Vinci, 1503–5, *La Gioconda (Mona Lisa)* (held by The Louvre, Paris).
40. Pater, 1986, 79–80.
41. *Ibid.*, 80.
42. Murdoch, 1988, 147.
43. Smith, 2005, 206.
44. *Ibid.*, 207.

45. Murdoch, 1997, Chatto, 255.
46. Smith, 2003, 6.
47. Smith, 2005, 252. Smith may be expressing her own feelings of "confusion about what [she] was wanting and what she was getting" (2008) as a student, and the extremes of theory-saturated academics. Murdoch's commitment to the idea of "negative capability," that the writer should rely on the imagination and refrain from pillaging life to feed plots, would have prevented her from overtly including personal experience to illustrate her point in this way.
48. Bronzino, ca. 1540–50. *An Allegory of Venus, Folly and Time* (held by The National Gallery, London).
49. Todd, 1984, 67. In fact, Todd has interpreted Paula's response to the overtly erotic painting as an indication that "sex comes to most of us with a twist." Dora and Paula are in the National Gallery, London, when they undergo their epiphanies with these paintings, which are both currently exhibited there.
50. Murdoch, 1954, 213.
51. Thomas Florentin Francine, 1624, *La Fontaine des Medici* (held by Jardins de Luxembourg, Paris).
52. *Ibid.*, 208, 206.
53. Flew, 1986, 42. Berkeley, 1940.
54. Murdoch, 2002 (1954), 208.
55. *Ibid.*
56. Murdoch, 1997, Chatto, 215.
57. Smith, 2005, 144. Rembrandt, 1632, *Dr. Nicolaes Tulp Demonstrating the Anatomy of the Arm* (held by Maruritshuis, The Hague).
58. *Ibid.*, 144.
59. *Ibid.* Simon Schama suggests that Rembrandt has smuggled himself conceptually into the painting merely to imply that the "painterly dexterity needed to bring off the painted anatomy lesson was analogous to the demonstration itself." This view might parallel the way that Howard would see the painting. See Schama, 2007.
60. Smith, 2005, 145.
61. Rembrandt, 1662, *The Sampling Officials of the Draper's Guild* (held by Rijksmuseum, Amsterdam).
62. *Ibid.*, 383.
63. *Ibid.*
64. *Ibid.*, 384.
65. Murdoch, 1997, Chatto, 291. This discussion is in Murdoch's important essay on the contemporary novel "Against Dryness."
66. See Murdoch, interview with Rose (Dooley, 2003, 16–29).
67. Smith, 2003, 6.
68. Murdoch, 2002 (1954), 189, 223. The critic Ronald Bryden writing in the *Listener* ("New Novels: Review of Iris Murdoch's *The Sandcastle*" 16 May 1957) suggests that Murdoch "imports at last into fiction the techniques of the great French moderns, bridging a gap in taste which has kept the novel in this country at least, a generation or more behind the visual arts. She writes as everyone since the Post-Impressionists has painted, to create form: joyously pulling reality about to yield the most brilliant surprising patterns of colour and relation" (80).
69. *Ibid.*, 267.
70. *Ibid.*, 257.
71. Rembrandt, 1660, *Self Portrait* (held by The Louvre, Paris).
72. *Ibid.*, 256.
73. Rembrandt, 1654, *Hendrickje Bathing* (held by National Gallery, London).
74. Smith 2005, 252.
75. *Ibid.*, 442.
76. Ibid, 433.
77. Rembrandt, 1658, *Jacob Wrestling with the Angels* (held by Gemaeldegalerie, Berlin).
78. *Ibid.*, 251.
79. *Ibid.*
80. *Ibid.*, 203.
81. *Ibid.*, 227.

82. Murdoch, 2002 (1954), 31.
83. Smith, 2005, 46.
84. Murdoch, 1997, Chatto, 215.
85. Thanks are due to Peter Conradi for clarifying this point.
86. Smith, 2003, 6. See Adamson, Freadman, and Parker, 1998.

5

Enchantment, Transformation, and Rebirth in *The Green Knight*[1]

SHARON R. WILSON

Iris Murdoch's novels do not always receive the acclaim that they deserve. Too often the 26 novels, extending over a 30-year period, are considered traditional or anti-modernist rather than postmodern, and the unreliability and irony of the third-person centers-of-consciousness are overlooked by philosophers who quote characters' dialogue to represent Murdoch's own views.[2] Murdoch's work has been limited by oversimplifications, such as the usual expectation that she always uses realism and refers to objective reality. She is thought to write tragedy rather than comedy,[3] be anti-feminist or non-feminist,[4] and is treated as English rather than as an Irish woman influenced by Irish writers and sometimes takes a postcolonial position.[5] Though most of Murdoch's characters feel enchanted, under a magic spell, and either awaiting rescue or salvation or assuming that they are able to rescue someone else, her myth and fairy-tale intertexts have particularly suffered from insufficient attention.

According to Conradi, Murdoch's references to fairy tales are only decoration for the plot and "contribute to ... atmosphere." He sees her use of myth as "deliberately incomplete, throw-away, and provisional" with "more the feeling of delighted play or joke than of any palpable symbolic design on the reader."[6] Elizabeth Dipple thinks that Murdoch's allusions to myth result in "overplotted, tricksy" novels.[7] Although Murdoch characters use myth and fairy-tale roles to deceive themselves that their lives are fated or scripted and that they are enchanted or imprisoned, paradoxically, myths and fairy tales also suggest transformation and rebirth. Comically, their transformations, like their love relationships, may be transitory. Nevertheless, most do awaken to see more clearly and do keep striving for goodness. Myths and fairy tales are stories and stories in Murdoch's texts ultimately suggest art, a way of creating meaning in a mysterious universe.

According to Murdoch,

> I think that people create myths about themselves and are then dominated by the myths. They feel trapped, and they elect other people to play roles in their lives, to be gods or destroyers or something, and I think that this mythology is often very deep and very influential and secretive, and a novelist is revealing secrets of this sort.[8]

Thus, the novelist or artist is in a sense the master magician. Slaymaker suggests that myths "provide fictional frameworks to support [Murdoch's] notion of the incomprehensibility and impenetrability of human action and motivations."[9] Myths frequently portray quests, such as for escape from a labyrinth or trap, to defeat or kill monsters, to defeat death, to become a hero, to win a prize. Regarding fairy tales, Lisa Fiander suggests that Murdoch's novels challenge and celebrate fairy tales' prescriptions for social engagement. Fairy-tale themes include unhappy childhoods, dangerous romances, the struggle between individuality and community, the journey toward community, and celebration of life.[10] In addition, fairy tales are about the search for identity, individuation, and healing and the transformation of individuals and their surroundings. Thus, Murdoch uses myth and fairy-tale intertexts, hardly just decoration, to convey the images, characterization, themes, and structures of her novels. These "novels" are actually closer to the genres of romance, fabulation, and the fantastic, with an interesting interlay of the money, manners, marriage, and morals tradition of the English novel.

Contrary to what most critics believe, although Murdoch admires traditional nineteenth-century Russian and English realistic novels and speaks of herself as a "traditional" writer, she does not necessarily write novels like Tolstoy and Dickens and is, in fact, only too willing to admit that she does not.[11] Instead, like contemporary writers including Margaret Atwood, Angela Carter, and Toni Morrison, she creates deceptive postmodern works that question her culture's master texts, including Plato, capitalism, Marxism, Christianity, mythology, and some canonical literary works. Despite/ because of her philosophical exploration of Plato, the world of her novels, filled with flawed human beings, lacks Reality and the Good. Like other postmodernists, she deconstructs national, social and cultural myths, as of fate or free will, and substitutes the concept of social construction for fixed concepts as of gender, identity, reality, or truth.[12] Stuck in a postmodern world of shadows and illusions, her characters still experience magical epiphanies that sometimes help them transform:

> A novel is a drama about people who are in some kind of confusion or illusion but are seeking enlightenment, freedom, seeking happiness of course, which we all seek, and the novel describes a drama which ends in catastrophe, falling back into illusion, or acquiring greater illusion or becoming more sensible, more enlightened or more free or something of this kind.[13]

Throughout her work, Murdoch's self-conscious centers-of-consciousness and first-person narrators chatter continuously about the stories they have been living and congratulate themselves on entering "reality" at the same time as they begin another fiction. Most readers have completely overlooked this metafictional dimension of her fiction, probably because it is almost totally dramatized and the implied author is at considerable ironic distance from the narrators. In *The Unicorn*, for example, Gerald and Effingham self-consciously comment on the life narratives which, by implication, are little different from the fiction we read. In their thoughts and dialogue, they reveal an awareness of choosing "art" over "reality," of creating and participating in aesthetic patterns or stories that may distance them from things as they are.[14] In *The Green Knight*, some characters do penetrate beyond illusion and use art to quest for enlightenment. In addition to metafiction, double-voiced irony, and self-conscious narration, Murdoch also uses other postmodern genres and techniques: antifiction, intertextuality, magical realism, parody, and openendedness or writing beyond the ending.[15]

Murdoch's penultimate novel, *The Green Knight*, has attracted almost no critical attention but illustrates well these postmodern techniques. Her fiction is nearly always metafiction, or fiction about fiction, and her narrators continuously call attention to their telling of stories. While Murdoch does not generally use full-fledged antifiction, which parodies traditional plot, structure, characterization, and even theme, her narrators do tell stories, such as that of Lucas's killing a mugger, that, like Atwood's *Surfacing* and *The Robber Bride*, unravel as they proceed. Regarding postmodern openendedness, Murdoch's plots are detailed and ingenious, and the novel gives an impression of every plot thread being tied together. But Murdoch makes no effort to explain Harvey's gothic incident in Tessa's house, probably an encounter with one of the women Tessa is attempting to help, but never spoken of and never related to the main action. Like the actions of Tessa, Emil and Clive, the Adwardens, Cora Brock, and Lucas outside of the main events, this event stands for the external world which cannot be perceived objectively but continues to be there, regardless of what happens to the characters we know. Finally, *The Green Knight* uses mythic and fairy-tale intertexts, my focus here, in a postmodern manner. Unlike Margaret Atwood, who sometimes in published work hides mythic and fairy-tale references more explicit in her manuscripts, Murdoch calls attention to her intertexts by sometimes naming them, in the book's title and in often parodic character descriptions, and she also gives her characters symbolic, sometimes mythic, names. These postmodern techniques puncture any assumption we might make that we are encountering reality in Murdoch's novels: instead, we are continuously aware of story, including its power and our addiction to it.

In addition to displacing the truth of traditional texts and shifting the point of view, postmodern intertextual tactics in *The Green Knight*, parodic until the end, include scenes based on mythic or fairy-tale intertexts and gender reversal, such as the sleeping Harvey being awakened by a kiss at Peter's party; symbolism that enlarges the meaning of the ordinary, such as Moy's cutting off her braid; writing beyond the ending to involve readers in plotting events beyond the book; genre blending; transgressive and ironic language; and surprising remythification, as when Moy realigns her personal world as she places the rock where it belongs. Fortunately, the two scholars who do discuss *The Green Knight* do briefly explain either a few fairy-tale or mythic references. Fiander notes "Hansel and Gretel" in reference to Harvey's fear of abandonment, "Cinderella" to characters aided and impeded by families, animal bridegroom tales, and "Beauty and the Beast."[16] Frankova briefly discusses "Sir Gawain and the Green Knight" and Green Man myth.

Many of the mythological and fairy-tale references are motifs or images that connect to "The Green Knight" and the Green Man. The same mythological patterns also underlie them. As Murdoch says, "The mythology, if you like, is made by the people in the novel themselves.... There are certain general patterns—for instance, the idea of an ordeal: somebody has to undergo an ordeal in order to become enlightened or even to succeed."[17] Ordeals—tasks to be performed or contests—figure not only in "The Green Knight" and the Green Man, but in many of the book's other intertexts: the Grail, Lochinvar, St. George and the Dragon, Perseus, Minotaur, Odysseus, Philoctetes, and other myths and on some level in most fairy tales, such as "Hansel and Gretel," "Cinderella," "Beauty and the Beast" and other animal bridegroom and monster (ogre) tales, "Blue Beard" or "Fitcher's Bird," "Briar Rose" ("Sleeping Beauty"), and "Rapunzel." Another general pattern is the quest, and Murdoch's characters are always questing for meaning, identity, goodness, love, metamorphosis or transformation, salvation, and a new era. Other mythic and fairy-tale motifs include spells and potions, sleeping, falls, injuries, dismemberment, enchantment, transformation, rescue, salvation, and healing. Other intertexts include those about the Great Goddess, Valkyries, Sibyls, the Delphic Priestess, Moira (fate), Silkies, Leda and the Swan, Circe, Daphne and Apollo, Andromache, and wizards. Literary (*The Tempest*), and biblical intertexts (Abel and Cain, Christ, Lazarus, Angels, Mephistopheles) also suggest general patterns in the book. Murdoch admits that she wanted to be a painter and, at the time of the interview, still wanted to be one (Lesser 13). References to painting, such as Rembrandt's *The Polish Rider* and Carpaccio's two *Saint George and the Dragon* paintings in this novel, are everywhere in Murdoch's work, and she recognizes that some of her visual images "carry a mythological charge." They and characters' surroundings are also symbolic, as everything is, because "people make things symbolic for themselves" and surroundings are "charged with emotional significance."[18] Magical objects and talismans—the bat, Peter's magic ceremonial sword (umbrella with hidden knife), characters' masks at the birthday party, the Anderson house (Clifton), Moy's stones, and Moy's braid—are also important. Significantly, however, while the many intertextual references might at first seem confusing, the same general patterns—the quest, the ordeal, transformation or rebirth—underlie all the intertexts.

In a book titled *The Green Knight*, the most evident mythological references are, of course, to the anonymous medieval romance, "Sir Gawain and the Green Knight," a poem that is already "a fusion of Celtic myths and Norman French stories;"[19] to the Green Knight myth; to the earlier, associated pagan myth of the Green Man, often a mask of a leafy man's face peering out of foliage that is displayed in European churches and pubs; and to the also earlier Great Goddess myths on which the other stories appear to be based.[20] The poem has a self-conscious narrator who draws attention to his telling of "as surpassingly strange a tale as ever Britain spawned."[21] It is about Arthur's "perfect knight" of the round table, Sir Gawain, first convincing Arthur to let him take Arthur's place and then accepting a challenge to exchange blows (play the beheading game) with the Green Knight. The Green Knight has green hair and skin, a green horse, a green axe, and green clothing, is associated with the green chapel, and is often referred to as the green man.[22] Gawain has characteristics of the Celtic sun god, including a diadem of golden hair, resembles Cuchulainn, Lug, and Gwri, and his strength waxes until midday and wanes afterwards.[23] After Gawain cuts off the Green Knight's head, the Green Knight picks up his head and says that he will return the blow in a year and a day's time, at the Green Chapel on the New Year. On the way to the chapel, Sir Gawain stops at Sir Bertilak's (Bercilak's) castle, where each agrees under the Gains game to give one another whatever he receives each day. While Bertilak is hunting, Gawain is tempted by his host's wife, who gives him kisses, which he passes on, and a green girdle or belt supposed to protect his life, which he keeps. At the Green Chapel encounter, the Green Knight, who is also Sir Bertilak, slightly injures Gawain on the third blow because Gawain does not tell the truth about the girdle, but he pardons Gawain for his love of life and Gawain keeps the girdle as a reminder of his sin.

The whole event is Morgan (Morgana) le Fay's test of Arthur's knights and, in goddess myth, her presiding over the death and resurrection of the rival year-gods as they behead one another in the life cycle.[24] Morgan, related to numerous river and lake goddesses, valkyries, and mermaids[25] as well as the Crone or Fate aspect of the Great Goddess (Moira-Moy in *The Green Knight*), dwindled in power by the late medieval romances, when she became Arthur's sister. Morgan ruled the Fortunate Isles where valkyries, associated with Aleph in the novel, ushered dead heroes to the afterlife.[26] The poem is about "chivalric virtues, temptation and chastity, goodness and truth.... The mysterious double figure of the pagan/Christian Green Knight/ Bertilak lends the poem an enigmatic quality," and, more significantly, appears to be the basis for the Peter/Lucas foiling and doubling in *The Green Knight*.[27] The poem and Green Knight myth link to pre–Christian Green Man myth, found in the many cultures throughout the world that depict foliate heads (including those of Dionysus, Osiris, Bachus, Al-kadir, and Jack in the Green),[28] because, like earlier goddess myth, both suggest the cycle of life, from death to rebirth to death and rebirth each Spring. Thus, the Green Man celebrates life and suggests fertility and Nature. He is also connected to the end of time, is the voice of inspiration to artists, and can come as a white light, a gleam, or an inner mood.[29] These mythic patterns, themes, character types, images, and mysterious tone translate to Murdoch's book and intertwine with other mythic, fairy-tale, and folklore intertexts in this metafairy tale beginning "Once upon a time there were three girls.... And they lived at the bottom of a well."[30]

Characteristic of Murdoch's tricky postmodern comedy, parody, irony, and frequent intertextual reversals, the preeminent "green man" in this book is a green woman. It can be argued, however, that many of the characters experience a quest, an ordeal, and a rebirth similar to that of the Green Knight or the Green Man and thus also enact these roles, sometimes both seriously and parodically. Beginning in an urban waste land reminiscent of T. S. Eliot's (partly based on Grail and other vegetation myths), Camus' *The Myth of Sisyphus*, and Sartre's *Nausea*, where many characters feel "shipwrecked,"[31] empty, hollow, wounded, and without purpose, most experience the growth and rebirth of the Green Man and the Green Knight. At the beginning, Peter is a confused manic depressive who almost dies, Lucas seems suicidal to his friends, Clement is deceived and tricked, Harvey is crippled and longs for a home, Bellamy longs for religious meaning but masochistically gets no further than punishing himself, Moy is drowning, Louise is passive, Sefton and Alethea seem caught in routine, Joan wants to be rescued, and all await a parodic apocalypse. Virtually all feel they have been enchanted by a spell, are unfree, and are asleep. They seek magical transformation and salvation. All experience comic deaths and rebirths.

The Green Knight and Green Man intertexts interlace with fairy-tale, biblical, other folklore, and literary intertexts, generally emphasized by the characters' own mythological associations. The obvious Green Knight to Lucas's Gawain,[32] Peter Mir, dressed in green and symbolically decapitated like the Green Knight, is actually a decoy, ironically dead at the novel's end. Thought of as a psychoanalyst and sorcerer or magician, and immediately the center of the book's social circle, Peter has an aura of power and prestige that is deflated when we discover that he is an escaped mental patient and butcher-fishmonger. The last name of Peter Mir, a man bent on revenge and punishment for a blow on his head which was assumed to have killed him, ironically means world peace. His first name suggests Simon Peter, the apostle of Christ, Czar Peter the Great, Robin Hood, and Peter Pan, who never grows up. Both Robin Hood and Peter Pan, like Robin Goodfellow and Puck, have historically been associated with the wild Green Man. In the eyes of the characters, Peter is also the minotaur in a maze of confusion (led by a green girdle), Odysseus, Lazarus, the biblical Saul and Paul, Mephistopheles, Mr. Pickwick, the beast of "Beauty and the Beast," a healer, a scapegoat some readers will identify with Jesus, a pirate, an artist, and Eros, who symbolically shoots arrows of love (through his "special" drink/ potion) that apparently effect each of the main characters except Tessa and Lucas, who are not present at the party.[33] In the second encounter of Murdoch's Green Man and Green Knight, Murdoch varies the myth by having the Green Man symbolically beheaded twice. Like the sun aspects of Gawain and the shafts of light (imagination) linked to the Green Man, Peter is associated with light the second time he enters the green world when, depending upon the viewer, a star or plane falls, he burns, he is hit by lightening, or he turns into an angel. Since Peter remembers his Buddhist religion when he is hit on the head for a second time with the baseball bat, he regains his Green Man reverence for life and plans charitable activities for the future before he dies in the mental hospital. Peter's unexpected clean stabbing (an ironic butcher cut) of Lucas with the hidden dagger causes no harm but completes the ritualistic cycle and indicates to Lucas that Peter is an artist.

Other male characters also share aspects of Gawain or the Green Knight in that they are comically associated with knights, warriors, or Trojan heroes and function within the book's cyclic design. Lucas Graffe, the parodic Gawain of the book,[34] whose first name suggests light, Lucifer, and luck, ironically lives in an always dark house. He is another Prospero sorcerer or wizard and secret Bluebeard, the ringmaster, Mephistopheles, the devil,[35] and Abel who prides himself on absolute power over his brother.[36] Although the reference to *Beowulf* suggests that this "shadow-goer" may enter the light[37] and both Harvey and Sefton feel that there is more to Lucas than we see, he seems to win the Lady of "The Green Knight" or Beauty (Aleph) without reforming his monstrous behavior. Ironically, his life is spared without his demonstrating a love of life. Clement, a Harlequin buffoon, Polonius, and juggler whose name means *merciful, gentle*, is the "parfit gentle knight."[38] He dreams that Lucas is offering him the Grail but fears it is poisoned.[39] Interestingly in a book by an author who thinks that Plato is the greatest philosopher, one of the Popes named *Clement* attempted to reconcile Platonic and Christian ideas.[40] Referring to Peter as the Green Knight and Lucas as having had an ordeal (implying that Lucas is Gawain), Clement recognizes that the two are linked and that perhaps justice is greater than the Grail.[41] Comically and ironically, he cannot recognize either the allusion to his being the supposedly murdered "third man" in the melodramatic shadows or the actuality that his brother tried to kill him.[42] Still, by the end he wakes to action in marrying Louise. Harvey Blacket, whose first name means *battleworthy*, is called Lochinvar after the poem about a knight carrying off a bride,[43] and he and Sefton-Sophia (history, order, and wisdom, masked as a Bishop and sibyl,[44] and linked to the amber necklace's qualities of luck and self-healing) (Holistic Qualities of Gems), do eventually decide to marry, but through much of the book he is crippled and immature, a Sleeping Beauty under a spell or curse and asleep in a fairy tale.[45] He also looks like a Greek *kouros* and feels like an abandoned Hansel, the snake-bitten Philoctetes, a puppet, and an androgynous Ariel, creator of illusions.[46] Probably the most comic of these questers, and reminiscent in his self-deceptions of *The Unicorn*'s Effingham Cooper, is Bellamy James, so unfocused and masochistic in his obsession with guidance, angels, and salvation that he causes Father Damien to lose his faith. Reunited with dog Anax (overlord, king) and forming a new relationship with Emil by the end, he finally manages to act in saving Moy from drowning. We know little about Emil except that he is German, rich, gay, initially in a relationship with Clive, writes books about art history, and appears to be more stable than the other characters.

On the other hand, Moy or Moira Anderson, whose first name means goddess of fate, who is part of the Great Goddess, and who is considered a witch in the novel,[47] actually represents the Green Man and the Great Goddess in her oneness with the earth. Contrary to what many feminists believe, folklore actually preserves information about the Great Goddess[48] and many other fairy tales ([besides "Cinderella"] e.g., "The Sleeping Beauty" or "Briar Rose")[49] are Goddess stories; the real mother of Ella (Hel or Helle) was the earth. The "fairy godmother" of later versions of "Cinderella"[50] represents "the dispossessed Great Goddess in retirement underground" and is still associated with the tree of life.[51]

Initially stuck in Clifton like a Rapunzel tower or Sleeping Beauty castle, feeling like a hump-backed dwarf, and close only to her beloved, Rembrandt's painting, *The Polish Rider*, she and her sisters (the Vestal Virgins) must, like the other characters, wake up from routines to experience life.[52] Attacked by a swan, explicitly recalling the myth of Leda and the Swan,[53] Moy is trying only to protect a duck and does not seek, as in Yeats' well-known poem, to put on the god's knowledge and power; instead, she worries that she may have hurt the swan. Moy wishes she had been the prince in "Sleeping Beauty" and awakened Harvey with a kiss. She is, however, the real Beauty of the book in being good, in being the first to recognize Peter's goodness, and finally in representing the union of Beauty and the Beast.[54] Privileged for a time with powers of telekinesis, one instance of the novel's real magic and use of magical realism, at the end Moy turns into a silkie (selkie, silky—in Shetland and Orkney Island myth, a seal who can take off its skin) and back into a person before she returns the conical stone to its original site. As Aleph recognizes early in the book and Moy repeats at the end, symbolically Moy is a girl on the land and a silkie in the sea, and the silkies are *her* people.[55] She is also able to commune with stones, spiders, and Anax and has reverence for all life. Rather isolated within her family early in the book, Moy cuts off her Rapunzel braid, becomes part of a new family with Bellamy and Emil, and is on the way to becoming one of Murdoch's special Buddhists. Peter's gift of a lapis lazuli necklace suggests psychic powers, the opening of a third eye, total awareness, and balance.[56] Significantly, she is the book's main artist. In love with Rembrandt's *The Polish Rider*, she sees him as "brave, innocent, chaste, good," a knight on a quest who is calm in the face of death.[57] Seeing Carpaccio's paintings of St. George and the dragon and also thinking of Perseus, she takes the side of dragons rather than captive princesses and thinks that princesses "should be careful and not make themselves attractive to monsters," the fate apparently in store for Aleph-Alethea (Truth), who also plays Andromache chained to a rock, Beauty of "Beauty and the Beast," the Lady of "The Green Knight," and a military Bluebeard, signifying the secret room of her relationship with Lucas.[58] The diamonds Aleph receives from Peter are traditionally associated with strength, eternity, and peace.

Moy's mother, Louise, who wears a moon mask and, like Aleph, is identified with a sacrificial victim, is also associated with a phase of the Goddess ("the great mother figure") and does signify happiness once she overcomes her symbolic paralysis and Rapunzel-like inability to reach anyone.[59] Joan, the doubled mother/ witch of "Hansel and Gretel," who ironically makes Harvey feel abandoned but sleeps in his bed and interferes with his becoming an adult, is Circe masked as a Delphic priestess.[60] Apparently lacking anyone else that she can manipulate or lean on, she ends up with Humphrey Hook, a man earlier spoken of as the last recourse. In keeping with the novel's amazing transformations, enigmatic Tessa Millen, a feminist who runs a woman's shelter and is also a sibyl, a body guard, "Hitler in knickers," and the witch of "Hansel and Gretel" — whose body is the delicious house — becomes a medical student.[61]

As is beginning to be evident, other myths besides the Green Knight and the Green Man and numerous fairy tales help shape the meanings of *The Green Knight*. Jeanne-Marie Leprince de Beaumont's "Beauty and the Beast,"[62] the more famous tale, is based on Gabrielle-Suzanne de Villeneuve's earlier, longer "The Story of Beauty and the Beast."[63] De Beamont's version is especially relevant to *The Green Knight* because the tale is about the superficiality of beauty: character, virtue, and kindness rather than good looks or wit create happiness. As all of Murdoch's works, both fiction and philosophy, suggest, goodness is what matters. Although Beauty's father is wealthy and her three sisters become arrogant and proud, he loses his money and the family is forced to be farmers in the country. When he is notified that his merchandise is safe and will journey to recover it, Beauty, unlike her envious sisters, asks only for a rose. The father becomes lost while returning home and enters the Beast's apparently deserted palace, where he finds food, a bed, and clothing. While leaving, he plucks a rose, only to be scolded by the Beast and told that he must die in three months unless a daughter takes his place. He returns home with a branch of roses, Beauty leaves with him in order to take his place, both he and the Beast are delighted with "the goodness of Beauty's heart," and the father reluctantly leaves. Beauty grows to respect the Beast, who does not eat her but wants to marry her, and recognizes that, although an ugly monster, he is "very good." Because she sees her father's grief in the Beast's magic mirror, she goes to see her father again and stays longer than a week, when the Beast nearly dies. Beauty returns to the Beast's palace, does not find him, and sees him unconscious in the garden from fasting in his grief. Beauty realizes that she does love Beast, he transforms into a prince "more handsome than Eros," the two sisters become statues until they recognize their faults, and Beauty and the Beast marry. Their relationship is based on virtue.[64]

"Beauty and the Beast" underlies *The Green Knight*'s characterization, themes, and motifs. Although this group of middle-class, educated people is mostly prosperous, they all feel a void in their material existences that fills through love. As Beauty prefers a rose to riches and realizes her love for the Beast in his garden, many of Murdoch's characters find healing and greater consciousness being in nature (the park, the sea, the second time on the bridge). Symbolically, both Peter (briefly) and Moy, like Beast and All Fur,[65] are able to remove their animal skin disguises[66] and, like both Beauty and Beast, dedicate themselves to a quest for the good.

In addition, the Grimms' tales, "Rapunzel,"[67] "Briar Rose,"[68] "Hansel and Gretel,"[69] "Fitcher's Bird,"[70] and "Cinderella,"[71] are among the most significant. "Rapunzel" and "Briar Rose" signify a movement from isolation to relationship that is echoed in the novel. Both take place in towers cut off from other people but surrounded by green nature. The tower in "Rapunzel" lacks door and stairs, and the witch/ sorceress strives to keep her treasured maiden for herself alone, paralleling the father in "Briar Rose" who encloses his daughter and cuts her off from the world to keep her safe from the curse. Although Clifton, the Anderson house, tall and narrow like a tower, is sometimes a center for social activities, most of the time each character occupies a separate room, and Louise certainly wants to keep her daughters and herself safe after their father dies. In "Rapunzel," because a woman covets Mother Gothel's private garden and steals some of the rapunzel plant, she loses her daughter. The witch insists on justice, like Peter Mir, and confines the girl in a tower. The girl still sings, as do Murdoch's Anderson sisters. When Mother Gothel discovers that a prince has been climbing up Rapunzel's hair, she cuts it off, exiles Rapunzel to a desolate land, and traps the prince climbing on the cut off braids. After the prince jumps off the tower and blinds himself on thorns in failing to rescue the princess, he wanders for years until he finds Rapunzel and the twins she has given birth to and regains his sight.[72] Harvey always feels that he is wooing a princess when he is in Clifton, but he initially pursues the wrong princess. Aleph is apparently already involved with Lucas, and Moy, who ironically considers becoming a nun even though she thinks she loves Harvey, never lets down her hair to him. She finally renounces Rapunzelhood by cutting off her braid and chooses to be an artist and a Buddhist. Harvey and Sefton plan to establish their own family.

Variants of the "Briar Rose," "Hansel and Gretel," "Cinderella," and "Fitcher's Bird" tales exist most places in the world.[73] "Briar Rose," "Cinderella," and "Fitcher's Bird" are about marriage, both "Briar Rose" and "Hansel and Gretel" are again partly about maturation to adulthood, and "Fitcher's Bird" is an upside down "Cinderella" story in which the ogre groom is caught in his own trap. *The Green Knight* is also about maturation and marriage in pursuit of happiness and a good life. Most of "Briar Rose's" major motifs—the curse and spell, the castle in the forest, the tower of isolation, the prick, sleeping, and the barrier of thorns—function ironically and parodically in Murdoch's novel, often in more than one sense. In "Briar Rose" a child reaches adulthood despite a wise woman/grandmother witch's curse. A king and queen who arrange a feast to celebrate the birth of their child invite only twelve of the thirteen wise women to the celebration because they have only twelve golden plates. The one who is not invited wants revenge and makes an evil spell so that the princess will prick her finger on a spindle and die. The last wise woman amends the sentence to a sleep of one hundred years. Although the king orders all spindles in the kingdom to be burned, on her fifteenth birthday the princess discovers a tower and unlocks a door to a room where an old woman is spinning. When the princess touches the spindle and feels the prick, she is overcome by a deep sleep. Gradually everyone in the palace falls asleep and a briar hedge encloses it for a hundred years, until a prince discovers that he can easily enter. When he discovers and kisses the princess, she awakes, they marry, and "they lived happily to the end of their days."[74]

Moy, too, has a birthday party (16th) and has a gift-bringing visitor, not initially expected, who changes the course of everyone's lives. Depending upon how one counts, the number of standard invitations might even total twelve. According to Joan, "Harvey ought to be the prince who hacks his way through the forest, but he can't be, he's *in* the castle!"[75] Harvey, both prince and parodic princess in *The Green Knight*, is "green" in the sense of naïve and innocent and certainly feels cursed, under a spell, asleep, and isolated, especially when he has to bypass Circe witch Joan and sibyl witch Tessa.[76] Still, Fiander's assumption, that in Murdoch's universe love means loving without too much knowledge,[77] seems oversimplified. While his pursuit of Aleph always seems barricaded with thorns, when he shifts to Sefton, who has already awakened him at Peter's house, he has the knight's experience of "Briar Rose": it is as if "the beautiful flowers opened of their own accord [to], let him through."[78] Disregarding the pun on *prick* that one is tempted to connect to Harvey and Sefton's first sexual experience, both prince and princess Harvey and Sefton, who have known one another nearly all of their lives, so suddenly become aware of one another that Harvey has to tell Sefton to "stop, stop, *wake up*" when she assumes Harvey must be in love with Aleph.[79] Several other characters—Peter, Moy, Bellamy, Clement, Louise—play Sleeping Beauty to the extent that they don't awaken to a real life purpose until late in the novel. As Louise says when she thinks she will descend into old age without romantic love, "for so long I was paralysed as if asleep."[80]

The Grimms' "Hansel and Gretel" and "Fitcher's Bird" (Perrault's "Blue Beard") both take place in a forest, as does "Briar Rose"; and, along with "Cinderella" and Green Man myth, thus suggest an origin in tree myth. The three tales involve trickery, betrayal, resourcefulness, and animal helpers; and both "Cinderella" and "Fitcher's Bird" involve transformation. "Hansel and Gretel" is about a child's movement from abandonment and anxiety about independence to self-sufficiency.[81] It is also about famine and greed, and some versions of "Fitcher's Bird" are about unnatural hunger—cannibalism. "Fitcher's Bird" also explores each person's "secret room," sexual politics, and transformation. *The Green Knight* is about all of these themes. Many of Murdoch's characters feel abandoned or unloved in childhood, resort to trickery and even betrayal, are greedy or covetous, and manage to keep parts of themselves secret. Some, such as Joan and Tessa, play games of sexual politics, and some manage to transform. Meals at Clifton are ritualistic,[82] may be offered instead of sex, and sometimes humorously puncture melodramatic dialogue, as when Aleph offers Harvey a prosaic lunch right after he suggests they are experiencing "a special moment in time ... like salvation."[83]

In "Hansel and Gretel," a woman convinces her husband to abandon two children deep in the forest when there is a famine. Although once they manage to find their way back by stones Hansel has dropped, the next time the birds eat the crumbs he hoped to follow and they are lost until a white bird leads them to a house made of bread, cake, and sugar. The mother's double, a wicked witch on a crutch, takes them in but plans to eat them, especially Hansel, whom she puts in a cage and tries to fatten up. Gretel manages to push the witch into the oven prepared for Hansel, releases Hansel, and they return to the forest, where they are helped across a river by a white duck. They return home to their father "and they lived together in utmost joy."[84] Specifically again Harvey, but, as stated, many of *The Green Knight's* characters, feel abandoned, Lucas by his parents when they have a "real" son, Clement by his brother Lucas, Joan and Louise by Clement, Bellamy by God, and Anax by Bellamy. Harvey, whose parents do leave him alone and hungry for affection, humorously plays the wicked witch on a crutch as well as Hansel but learns to take responsibility for his actions. Although *The Green Knight* is not really moralistic because of the parodic undercutting, all of the characters resemble Gretel in using their wits and moving beyond self-obsession to concern about at least one other person.

"Fitcher's Bird" is the Bluebeard tale about a wizard who enchants girls into jumping into his basket and dismembers them when they open the door into a forbidden room with dead bodies. This tale, associated with animal bridegroom ones,[85] is obliquely suggested by the wizard-like power, which sometimes seems mock-gothic, that Lucas and Peter exercise over other characters. Restitution for a wrong committed is the theme not only of "Gawain and the Green Knight" but of animal bridegroom tales.[86] Lucas, the "ringmaster" who seems to manipulate everyone behind the scenes without feeling anything for anybody, remains a mysterious ogre. Fiander suggests that Lucas is a borderline psychotic,[87] and he certainly behaves in a beastly way to everyone.

In opposition to "Cinderella," where a girl in the ashes rises in fortune to become a princess, the third sister in "Fitcher's Bird" discovers the underside of a fairy-tale marriage: she outwits the wizard by not getting her egg bloodied in the forbidden room, disguises herself as a marvelous bird, uses goddess power to re-member her hacked-apart sisters, and survives while the wizard is punished. Comically in *The Green Knight*, Lucas secretly succeeds with successive women, appears to murder without consequence, and gets away with the beauty. Aleph's family worries that he may destroy her. Peter, who is his own secret room, dies before he is able to carry off a maiden. Sexual politics, between men and men as well as men and women, emerges in dominance-submission games between Magnus and Bellamy, Lucas and Peter, and Joan and Clement. Moy seems to possess the third sister's, the Green Man's, and the Great Goddess's power to heal and resurrect. Symbolically under the well at the beginning of the book, she emerges from "drowning" at the end.

To a greater extent than in some of Murdoch's early novels, most of the characters of *The Green Knight* do experience a comic rise in fortune to celebrate life, and in most cases, even though sudden, these characters' epiphanies show greater awareness. As in the money, manners, marriage, and morals tradition and many fairy tales, there is a movement from loneliness to partnering, and many of the characters marry or plan to marry. While human instead of perfect, their happiness appears more genuine than illusory and likely to last longer than their previous experiences. Although still young, Moy possesses the Green Man's artistic inspiration and shows insight and capacity to do good. Clement and Louise have known one another well for a long time and seem to have realistic expectations, and Harvey and Sefton will continue school and postpone marriage for a while. Tessa has chosen a useful career, and Aleph acts on a dream. Less can be said about the chances of Bellamy, Lucas, and Joan, but each is at least in a relationship and not mired in self-pity or selfishness.

Murdoch's fairy-tale and mythic intertexts thus are integral to every aspect of her novels: they supply the unforgettable, magically real images—the bell in *The Bell*, the sea monster in *The Sea, the Sea*, and in *The Green Knight*, the shaft of light surrounding Peter as he is "beheaded" for the second time and the conical rock returned to its place on a hill beside the sea. They reveal the comic and parodic but still likable characters who spend their lives questing; they depict ways of creating meaning in a mysterious postmodern universe.

NOTES

1. A slightly different version of this article appears in Wilson's 2008 monograph, *Myths and Fairy Tales in Contemporary Women's Fiction: From Atwood to Morrison*.
2. Gordon, 1990, 115; Duddy, 2006, 2287.
3. Lesser, 1985, 15.
4. Rowe, 2005, Review 352; Fiander, 2004,8, 10–11. Fiander says, "Murdoch almost never

portrays liberated women in her novels" (10), but ironic writers rarely use characters as author surrogates. For an analysis of Murdoch's questioning of gender identity and transgressing gender boundaries, see Johnson (1); for feminist themes, see Weese (634). Murdoch actually "feels very strongly about the liberation of women" (Sagare interview, 707). Murdoch was born in Ireland and even sets one of her novels, *The Red and the Green,* at the time of the Easter Uprising.
    5. (Gerstenberger, 1975, 79; Rowe, 2005, "Dame," 316–20; Weese, 2001, 648).
    6. Conradi, 1986, 11, 126, 250.
    7. Dipple, 1982, 3.
    8. Bellamy, 1977, 138.
    9. Slaymaker, n.d., 166.
    10. Fiander, 2004, xii, xv, vii.
    11. Sagare, 2001, 698. Margaret Moan Rowe admires Murdoch's talent for concealing as much as she reveals in interviews, often being "guarded and gnomic" in her responses (2005, rev., 351).
    12. Holman and Harmon, 1986.
    13. Sagare, 2001, 698.
    14. Wilson, 1976, 95.
    15. Holman and Harmon, 1986.
    16. See Fiander, 2004.
    17. Sagare, 2001, 705–06.
    18. Lesser, 1985, 13.
    19. Frankova, 1995, 77.
    20. See Miyares, 2002, 185, in which the goddess represents "Nature, Fate, Time, Eternity, Truth, Wisdom, Justice, Love, Birth, Death" (Walker, 1983, 346).
    21. Raffel, 1970, 49.
    22. *Ibid.*, 52–61.
    23. Leach and Fried, 1984, 442–43.
    24. Walker, 1983, 674.
    25. Leach and Fried, 1984, 746–47.
    26. Walker, 1983, 675; Leach and Fried, 1984, 746.
    27. Frankova, 1995, 79.
    28. Jack in the Green was part of a May Day pageant in England and probably a relic of tree worship, resembling Eastern European Green George on St. George's Day (Leach and Fried, 1984, 534).
    29. Anderson, 1990.
    30. Murdoch, 1993, *Green,* 1.
    31. *Ibid.*, 327.
    32. *Ibid.*, 456.
    33. *Ibid.*, 195, 343, 117, 297, 195, 213, 338, 91, 421, 319.
    34. *Ibid.*, 456.
    35. *Ibid.*, 252.
    36. *Ibid.*, 88.
    37. *Ibid.*, 422.
    38. *Ibid.*, 11.
    39. *Ibid.*, 84, 87.
    40. Clement, Behind the Name.
    41. Murdoch, 1993, *Green,* 456.
    42. *Ibid.*, 94.
    43. *Ibid.*, 112.
    44. *Ibid.*, 141.
    45. *Ibid.*, 467.
    46. *Ibid.*, 32, 111, 112, 59, 245.
    47. *Ibid.*, 49.
    48. Gimbutas, 1991, 226.
    49. Von Franz, 1972, 20.
    50. Thompson, 1955 (Motif F311.1).
    51. S. Wilson, 1993, 20; Walker, 1983, 168; Von Franz, 1972, 9–10.
    52. Murdoch, 1993, *Green,* 386, 49.

53. *Ibid.*, 202.
54. *Ibid.*, 213.
55. *Ibid.*, 16, 467.
56. Lapis Lazuli, Holistic Qualities of Gems.
57. Murdoch, 1993, *Green*, 20, 386.
58. *Ibid.*, 203, 112, 208.
59. *Ibid.*, 205, 206, 371, 218.
60. *Ibid.*, 107, 207.
61. *Ibid.*, 133, 5.
62. Aarne and Thompson, 1987, 425C.
63. Zipes, 1989, 231–32.
64. *Ibid.*, 233–45.
65. Zipes, 1987, *Complete*, 263.
66. Thompson, 1955 (Motif K521.1).
67. Aarne and Thompson, 1987, 310.
68. *Ibid.*, 410
69. *Ibid.*, 327A.
70. *Ibid.*, 311.
71. *Ibid.*, 510, 510a.
72. Zipes, 1987, *Complete* , 46–49.
73. Aarne and Thompson, 1987, 138–39.
74. Zipes, 1987, *Complete*, 186–89.
75. Murdoch, 1993, *Green*, 11.
76. *Ibid.*, 334, 133.
77. Fiander, 2004, xiv.
78. Zipes, 1987, *Complete*, 188.
79. Murdoch, 1993, *Green*, 421.
80. *Ibid.*, 336.
81. Bettelheim, 1976, 98.
82. *Ibid.*, 309.
83. *Ibid.*, 264.
84. Zipes, 1987, *Complete*, 64.
85. Fiander, 2004, 73.
86. *Ibid.*, 68.
87. Murdoch, 1993, *Green*, 67.

6

Messy Is Flourishing Is Sublime

M. F. SIMONE ROBERTS

"Love is the perception of individuals."
— Iris Murdoch

"We still fall short of the human."
— Luce Irigaray

In "The Darkness of Practical Reason," Dame Murdoch offers one of many summaries of her ethics, and doing so makes a statement Luce Irigaray would agree to but qualify with respect to gender ideology and gender ontology. Murdoch reminds us of a truth poststructuralists take for granted:

> The world which we confront is not just a world of "facts" but a world upon which our imagination has, at any given moment, already worked; and although such working may often be "fantasy" and may constitute a barrier to our seeing "what is really there," this is not necessarily so.[1]

While Murdoch's investigations of these blinding fantasies have to do with neurosis as she finds in the work of major philosophers (taken as avatars of their eras) and the psyches of individual people as informed by their era, Irigaray examines cultural fantasies concerning gender in both philosophy and psychoanalytic theory. Their arguments run along similar lines. Both women would agree that to "be human is to know more than one can prove," but Murdoch focuses in a generally humanist way on philosophy's tendency to assume a world "living strictly by extremely general rules" that leave "no place for the morally complicated or eccentric" persons or cases we encounter in the mess and muddle of life.[2] Irigaray would qualify "complicated and eccentric" to mean the feminine both as women and as a mode of human being excluded by a culture and philosophy historically written by and (she assumes) to suit men and the masculine. The philosophers propose similar solutions to these structurally parallel and possibly related problems: in Murdoch's words, "We have to *attend* to people, we have to have *faith* in them, and here justice and realism may demand the inhibition of certain pictures [of humans], the promotion of others."³ Both lay the responsibility for changes and reimagining we would like to see squarely on our own shoulders. Irigaray argues that women must discover/imagine and culturally codify a positively defined grounding sense of the feminine as men have had the chance to do (to their advantage *and* detriment). Murdoch argues similarly that we all "have partly willed our world when we come to look at it; and we must admit moral responsibility for this 'fabricated' world, however difficult it may be to control the process of fabrication."⁴

In addition to their attitudinal sisterhood, I would like to read these two philosophers next to each other because their habits of mind are also similar. Both engage the history of philosophy in order to increase methodological room for what it brackets off (the mess, the particular, the feminine). Both stand outside of and alongside the schools of thought present in their own intellectual milieus. It is not a simple thing to call Murdoch a humanist, nor to call Irigaray a poststructuralist; though it is fair to call Murdoch a moral philosopher (unqualified) and Irigaray a moral philosopher of gender. Both are simply titanic women: Murdoch as a philosopher and novelist, Irigaray as a philosopher, linguist, and psychoanalyst (she holds degrees in all three fields and employs them in her work).

The study of moral philosophy makes one thing (if not much else) clear: Nothing Good Just Happens. Nothing bad just happens, either, and I am fairly certain these two women would consider my placing them side by side at least a little bit bad. Murdoch would object to Irigaray's "structuralism" as walking dangerously away from necessary grounds for truth. She would be partly correct in that Irigaray argues having only one (masculine) transcendental signifier is half the story and we have not yet made up the other half (a space for moral imagination if ever there were one). Irigaray holds that sexual difference implies/requires two truths. Irigaray would object to Murdoch's universalist liberalism and grounding of her discourse on a "neutral" transcendent term, The Good, whose neutrality remains too much within the masculine symbolic order, thus erasing (again) women and the feminine from what could be a balanced symbolic order (though we often feel that just the impossibility of the Good is demand enough). And, if they were to sit down together, they would likely have a long hot talk about these problems.⁵

Still, the points of resonance in their thought compel me to stand both outside and alongside them. Their critically constructive work on other thinkers leads Murdoch to describe the constriction of the liberal personality as found in Kant, Hegel, and Sartre by fantasy or neurosis; while Irigaray reads in many of the same thinkers evidence of a neurotic and delusional patriarchal (or masculine) subject. Both agree that such neuroses do a great deal of very real damage, the one more focused on the individual, the other on the cultural flows of this damage. Both philosophers focus on the workings of love and attention to the particular or the gendered other as a path that is also the goal in living ethically; both accept the paradox of that goal-path. Unselfing is nothing if not a goal and a process. Being-two is, equally, work we simply undertake and attempt to perfect. Murdoch and Irigaray want us to engage in the process of reshaping our desire for the sake of other people. And lastly, I see in the later Irigaray positive descriptions of gender and its dynamics as detailing some of the flows in the mess Murdoch takes us to live in and celebrates. Though Irigaray goes further in her philosophy than Murdoch does, both philosophers offer their analyses and imagination for the sake of more robust human flourishing. One could say that Murdoch and Irigaray are existentialist mystics.

Beginning in the Mess (Because where else is there?)

For all the crystalline brilliance of much philosophy, there is something troublingly dead about it for Murdoch and Irigaray. For Murdoch, it is so clean and self-contained that it fails to address itself to the ambiguities and contingency of life — or when it does, finds itself alternately angrily horrified and overwhelmed, or determined to absorb all that otherness. She argues that this cleanliness is a sign of either narcissistic or neurotic fantasy, or both. Irigaray argues that in philosophy, and life, this particular dysfunction is of the masculine (culture, and in men and women). In several texts she casts the question of being-two or sexual difference as a matter of nearly global life or death. For both philosophers, life is far richer, more particular, textured, more contingent and surprising, and possibly more nourishing than much of the history of philosophy would allow us to imagine. The lovely thing about contingency is that it means this: whatever the case is, it can change. We can throw our weight around.

MURDOCH AND THE BIG THREE

Against these self-enclosed systems, Murdoch offers philosophy in and embracing of the mess, the particular, and Irigaray offers the thinking of sexual difference or being-two. The concepts compliment and strengthen each other especially when we consider the role of attention or perception that each philosopher describes as their versions of moral vision.[6]

Both the ravishing and the repugnant aspects of contingency Murdoch calls "the mess," a word she uses less often than contingency, but one I prefer. Contingency connotes rectification and contractuality, where one mess might get cleaned up even as we know another one is coming; moreover, contingency sounds like a tidy philosophical concept while mess sounds earthly and particular, human. In Murdoch's view, much of philosophy fares poorly at encountering this mess (history, cultural differences, the moods and will of other people, traffic jams), but this encounter is essential to her view of love and ethical being. "Real people are destructive of myth, contingency is destructive of fantasy and opens the way for imagination" which, she argues elsewhere, is an element of love.[7]

Myth and fantasy, like narcissism and neurosis—her oft repeated charges against previous philosophers—are dodges around paying attention (to particular, opaque other humans who require of our theories "a new vocabulary of attention"[8]). The mess, and contingency, she urges, "must be defended for it is the essence of personality."[9] In "The Sublime and the Good," and "The Sublime and the Beautiful Revisited," she takes Kant, Hegel, and Sartre (with a nod to the Symbolists and ordinary language philosophers) to task for various attempts at avoidance of this attention—for, that is, various degrees of fantasy, narcissism, and neurosis in that their systems work very hard to form closed circles defending them from the other. Quickly: Kant gives us a moral philosophy that equates virtue : freedom : reason. Virtue is, on her reading here, "an ability to impose rational order" that leaves out "the messy and ambiguous region of the emotions" and our many conflicting motives, the contexts in which we feel our desire, aversion, rage in favor rational choice.[10] That which complicates those choices (that is the personality which needs defending in its contingency and particularity) is outside the realm of Kant's system. In a later discussion of the Symbolist abhorrence of "messiness," Murdoch punctuates her characterization of Kant's Rational Man: "a fear of contingency, a yearning to pierce through the messy phenomenal world to some perfect and necessary form and order."[11] This is no easy task, to be sure. A fantasy troubled with convention, and it is that convention that precludes or retards the flexibility Murdoch finds necessary for loving other subjects in the mess.

Hegel's Romantic Man[12] does not experience a defeat of reason, as Rational Man might when faced with the sublime.[13] The reason of Romantic Man can "close the circle of knowledge, no agnosticism here, no limit." Rather, for Hegel virtue is freedom is self-knowledge. "There is only one being in the Hegelian universe," Murdoch summarizes, "a whole which cannot allow anything outside itself and which struggles to realize all that is apparently other."[14] This man refuses the risk of contingency by retreating to narcissism. For him, "potentially separate [centers] of significance [are] necessarily a menace..., something to be internalized in a battle of consciousnesses just as discrepant centres in oneself are to be overcome by reflection."[15] Engagement with internal otherness is for the purpose of self-realization and its continuance unto the Absolute.

Sartre's Totalitarian Man works around the mess by yet another route, a kind of glorified neurosis with hints of rebellion. Sartre's man, Murdoch argues, "represents the surrender to neurosis" even though his moral agent is as solitary as Kant's rational chooser and embedded in a struggle for self-realization as dramatic as Hegel's Spirit. Totalitarian Man is "entirely alone," suffers *angst* making his choices "against the apocalyptic background of the modern world" and the resistance of other people who are "not real contingent separate other people," but "organized menacing extensions of the consciousness of the subject."[16] Worse for him, this man has given up on the "confidence in universal reason" and its "dignified and exultant aspect." There is no *Achtung*, but rather for him virtue is "sincerity, courage, will: the unillusioned exercise of complete freedom."[17] He feels terror or revulsion at "anything which encloses the agent or threatens his supremacy as a centre of significance." Pushing his way out of convention, he is left in neurosis, even a hint of paranoia.

What all these kinds of moral subjects have in common is a characterization Murdoch lays on the Symbolist poets:

> What is feared is history, real beings, and real change, whatever is contingent, messy, boundless, infinitely particular, and endlessly still to be explained; what is desired is the timeless non-discursive whole which has its significance completely contained in itself.[18]

Not insignificantly, we will see later, this is a good paraphrase of the charge Irigaray lands against the Masculinist Personality: trying very hard to be his own alpha and omega, a perfected circle lifted "out of the fallen world of existence."[19] The everyday world, including that of other embodied, vulnerable humans, is too dirty, too complicated (non-philosophical) and therefore terrifying, and in any case: to be avoided.[20]

Avoidance is not attention. Attention wakes us up right in the midst of the mess; but its attendant, love, gives us a chance at vision, at perception in Irigaray's terms. Both of these women find that one does not first become secure enough for this generous attention and then offer it. One practices attention/perception and finds that security and love for the other come into being with it. This is a paradox, and philosophy categorizes paradox as part of the mess. However, we are in the mess, and paradoxes must be taken up honestly because they are true, if a bit irrational: for instance, Irigaray's desire for (at least) two sources of meaning in the symbolic of culture/religion/politics/art or Murdoch's sense of unselfing as both painful and an act in love.

Of attention, Murdoch would like us to understand several points. Turning ourselves "toward the great surprising variety of the world" is no easy task.[21] It involves a patient dismantling of the "anxious avaricious tentacles of the self" along with the fact that life and the other people in it will not be waiting for us to finish untangling before engaging with them, and Murdoch admits that "[success] in fact is rare."[22] The process is linked with detachment, obedience, and discipline requiring "a refined and honest perception of what is really the case, a patient and just discernment and exploration of what confronts one" as we come to experience and think in terms "of degrees of freedom, and to picture in a non-metaphysical, non-totalitarian and non-religious sense, the transcendence of reality."²³ Morality is less a matter of choices made within particular rubrics and more a matter of a posture, an attitude:

> ... if we consider what the work of attention is like, how continuously it goes on, and how imperceptibly it builds up structures of value round about us, we shall not be surprised that at crucial moments of choice most of the business of choosing is already over.²⁴

Murdoch's figure for this moral agent is the great artist and the good critic, both of whom arrive at their subjects in order to see them in their particularity, without any assumed (narcissist or neurotic) background theory or overdetermination.²⁶ When we attend, we must also welcome that fact that not everything or everyone will suit us, fit our scheme — indeed, it is our obligation *not* to require that fit. This, as Murdoch famously reminds is, is painful but also in the case of love and art, often beautiful, possibly a source of flourishing.

We always encounter the other and the world in the midst of our own narratives and histories, and in the midst of theirs. Attention contains that sense of attending: an active and passive process of looking/reading and waiting for further revelation from the other. Where the artist has the luxury of focusing their and our attention on one scene as in painting, one moment of realization as in poetry, or one slice of time in characters' lives as in the novel, their work is only a training ground because the work of art itself is static.²⁶ Our refinement of attention might draw lessons there, but we must then go on outside in the mess of our *in medias res* to shed illusions and see the other clearly as they also, we hope, go about shedding theirs in order to see us. There is a lot going on in the mess even if one is loving. It takes, I think literally, a great deal of imagination to begin to understand oneself as "grounded" and replete enough for this generosity and to begin to hear and respond others' being in love. It requires that we feel love to be both a goal of our effort and its path — paradoxically.

Irigaray's Attention

In her essays and comments on perception, Irigaray limits the field of the mess to sexual difference, one aspect of the mess that is most persistently troubled (in life) and covered over (in philosophy). In the context of sexual difference, Irigaray elaborates a number of terms that I read as figures for the mess: the interval, the double-loop of subjectivity, active-passive being, the sensible transcendental, all of which are kin to what she calls the Diotiman dialectic. She reads this dialectic out of Plato's *Symposium*:

> There is an intermediary that allows for the encounter and transmutation or transvaluation between two. Diotima's dialectic is in at least four terms: the here, the two poles of the encounter [between subjects], and the beyond — but a beyond that never abolishes the here. And so on, indefinitely. The mediator [the interval, love] is never abolished in an infallible knowledge. Everything is always in movement, in a state of becoming.²⁷

To summarize radically, sexual difference is the principle that in philosophy and culture (the symbolic) we have a long history of elaborations of the masculine that erase the feminine or define it for purposes of the masculine's own. Because we inhabit a history in which the feminine was never elaborated on its own terms and for itself, our culture is out of balance and so are our psyches. Irigaray proposes her thinking of sexual difference an establishment of the feminine symbolic as both the ground of feminine identity and as a balance to the masculine symbolic in a culture of being-two. In sexual difference there would be two poles of encounter, masculine and feminine as persons and principles in culture. Where Murdoch then would argue that philosophy fails in the face of the mess and the neutral individual, Irigaray argues that it fails in the face of the feminine and sexual difference, and I find that the rejected terms are quite similar.[28]

Where Murdoch argues that our unselfing takes place in relation to a world and other persons horizontal to us, Irigaray argues that this process is also gendered. As with Murdoch, love and attention (perception) are the goal-paths Irigaray promotes while qualifying that process: women must create a Feminine that balances the Masculine while men must revise the Masculine in light of this developing Feminine. Because her focus is on gender as it might be imagined and lived rather than as a stable social category, Irigaray's figure for the moral agent is dual: the lover-masculine and the lover-feminine, neither reduced to an object of the other's personal or cultural fantasy.[29]

In a late and summative work, *To Be Two*, Irigaray addresses perception and the caress as two modes of ethical being that involve an opening of the self to the being and becoming of the particular other. Perception and caress involve ethical energies akin to Murdoch's attention and unselfing. Irigaray explicates and imagines interactions as gendered ontologically, phenomenologically, morally/culturally, and psycho-spiritually. For Irigaray the caress is the physical/real expression of perception which is ideal/symbolic.

In "The Wedding Between the Body and Language," Irigaray opens one discussion of perception with observations of philosophy in general and Sartre in particular that mirror Murdoch's:

> Man prefers a relationship between the one and the many, between the I-masculine subject and others: people, society, understood as *them* and not as *you*.
> ...
> For ... Sartre, the body of the other is a "facticity," a fact, a present objective reality which is beside me.... But the other is more than facticity, the other is consciousness: of-itself, for-itself, consciousness of the world, even.[30]

Due in part to this misperception of the other, Totalitarian Man has two choices: absorb the other, or fight them. Love is out of the mix. The subject that cannot admit of other consciousnesses, modes of being human, desires only "the same" (familiar, consoling) and "cannot escape conflict in order to appropriate the other's transcendence" (the other gender's relation to time, history, the world).[31] Like Murdoch, Irigaray argues that this dismissive/possessive will "corresponds to a solitary and solipsistic dream which forgets that your consciousness and mine do not obey the same necessities" because we are of different genders.[32] What is to be done? How is one to perceive and then respond in love to the other? There too, we are in trouble for "we lack a culture of perception, and because of this flaw, we fall back into the realm of simple feeling" or of fantasy and spectacle.

However, perception does present us with a mode of "sensing the other, respecting him as subject, and it also allows me to remain a subject while perceiving the other."[33] This kind of perception would establish consequential links between the other and the world out there and my subjectivity, intentions, becoming. Irigaray calls this the "sensible perception" our culture lacks.[34] Irigaray discovers practices in Tantra and the yoga sutras that hone sight, smell, touch, taste, hearing as conduits for contact with the world, as modes of engagement trained to be conscious, intentional. The intention is mutually sustaining and uses these practices and descriptions of the genders to modify our ethics to see "each other between us: as life, as freedom, as difference."[35] It is to the concrete particularity of the other that we owe our perception and opening, but also to that other as a member of a gender, with a history and a relation to the community and future that are not the same.

Perception operates ideally, while the caress operates corporeally (part of our work in an Irigarian ethics is to align mind/spirit and body in the work of love and becoming).[36] In this ethical caress there is no

> ensnarement, possession or submission of the freedom of the other who fascinates me in his [or her] body. Instead, it becomes an offering of consciousness [one hears the Tantric echoes here], a gift of intention and of word addressed to the concrete presence of the other, to his [or her] natural and historical particularities.[37]

Our perception and caress, our ideal and carnal relations to the other should not only recognize the particularity of the other — as that recognition can mean conflict — but seek to preserve and enhance the becoming of the other and ourselves. In this alliance, something of friendship and even flourishing is possible, but as with Murdoch's attention, much illusion and trouble in our own subjectivity and in our philosophy must be addressed. The difficulty there is that that there is no thinking through before beginning to live it. The mess, our meeting each other as gendered and in *medias res*, means that we cannot solidify a plan before loving the other.

Perception is both an active and a passive process, both a careful regard of the other and open reception of their being and becoming in time. It is also a process of self-questioning, of checking one's desire/assumptions/illusions against the reality presented by the other. Perception, like attention, is not only seeing, but a cultivated activity, consciously developed for the sake of the other: it is an intention. In the symbolic of masculinist culture, it is the masculine that perceives and the feminine that is perceived (or assigned to abjection, contingency, fluid modes, the messiness of embodiment). It is a process of interpretation:

> We still ignore the possibility of giving up a centered gaze, a fixed sight, a renunciation which would leave space and air around and within the other.... A body that is in love does not endure being fixed as an object. Cutting it out of space and time destroys that carnal immersion required by a loving relationship.... Perception should not become a means of appropriating the other, of abstracting the body, but should be cultivated for itself, without being reduced to a passivity or an activity of the senses.[38]

In Irigaray's lexicon, that "centered gaze" is the point of view of subjects that Murdoch would describe as trapped in fantasy or narcissism or neurosis, subjects that find others-with-gaze a source of enmity rather than felicity. To leave 'space and air' around and in the other is to imagine them (her) to be fully alive, and cutting that other in a (her) body out of space and time, life and a relation to her own transcendence or becoming, in imagination or desire destroys contact with her particular reality, and so destroys the possibility of love, even of our own becoming.[39] Perception does not only work for the other, however: if done lovingly (it's both the condition and the act of love), perception allows the self becoming as well. The other is a negative to me, a limit and transcendent to me, my engagement with this other can enliven my own becoming. This is not always comfortable, certainly, but the discomfort tends to come when the other fails to respond to my reality, or when I resist the becoming demanded by their reality.

Flourishing
(It's more fun than dysfunction!)

Unlike most moral philosophers, Irigaray does not take the demand of the other's reality to be (only) a burden/threat to the vitality of the self. While the other is certainly a limit, a horizon, a negative, transcendent to myself, that otherness can be a catalyst to flourishing for both of us. Irigaray realizes that flourishing is not a zero sum game. My becoming needn't be at your expense. The masculine need not become as the expense of the feminine. It *can* be a zero sum game, as in the case of a masculine that debases the feminine in order to legitimate itself, or in the case of the variously dysfunctional liberal subjects Murdoch criticizes, but not necessarily because "looking at the other as a precise objective [a fact] and looking at the other with respect to his [and her] intention and ... interiority are quite different things."[40] The first is often combative or appropriative, the second is a fecundating being-two and opens an as yet unrealized horizon for flourishing.

Being-two is a mutual project, for persons and genders, that is focused on the becoming of each and takes place between them (not above or below, not blending them into one, not later) and includes each one's relations to time, to space, to spirit. Being-two assumes that other is nearly inscrutable, will always have a reserve/remainder/surplus of being that the self has no access to — and finds this to be a very good thing indeed. The fact that our interiority is invisible to each other allows us to relate at all. Were it all externalized, or all deferred to the future or heaven, or melded into one, there would be no relation, no fecundity, no life: there would be stasis. For Irigaray, as our sexed bodies fecundate new physical life in the real, so our sexuate or gendered selves can fecundate our being in the imaginary and symbolic, in spirit even.

In "I Announce to You that We Are Different," Irigaray compares the Western and Eastern views of the physical natures of men and women. Aristotle, for instance, finds that woman is cold (not quite completely cooked: potential) while men are hot (completely cooked: actual). Some Eastern traditions, like Tantra, teach that "woman is hot inside and cold outside, while man is cold inside and hot outside," and that they can each bring the other into balance.[41] The whole system of Tantric thought and practice is concerned with these reciprocal differences and their harmonization, and that harmony allows each to flourish in their own way and together.[42] The ability to do this requires something like Murdoch's Weilian unselfing: "To remain between two requires the renunciation of this sort of unity: fusional [subsumption into one], regressive [as into childish dependency], autistic [a fall into unconsciousness and inarticulation], narcissistic [the other serving as a prop for the self]."[43] This fusion, or regression, or autism, or narcissism are strategies to avoid unselfing and the very real contact with others that process opens up. Call it unselfing, call it growing up, Irigaray calls it being-two, a kind of abiding with the other.

Its practice and purpose is always horizontal and vertical in Irigaray's descriptions: addressing body and spirit, real and symbolic. It must begin here and now, and it must just begin — there is no preparation, no future in which we will have become able to do this without doing it. To be two, she describes:

> means to help each other to be, to discover and to cultivate happiness, to take care of the difference between us, not merely because of its role in [sexual] generation, ... but in order to achieve happiness and make it blossom.[44]

Irigaray does not mean the happiness of a new purchase; she means the replete well-being of the bodies and spirits of the lovers, the friends. She is interested in what she calls "a felicity in history," in the subtitle to her book on Hegel. Why the emphasis on the here and now, on the physical? Women have been assigned the bearers of these halves of dichotomies. In the logic of the Same Man is mind, woman is body, Man is reason, woman is emotion, Man is good, woman is sin, Man is actual, woman is potential, Man creates the symbolic, woman achieves only the imaginary, etc. (When Irigaray uses the post-structural term the Same, she is both irate and smirking.) So, her interest is in setting man and woman and the masculine and feminine up as cooperative transcendences in what she calls the sensible transcendental: A physical and ideal/spiritual relation, in time, on earth, in the midst of history. To achieve this, we "take care of our differences," that is we engage in care of the self and the other such that we have reserves from which to approach each other with the degree of confidence and generosity (and it is a large degree) needed to engage in ethical love in the contingent world.

Righting a Lack of Balance

The liberal personalities Murdoch criticizes know very little of these kinds of attention, perception, or being. The traits she fears they demonstrate or imply are traits Irigaray would identify as part of a dysfunctional and culturally dominant masculine personality. Each of the three avatars of Man — Rational, Romantic, Totalitarian — fails Irigaray's demands by remaining, ultimately, diabolic: "The diabolic ... delights in enclosure.... Miming the living, the diabolic does not breathe [relate to the other], or does not breathe any longer. It takes away air from the other, from the world. It suffocates with its sterile repetitions...."[45] One way or another, the Same boomerangs in on itself or skips over the (feminine) other on its way to an always frustrated relation to a transcendent Other: Duty, God, Absolute, Freedom, The Law of the Father. Each of the three avatars fails due to this diabolical enclosure, this narcissism or neurosis differently.

Murdoch's Kant understands us to respect each other as "co-equal bearers of universal reason" but not as "particular eccentric phenomenal individuals" and thus leaves all the messy "feminine" out of his equations, the "entire world of our emotions and desires is irrelevant to morality."[46] Kant's subject relates to others who are very much like it: creatures of reason, masculine. Rational Man's enclosure is in the cleanliness of a system that does not admit of all that so troubles and that could enhance morality. Rational Man can relate to others in so far as all are participating in *Achtung* and duty.

Murdoch's Hegel imagines a subject sunk in a conditioned social world seeking to close the circle of self-knowledge, and become absolute. Permanent and co-equal otherness is unimaginable/intolerable. Romantic Man is neurotic, every interaction whiplashing back to inform him about himself in a struggle for becoming.

Murdoch's Sartre imagines the least open of the three avatars. Totalitarian Man surrenders to "convention and neurosis, the two enemies of understanding, ... of love" and is entirely alone.[47] Or, would prefer to be, given Sartre's sentiments on the subject of hell. Others are "organized menacing extensions of the consciousness of the subject" so that he remains diabolically enclosed, and paranoid to boot. Totalitarian Man finds "others" a limit on his becoming, but not transcendent to him, except as a threat.

The difficulty we inherit from these philosophical subjects is that human beings exceed our rational ability to compass them, to fit them cleanly into a total system for us. Others, frustrating to the three avatars, have their own becoming and that becoming defies form. In "The Sublime and the Good" Murdoch turns to great and tragic art to explain the call we make to others and they to us:

> What makes tragic art so disturbing is that self-contained form is combined with something, the individual being and destiny of human persons, which defies form. A great tragedy ... leaves us in eternal doubt. It is the form of art where the exercise of love is most like its exercise in morals.[48]

In great art we lose our certainty because we learn that the other is as busy meaning as we are interpreting them. They have a relation to the real (in their sex), to history and their own history, to an undeterminable future, and to the vertically transcendent in ways that we cannot know, or contain, or control. It is that other people have their own becoming, and that it can go awry, that we are transcendent to them and they to us. Love is attention to this complexity; and unselfing is a matter of living in it.

What is lacking in Murdoch and Irigaray's views is balance provided by the particular, the unruly, the contingent, the feminine as a source of something other than unease. In her acceptance of the genders/sexes as both socially and ontologically different, as the ultimate horizontally transcendent others to each other, Irigaray finds room to think that unselfing can be more than painful, but a fecund and complex adventure. Irigaray proposes that we set about creating balance. The result is health, more life. Maybe not happiness like the uneasy consolation of the narcissist/neurotic boomerang attention; and maybe not the constant state of womb-like fulfillment we dream happiness to be: but more life, something more vital and vibrant.

However, we cannot set everything about sexual difference right and then go about living in it. Going about living being-two will work its way to setting things right. Unselfing is like this: we don't get to step away from relations to other people in order to get over ourselves; we get over ourselves in relations to other people. Nothing short of a refounding of society is the limit of Irigaray's imagination: a society in which woman/the feminine is a full partner in culture and history, not only in private, and not only as a mangled version of man.

Being-two is that refounding: meeting with the other, "the man or the woman that I must horizontally recognize as equivalent to me in the radical respect his or difference(s)." We are inassimilable — we cannot be exchanged for each other.[49] Being-two might be being happy, but more than that it means becoming, consciously and culturally more completely human, opening up a future unavailable by any other means:

To affirm that man and woman are really two different subjects does not amount for all that to sending them back to a biological destiny, to a simple natural belonging. Man and woman are *culturally* different. And it is good that this is so.... The subjectivity of man and that of woman are structured starting from a relational identity specific to each one, a relational identity that is held between nature and culture, and that assures a bridge starting from which it is possible to pass from one to the other while respecting them both.[50]

Rather than an agon of fantasized totalities, Murdoch and Irigaray would have us retrain ourselves, our ego and subjectivity, our desire into a resonance of partials. Of course, where that leads will ultimately be a surprise. That is after all what contingency means: even the best gesture is risk. The nature of the risk reshapes itself: rather than securing (however fraudulently) my own being at your expense, we each enter an active and passive relation between us that is our uncertain becoming. The mess, that is.

Sublime
(The transcendent is/in the immanent.)

What I like best in Murdoch and Irigaray is that they both retain a sense of a beyond, both transcendent and futural, whose claim on us is no greater than and never replaces their sense of the here and now, the earthly, and its claim on us—our relations to them. What has often amazed me is how few philosophers think of the human other, man and woman, as sublime. I think that is what both Murdoch and Irigaray ultimately do. Like Kant, I have been paradoxically humbled and ennobled before mountains, the aurora borealis, the work so many do to secure life and health for others, the Grand Canyon, the smoking rubble of the Twin Towers, the on-going avid hunger for power through death. Humans have a capacity for ambiguity and paradox far surpassing even that of nature whose work is the creation and destruction of life. Like the sublime, humans are both a call to greater becoming, and a threat to that potential. But, then, so am I to my others. This is part of the meaning of our embodiment, of our subtle and dynamic complexity that plays out on small and large scales.

Murdoch's Everyday Sublime

On the sublime, Murdoch summarizes Kant in "The Sublime and the Good," beginning with Kant's scheme that imagination serves reason, that faculty that "seeks systematic wholeness and abhors incompleteness or juxtaposition." In the presence of massive natural phenomena usually located above a human's relation to the horizon, "imagination strives to its utmost to satisfy" reason's requirement for this wholeness, and fails. At this failure of imagination to provide reason with assurances (that I can know, compass Mont Blanc, the universe of stars) we feel distress and "exhilaration in our consciousness of the absolute nature" of reason's prerequisite that draws us beyond what "mere sensible imagination can achieve." This shock that we do not have the whole picture is "very like *Achtung*, the experience of respect for the moral law," in which we feel "pain at the thwarting of our sensuous nature ... elation in ... our rational nature: that is, our freedom to conform to the absolute requirement of reason" and its desire for tidiness and a possibly dangerous kind of convention.[51] Imagination makes better contact with the mess, in its risks and joys, both quotidian and of dramatically high stakes.

Imagination is not good at satisfying reason partly because, as we learn in the arts, it adores paradox, juxtaposition, ambiguity. Kant misses the last step and Murdoch gently corrects him: yes, the sublime destabilizes us, but we particular messy persons also confound and defeat reason and imagination for each other. Instead of hopping over the concrete toward the absolute, Murdoch brings Kant's sublime down to earth between us:

> Kant was marvelously near the mark. But, he thought of freedom as the aspiration to universal order[52] consisting of a prefabricated harmony. It is not a tragic freedom. The tragic freedom implied by love is this: we all have an indefinitely extended capacity to imagine the being of others. Tragic because there is no prefabricated harmony, and others are, to an extent we never cease discovering, different from ourselves.... Freedom is exercised in the confrontation by each other, in the context of an infinitely extensible work of imaginative understanding, of two irreducibly dissimilar individuals. Love is the imaginative recognition of ... this otherness.[53]

In this move, Murdoch relocates the sublime right down here with us, *as* us. She and Irigaray both locate, as the Eastern traditions sometimes do, the transcendent in the immanent. Revisiting the sublime and the good, Murdoch gives us Murdochian Man, who feels the sublime on this horizontal scale, who can unself and be-two:

> ... the man that I have in mind, faced by the manifold of humanity, may feel, as well as terror, delight, but not, if he really sees what is before him, superiority. He will suffer that undramatic, because unself-centered, agnosticism which goes with tolerance. To understand other people is a task which does not come to an end. This man will possess "spirit" in the sense intended by Pascal when he said, "The more spirit one has the more original men one discovers. Ordinary people do not notice differences between men." And a better name of spirit here is not reason, or even tolerance, but love.[54]

While ordinary people do not register differences, neurotics do but only to covet them or to seek to negate them. People with spirit, in this general still-humanist line of thinking, do discover other "original men," others' differences of mind, talent, soul, and can celebrate them. Implicit in this statement is an inkling that unselfing, while humbling/painful, is also delightful/enlivening and might move the ego, the Subject, the various truncated avatars of man into having enough spirit and sense of their own actual becoming to enliven and even celebrate that of others.

IRIGARAY'S EVERYDAY SUBLIME

Enlivening and sharing are key to Irigaray's sense of the sublime that we are. In Irigaray's ethics our sensuous nature, our embodiment, is not a problem to be thwarted, but an ally that can be called to our assistance in being-two. A mind or body neglected, left to feel impoverished, cannot have enough of Pascal's spirit to grant the reality, neat or messy, of other people. Staying with that metaphor of spirit, take Irigaray's thinking about breath and air, for instance.[55]

Breath and air, like many of her concepts, is to be taken both ideally/symbolically and ontologically/phenomenally. Irigaray will slide from one register to the other, or harmonize them as suits her meaning at the moment. So, breath and air are resonant with her concept of the sensible transcendental, an alliance between the body and spirit, even the divine, in a "spiritualization of the body and of the senses" that is part and parcel of her understanding of perception and being-two.[56] Breath is the exchange of air between the self and her/his world and context, and with the other in relation. It is the most elementally shared of our media, and the most unconscious. She uses it to describe relations between subjects in difference because it "maintains life and health" and can be trained spiritually as in the yogic and tantric methods. More, in its sustenance of all persons, air is a figure for the interval that protects the subjectivity of each and allows their relation, as well as what she calls a "passage to humanity as such"—something akin to unselfing, though delineated as being-two, masculine and feminine.[57]

In *Between East and West,* Irigaray attempts to work out a relation between Western and Eastern spiritual practices that might bring a (in her estimation) nearly dead West back to life.[58] Central to this work is her thinking about breath and air as both material and spiritual modes and media for being-two. To Irigaray's way of thinking sexual difference and the sensible transcendental, desire is both carnal and spiritual, "an awakening" of perception, attention, consciousness, rather than their occlusion.[59] Her work in philosophy, psychoanalysis, linguistics, aesthetics and politics brings her to statements as strong as this in "The Way of Breath":

> Sexual difference is, in fact, the difference that can open a transcendental horizon between humans, in particular between man and woman.... [In it] the split between human and divine identities can be overcome, thanks to the cultivation of energy [breath, awareness] ... including carnal love [that] corresponds to ... a soul. A soul not localized and enclosed, as the masculine soul is,

but one that opens on a "culture of life and of love."⁶⁰ In this respect for the gendered other, we have a new task, a new imperative. Transcending to reason, to the absolute, to an unencumbered freedom is less our work than transcending to a Good left open and sustaining:

> Articulation between nature or life and transcendence becomes a new task incumbent upon us. A transcendence which now remains alive, sensible and even carnal. [It] cannot be reduced to a mental idea or a belief, but is incarnate, also in the other. Transcendence in this way always remains a mystery for us.⁶¹

That is, sexual difference is an enlivening and cooperative difference between the sexes. In the living of it, we become sublime to each other. But, before we celebrate our arrival at the sublime too enthusiastically, we remember that difference is not without friction, doubt, effort, ambiguity, juxtaposition, all the consternation of the sublime. It is a complicated relation. No more I-subject to you-object: but "a double desire" between I-subject and You-subject, "establishing a chiasmus or a double loop in which each can go toward the other and come back to itself ... a double pole of attraction and support."⁶² What has changed in Murdoch's horizontal sublime and Irigaray's intensification of it (as I have structured matters here) is that we do not skip over each other to some Absolutely Other Holder of the Sublime, but attend here with and to each other in the messy, convoluted, delightful, threatening, sustaining everyday world.

A Messy Flourishing Sublime

A complex resonance plays between Iris Murdoch and Luce Irigaray as much as it plays between each of us. Beginning to read them side-by-side as I have here, it becomes clear the attraction their ardent readers have for each of these women: they write a philosophy that re-opens the future for us. One senses in their work that we and the world we create are still possible, that nothing about our being is enclosed in old descriptions. The last century slid away from the devolution of Western Civilization into Nazi ambitions and the Holocaust — the utter failure of our best faith and philosophy it realized — and out of it we wandered still bewildered into this new millennium with its plethora of threats natural, social, geopolitical, and all fairly immediate in their call for our best imagination.⁶³ Murdoch and Irigaray seem to assure us that we have the capacity for renewal, for the opening of a new human horizon, and that we might just pull ourselves out of the frying pan and into flourishing.

I have here addressed relations between their work only on the most general level. I have only performed a kind of handshake between them. Other points of cooperative difference wait to be explored. How might we read Murdoch's loving couples in Irigarian terms? Might we be surprised to find models for learning to be-two in some of Murdoch's stories? Or, similarly, how might we apply Irigaray's analyses of crippled subjective expressions of the masculine and feminine in Murdoch's more demonic men and women? Murdoch and Irigaray are both discussed in religious studies (though Irigaray has much more to say about the divine — a divine in difference *per se*— than Murdoch); perhaps a comparison of their thinking of the transcendent or divine would be profitable. It would be incredible fun to read Irigaray's *The Marine Lover of Friedrich Nietzsche* alongside Murdoch's *The Sea, the* Sea, or Irigaray's *The Forgetting of Air in Martin Heidegger* with Murdoch's Heidegger manuscript. Both women take some degree of inspiration from the East, so perhaps careful tracings of their faith with and diversions from those traditions might be useful to understanding their thought and our own paths for becoming.

Perhaps most compelling is their interest in art. Murdoch and Irigaray take the great artist or strong poet to be partial models for the subjectivity they ask us to develop. These subjects know how to marvel, how to wonder at reality and others. The serious artist, Murdoch notes, "looks at the world and sees more of the world ... the marvels which selfish anxiety conceals from the rest of us."[64] That anxiety, and being "enclosed in a fantasy world," disallow imagination, whereas love is "an exercise of the imagination."[65] Art requires consciousness, deliberation, the examination of one's desire and of the reality confronting us. Irigaray's being-two is a kind of living artfully, but in a necessarily open-ended manner. In the introduction of *An Ethics of Sexual Difference*, she calls for a new poetics, and we see in reading that text that she means a poetics of the self, "a new era of thought, art, poetry, and language: the creation of a new *poetics*."[66] This artful being and art itself can recognize reality and "transfigure" it, even "create another reality which could allow us to live in a more beautiful and happy way," might be a path for passing from "animality to humanity."[67] Such an artful living would require wonder, marveling, experimentation, discipline, and the guts to begin in the mess without prerequisites.[68] These ideas of living-as-artists are not about the controlled presentation of a shapely life to some passive and admiring audience, but a real artful engagement with reality in a process of creating ourselves and supporting other's creations of themselves. It happens as we go along, starting when and where we start, and would reconfigure reality because each gesture of love and unselfing changes the contingent world in which we are becoming.

Just between these two women there is already a rather messy space of possible flourishing. They clearly wish no less for us. Even if we try, personally and culturally, to live imaginatively into seeing reality and being-two, we will go wrong from time to time. Our own stubborn old habits of being will trip us up, send us spectacularly awry. It is part of our sublimity that we are so complex, so uncertain. The opening of a new horizon for humanity, whether a humble recognition that love is devotion to the reality of others, or that love is devotion to the reality of difference on every level, is only a chance to reshape ourselves, incrementally, generationally, beginning here in the mess. Neither Murdoch, nor Irigaray, nor I ignore that risk. We know at least this: now that a desire for the Good and love, and for living in difference has been articulated, we have fewer excuses. And I submit that we must try. Murdoch reminds us of the stubbornness required for these attempts:

> We should always be aware of doctrines of necessity which show us (with professions of regret) the eminently desirable, the good, as being, alas, the impossible.[69]

We must try in honor of our own embodied sublimity and that of other people right here in everyday life. If we don't, there is a better than off chance that no one who lives through it will have the luxury of time to write the epic poem of our failure.

Notes

1. Murdoch, 1997, Penguin, 199.
2. *Ibid.*, 215.
3. *Ibid.*, 199.
4. *Ibid.*, 201.
5. That conversation would enrapture most readers of this book. Both of these women possess a nearly encyclopedic knowledge of and engagement with modern philosophy from Kant right through the twentieth century. They would be beautiful to watch, both engaged as they are with the Continental tradition and Murdoch having more insight into analytical philosophy, while Irigaray is (in writing at least) more engaged with the Romantic philosophers, their various choices of focus in the twentieth century would only enhance the tapestry. Both have a great deal to say about art and literature, and many of their readers have employed their ideas in those fields. The possible connections are very many indeed. Here, however, I shall perform only an introduction with handshake.
6. If you are beginning to feel that I am working out a rapprochement between these two women of the sort that Stanley Cavell creates between deconstruction, analytical, and other philosophical tacks, you are right on target. Congratulations! If not, I strongly recommend reading Cavell. He is delightful.
7. Murdoch, 1997, Penguin, 294.
8. *Ibid.*, 293.
9. *Ibid.*, 285.
10. *Ibid.*, 262.
11. *Ibid.*, 273–74.
12. Murdoch and Irigaray both take the philosophy written to represent the spirit of an age, of the ages, as not just descriptions of what we are involved in but of what we are.
13. I will come back to Kant and sublime in the third section of the essay.
14. *Ibid.*, 264.
15. *Ibid.*, 269.
16. *Ibid.*, 268–68.
17. *Ibid.*, 269.
18. *Ibid.*, 274.
19. *Ibid.*, 135.
20. I realize that to pick up and elide Murdoch's characterizations of the philosophers this way gives the sense that she does not admire them. This is not the case. But it is the case, as these condensations of mine show, that taken together she is sure that their descriptions of the moral world and the moral agent are at least insufficient, and at most quite damaging.

21. *Ibid.*, 354.
22. *Ibid.*, 385, 358.
23. *Ibid.*, 330, 293.
24. *Ibid.*, 329.
25. Not having a theory is, of course, impossible. It's like not having an ego or a self. What is required here, as we will see more clearly in the following discussion of Irigaray, is that one must be aware of and flexible in the application and adaptation of this theory/ego in the encounter with the art or other or world with the intent of perceiving that reality on its own terms rather than simply according to its proof of our rightness or to its use for us. That sentence wades into a massive debate over matters philosophical, methodological, psychological — and yet, I shall have to let that statement stand.
26. Not just any work, but great works, and these render a sense of tragedy, of the small particularity of individual humans — that the world is bigger than we are, arranged without our permission, over-against us — and also a pathos that simultaneously makes audiences see that particularity and feel less terribly isolated in their own.
27. Irigaray, 1984, 21.
28. Nearly every statement in this paragraph has a long history of elaboration in Irigaray's own work and is both explicated and contested by her readers and critics. Especially useful in entering this area of thought are the following texts (full reference details in the bibliography): Whitford's *Engaging with Irigaray*, Cimitile and Miller's *Returning to Irigaray*, Braidotti's *Nomadic Subjects*, Grosz's *Volatile Bodies*, Irigaray's interviews in *Je, Tu, Nous*, and *Why Different?*, and Deutscher's *A Politics of Impossible Difference*.
29. For more thorough explication see my essays "Irigaray's Eastern Turn: Tantra and *An Ethics of Sexual Difference*" and "Burn the Panopticon: Irigaray's Ethics, Difference, Poetics." See for other views Joy's *Divine Love* and Hollywood's *Sensible Ecstasy*.
30. Irigaray, 2001, 17.
31. *Ibid.*, 18.
32. *Ibid.* Or cultures, or sexualities, but Irigaray does not address these points of difference. Hers is a project devoted to sexual difference, rather exclusively.
33. *Ibid.*, 22.
34. *Ibid.*
35. *Ibid.*, 23.
36. Irigaray is responding to and deconstructing Merleau-Ponty's writing of the caress. See also "The Invisible of the Flesh: A Reading of Merleau-Ponty, *The Visible and the Invisible*, 'TheIntertwining — the Chiasm'" in Irigaray's *An Ethics of Sexual Difference*.
37. *Ibid.*, 26. These passages references to the other as masculine might seem a bit confusing, but these are some in which Irigaray is writing back at male philosophers as a woman-subject particularly. Irigaray's rhetoric is integral to her arguments.
38. *Ibid.*, 42–43.
39. To be sure, women and the feminine can view men and the masculine in this stultifying way, fixing them in time, defining them conveniently. This is, Irigaray would argue, a masculine and either neurotic or narcissist operation no matter the sex of the person doing it.
40. *Ibid.*, 42.
41. *Ibid.*, 55.
42. This is one radical summary. My essay "Burn the Panopticon" cited above clarifies these claims.
43. *Ibid.*, 57.
44. *Ibid.*
45. Irigaray, 2004, 166.
46. Murdoch, 1997, Penguin, 262.
47. *Ibid.*, 268.
48. *Ibid.*, 219.
49. Irigaray, 2004, 25.
50. *Ibid.*, 26–27. It has been the work of Irigaray's entire career to discuss the sources of and views concerning these differences. Perhaps especially useful in the context of this quotation would be to see her *To Speak Is Never Neutral*, a collection of her analysis of linguistic habits of men and women the world over which shows that our habits of relation are quite different.

51. Murdoch, 1997, Penguin, 208, inclusive.

52. Significantly, this universal does not include the feminine, or women. Both are beautiful, sensuous, sentimental. In *Observations on the Feeling Beautiful and Sublime*, Kant pauses to consider sexual difference:

> Laborious learning or painful pondering, even if a woman should greatly succeed in it, destroy the merits that are proper to her sex, and because of their rarity they can make of her an object of cold admiration; but at the same time they will weaken the charms with which she exercises her great power over the other sex. A woman who has a head full of Greek, like Mme Darcier, or carries on fundamental controversies about mechanics, like the Marquise de Châtelet, might as well even have a beard [78].

It's a real Don Imus moment of clunking bias, showing that the limits of Kant's reason are overdetermined by the conventional axioms of patriarchy. The women who fit in this system's fantasy are politely delicate and well trained beauties, domesticated manageable others. That is, the realities of these women simply don't work *for* Kant's system.

53. Murdoch, 1997, Penguin, 216–17.
54. *Ibid.*, 283.
55. Readers familiar with Irigaray's later thought and its relations to Tantra and yoga will know that I am avoiding the discussions concerning the body's relation to spirit, the care with which she elaborates the relational, psychological, and cultural differences in the men's and women's modes of self-care. I address these in the essays cited above in note 29.
56. Irigaray, 2002, ix.
57. *Ibid.*, x.
58. Irigaray's appropriation of these traditions is a topic of some debate among her interlocutors, some reading it as a repetition of a gesture often made by teachers from Eastern traditions, others as a more or less imperial poaching of the cultural other for the sake of the West. For the latter, see Penelope Deutscher's "*Between East and West* and the Politics of 'Cultural Ingénuité': Irigaray on Cultural Difference," in Cimitile and Miller's *Returning to Irigaray: Feminist Philosophy, Politics, and the Question of Identity* (137–50).
59. Irigaray, 2002, 82.
60. *Ibid.*, 90–91.
61. Irigaray, 2004, 148.
62. Irigaray, 1984, 9.
63. Both these women lived in the shadow of the Nazis' desires, a kind of technologically perfected exercise in the dominance of one self over all others. Irigaray was a young girl in occupied France, Murdoch a young woman living through the Blitz. The worst of the masculine, the most perverse sense of reason and perfect realization in history is for Irigaray, and was for Murdoch, a very real thing. The nightmare visited on whole peoples and societies finds fresh treatment in Richard J. Evans' *The Third Reich at War* (Penguin 2009). Just the horrors noted in William H. Gass's review in *Harper's Magazine* is enough to remind us how vitally important is the real reshaping of our ego and desire. See "Kinds of killing: The flourishing evil of the Third Reich," in *Harper's Magazine*, August 2009: 75–82. One wonders how Evans's psyche survived the research and writing of this book, and offers thanks that he did.
64. Murdoch, 1997, Penguin, 28–29.
65. *Ibid.*, 216.
66. Irigaray, 1984, 5, emphasis in original.
67. Irigaray, 2004, 98.
68. Several critics have applied Irigaray's ideas on art, especially in a feminist context. One excellent example is *Reading Art, Reading Irigaray: The Politics of Art by Women*, by Hillary Robinson.
69. Murdoch, 1997, Penguin, 272.

7

Domination, Resistance, and Anglo-Irish Landlordism in *The Servants and the Snow*

WEI H. KAO

Iris Murdoch's position in the Irish literary canon has always been ambivalent, as the writer, unlike her mostly male Irish peers, did not write a substantial number of Irish-flavored works, nor remark frequently on Irish cultural and political matters. Her novel, *The Red and the Green*, set on the eve of the 1916 Easter Rising and concerning an extended Anglo-Irish family during the political emergency, is identified as her only serious Irish work.[1] As might be expected, her close connections with the literary and academic circles of England did little to define her as an Irish writer, particularly given her politically incorrect Anglo-Irish origin. However, some critics, such as Donna Gerstenberger, argue for her implicit Irishness in her "consciousness of national materials," and portraits of lower-class Irish people in their troubled homeland, despite not all of them receiving full characterizations in her works.[2] Although she is not widely perceived as an Irish author, Murdoch was anxious to defend her non–Englishness to Peter Conradi, her biographer — "You could cut with a knife [my Irish accent]. I may have misleading Oxford overtones — but the vowels are Irish" — and often introduced herself as an Irish person in conversations with friends and colleagues.[3] If the nationality of a writer lies in one's birthplace, it is peculiar about Murdoch, born in Dublin, that she is left out of the Irish canon; whereas her near contemporary, Mary Lavin, born in New England, is a canonic figure in many Irish anthologies. What differentiates them, presumably, is that the latter dealt with universal experiences *predominantly* through an Irish lens, where the former often explored them not for their particular Irishness but relatively through a philosophical approach to Irish life.

To define Murdoch's position within Irish literary context, this article examines her nearly forgotten play *The Servants and the Snow*, and situates it in a colonial framework to critique British dominance over Ireland — through an impending riot of servants in an Anglo-Irish residence. In this residence, the struggle for power — testifying to a Master-slave dynamics, between the Protestant, landowning minority and the Roman Catholic, Irish, rural majority — is practiced almost permanently. Symbolically, a series of incidents taking place in this residence suggests how the playwright observes colonial oppression of the colonized, the cultural sadomasochistic mentality that undermines anti-colonial movements, and, more significantly, the "emotional ambivalence" that maintains authoritarianism from one landed generation to another. This play profoundly dramatizes the playwright's concerns about class struggle and her Hegelian assessment of not only the Master-slave relationship in a colonial context but also the existence of God in a Catholic land, when prayers become ineffectual as exploitation marches on.[4]

The premiere of *The Servants and the Snow* took place at the Greenwich Theatre, London, on 29 September 1970, but it did not receive much critical attention, and was not selected for staging at more up-market theaters. Not until September 1980 was *The Servants* adapted into an opera libretto by the composer William Mathias and performed by the Welsh National Opera for a short run. The ten-year gap suggests that the play had some significance and was not entirely forgotten after its premiere, though it has been absent from the portfolios of both Irish and Murdoch studies.[5] The general disregard for her theatrical achievements, along with her ambivalent (Anglo-)Irish identity, makes *The Servants and the Snow* a nearly ignored piece. One can argue that the neglect of this play stemmed from an Irish *mise en scene* too implicit to attract critical attention from Irish critics. Indeed, the play was not first performed in Ireland and the playwright failed to specify an Irish locality, only "[a]n old isolated country house in winter."[6] However, the argument for the unspecified locality might not be tenable, as the Irish qualities of the play are discernible — with Irish characters, traditional practices, and settings peculiar to the Anglo-Irish Ascendancy and the Irish tenants. That Murdoch did not clearly indicate its Irish context might have been due to her concern to find a larger audience in England, and to present an Irish tragedy within a more universal framework.[7] She might also have been responding to the limited opportunities for women playwrights in Ireland before the 1970s, so she had to resort to fringe theaters in England, and could not regard Irish people as her only target audience.

This article intends to break fresh ground for this play by introducing a Hegelian and psychoanalytic reading. Before doing so, it might be useful to contextualize Murdoch in the Anglo-Irish tradition. She was born to Anglo-Irish parents in 1919, within a few years of the Easter Rising that led to the caesarian birth of modern Ireland.[8] Like many Anglo-Irish people before and after her generation, she went to England (Bristol and Oxford) for her education, but returned periodically to Ireland for her summer holidays. Being a member of the upper middle class, Murdoch was particularly sensitive to the ways the gentry managed their landownership, and was attentive to those who relied on the fringe benefits life in the "big house."[9] Her experiences and perspectives would therefore be different from those of James Joyce, for instance, who came from the lower or middle Catholic stratum, but would be absorbed into the "big house" literary tradition to which Maria Edgeworth, Somerville and Ross, Elizabeth Bowen, and Molly Keane contributed as women novelists. *The Servants and the Snow* should be worth a fairly high position in the tradition of Irish big house writing, as the playwright, considered alongside her novelist predecessors and contemporaries, is no less concerned than they were about the bitter history of the Anglo-Irish dominance over Ireland, particularly when viewed through female perspectives.[10] In an attempt to challenge the aristocratic system, Murdoch dramatizes the Anglo-Irish experience from the perspectives of both privileged and unprivileged women in regard to their often profitable marriages in a patriarchal society.

Although Murdoch left Ireland at an early age, *The Servants and the Snow* reflects her close observations of the economic and cultural practices of her privileged class, and considers the historical heritage of her cultural origin especially as that society was becoming industrialized and traditional landownership was at stake. In particular, the landowner Basil and his servants are learning to cope with an Ireland transforming from a colonial to a more liberated state at a time when the Industrial Revolution was distantly but significantly influential in all parts of Europe. This social transformation was accompanied by belated individual awakenings which, in the play, cause anxieties both for the landlord and the servants. The difficulty of adapting to these social changes, however, inspired Murdoch to examine how existentialism, on which she elaborated in many of her publications, applies to an Irish drama. This article, then, enters into her philosophical inquiry of the Master-slave relationship in an Anglo-Irish residence and the significance of God to colonial subjects.

It might be necessary to first clarify the rather implicit Irish characteristics of *The Servants and the Snow*. Specifically, Patrice, a "gypsy," is a minor but essential Irish character. With his "Irish accent" as Murdoch specifies, Patrice is ethnically different from those Romani people traditionally nomadic in Central and Western Europe, and the Middle East. Patrice belongs to very small Irish minority that often appears in Irish literature and folklore as tinkers or Pavees.[11] By featuring Patrice and the lifestyle of these wanderers in the play, Murdoch repositions this silenced ethnic group from the social margin to a more critical position, to represent their voices and redress social prejudice against them. Hans Joseph, a servant, exemplifies this prejudice by a derogatory description of "gypsies" to his master, Basil, explaining that they "spend the summer on the plains, in the nomad camps, and then when it gets cold they attach themselves to big houses and creep inside like rats and live there by stealing."[12] On the lowest rung of the community, Travelers were seen as little more than shooting targets for landlords for their being "parasite[s] and thie[ves]."[13] The inhuman exploitation of Irish tinkers—approved by Anglo-Irish landlords and assisted by their servants—can be examined from an existentialistic standpoint about the power hierarchy in a community long dominated by the Anglo-Irish Ascendancy. In Hegelian terms, the ruler's violence is necessary for the initiation and maintenance of individuation and self-authentication, as

> it is only through staking one's life that freedom is won; only thus is it proved that for self-consciousness its essential being is ... only pure being-for-self. The individual who has not risked his life may well be recognized as a person, but he has not attained the truth of this recognition as an independent self-consciousness.[14]

In other words, the landlord and the servants recognize and maintain their status at the cost of the lives of "gypsies"; the former two tend to negate the existence of the latter in order to reinforce the legitimacy of their given power, while the landlord owns the sovereign right to abuse both the servants and gypsies in this hierarchal system. For instance, the landlord hires Grundig as a rent collector who ensures the self-sufficiency of this feudal community. People like him are often given full powers by absentee landlords. Grundig may evict tenants who are behind with the rent, and makes a profit from the collected rent. Apart from this, the feudal lord, Basil, claims total jurisdiction within his lands—going beyond proprietorship even to the extent of the ancient *droit de seigneur*: the right to sexual relations with the brides of his tenants on the wedding-night. The claim of rights contributes significantly to the stability of the feudal system and justifies the hierarchical domination and its violence. In her discussion of Hegel's "Master and Slave" discourse, Murdoch indicates that, although those in the master's power are

> vital and yet unsatisfying and also dangerous to us.... [T]hey are dangerous in that they may stabilise us as something which we do not wish to be.... [W]e cannot be certain of their steadfastness, and in trying to hold them to their task we objectify them and destroy the freedom.[15]

The eviction of unpaid tenants as punishment, and the practice of *droit de seigneur* as a justifiable act, are thus measures that reconfirm the inherited social position of each member of the community. By presenting the power structure *within* the Anglo-Irish estate, Murdoch, on the one hand, documents and uncovers the way in which Anglo-Irish (absentee) landlords managed their properties through exploitation of the lower classes. On the other hand, she introduces an existential approach to the colonial issues to penetrate human complexities during wartime, particularly as the Northern Ireland Troubles that had broken out at the time of this play's production.

We can read *The Servants and the Snow* as a (anti-)colonial allegory not only because of the Irish setting but also the violence accumulated and passed on from one governing stratum to those below that keeps "the other" in place or on the social margin. The Master-slave violence operates on both the physical and social levels, reinforcing the stability of the colonial system (Anglo-Irish landlordism) as an extension of colonial power. Take, for example, the practice of *droit de seigneur*. This practice is an expected community code through which social oppression is redeemed by the master's patronage of newly-wed brides. The sexual violence to female subjects, though "dangerous," immediately confirms the master's supremacy: "Who can rule without it? And sometimes, by some people, magical power can be transformed into spiritual power."[16] This institutional sexual violence also informs the sense of morality of some lower-class women. They can claim a higher position, or end the slavery of their family, should they make their beds available for their masters. Since the community admires the sacrifice of these heroines, as Murdoch describes, there is tacit permission for the master's domination over the bodies of his women servants in a physical act of colonialism, defining authoritatively the roles of the colonizer and the colonized.

The Servants and the Snow was produced at a time when postcolonial critics were starting to make their observations on the power struggle between the colonizer and the colonized, and to analyze the traditional colonial view from which the colonized were regarded as perpetually inferior.[17] Murdoch seems to have noted that Hegel's conceptualization of "lordship and bondage" functioned as a source of the emerging postcolonial discourse; the difference being that Murdoch highlights the reciprocal relationship between the master and the servants as her dramatic response to relevant issues. Specifically, the *droit de seigneur* and other community codes are probably the result of reciprocation between colonizer and colonized in this Anglo-Irish residence, including more than merely physical abuse exerted by the master over his subjects. That is, when the servants in this power relationship strike to achieve recognition from the master, they confront an "existential impasse," for "the master is nothing without the slave; well, not much," and *vice versa*.[18] They become more attached to each other, in that the servant approaches the master not with "an independent consciousness, but a dependent one. [The master] is, therefore, not certain of being-for-self as truth of himself" but has to meet the demands and challenges coming from the slave.[19] Presumably, this play, among other of Murdoch's literary works, dramatize this Master-slave dialectic, and allows the audiences to examine in more detail the interpersonal relationships that complicate colonial politics.[20]

The Master-slave attachment, however, is a balance of terror, since the subjugated are not interminably submissive and riots are always on the horizon. In *The Servants and the Snow*, an imminent riot informs the background action and the tone of the play. It involves nearly two hundred servants in this Anglo-Irish estate, when Basil and his town-bred wife, Oriane, return to their ancestral residence, after Basil's tyrannical father dies. Having not been there since his youth due to a rupture with his father, Basil intends to democratize and liberalize the community, following on the political trend in the city. Servants, however, do not interpret his gesture as progressive, but see it as a sign of incompetent leadership compared to the severe domination enacted by Basil's father. Still, and ambivalently, the threat of riot seethes in some servants' resentment at torture by his father, as no one can "suffer as (the servants) have suffered and then declare a new day."[21] Part of their resentment results from the murder of their colleague, Francis James, killed by Basil's father because of his desire to take Marina, Francis's wife, as his mistress. The servants suffer a strong sense of guilt for having tolerated the murder, though they have little choice but to keep silent.

It can be argued that the murder of Francis James and the *droit de seigneur*, as discussed earlier, are two measures that create fear, even terror, with which the landlord subordinates servants unconditionally. The nature of domination exerted by the ruler comes, ostensibly, from the violation of normal social taboos; the killing of the insubordinate, and the demand for access to female sexuality, which reinforce the authority and authoritarianism of the landlord. In other words, coercion and fear are convenient but unstable forces for ruling/colonizing the underclass because of "emotional ambivalence," a term coined by Sigmund Freud to explain the mechanism of the Master-slave dialectic. As Freud suggests, the "emotional ambivalence" of the ruled arises from their mixed sentiments towards taboos "sacred" and "dangerous," or "consecrated" and "forbidden."[22] They are either unable to challenge the taboos or they violate them by imitation of the Master. The emerging riot in the play is an act by which the ruled intend to take revenge on the ruler for having tortured them, while they will not accept Basil's moves toward liberalization of the estate's social codes and structures. This anti-colonial sentiment corresponds to what Freud suggests, "Anyone who has violated a taboo becomes taboo himself because he possesses the dangerous quality of tempting others to follow his example."[23] Postcolonial research has shown that the formerly colonized often imitate the violence the colonizer imposed on dissenters, form a new privileged class, and "re-colonize" the new state no less hierarchically. The inherent "emotional ambivalence" transfers from one ruling class to another by changing the identity of the Master, but not upsetting the Master-slave relationship. In this drama, the servants' sense of guilt and resentment, their demands for "[an] eye for an eye, a tooth for a tooth," and their belief that "blood calls for blood," counteract their emotional attachment to the ruler, thereby potentially healing the traumas they experience.[24]

What makes the play more complex is the complicity of some of the servants in the oppression. One of the senior servants, Peter Jack, who becomes engaged to Marina after Francis's death, encourages Basil to perform the *droit de seigneur*, claiming that the servants would thus be appeased and the landlord's authority reasserted, even though the practice is never fully justified by the servants. Abhorred by and resistant to the proposal at first, Basil later finds he is attracted by Marina's charisma. An added complication is Marina's conviction that her sexual relationship with the master will be "an action of reconciliation and healing" and a "duty" she must perform for her community.[25] Anticipating Marina will secure a special status within the big house hierarchy, her fiancé, Peter Jack, is very supportive of her "sacrifice," or this internalized oppression, expecting he will also gain esteem from other servants who have no access to the echelons of the upper class. Peter Jack's "generosity" may imply his twisted value judgment in this Master-slave scenario. In other words, his position as head of the servants would be reconfirmed by allowing the abuse of his fiancée by his master. The *droit de seigneur* is not viewed as an act of sexual abuse, but as Basil's patronage over selected female servants in the community. Having loved Marina since childhood—"You know that I've always loved you, always, since childhood, right from the start"—Peter Jack may have suffered an internal struggle at the proposal of the *droit de seigneur,* but still succumbs to the beneficial prospects of this sacrifice.[26] His struggle, however, cannot be simplified as a personal affair, nor is it ever an obligation for him to surrender his fiancée to Basil as Murdoch presents their interaction. His struggle is thus an embodiment of the Master-slave interdependence, or two sides of the same coin, for Peter Jack is both a slave (of Basil) and a master (of the servants). According to Murdoch, the intricacies of Hegel's Master-slave dialectic are more than a "struggle between persons" but "really a struggle within the mind of a single character."[27] Peter Jack, to reinforce his pseudo-privileged position in this Anglo-Irish estate, chooses to set aside his conscience and buttresses the vicious circle of power and abuse.

A cross-hierarchical relationship also exists between Oriane and her personal valet, Frederic, from the city. Frederic's intention of maintaining a sexual relationship with his female employer is not for the sake of romance but to purify his low-bred origin: "I was born in a city slum among horrors which you would faint even to hear of."[28] Oriane takes sexual advantage of her servant to alleviate her boredom at living in the big house by challenging social taboos: "It amused me to hear you use my Christian name, because you are a valet. It is sometimes exciting to break a taboo."[29] The servants' violation of taboos through fornication with their superiors, on the one hand, alleviates their ambivalent sentiments towards their masters, and confirms their privileged positions within the servant class. On the other hand, by taking pleasure in complicity in this oppression, both the servants and the master reinforce their bondage with each other. Their reciprocal relationship cannot be changed despite the fact that the new landlord, Basil, has made such an attempt.

How *The Servants and the Snow* functions as a colonial allegory, and how it testifies to Murdoch's Hegelian and Marxist approaches to the dominance of the Anglo-Irish Ascendancy in Ireland, aligns with the playwright's philosophical alliance with the socialist movement and its "moral energy."[30] As Murdoch puts it, the energy ignites "the desire for human equality ... the desire to tidy up society, sweeping away metaphysical obscurantism and outdated tradition."[31] The play evolved with these desires to disclose the miseries borne by the exploited in this Anglo-Irish residence during the colonial period. More specifically, in this drama, although Basil has complete power over his properties, including his servants, the economic exploitation is effectually conducted almost singlehandedly by Grundig, the land agent. As an intermediary, he has accumulated a large fortune by trickery of both sides, and he uses this money to run a "little opera house" in town.[32] The agent and the landlord form an allied relationship according to which Grundig will do or say almost anything to pursue the ultimate interests of both parties. The "little opera house," therefore, functions not only as a personal place of leisure but also as a symbol of power and class oppression. Specifically, Basil has to rely on Grundig, a middleman, in order to afford at least two hundred servants, by getting the rents paid regularly and punctually. The fear of being evicted makes the tenants acquiesce to the abuses of power. More significantly, the exploitation fortifies the colonial superstructure in which social values, economic activities, interpersonal relations, and religious beliefs, are subject to landlords and middlemen—both closely and distantly. Although Murdoch was a Marxist only for a short period of time at a young age, her approach to the social and economic foundations of this Anglo-Irish residence reveals her sympathy for the exploited classes.[33] The sexually abused women servants and physically tortured male workers are matters of concern to her for their being on the bottom rung of economic production and exploitation.

Although Murdoch expresses her profound concerns for the underclass in this play, she does not oversimplify matters and imply that only the ruled experience oppression. Women in the ruling class are not exempt from patriarchal domination and sometimes become part of it. Take Oriane, the wife of the landowner, for instance. She is obviously an object who can be maneuvered by patriarchal forces but she can also unconsciously victimize women on the lower social strata. For example, realizing that Frederic's wife chooses not to follow her husband but to remain in the city, Oriane judges, probably resentfully, that, "a wife should go where her husband goes even if she doesn't think she'll enjoy it."[34] Unhappy about her own marriage, she is unsympathetic to Marina's idea of staying single and avoiding "do[ing] what [my] husband wants and not what [I] want."[35] She thus demands "the sooner you get married [to Peter Jack] the better!"[36] Oriane seems to put herself forward as a patriarchal instrument that seeks to dismiss any rebellious thoughts on the part of her womenfolk. Specifically, women like Marina can be passed on as objects from one master to another with at least six male superiors who have all desired to either condemn or sexually dominate her: Francis James, Basil's father, Basil himself, Peter Jack, Patrice, and her son Maxim. Having Marina surrounded by these men with disparate expectations, Oriane arrogantly joins in with the patriarchal and hierarchical violence more unconditionally than her husband, who wants to liberalize the underclass. Oriane represents ruling-class women who complement colonial domination by taking advantage of the women who are ruled and her own privileged position granted by a patriarchal society. Without recognizing that male superiors determine both hers and Marina's positions, she argues with her husband: "Nonsense, [the servants] love [being treated harshly...]. I think after all I shall fit into this scene better than you will!"[37]

Both Oriane and Marina suffer from patriarchal domination, although the latter, as a member of the servant class, is much less able to resist its violence.[38] The irony is that Marina, being adept enough, has to make good use of her charm to survive the constant social abuse of her body and earn respect, or some "spiritual power," from her class peers, should she make herself available to her masters.[39] Her "pleasure" from this Master-slave relationship may, dialectically, build to her private and public recognition by "undergo[ing] a reformation by virtue of ... servile work," and be largely "due to the fear of death and the love of life, mere life, that the slave succumbed to the master in the struggle for recognition."[40] Marina might have realized that what marriage means to her as a woman in servitude is that she still has no choice but to marry Peter Jack, while also consenting to be the mistress of Basil, instead of eloping with Patrice, the tinker, who promises to bring her freedom after leaving the big house. Her choice to marry might be because she judges, sensibly, that Patrice cannot exempt her from patriarchal subjugation. The power she can wield is therefore sexual, and secures for herself a relatively higher status among the ruled, although she knows that she is being treated as a commodity.

Murdoch's concern for the issue of gender equality can be understood more explicitly if readers take into account the context of *The Servants and the Snow* in the 1970s, during which second-wave feminists had been demanding the end of discrimination against women in both public and private arenas, and were seeking to promote equal rights through legislation.[41] Murdoch, being conscious of gender inequality and having featured relevant issues in her novels, might have intended to bring to public attention the social marginalization of women who suffered from the abuse of power, by dramatizing a claustrophobic Anglo-Irish big house. Having acquired the Hegelian and Marxist approaches to the capitalist exploitation of the proletariat, and having been a prolific philosopher and social critic herself, Murdoch likely viewed drama as another medium with which to pursue "Benthamite efficiency," which aims at "a general revolt against convention, the resistance to the nineteenth-century father-figure in his many guises, the revolt against sexual taboos and restrictions, the movement for the liberation of women."[42] *The Servants and the Snow*, evidently, illustrates a mixture of these agendas, providing the audience with more critical distance from the oppressions of one social stratum on another, and testifying to the tenability of these philosophies in a dramatic form. Interestingly, the play does not appear to be at the service of Marxism but exhibits the more perplexing nature of gender and colonial politics, telling the failure of both the forthcoming riot and Basil's liberal aspirations.

Given a Hegelian and Marxist reading of the tragedy, what frustrates the riot so profoundly can be further understood by applying a Freudian approach to this power struggle, or Master-slave dialectic. For instance, a hidden Oedipus complex may be the primitive sentiment that not only causes suffering to the protagonists but drives them to behave or be fearful in ways that support the existing colonial system. In regard to gender politics, women of both classes in this play can only with difficulty escape from patriarchal subjugation or obtain assistance from outside the estate. This is particularly difficult for female servants like Marina, since she "[has] never left this place; I've never been across the river."[43] What blocks Marina's freedom to reach the outside world, however, is not her lack of courage but the Oedipus complex to which her male colleagues and family members are also subjected. More specifically, Maxim's request of his mother's chastity suggests *his* exclusive, nearly inhuman, expectation of his mother's monogamy, and his intention, as a man, to protect her from harm. That Peter Jack becomes engaged to Marina, the mistress of his former master, is partially the result of an Oedipus complex. Their relationship is no longer born out of romance, as Peter Jack once claimed, but, metaphorically fostered to bring him closer to the "spiritual power," or center of the patriarchal mechanism and position of the landlord/father, as he has been regarding his fiancée as a prostitute. He reasons with Basil: "A great prostitute is a great symbolic force."[44] His desire for power through the former mistress of the deceased master hints at how the Oedipus complex of the servant class cooperates with the Master-slave relationship to buttress the patriarchal community. That is probably why Peter Jack does not mind "sharing" Marina with Basil, the new master, as long as he can earn respect from the servants. Interestingly, compared to the male servants' Oedipus complexes, Basil seems to be more possessed about this, choosing keep the power mechanism in operation. Basil's carnal relationship with Marina aims, ostensibly, to "resolve the crisis in my authority which has arisen out of the actions of my father" for "the benefit of the whole community."[45] In other words, the fact that he quickly adapts himself to the chauvinism that only favors the master by abusing the inferior reveals the hypocrisy in Basil's political rhetoric about liberating the servants from the legacy of his forefathers.

Although Basil claimed he would be a modern and liberal master, in practice he is reluctant to give up the *droit de seigneur*, once Marina offers to devote herself carnally. All Marina can do, upon Basil and Peter Jack's request of her "first" night with the master, is to keep repeating: "Yes," "Yes, your honour," and "I am — yours."[46] The carnal relationship between the master and the servants, observed in a colonial context, completes the exercise of power over the ruled through economic, political, and bodily oppressions. Moreover, the servants justify the master's domination over not only female bodies but also their mentalities. Marina, for example, cannot resist Basil's expectation of being his submissive companion, and neither can Oriane, his wife. Their submissiveness stems from the servants' feeling of "emotional ambivalence" about their masters. Peter Jack describes this double bind to Basil about the servants' attachment to his father: "It may seem strange to you, but your father was admired even though he was feared, and loved even though he was hated. People prize what is big."[47]

The Anglo-Irish landlord's domination over economic production combined with forced carnal relations between the ruler and the ruled enables the colonial mechanism to operate systematically. Those who attempt to challenge or break down the system will be dealt with by the "spiritual power," as Peter Jack implies, and sometimes to the point of being killed.[48] Violence and the threat of it maintain the "spiritual power" and distribute it assertively from one level to another. The *droit de seigneur* of Basil and his father over Marina, though unethical, is politically compelling in that Marina can "confer that power [of Basil's father] upon [his son]" by being mistress to both, in spite of the fact that she has been "regarded with resentment ... but also with respect, even with awe" by the servants.[49] The servants, tenants, and peasants who are subject to Basil's dominance therefore suffer unrelentingly in the colonial hierarchy, as both the land and power confer from the father to the son symbolically, through Marina's intimacy with both of them.

The abiding Master-slave dynamics in this Anglo-Irish residence bear additionally some elements of a sadomasochistic complex, given that the oppression that flows from one servant to another, and to the even more inferior Patrice, is never unilateral but often imitational. This means that the slaves acquire the violence of the master, justify it to themselves, and reapply it towards one another. They do not have to agree upon the employment of violence on their own kind, but they practice it whenever applicable, finding "pleasure" and/or receiving a sense of recognition when they do so. The imitated violence, consequently, prompts a sadomasochistic circle which, in Hegelian terms, reflects "the double movement of the two self-consciousnesses."[50] This split or halved mentality lingers in this Anglo-Irish residence, self-contained and strictly controlled for generations, in that

> each sees the other do the same as it does; each does itself what it demands of the other, and therefore also does what it does only in so far as the other does the same. Action by one side only would be useless because what is to happen can only be brought about by both.[51]

In *The Servants and the Snow*, although the servants detest the landlord's tyrannies, they also believe in the necessity of brutal practices as the moral code that keeps the community in order, that creates the 'pleasure' of a kind of safety. The devotion of the ruled to the ruler, and exploitation within the community of the socially disadvantaged, for example, the servants' rejection of Patrice the Traveler from their community, are greater than their "emotional ambivalence" about their masters. Although the servants can create their own recognition system by identifying Patrice as of an even lower class, one alternative explanation for the internalized oppression within their own hierarchy is, metaphorically, the presence of a sadomasochist mentality both they and the colonizer display in this Master-slave relationship. This mentality manifests in their daily mannerisms and seems to be invariable. Specifically, the servants voluntarily kneel at the master's feet and kiss his hands on all occasions, even though, as in the case of Basil and Peter Jack, they are the same age and were childhood companions.[52] Two hundred servants drop to their knees when Basil unexpectedly appears during their mealtime in the servants' hall, albeit they harbor strong resentments against him. The voluntary kneeling of the ruled suggests their bodies have long been conditioned by the colonial customs which they are unable to question. The ruled also appear to feel a sense of security in following the custom, despite the fact that the practice is forced upon them. This explains why they can endure and justify all the atrocities that have happened to their class now and previously. Put another way, their discrete "pleasure" accrues from making themselves *never* a target for punishment but following what is the secure path at that moment.

In the case of Marina, who undergoes less than freely chosen sexual intimacies with her superiors, her perception of love bears some traces of being culturally sadomasochistic since her "love" for her masters is mixed with fear of their power, and she somehow mistakes this love for romance. The *droit de seigneur* has not only distorted her sense of love but deprived her of subjectivity; she enjoys being cared for by men but is more anxious that their love might fade away: "I love his honour, I love him. But — Oh Peter, I'm so terribly frightened for his honour."[53] Her difficult choices, nonetheless, confound her son, Maxim, who condemns his mother's promiscuity: "Oh if you knew how my shame for you has weakened me! All women weaken a man through shame;" "you seem to have two husbands here, do you want a third?"[54] His condemnation of Marina might be due to his failed attempt at rescuing his mother from her sexually abused condition. What he finds hard to understand is that the patronage of the masters over his mother can help to stabilize the community, in that she builds the "spiritual power" that the ruled need to pass from one master to another.

The culturally sadomasochistic mentality is further demonstrated by examining the servants' own discrimination against Patrice, the "gypsy," or Irish tinker, particularly about whether he should be referred to the police when suspected of stealing Oriane's ring. Because of his passion for Marina, who actually put the ring on her finger by mistake, he covers her error and confesses that he was the thief. Hans Joseph (as Marina's father), and Peter Jack, are both excited about punishing Patrice physically, and say that he should not be sent to the police "miles and miles away.... It's far simpler and better to beat him."[55] They obviously have little sympathy for him as socially marginalized in relation to their own class status. By maltreating Patrice the servants can enjoy a privilege that they would never have in the usual course of events, elation at holding the power of torture that their masters hold over them. Peter Jack and Hans Joseph, along with their master, represent the vested interests, ignoring the fact that they are servants subject to slavery in the wider Anglo-Irish hierarchy. On the one hand, their abuse of the "gypsy" partially compensates for the traumas they have experienced.[56] On the other hand, the physical abuse of Patrice illustrates how the Oedipus complex and cultural sadomasochism operate together, since Marina and her "spiritual power" are protected from Patrice's love and her possible choice to love him that the supreme, patriarchal dominance over the ruled is steadfastly secured. The complex interactions between the ruled and the ruler in private and public domains, as Murdoch explained to Alun Vaughan Williams, the director of the play in 1970, aim to explore the relations between "Eros" and political power.[57]

More complexly, Peter Jack and Hans Joseph's abuse of Patrice can collectively, also imaginatively, reverse their social position from colonial object to subject, and temporarily challenge, in a self-centered manner, the hierarchical binaries of active/passive, the ruler/the ruled, male/female, in control/vulnerable, aggressive/submissive, and so forth. The limited reversal of their position, on the one hand, suggests the problematic nature of such cultural designations. On the other hand, observing Patrice abused and Marina sexually dominated releases the servants' repression and sexual desire. Peter Jack, for instance, who encourages his more experienced age-peer Basil to claim the *droit de seigneur* to "deflower" his fiancée Marina, has been a virgin all his life.[58] His virginity suggests that he has long been sexually repressed by prevailing moral codes, never sexually content, and would be less frustrated if he could politically subjugate the powerless "gypsy."

Regarding the characters' fascination with physical abuse, Gary E. Holcomb has argued that the colonized are often captivated by the power they cannot hold. Their pain at being the ruled and "the enforcement of discipline are [thus] the source of endless fascination [... with] power beyond [the] means available to the colonized."[59] The simulation of abuse and pain — to be imposed on Patrice — stands as analogous to that of colonial oppression and representing the "ideological instrument of that oppression."[60] What is ironic is that Patrice suffers under those who are traditionally punished, the servants; control over his body can only momentarily liberate them from the memory of being scarred during the "regime" of Basil's father. Marina's sexual devotion to the new master can briefly erase the grief of losing her former husband — murdered by Basil's father — without her sensing this ongoing sexual exploitation within the power mechanism that Basil conducts. Although the underclass can somehow temporarily reverse and compensate for the political binaries between the active and the passive, ruler and ruled, the self-abuse within their own community further reinforces the class divisions. As Hegel remarks, the temporary reversal of their positions cannot annul the Master-slave relationship, but redefines it: "The bondsman undergoes a formation by virtue of his servile work ... compelled to work for the master ... gets rid of [slavery] by working on it."[61] In other words, the use of punishment as an approach to defining their relationship with the ruler will only lead to stronger operation of the social mechanism. Peter Jack and Grundig's belief that "[h]uman rights are hopelessly frail," and their insistence that Basil use force to discipline the underclass, illustrate their shared culturally sadomasochistic mentality. The servants thus become the "bottomless bottom" who "can never be satisfied," and continue the vicious circle of being abused and abusing one another.[62] What we should note is that an abuser such as Basil is, to some extent, under the control of the abused, namely the servants, in that they often instruct him, step by step, to follow the tradition maintained by his forefathers. In this case, Basil becomes a slave dominator — with no real pleasure to himself. His death by accident is therefore the consequence of "step[ping] into" the trap of cultural sadomasochism.[63]

The sadomasochistic practices performed on the bodies of the underclass are an imaginative redrawing of the map of colonial politics. That is, the bodies of Patrice and Marina are consumed as objects desirable to the colonizer, who colonizes not only foreign territories but their bodies through punishments exacted on the underclass that serve as a disciplinary signal to other colonized objects in the entire colonial empire. Regardless of their gender, the ruled, being powerless, are feminized in the redrawing, or redistribution, of the colonial power. In *The Servants and the Snow*, the only figure who can partially overcome the sadomasochistic control might be Patrice. Differently from the servants, he is outspoken about his preference for being a social outcast, refusing to work for the estate for food, and explicitly critical of the slavery that Basil and Oriane have plunged themselves into by inheriting the big house. He elaborates his alternative understanding of slavery in a rather philosophical tone as follows, illustrating the cultural sadomasochistic condition to which Basil is bound but unaware of:

> PATRICE: Other people contribute out of self interest because they are ambitious enough not to mind being slaves. I am not ambitious and I have no taste for slavery. I steal out of self interest only the little bit that I need. And there are so many slaves working so hard that society can easily spare that little bit for unambitious men like myself who prefer to be free.
> BASIL: But if society catches you, you may suffer.
> PATRICE: Yet even in suffering I remain free.
> BASIL: Free! A rather philosophical gipsy. You knelt down in front of me just now.[64]

Patrice's kneeling is not exactly an arguable point here, as this practice has been regulated by Basil's forefathers as expected practice in the presence of their betters. What is significant, however, is Patrice's anti-capitalistic implication about the cause of self-slavery to which both master and slave are drawn: a self-interest shaped differently than his own unambitious sort. His marginalized social position, nevertheless, enables him to be remote from economic and physical exploitation, in that he is free to come and go to and from the big house. Interestingly, according to Hegel, we can see Patrice's self-consciousness is secured with the acknowledgment of an "other," which to Patrice is his master and the servant class above him. The freedom he tries to assert is thus through "dominat[ing] that other and forc[ing] acknowledgment of its dominance."[65] As a nomadic Irish tinker, Patrice is able to claim dominion over his own body, and freedom, in contrast to those centering around Basil: the servants, the land agent, and the privileged wife and mistress — even Basil himself. His reliance on the few benefits that come to him from the big house makes him a "parasite," and his speech against slavery contradicts his later behavior after he confesses to pilfering the ring that Marina actually takes, and acting extremely humbly, almost cowardly.[66] He implores that he not to be sent to the police, falling down on his knees *three times* in front of Basil and the servants, and showing no trace of the arrogance of his discourse on freedom. Nonetheless, his humility seems to be an extenuating choice, as "[they'd] just put [Patrice] in prison and forget about [him] forever!"[67] His changed attitude implies how precious and fragile freedom is in a strictly controlled "feudal" society, and he would pay any price, including his own dignity and bodily pain, to be a *free* social outcast. Being a social outcast, he is self-determined only thanks to the freedom he solicits from the fringe of the big house — by inhabiting an undersized "cupboard" in the company of rats.[68]

In the final scene of the play, Patrice has to depart, in the snow, from the estate after realizing Marina's lack of interest in his plan to elope with her, and after Oriane's shooting of Basil, and General Klein's arrival and show of iron-handed control over the estate. Frederic moves into the cupboard that Patrice leaves, and loses his position with Oriane, the privilege of whose solicitude he used to be so fascinated with. However, his withdrawal from the servant class to become a social outcast is not comparable with that of Patrice, as Frederic makes a Hobson's choice. He intends to follow in Patrice's steps but cannot, as he has been a trained domestic servant all his life and has never learned how to lead an itinerant lifestyle and survive like Patrice as an Irish Traveler. He cannot walk easily through the frozen wild. Only Patrice has learned how to "go through the snow. You couldn't. I can. My feet will melt it like the feet of the saint in the story."[68]

Irish tinkers such as Patrice are rarely protagonists who are dealt with seriously in Irish literature and drama, and in reality they are placed on the social margin without individual voices. This play, however, contextualizes Patrice within the power dynamics of this Anglo-Irish estate. Being on the lowest rung of the social mechanism, he is symbolically the nexus of all the power conflicts. He is not only the most deprived in the economic production hierarchy, relying on leftovers, but also the sufferer most subject to the sadomasochistic mentality of all his superiors. The mistreatment of his body contributes significantly to the stability of the class divisions.

The play ends with Maxim's and Oriane's assassination of Basil, due to their disgust at Basil's inherited power, the *droit de seigneur*, and resentment against social division and suppression. They are relatively more capable than Patrice of defending their own interests in that they are at least *within* the power hierarchy. Peter Jack's protection of Basil from getting Maxim's bullets reflects his distorted value judgment arising from an aristocratic regime, since the *droit de seigneur* has meant to him "the primitive ideas of justice" and should be continued as a traditional practice.[70] His voluntary sacrifice for Basil, though seemingly for the benefit of the whole community, likely results from his sadomasochistic mentality and emotional ambivalence as a member of the colonized servant class.

One minor but important figure worthy of notice is Father Ambrose, and particularly his Christian standpoint regarding the ongoing savagery. Unable to be a proper shepherd for God, and having also lost his faith, Father Ambrose boldly confesses to Basil that the Christian God is no longer working here and will be replaced by pagan gods: "When I die, which please God will be soon, these people will revert to a paganism which is very much more natural to them than the religion which I have preached and failed to practice."[71] This confession is striking when uttered by a lifelong clergyman, but it echoes Patrice's criticism about the ambivalent role that Father Ambrose leads in his political preference for the exploiter:

> If you expect any other kind [of human love] you are the friend of tyrants. If you make humiliation holy you are the friend of tyrants. Your big God is dead and your little gods are dying. And you are mortally sad because you have forgotten nothing and because you know that even though you willed all manner of good things and hoped all manner of good things you have still been all your life the friend of tyrants.[72]

The negative illustration of failed Christianity implies how Murdoch has tried to question the hierarchical natures of both religious and feudal establishments. They endorse each other in the name of social stability, while the former eventually tolerates the tyrannical actions of the latter, above or below the table. Thus clergymen, here symbolized in Father Ambrose, are not necessarily the guardians of social justice but are impelled to join the disciplinary forces of the landlords, contributing to the pervasion of colonial/political control over foreign lands. Father Ambrose not only betrays his Christian teaching, but also justifies the ferocities of the landowners. Nevertheless, Father Ambrose is probably the only character who can feel his conscience being tortured in the face of others' suffering, and was prompted to murder Basil's father to put an end to all the savagery.

Murdoch engages with two existentialist theses through the characterization of Father Ambrose: the absemce of God and the limits of conscience. For God's part, the servants' prayers never lead to a miraculous stop to the injustice they suffer. Father Ambrose is still, and has to be, God's device in testifying to His existence — at a distance from but not ignorant of human suffering. The limitations of both manifest in the fact that the only church in the community has been "ruined" without worshippers, and Father Ambrose utters "God does not exist" to Oriane in his despair.[73] His murder of Basil's father may result from his personal choice, while it can also be seen as one approach to experiencing God, in that the killing of a tyrannical landlord may convince us that "[he] does exist and is constantly experienced and pictured," as Murdoch explains even if "God does not and cannot exist."[74] Ambivalence and violence extend everywhere in this play. As to the limits of conscience, Father Ambrose may exemplify one existentialist claim: "[Conscience] is [a] term we use for the kind of moral conviction that will sometimes lead a person to reject the accepted standards of his society in response to what he believes to be a more deeply founded imperative."[75] The tyrannicide that Father Ambrose commits may imply that God exists only when the conscience vibrates with disquiet or satisfaction; God cannot exist if the conscience hibernates.

At the conclusion of the play, the small openings out of tyranny, if not the many valences of ambivalence, close. Patrice's departure coincides with the unexpected arrival of General Klein, Oriane's brother, as a *deux ex machina*, after Peter Jack takes Maxim's bullets to protect his Basil, and Oriane shoots her husband dead out of her jealousy of Marina. The order of the Anglo-Irish community is re-established with the terrors reintroduced by General Klein, who not only puts Maxim in chains but demands "kneel when you address me, you swine...."[76] What is interesting is that General Klein, according to Murdoch's stage directions, is "played by the same actor who plays Patrice."[77] The two characters with very disparate social backgrounds — to be played by the same actor — can however provoke profound effects on the audience. That is, Patrice is a social outcast — much debased in the feudal hierarchy — whereas General Klein is a "master," installed directly into Basil's estate. The two characters will be received differently, because of their dissimilar costumes and demeanors though they are performed by the same actor. Murdoch might have intended to interrogate the superficial differentiation of human values, and the divisions between the upper and lower classes that can be reversed and disguised simply by a change of costumes. The contingency of social divisions thus becomes manifest, although, ironically the characters in the play are insensitive and continue the vicious interlocking circles of abuse.

The Servants and the Snow has been a largely ignored text in the Irish literary canon, as its Irishness is rather implicit, although Murdoch illustrates a cocktail of Irish human dilemmas that goes beyond mere politics. Her exclusion from the Irish canon, in part, rests on the nature of modern Irish literature, which tends to "register alienation," as Seamus Deane observes.[78] Women writers are inclined to be alienated "from self-expression, from self-determination" in this male-privileged canon.[79] A distant onlooker of Anglo-Irish culture and historical experiences, Murdoch has presented her observations on the political and economic connections of her Anglo-Irish community by the (anti-) colonial operations in this play. She both sympathizes with the colonized Irish who were often silenced and alienated from mainstream society. She is also alert to the complex dynamics that undermine their resistance to domination, testifying to what Frantz Fanon calls the "hierarchy of cultures."[80] If the victims of power and abuse misuse it against one another, no one, including the masters, can really escape servitude.

NOTES

1. Other works that are set in Ireland include *The Unicorn* (1963) and the short story "Something Special" (1957), while *The Red and the Green* is the one that more closely deals with Irish politics.
2. Gerstenberger, 1975, 70.
3. Qtd. in Bostridge, 2008. In a 1978 interview, Murdoch also emphasized, "My Irishness is Anglo-Irishness in a very strict sense.... I'm profoundly Irish and I've been conscious of this all my life, and in a mode of being Irish which has produced a lot of very distinguished thinkers and writers" (qtd. in Conradi, 2001, 27).
4. I am much indebted to Alison and Michael Scott-Baumann, and M.F. Simone Roberts for their suggestions in deciphering the colonial context of this play through this Hegelian approach, and their valuable advice.
5. Only four reviews are traceable, as surveyed by John Fetcher. Apart from *The Servants and the Snow* and *The Three Arrows* (1973), Murdoch has adapted three of her novels for theatrical performance: *A Severed Head* (1964), *The Italian Girl* (1967), and *The Black Prince* (1987). There has been little critical writing about Murdoch's theatrical contributions other than John Fetcher's "A Novelist's Plays: Irish Murdoch and the Theatre."
6. Murdoch, 1989, *Servants*, 12.
7. According to Christopher Fitz-Simon, the Abbey Theatre from 1941 to 1969, under the managing directorship of Ernest Blythe, did not "actively search for innovative works" but "displayed that paralyzing trait" which failed to respond "positively" to social change by commissioning plays from a younger generation (xiii). Murdoch belonged to this "younger" generation that was unable to raise the eyebrows of Blythe and other theater managers.
8. Specifically, Murdoch's mother was Irish, and her father was an English civil servant based in Dublin. Her family connection to, and experiences with, both ethnic groups in Ireland might have brought her a critical viewpoint beyond the ethnic divisions. Her critique of both Anglo-Irish ascendancy and Irish republicanism is *The Red and the Green*.
9. The "big" houses, however, were not castles or palaces, but can be contrasted to the peasant cottages from which their tenants could be evicted.
10. Maria Edgeworth's *Castle Rackrent* (1800), Elizabeth Bowen's *The Last September* (1929), Somerville and Ross's *The Real Charlotte* (1894), and Molly Keane's *Good Behaviours* (1981) are their representative works, among others, about the decline of the Anglo-Irish locations where they grew up.
11. Murdoch, 1989, *Servants*, 30. People of this minority group are also known as the Pavees, Knackers, Tinkers, Gypsies, or Irish Travelers. Travelers such as Patrice are/were a nomadic people of Irish origin, believed to have their own customs, music, dialects, storytelling, and celebration, and are identified in English law as an ethnic group, while only a "social group" in the Republic of Ireland. Adopting an itinerant lifestyle, they were inheritors of the Irish oral tradition, as most of them were illiterate and thus dismissed in the literature of "The Great Tradition" (Gmelch 14).

W.B. Yeats's *Stories of Red Hanrahan* (1904), and J.M Synge's drama, *The Tinkers' Wedding* (1909), for example, are two literary examples, among others. For further information, see Sean Maher's *The Road to God Knows Where* (1972), Sharon Gmelch's *Nan: The Life an Irish Travelling Woman* (1986), and Aoife Bhreatnach's *Becoming Conspicuous: Irish Travellers, Society and the State 1922–70* (2003).

12. *Ibid.*
13. *Ibid.*
14. Hegel, 1977, 114.
15. Murdoch, 1997, Chatto, 147.
16. Murdoch, 1989, *Servants*, 92.
17. Postcolonial criticisms— published before this play was produced — include Aimé Césaire's *Discourse on Colonialism* (1950), Frantz Fanon's *Black Skin, White Masks* (1952), *The Wretched of the Earth* (1961), and Albert Memmi's *The Colonizer and the Colonized* (1965).
18. Sekyi-out, 1996, 58.
19. Hegel, 1977, 117.
20. For instance, *The Red and the Green*, which portrays the experiences of an Anglo-Irish family and its mixed reactions towards the Easter Rising, is based upon this master-slave dialectic. This landed family is much troubled by an identity crisis in which some of its members have sympathy for Irish nationalists and some are diehard unionists. Their conflicts arise from the inferior/superior complexes through which they understand the political situation: "it's always easy for the top dog to extend his sense of identity over his inferiors. It's a different matter for the inferiors to accept the identification" (34–35).
21. Murdoch, 1989, 37.
22. Freud, 1919, 75.
23. *Ibid.*, 86.
24. *Ibid.*, 73.
25. Murdoch, 1989, 96.
26. *Ibid.*, 38.
27. Murdoch, 1997, 279.
28. Murdoch, 1989, 93.
29. *Ibid.*, 101.
30. Murdoch, 1997, 171.
31. *Ibid.*, 172.
32. Murdoch, 1989, 15.
33. Asked about her political leanings, Murdoch admitted in an interview that she "became a Marxist at the time of the Spanish Civil War.... But I became quickly disillusioned with Marxism; the ideals were OK but what was being done in its name was awful" (qtd. in Cowley, 1999, 15). She did abandon it, but Marxism's values have been a decided undercurrent in her works.
34. Murdoch, 1989, 22–3.
35. *Ibid.*, 52.
36. *Ibid.*
37. *Ibid.*, 50.
38. Her charisma, according to John Fetcher, resembles that of Blanche DuBois, a female protagonist in Tennessee Williams's *A Streetcar Named Desire* (1947), whereas her beauty and social class are largely the sources of the resentment aimed at her.
39. Murdoch, *Servants*, 1970, 92.
40. Hegel, 1977, 117.
41. It has long been known that the first concerted movement to reform women's social and legal inequalities began in the nineteenth century. Mary Wollstonecraft (1759–1879) was one of the leading activists. However, it was not until the 1850s that a more organized feminist campaign started in Britain, followed by the suffragette movement in the end of the nineteenth century. The "second wave" of feminism was a phrase coined by Marsha Lear, referring to the widespread and growing feminist activities in America, Britain and Europe from the late 1960s onwards (Lear 1968 as cited in Humm 1995, 251). The objectives of this movement include: equal political influence, improved working conditions, equal pay, more occupational choices, child care, and abortion rights.
42. Murdoch, 1997, 172.

43. Murdoch, 1989, 65.
44. *Ibid.*, 91.
45. *Ibid.*, 97.
46. *Ibid.*
47. *Ibid.*, 90.
48. *Ibid.*, 92.
49. *Ibid.*, 91.
50. Hegel, 1977, 112.
51. *Ibid.*
52. Basil and Peter Jack remark on their ages on page 14.
53. Murdoch, 1989, 89.
54. *Ibid.*, 56, 109.
55. *Ibid.*, 68.
56. That the servants also try to restrict Marina's freedom of speech is readable as a symptom of sadomasochism. Peter Jack demands that Marina remain silent about her father's murder by Basil's father: "Be silent! There is nothing you can do. You cannot give life to the dead. Let this thing remain between us in this room" (Murdoch, 1989, 72). He apparently dismisses the fact that the other servants have all been suffering a sense of guilt for tolerating the murder of her father, but still he forces Marina to continue to cover up the scandal and violence, keeping the pain among his own ranks.
57. Conradi, 2001, 531.
58. Murdoch, 1989, 90. See page 20 for the mention of his virginity.
59. Holcomb and Holcomb, 2002, 974.
60. *Ibid.*
61. Hegel, 1977, 117.
62. Stoller, 1991, 15.
63. *Ibid.*, 20. Oriane had been unwilling to return with Basil to the countryside residence, although she did not have a free choice — due to her husband's insistence and position.
64. Murdoch, 1989, *Servants*, 32.
65. Baird, 2000, 3.
66. Murdoch, 1989, *Servants*, 30.
67. *Ibid.*, 68.
68. *Ibid.*, 31.
69. *Ibid.*, 107.
70. *Ibid.*, 72.
71. *Ibid.*, 59.
72. *Ibid.*, 57–8.
73. *Ibid.*, 60, 102.
74. Qtd. in Cowley, 1999, 15.
75. Macquarrie, 1973, 210.
76. Murdoch, 1989, Servants, 112.
77. *Ibid.*, 12.
78. Deane, 1979, 244. In other words, the experiences of exile from the social and religious mainstream provided nutrition for male Irish writers. James Joyce, for instance, "named exile as one of the conditions of his artistic life" (Leeney, 2004, 150). Modern Irish literature is therefore criticized for male writers' depictions and celebrations of their own self-alienation.
79. Leeney, 2004, 150.
80. Fanon, 1970, 41.

8

Nausea Under the Net

ALISON SCOTT-BAUMANN

In *Sartre: Romantic Rationalist* Murdoch studies Sartre's writing styles—in his work as a novelist, as a political polemicist and a philosopher — in order to look at his belief system. She takes him at his word; "Sartre has recommended moral concern as a recipe for good writing," and she finds a discrepancy between Sartre's idea of moral concern and his views on good writing.[1] This discrepancy is at odds with her own understanding of morality, and can be illustrated by Sartre's handling of negative thought. Of course she admires his negative worldview of the twentieth century horrors of Hitler and Stalin, recognizing him as a co-witness with her, and yet she becomes wary of his search for a remedy to these horrors in modern socialism. She also becomes wary of his powerful use of description: in her analysis of his most famous novel *Nausea*, she shows us how he describes phenomena in such a way that he *also interprets*, going beyond description and giving us negative meaning that we cannot easily challenge because it *seems* synonymous with reality. We know that Murdoch sees this interpretative capacity as a wonderful aspect of language, and uses it herself, sometimes to excess.[2] Yet she finds "a lack of frankness in the way Sartre has moved on from description to recommendation" in order to create interpretative meaning based on negative values.[3] In tribute to his desire to improve upon the past by combining theory and practice she describes him as a good writer who respected the novel with the beliefs of "a sincere propagandist in a powerful weapon."[4] However her reservations about Sartre's novels are significant and include his socialist polemics and his exaggerated use of language, exemplified in her analysis of Sartre's negativity:

> Sartre's great negatives are not the negatives of cynicism, but of an obstinate and denuded belief, which clings to certain values even at the expense of seeming to make them empty. The Marxists revile Sartre because he describes man as a fundamentally non-social, non-historical individual. But what Sartre wishes to assert is precisely that the individual has an absolute importance and is not to be swallowed up in a historical calculation.[5]

Here Murdoch identifies and analyses the contradiction at the polemic core of Sartre's work: he argues that Marxism is fatally flawed and yet she believes that he cannot resist the attraction of metaphysical myths (in this case Marxism) that provide meaning. She sees two levels of myth-making in Sartre; Marxism is his myth at a systems level, and at an individual level she notes his attraction to the myths of "bad boys" of literature like Genet.[6] She also celebrates what is perhaps his greatest legacy: against the horrors of the Second World War Sartre insisted that the individual person has choices and these must not be negated by the pogroms of history. After 1956 he used this debate about individual capacity for change in his struggle with the Stalinist domination of the French communist party (PCF). Here she criticizes his assertion that, at both systems and individual levels, "in an oppressive society only violence is honest," by which he often seems to mean the violence of language.[7] I will discuss Murdoch's view of Sartre as a moral philosopher, analyzing her work through the lens of her writing on Sartre, and focusing particularly on her handling of Sartre's approach to negation.[8] I propose to demonstrate how the vitality of Murdoch's engagement with philosophy allows her to challenge Sartre's use of literature to support socialism: she shows us how Sartre was trapped between Kantian and Hegelian impulses and that this necessitates our engagement with the negative.

I will analyze the importance for Murdoch of Sartre's existentialist relationship with *negativity, denial, lack, loss* and *nothingness*.[9] This will enable me to focus on the centrality of morals for Murdoch's own writing. The negative approach deserves attention because it is a very different position to Murdoch's and also because of its dominance in modern philosophy. As Roger Scruton comments,

> This arrest of the soul in the posture of negation is worthy of study, since it is at the root of much that passes for philosophy in a modern university ... the proof that there is no source of law, no value and no meaning.[10]

We can reject Scruton's commentary for its sweeping generalization, yet there are interesting connections between Murdoch's work on Sartre and Scruton's proposal that we engage with ideas that we wish to negate while simultaneously resisting their powers. Engagement with Sartre's work is an integral part of Murdoch's intellectual development, yet neither her philosophical writing nor her novels are Sartrean (by which I mean that she resists his pessimistic existentialism). Nor does she engage in socialist polemic. How did she achieve this ambivalent relationship with Sartre and the negative? One possible answer lies in the importance of another, hitherto under-explored element, namely her use of the work of Gabriel Marcel whose style she saw as uncontrolled yet moral. With Sartre, in contrast, she identifies various moral dilemmas that she believes are created by Sartre's stylistic excesses and his desire to control our thoughts as readers. She sees this in his evocation, for example, of nausea and the slimy viscosity of life and this facilitates analysis of her belief in the morality of literary style.

In order to move to and fro between examining Murdoch's literary critique of Sartre and her philosophical work on him, we first need to analyze briefly the philosophical milieu of Europe at that time.

Philosophies of Existentialism

Unlike those who may have carried Sartre's books around on the 1960s university campus to impress others, Iris Murdoch actually read *Being and Nothingness* and *The Critique of Dialectical Reason*—in French—and wrote incisively about them.[11] She was trained in Oxford analytical philosophy and also worked alongside the British ordinary language philosophers; both of these traditions insist upon clarity. She also immersed herself in the continental philosophers characterized by Husserl and his descendants, and their insistence upon complexity. She made critical choices and then set herself apart from all three lineages and developed a moral philosophy that respects clarity *and* complexity. I believe Murdoch is underestimated as a philosopher, partly because she should be measured against criteria that reflect the hybrid philosophy that she developed, and the way in which she steeped herself in European thought. Murdoch insisted upon a rich fusion of different sources, from Plato to Kant and Sartre and the modern novel.[12]

Her work urgently deserves contextualization within European philosophy. Conradi provides us with excellent archival evidence, showing us how *excited* Murdoch was by reading Sartre, by his versatility and his contrast to the colorless liberalism of contemporary Oxford philosophy. By 1945 she was reading *Being and Nothingness* and feeling invigorated at the possibility of doing philosophy again after the war years.[13] Conradi also shows us how naïve Murdoch was, joining the communist party in 1938 and not voicing concerns about Stalin until 1945.[14] Strong commentaries in the Anglo-American tradition come from Antonaccio, Diamond, Mulhall and Schweiker on Murdoch's debate about *fact* and *value*, about *is* and *ought*.[15] In order to understand Murdoch properly, we also need a European commentator on existentialism and on Sartre; so much of the social tragedy and literary action to which Murdoch referred was in continental Europe. Paul Ricoeur, one of the greatest modern Western philosophers, is valuable for this purpose.[16] Ricoeur's approach to Sartre resembles that of Murdoch, and he experienced the same concerns as Murdoch and Sartre did about the dominance in France of Stalinist communism, the despair caused by the Second World War and the limitations of existentialism.[17]

In order to consider the importance of Sartre's work and of negation, we need a brief contextualizing commentary on existentialism, that Ricoeur, Sartre,

Beauvoir and to some extent Murdoch all developed and experienced at first hand and, to varying degrees, acted upon. Paul Ricoeur summarizes the problems, by endowing existentialism with three characteristics.[18] First there is the "owned body" of Merleau-Ponty, who, in emphasizing the vital role of perception, attempted to overcome Cartesian dualism by joining body and mind.[19] Secondly there is the idea of freedom as the annihilation of the past, the negativity of being. This owes its strength to Hegel, who "took possession" of the negative and integrated it fully into his philosophy as a creative force. This negation formed part of what came to be known as the dialectical method, comprising thesis and antithesis (ideal versus real, positive versus negative), leading to synthesis, which Murdoch discusses in the context of Sartre's own dialectic. Thirdly there is the Sartrean idea of the Other. Sartre, writing at the same time as Murdoch (and Ricoeur) in the 1950s, experienced the Other as adversarial and negative; as Murdoch put it "the other person (envisaged by Sartre as the enemy) sees me and may turn me to stone."[20]

Ricoeur asserted that negative thought has become prevalent: Hegel, Kierkegaard and Nietzsche provide us with a modern philosophy of negation that makes Sartrean existentialism possible. Through them it may be understood that negative thinking has become a problem that threatens our human identity, whereas with the ancient Greeks negative thinking was more of an epistemological and also an intellectual position. Classical philosophy was refreshingly free of solipsism, the conviction that the individual is the only real, albeit increasingly fragile phenomenon in the world. However, there was also debate even within classical philosophy about being and nothingness.[21] Negation was seen as several things: in a Socratic way as *lack* or *loss* (of understanding), in a Platonic way as *not* being able to understand (the other person) and, through Plotinus and the neo–Platonists as a way of conceptualizing both the negative *and* the positive.

Kant challenged Descartes by arguing that I will never be at one with myself; discrepancies between who I want to be (moral and strong) and who I am (fallible and weak) will never be resolved, but at least I can attempt to be aware of these and use reason in order to behave morally. Hegel developed Kant's views about perception further; we are the *subjects*, and the *objects* around us belong to our world because we define them, we imbue them with meaning.[22] Hegel gave us negation as half of this bipolar condition of *being* and *owning*; freedom and negation are inextricably connected and, by defining each other, serve both to liberate and to chain each other as with the Master-slave dialectic. The master dominates the slave, yet needs the slave as justification for existing and this makes it hard for the slave to be free. The problem is to decide whether the world around me is the master, or can I be in control? Roquentin, anti-hero of *Nausea*, experiences many nightmare moments of trying to achieve this Hegelian totalization, a sense of trying to control the world and feeling its negative pull.

Murdoch's "unselfing" shows us a very different solution, where activism and inwardness are both transformed by love, and finds this missing from Sartre. She analyses how dependent Sartre was on Hegel: Sartre uses Hegel to develop Descartes" unreflective cogito and the idea that freedom is the means by which the progressive revelation of the truth will emerge.[23] Murdoch, as novelist *and* philosopher, was particularly interested in Sartre's rather grim interpretation of Hegel's conviction that societies improve.[24] The paradox is that we need to free ourselves in order to carry out actions that are somehow ordained. Too much inwardness, contemplation about our intentions will impede our capacity for free (i.e., according to Hegel, not free but determined) action, so Sartre isolates both inwardness and activism from each other, thereby *denying* both the benefit of the other. Such a negative position leads to "the half-conscious, unreflective self-deception, which he calls bad faith."[25] Using Kant, he argues that we always see things from a limited point of view, so neither our perception nor our understanding can be good enough to allow us to transcend our personal perspective. Thus, by the limitations of our own perception we are forced to negate the possibility of absolute truth. All that we have is Hegel's belief that, any society will improve upon previous societies. Either way we are not free, unless, as Sartre hopes, he can fuse existentialism and socialism in the individual's actions. These actions will involve other people, through (for Murdoch) love; yet instead of love Sartre shows his negative approach again.

THE EXISTENTIALISMS OF MARCEL AND SARTRE

Murdoch shows us in 1950 that for Sartre nothingness goes to the heart of being: that third element of Ricoeur's analysis of existentialism shows Sartre negating the Other; not merely the other person, but the other part of me, consciousness as opposed to just being alive. "The thing is in-itself, *en-soi*; the consciousness is for-itself, *pour-soi*. That is, it *is* nothing; it is not a substance and it has no meaning, although it is the source of all meaning."[26] The *pour-soi* is nothing because it is spontaneous and free, the *en-soi* is inert and trapped. This is Sartre's dialectic: despite Sartre using it as an idea to try and free France's collective conscience from the horrors of the war, this dialectic cannot resolve itself into the higher form of civilization as envisaged by Hegel, because Sartre's individual feels trapped.

By contrast Gabriel Marcel developed a very different form of existentialist thought.[27] In the 1950s Murdoch developed an interest in the work of Marcel, who "coins new and persuasive concepts" and whose work gives her a more positive paradigm of existentialism.[28] Murdoch found Marcel's thinking attractive because, like her, he was interested in the transformative power of love and because of the challenges he set us; is it possible to be oneself and also reduce the distance between oneself and the other person in such a way that we can address each other's needs at least to some extent? Marcel accepts the risk of acknowledging that others have different views. Sartre denies it by negating the possibility of understanding oneself through the Other, who will, in fact, sap my meaning from me. Two people can never understand each other. Gabriel Marcel, on the contrary, saw the need to *hope* that two people can understand each other. Marcel was of great importance to both Murdoch and Ricoeur, and yet we will see how Murdoch sets him to one side after a while.

In her short essay from 1951, "The Image of Mind," Murdoch provides us with a clear picture of Gabriel Marcel, his strengths and weaknesses and his book *The Mystery of Being*.[29] Murdoch admires his concern with ethical and religious matters, his interest in the phenomenology of everyday life (how do we perceive the world round us?) and his capacity to convey the sense of mystery and revelation in being human. She prefers Marcel as a philosopher to a thinker like Ryle, with the "hygienic and dehydrated analysis of mental concepts" that she believes to be characteristic of Oxford philosophy, and yet she finds fault, as do many others, with the impressionistic, rambling nature of Marcel's text and his use of metaphors that he fails to clarify.[30] Conradi comments that she contrasted Sartre with Marcel and preferred Marcel for his belief that we can and must seek meaning.[31]

She admires Marcel's work, and yet she wishes that he would write more clearly. It is interesting to see possible parallels with Marcel and the characters in Murdoch's novels: when Murdoch's characters are good they are often inarticulate, and they contrast sharply with the self-centered characters who are often highly articulate. Marcel's approach to negation, often implicit, was of interest to her as was his postulation of the *surplus* of meaning by contrast with Sartre's rejection of the surplus of meaning. This may provide us with insight into her assertive approach towards challenging negation: Murdoch explains how Sartre postulates a void at the centre of existence, like his character Mathieu's cold anger at himself for abandoning his pregnant girlfriend *for nothing*, in *The Roads to Freedom*.[32]

Kant's Antinomies

For Sartre, man is an emptiness poised between two inaccessible totalities. Murdoch detects here that "this rather bitter view of objective reality as "fallen" is a persistent feature of existentialist thinking."[33] To replicate this feature he creates in his writing this sense of a void at the centre of the dialectical oppositions. The problem, as Murdoch describes it, "is to find a middle way (a third force), between the ossification of language and its descent into the senseless."[34] Sartre uses Kant's analysis of antinomies; these are opposites that seem reasonable ways of categorizing our world until they are juxtaposed with each other, at which point they create dogmatic or skeptical polarities that are still inherent to reason yet must be grappled with in an attempt to bring them into some sort of harmony (reason and emotion; infinite and finite; good and evil; male and female, in Hegel, master and slave, in Sartre *pour-soi* and *en-soi*). This attempt to combine opposites will always fail; there is no hope of resolution but we must try. She shows us how he uses Kant to challenge Hegel: on the one, Kantian, hand the world of intelligible being is unattainable; on the other, Hegelian, hand the world of objects is impenetrable, even contradictory.[35]

In order to clarify the difficulties posed by Hegel, Sartre uses a bleak, irresolvable version of Kant's antinomies.[36] The human can move, albeit with difficulty, between Kant's antinomies (related opposites), but Sartre's contrasts are too extreme and will condemn him to the polarization on the one hand between gritty, realist street barricade action and, on the other hand, the metaphysical ideals of a perfect Marxism. A revolutionary must act in order to have meaning. Murdoch, starting in 1950, explains to us how "Sartre presents in dramatic and polemical form his view of the 'non-existence' of value prior to action."[37] There is no possibility of metaphysical value; it must all be grounded in action. Yet although Sartre negates metaphysical aspirations, he longs for them: he hopes that the action of manning the barricades, protesting, demonstrating, striking and distributing pamphlets will lead to implementation of the ideal of pure socialism. Birchall, in his book *Sartre Against Stalinism* shows us how absolutely convinced Sartre was that action in the present would liberate the masses from oppression.[38] He seeks by action to both heighten and resolve the contradictions between the real and the ideal, whereas Murdoch's characters are only too conscious of the unintended consequences that may emerge from actions.

In "The Existentialist Political Myth" Murdoch establishes a clear philosophical challenge to Sartre's heightening of antinomies and attempts to fuse them by examining his argument about reality.[39] For Sartre we are at the centre of the perceptual world: we make our reality and this is both narcissistic and negative because it involves awareness of value and we know we cannot live up to our values. Bad faith (*mauvaise foi*) is one manifestation of this tension, i.e., to blame inaction upon one's surroundings and circumstances and the failure to understand oneself as capable of acting. Many characters in Murdoch's novels manifest bad faith, for example Bernie in *The Red and The Green* is bad faith incarnate. The flaw in all of this, for Murdoch, is that she believes emotional development ("man the barricades!") and rational argument (mankind will follow socialist thought) are not compatible. She challenges the way in which Sartre bases his writings on the possibility of just such compatibility, especially when so much of his philosophy provides enough negative force to make this impossible. She argues, moreover, that he endangers the development of ideas with his use of melodrama, hyperbole, exaggeration and other stylistic devices. We can now adopt her philosophical wisdom to consider her analysis of negation in Sartre's *oeuvre*.

Sartre: Romantic Rationalist

Murdoch's 1953 monograph *Sartre: Romantic Rationalist* is her most sustained challenge as a philosopher to Sartre. It was the first English language response to the cultural and literary phenomenon that was Jean-Paul Sartre, and it is still fresh and vibrant more than fifty years after she wrote it, especially with the complementary introduction that she wrote for its re-issue in 1987. Conradi comments on the lapidary, compressed brilliance of *Sartre: Romantic Rationalist*: "It revealed a novelist's capacity to sink and merge her personality within the mind of another, and criticized Sartre's ideas and novels accessibly."[40] Life has no meaning, Sartre asserted, except that which we give it; moreover this enterprise is doomed because we only make meaning by taking action. Our actions will go wrong more often than they go right, even if we attempt to implement the principles of European socialism, as recommended by Sartre.

We know from Sartre's depiction of Roquentin, the anti-hero of *Nausea* that Sartre makes much use of something like Scruton's "arrest of the soul in the posture of negation," and Murdoch is greatly exercised by this phenomenon. The danger of negative thought is that the active person may become trapped in inwardness.

Neurotic Characters

Murdoch is respectful yet critical of Sartre for the characters he creates because she believes they are more identifiable as the embodiment of a particular moral problem than they are as people.[41] She sees this as the consequence of being rational about emotions and believes that it creates a didactic distance between reader and character that weakens Sartre's impact.[42] Moreover each of those problems is contextualized within situations that are fatally flawed and peopled by those who are doubtful and insincere, yet desperately seek meaning. Hence Murdoch sees no real dialectical choice for the reader: "We are offered things or truths. What we have lost is persons."[43] Another problem is caused by the interior monologue; while Murdoch agrees with Sartre that this is the best way to develop a character, she also feels that Sartre's over-intellectualization of internal struggles will discourage the reader, who becomes exhausted by the "drying and emptying effect of the perpetual analysis."[44] By discussing literary creations such as Mathieu (the hero of the political trilogy *The Age of Reason*) who is possessed of a "chill self-consciousness," and stylistic effects such as her own and Sartre's use of interior monologue, Murdoch the young author initiates and maintains a fascinating debate about philosophical and novel writing.[45] Clearly Sartre is a major influence on her.

While writing *Sartre: Romantic Rationalist* she is presumably already working on *Under the Net*, considering Sartre as an equal and one who shares her own interests in philosophical novels and in writing philosophy.[46] She weaves together here an astute awareness of the technical craft of writing and its desired effects on the reader, citing the need for what George Eliot called "an equivalent centre of self from which the shadows fall with a difference" and suggesting that, in contrast, Sartre interprets the human individual as unmanageable and "fears, not loves, this notion of a volcanic otherness within the personality."[47] Whereas for Murdoch, as for Socrates and Plato, dialogue with others is the essential creative force that allows us to become better at living the good life that seems unattainable for all of us, this is unattainable for Sartre's characters. Here we return to the sense of absolutism that pervades Sartre's writings, together with revulsion towards other people for their unpredictability, their bodily presence and the sheer otherness with which their flesh endows them. This is balanced by self-loathing: self-knowledge is negative and destructive.

Of course Murdoch also sees utility in this version of existentialism; "dramatic, solipsistic, romantic and anti-social exaltation of the individual," and as her writing develops, her novels contain significant neurotic characters.[48] In 1959 Murdoch sketches for us her analysis of this; she calls it the "neurotic Romantic literature" in which "a single person has swallowed up the entire book" as first person male narrator.[49] By its combination of dynamism, negativism, self-indulgence and the will to deprive others of their freedom, such an approach provides a model for many of Murdoch's charismatic men: Carel, Julius, Bradley Pearson. By contrast she challenges us to admire the many memorable characters in the novels of great writers, (citing Tolstoy), and she recommend that we avoid both the neurotic Romantic with his omnipotent voice and the didactic characters from Sartre, Camus and Beauvoir. In their different ways they deny us our imagination. For Murdoch, "neurotic" and "didactic" represent errors in style.

The Literary Style of a Romantic Rationalist

NAUSEA UNDER THE NET

Given the Kantian and Hegelian tensions that preoccupy Sartre, it is no surprise that Roquentin, anti-hero of Sartre's novel *Nausea,* feels such disgust at himself, at his girlfriend and at existence, raising existential questions that are discussed by Sartre in 1943 when he publishes *Being and Nothingness,* which is his philosophical analysis of the ideas in *Nausea.* Hence in her 1953 book on Sartre, Murdoch calls *Nausea* "the instructive overture to Sartre's work."[50] *Under the Net,* Murdoch's first and highly successful novel, is a sort of reply to Sartre's *Nausea.* Her title refers to the constraints and also the structure afforded us by language, using a phrase from Plato. The beginning and end of *Under the Net* are reminiscent of Sartre's *Nausea*; the main protagonist in each novel (Roquentin in *Nausea*, Jake in *Under the Net*) is a writer experiencing difficulties in writing at the start of the story, who by the end of the novel, is planning to start writing again. In both cases the novel they plan to write turns out, perhaps, to be the one we have just read. Another Sartrean influence upon Murdoch is the existentialist anxiety that characterizes Jake's attempts to make sense of the world, but Murdoch transforms this into productive excitement; *Under the Net* is suffused with the surprise of life, the mysteries that are other people and Jake's gradual understanding that other people are extraordinary and different from us and that he must not impose upon them his own fantasies. Sartrean influences recur, as in *The Sea, the Sea*.

At the end of *Nausea* Roquentin is attempting to recover from his perpetual sense of nausea: he is mesmerized by the song in the café and the possibility that he could create a novel as beautiful, hard and enduring as steel, not slimy like the cold semen of spent reality.[51] As a counterbalance to Roquentin's café scene, near the end of *Under the Net* Jake hears Anna singing on the radio in Mrs. Tinckham's shop and is transported. Yet this dialogue, created by Murdoch with Sartre through her recognition of the value of *Nausea*, seems more like a subtle heuristic device than imitation as a form of homage. *Under the Net* provides a penetrating critique of *Nausea* as Murdoch offers a more productive alternative to negation than Roquentin's despair. *Nausea* is a study of a world without meaning and ends on a depressing note of self-doubt with Roquentin longing to be able "to recall my life without repugnance."[52] Conradi summarizes the contrast between the two novels: "where *La Nausée* presented the contingency of the world as the enemy, *Under the Net* presents some healing surrender to its otherness as a precondition for happiness and creativity alike."[53] This sounds to me like a neo–Platonist approach to negation: we cannot ignore dialectical tensions and actually we need polarized tensions because trying to understand one polarity will help us see what the other is not. Jake realizes how important it is to accept that negation as nothingness is a necessary preliminary to moving on:

> All work and all love, the search for wealth and fame, the search for truth, life itself, are made up of moments which pass and become nothing. Yet through this shaft of nothings we drive onward with that miraculous vitality that creates our precarious habitations in the past and the future.[54]

Murdoch's concern as a philosopher is to depict the possibility of hope, not despair, and we see this with the transformative power of texts such as *The Sovereignty of Good*, as well as many of her novels.

Style and Value in the Modern Novel

Sartre uses a highly evocative style of imagery to describe exaggerated states of despair: this is an eidetic approach, i.e., he conjures up a convincing, intense world of powerful sensory input. Then he challenges the accuracy of our perceptions by telling us *we* are deceived and *he* can therefore tell us what to think. He "has recommended moral concern as a recipe for good writing" yet we will see how, for Murdoch, *he* deceives *us*.[55] There is a flickering that gives our perceptions some febrile sense of the complexity of life; I close my eyes briefly and reality is switched off, I open them and there is something there that is in fact nothing at all. Sartre depicts this feverish flickering through Roquentin, who experiences disorientation at the existential complexity of trying to make meaning through the objects in his daily life. By contrast Murdoch develops a world for us in *her* novels, of perception as a moral discipline and description as a moral obligation:

> If we attempted to describe this room our descriptions would naturally carry all sorts of values. Value is only artificially and with difficulty expelled from language for scientific purposes. So the novelist is revealing his values by any sort of writing which he may do. He is particularly bound to make moral judgements in so far as his subject matter is the behaviour of human beings.[56]

In "The Sublime and the Beautiful Revisited," Murdoch tells us about her evolving style as a novelist by showing us her approach to Sartre's philosophy: she contextualizes him within the modern development in the novel form that loses its impact by trying too hard to be didactic.[57] She cites, as she has done since the early 1950s, the power that ordinary language philosophy exerts over language in what she regards as a futile attempt to cure it of its polysemic messiness. Yet for Murdoch, Sartre also represents something even worse; totalitarian man as the neurotic who seeks to cure himself by developing a myth about himself, when in fact he knows that there is no cure for his condition because a cure requires belief in something beyond the immediate situation and is therefore disallowed. In his trilogy *The Roads to Freedom* the cure is communism, yet the sickness seems too deep: his trilogy is unfinished and flawed, peopled by characters who represent impossibly abstract ideals, and do not seem believable. Sartre really is trapped, wedged, stuck between Kantian antinomies of attempting to offer a moral solution through combining emotion (revolutionary acts) and reason (the belief in theory) and failing; yet this myth of the solitary moral agent remains fascinating for us, perhaps precisely because there is no solution. We cannot act better than we do, because we are trapped by circumstances, even if we reject "bad faith" at an intellectual level. We are individuals enamored of the modern novel, the personal drama that features us in the starring role, often as the victim of destiny or Sartre's favorite "romantic figure of the gratuitous loser."[58]

ORDINARY LANGUAGE MAN AND TOTALITARIAN MAN

Murdoch describes the individualism of the modern novel as a seductive form that we embrace in spite of ourselves, "the triumph of neurosis, the triumph of myth as a solipsistic form."[59] We are seduced by such writing, whether we resist or not, and thereby relinquish the possibility of standing back and understanding the difficulties that underlie this phenomenon, which are mirrored in Sartre's existentialism and Wittgenstein's (linguistic) empiricism.[60] Murdoch believes that we identify quite closely with these characters whom she names Totalitarian Man (Sartre) and Ordinary Language Man (Wittgenstein), despite the existence of those who criticize them and to whom we should pay even more attention. We may ask ourselves why we find the work of Sartre and Wittgenstein, for example, so attractive? Murdoch believes regretfully that we identify with the clear, well organized and organizing ideas of Totalitarian Man and Ordinary Language Man, rather than with those of their critics such as Marcel or Weil, whose ideas are more productive yet also more ambivalent and morally demanding and in whom we do not see ourselves reflected ("they do not at all represent what we take ourselves to be").[61]

Murdoch contrasts the open tolerance of the great nineteenth century novels of Tolstoy and others, teeming with life, with the modern novel that is often a clear, precise and well organized myth-like creation, beautiful in its own way yet constrained by its didactic intent, like Camus' *The Stranger*, or Sartre's *Nausea*.[62] A key characteristic of such novels is the attempt by their authors to manage, control and reduce contingency, whereas Murdoch relishes the fecundity of chance events, as shown for example in the ways her characters meet and fall in and out of love (*Bruno's Dream* and *The Book and The Brotherhood* show this well). Denial of contingency, of chance, of the unexpected, entails denial of new meanings and condemns us to passive acceptance of the other person's viewpoint, feared by Sartre as unavoidable. The first person male narrator in six of Murdoch's novels is a challenge to this, a potent amalgam of several "otherings": we are not allowed to read the book as ourselves and we are being told what to think about how we feel and what is of value. She then goes beyond Sartre, urging us to detect the discrepancies that appear between our views and those of the male voice.[63]

Again, Murdoch analyses Sartre through her philosophy. If we return to her 1950 essay about Sartre's outline of a theory of emotions, Murdoch clarifies her challenge to his ideas about emotion and rationality by critiquing his two theories, as she describes them; one theory is that emotion is purposive. My emotions are targeted towards achieving certain goals. The other theory is that we are conscious of this purposiveness, i.e., I know what I want and I believe that I know how to get it. Hence Sartre believes that we know what our emotions are and we also know what these emotions mean, i.e., we can be rational about our emotions.[64] Murdoch reminds us that Sartre rejected psychoanalytic models of repressed thought, insisting that "what occurs in the consciousness ... can receive its explanation only from the consciousness."[65] She sees Sartre as using a Cartesian model of perception, with the cogito being unreflective and focused upon perception as a reliable form of knowledge.

Again, Murdoch detects a problem in that Sartre is arguing that emotions are stable and measurable and at least theoretically open to rational analysis: as Dosse words it in his excellent *History of Structuralism,* "Sartrean existentialism, [was] articulated around the notion of a constituent, transcendental, omnipotent, and completely abstract subject from which everything and all meaning proceeded."[66] For Murdoch, by contrast, emotions are complex, changeable, reciprocal and often impossible to understand, yet by no means necessarily coated with Sartre's slime.

Moreover she detects a flaw internal to Sartre's own argument; the Sartrean assertion that emotions are fixed is absolutely incompatible with his related assertion that he is able to separate conscious activities from the reflective activities that attribute values to what we perceive. I believe we see this in Sartre's discussion of gluey viscous matter in *Being and Nothingness.* With nearly forty years between her two books, in *Sartre: Romantic Rationalist* and in *Metaphysics as a Guide to Morals* she discusses his famous section on gluey viscosity, sliminess, from *Being and Nothingness.*[67] Barnes, the translator of *Being and Nothingness,* gives us 'slime" rather than viscosity. Sartre discusses the psychic nature of the slimy as being "identical with the symbolic value which the slimy has in relation to being-in-itself."[68] We lose something in translation with Barnes" use of the term slime—closer is the gluey stickiness of refusing to separate oneself from one's situation in order to act well for oneself and for others. Murdoch read *Being and Nothingness* in French and her rendition of *visqueux* as gluey gunge in which we become trapped in bad faith, defies possible translation problems. We see by this argument how prescriptive Sartre can be; he can argue that the essence of meaning is there clearly to be seen, as with the unattractive, indeed repellent nature of gooey substance, from which even infants recoil, he tells us.[69] By focusing in such great detail on a phenomenon that he tells us is both natural and universally identified as abhorrent, Sartre is determined to show us that "sliminess" is not just an example after all; it represents the aberrant core to our being. Indeed he proposes as much; "In its own way it symbolizes being: that is, as long as the contact with the slimy endures, everything takes place for us as if sliminess were the meaning of the entire world."[70] Being stuck in glue is reality: one way of interpreting this is that the world is real, we are stuck, glued into our little bit of the world and hence we manifest bad faith. He has made glue into an image of reality that is melodramatic, hyperbolic and negative.[71]

In Chapter 4 of *Sartre: Romantic Rationalist* Murdoch analyses Sartre's understanding of value: by contract with gunge it is something special and must not be seen as part of daily humdrum life, or else "the contingency of being kills the value."[72] The special nature of value is to be found in a perfectly balanced combination of being one's daily self (*être-en-soi*) and also being completely stable in one's conscious mind (*être-pour-soi*). This is being *en-soi-pour-soi* and is clearly unattainable. Thus, fixing gluey viscosity as the core of human existence is part of Sartre's attempt to create a *total* picture of the broken totality of the world, and it must fail, not least because Sartre knows (and has told us through Kant) that there is no total picture available. Having a sense of value means knowing that value is unattainable, thereby engendering a sense of *lack*.[73] Murdoch does not mind so much about such failure, as she sees failure as an inevitable component of all philosophical endeavors. What she minds about is what she calls "a sort of logical loneliness" in which for Sartre "meaning is suddenly seen as withdrawn not from a world of objective values, but from physical objects themselves."[74] Murdoch sees this reflected in Sartre's use of melodramatic language which alienates the reader from their experience of reading Sartre's novels, and which constitutes, for Murdoch, an abnegation of responsibility on Sartre's part.

Denying the Dying Child

By 1992, in *Metaphysics as a Guide to Morals*, we read a damning indictment of Sartre: according to the mature Murdoch it may be impossible for us, through Sartre, to understand ourselves, because if we read *Nausea* we experience the "horror of those who can no longer love or attend to or even really see the contingent, and fear it as a threat to their imaginary freedom and self-reading authenticity."[75] Conradi sees this as a demonic Sartre, and certainly Murdoch condemns Sartre for his hyperbolic, narcissistic prose. Her criticism goes beyond stylistic considerations, because she uses critique about style to show us how Sartre uses his moral positions in literature.

To help me here I enlist the work of Toril Moi with her discussion of Sartre and Beauvoir, one of the most famous couples in modern western literature, and their contrasting view of the value of literature: in 1964 Sartre commented, regarding the impending publication of his autobiographical text *Words* that "faced with a dying child, *Nausea* isn't worth much."[76] Moi contrasts this with Beauvoir's statement at around the same time, in *Force of Circumstance*, that "I am an intellectual, I take words and the truth to be of value."[77] Moi uses the work and vocabulary of Stanley Cavell on skepticism to propose that Sartre insists upon taking the risk: being "melodramatic" in a counterproductive way, as opposed to the more moderate intent of Beauvoir's "ordinary" register. Firstly Moi sees Sartre's use of melodramatic style as a possibly honorable attempt to expose the fantasy of the omnipotence of writing, an attempt which insists upon believing either that literature is enormously powerful, or absolutely worthless: with his denial of its value "the affect has shifted, from exuberant jubilation at the omnipotence of writing to abject disappointment and guilt at the failure of writing."[78]

Secondly however, as Moi points out, Sartre's statement is a negation, and can even be construed in a Freudian sense of repression, although Sartre would reject any psychoanalytical analysis. Moi feels that Sartre risks irreparable damage to his political aspirations, by setting up excessive expectations that he then destroys—what good can I do a dying child, just by writing? In fact, what good *can* I do, by the power of words, to comfort others and to survive grief? This is consistent with Cavell's work in *Contesting Tears* about the use of skepticism as a form of metaphysical thinking that takes upon itself a form of deterministic hubris: after all, we should perhaps ask ourselves; "how do you know that you are *not* helping a child?"[79] Moi's analysis of Sartre's use of negation resonates with Murdoch's views about his extreme hopes that are denied because they are unrealistic and which therefore then need to be destroyed, in his pessimistic version of dialectical contrasts. This may infect the reader with depression, *as if* the novel were suffused with immorality. Murdoch has pointed out to us already that Sartre's aspirations are both so high and so low that he makes three mistakes that are common in philosophy; we cannot make emotions empirically clear and stable, we must constantly try to discuss what we mean by value and truth and we must try to balance some sort of holistic understanding with empirical evidence.[80] Sartre's extreme form of negation creates a vacuum and plays a crucial rôle in negating the possibility of all three. I will go even further and argue that this is a negation of the Other; Sartre seems to be denying the child help, so that in this case his hyperbolic excesses negate the dying child, and the death of its needs and its wishes, the child in all of us.

Denial of the Other Person

To address such a shocking assertion we need now to review Sartre's idea of human existence as emptiness poised between two inaccessible totalities. Sartre describes the reciprocity of denial; "the Other on principle denies that he is I as I deny that I am he."[81] Murdoch sees the consequence of this in *Sartre's Critique of Dialectical Reason*, which she finds paradoxical as a book; she sees it as lacking in morality, and without morality therefore its language is destructive, because, from her point of view "almost all our language is value language."[82] She finds value concealed therein, however, namely the concept of a world-dominating will, which she rejects as a response to Marxism and to the human condition. At a broader social level this plays itself out as a state of denial that measures itself by its own standards because it seems to define itself in denial:

> The ambiguity of all past and present morality is that it makes its appearance in a world of exploitation and oppression, a state of negation (of humanity) which morality then negates. Morality is thus a pseudo-positive, being a negation of a negation.[83]

Since Hegel, this has become much more dominant — negation has become the core idea that defines us; and we see an extreme and depressingly circular form of this in Sartre, for whom freedom is created by the nothingness that gives me freedom to act.[84] Existential negation of a Sartrean sort appears first as a difference between me and another, then as a difference internal to me, then as a sad finitude, a blocking of possibilities, defeatism.[85]

Taking this negation to an irrevocable depth of negativity would preclude affirmation, and this is what Sartre chooses; his versions of the negative are doubt, anguish, rejection of the other and validation of negative psychological states, as in Kierkegaard. For Sartre, reflection, inwardness is a form of negation because it is the same as refusing to act. Activism is the key. One of the reasons for Sartre's popularity during and after the Second World War was his rejection of reflection upon the meanings he and his fellow French inherited from their past.[86] It was seen as necessary to abolish the truths of the past; the war, collaboration, the inheritance of loss. However, what can we then fall back on? Is there nothing left to believe in? Murdoch describes how Sartre writes about "the situation of a being who, deprived of general truths, is tormented by absolute aspiration," i.e., the vain hope of finding worthwhile meaning. Murdoch finds here the three characteristics of existentialism discussed earlier; first she believes that Sartre would like to overcome the Cartesian mind-body split, which Merleau-Ponty attempted; secondly Sartre saw, like Husserl in his late works, that this is impossible, and thirdly he depended a great deal on the concept of the Other as alien.[87] However, in all this he is recognizable as a product of the Romantic tradition, and therefore in that sense closer to Murdoch's affections than Marcel.

In returning to Marcel, we note that by 1992, Marcel hardly merits a mention, and Murdoch decries the utility of the Marcelian idea that moral problems can be dissolved in a relationship with God.[88] Yet she is always much more Marcelian than Sartrean, filling her novels with the joy and the mystery of life and nature. She describes how the good man is the one who "nothing himself, lets other things be through him," through the "continual expelling of oneself from the matter in hand."[89] This is an insoluble problem, that goodness is a form of negation *of the self* that is unselfing, self-effacement. Goodness as negation, as self-effacement is not compatible with a plot line as it provides no spectacle or story but a negation of the self as a manifestation of goodness, an avoidance of melodrama or hyperbole. Arthur in *The Word Child*, Tallis in *A Fairly Honourable Defeat* and Bledyard in *The Sandcastle* are good characters who are inarticulate and who must therefore remain minor. She cannot write like Marcel or express arguments like Bledyard and be confident that we will continue to read, because goodness can seem inarticulate or lacking in challenge or both.

Murdoch is well aware of this problem, arguing that we are more attracted to Sartre and Wittgenstein than to Marcel or Weil. Sartre and Wittgenstein present an exaggerated negation of depth; this manifests itself as a force that develops a positive charge, energy through narcissistic, solipsistic myth making, and linguistic posturing. Thus we find Murdoch's Ordinary Language man (Wittgenstein) and Totalitarian Man (Sartre) melodramatic and irresistible. In her philosophical writings she can analyze this phenomenon yet not easily refute it, even though it has been with her since she first met Sartre in 1945: Conradi shows Murdoch identifying the demonic in Sartre as early as 1947.[90] In her novels she can get much closer than is possible in philosophical writings, to challenging our narcissism and suggesting the strengths of unselfing, by creating characters who seem free to act despite plots that create chaotic situations driven by chance occurrences; "contingency must be defended for it is the essence of personality."[91]

Excesses in Style and Socialism

Iris Murdoch, like Sartre, was a novelist, playwright, philosopher, political commentator, critic and teacher. Here I have studied Murdoch *through* her study of Sartre in order to gain valuable insights into the stylistic manifestations of negative thought: *negativity, denial, lack, loss* and *nothingness*. Two major phenomena in Sartre's work remain a focus for Murdoch up to her writing of the new introduction for *Sartre: Romantic Rationalist* in 1987, because she regards these two phenomena as highly significant for Sartre's moral profile. Sartre denies Kant's antinomies, and also soars above and beyond them into an exaggeratedly idealistic zone of socialist hopefulness. Yet this sense in which Sartre can also be interpreted as going further than Kant may be a useful form of human rights: existentialism is humanism and if I will freedom for myself, I will it for others. Murdoch is not deceived by Sartre's bad boy image; he does *not* negate the needs of the dying child, but he must be challenged for the use of such imagery, because Murdoch believes that it violates the morality of literary style and the writer's responsibility to the reader.

She sees his intensely moral vision and she makes clear his admiration for socialism, which she believes he preferred to Marxism:

> Value is produced at the level of basic praxis [that is, in Sartrean Marxism, purposive consciousness...]. Thus, in the Soviet Union, moralistic talk, the utterance as values of moral generalities common to all, should not conceal or be confused with the collective praxis which is creating socialist society.[92]

After her own initial enthusiasm, Murdoch left her Marxism behind by the mid 1940s and was profoundly shocked when communism betrayed socialist ideals in the Russian 1956 invasion of Hungary. Sartre became, if anything, more devoted to the socialist cause, whilst also regretting the injustices of Soviet imperial power. Birchall shows us that Sartre was more in sympathy with the anti–Stalinists than he chose to reveal, perhaps because of the dominance of Stalinist thought within the French communist party.[93]

The dominance of Stalinists after the Second World War is still debated in French intellectual circles, as Badiou demonstrates in 2007.[94] Murdoch chooses not to analyze the complex conflicts within French communism, and definitely sees Sartre's socialism as a manifestation of much more than a political predilection. She argues that one should neither polarize activism and inwardness nor feel that "one is bound to swallow the other."[95] To Murdoch, Sartre attempted in vain to combine Kantian antinomies with Hegelian totalization and to attempt, against the odds, the swallowing up of his Sartrean idealism within Sartrean socialism. Murdoch finds Sartre's political struggles interesting (as we see in *Sartre: Romantic Rationalist*). She also asserts in "The Sublime and the Beautiful Revisited" that his literary charms must be analyzed, unlike those of Marcel, whose writings are more morally interesting yet less stylistically attractive and therefore less emotionally moving. She herself is a sort of existentialist, more along the lines of Marcel's moral existentialism and perhaps, as Conradi believes, both her novels and her philosophical writings reflect her desire to engage with Sartre (and others) in penance for her youthful political naivety.[96]

She challenges Sartrean existentialism through her novels, through willful characters like Carel in *The Time of The Angels,* Austin in *An Accidental Man* and Julius in *A Fairly Honourable Defeat*.[97] Murdoch takes Sartre's negativity and populates his "void at the centre" with characters that play out the tension between *his* negativity and *her* love of life.[98] She creates many inarticulate yet good characters, reminiscent perhaps of Gabriel Marcel: Arthur in *A Word Child,* Tallis in *A Fairly Honourable Defeat,* and Bledyard in *The Sandcastle.* Through these characters she sees Sartre's nothingness as "more like an exciting springboard than a void."[99] She responds positively to his critique of the horrors of the century while seeing his use of hyperbole as a denial of the moral importance of perception, imagination, consciousness and their representation in literature. She believes that his stylistic excesses also distort the impact and reduce the importance of his work.[100] As a philosopher she cannot deal head-on with Sartre's negation because he refuses love and happiness and thus disallows their counterpart, negation and nothingness. As a novelist she provides a polysemy of characters who create challenges to Sartre's negation and to his exaggerated gestures and hyperbolic emphasis on nothingness. As a philosopher she also gives us the transformative power of texts like *The Sovereignty of Good.* Sartre's powerful language and his disclaimers, his colorful negation of so much that gives purpose (including love), must also be dealt with through her novels, as Sartre's arguments are too attractive to be fully dismantled in philosophical language. Only by attending carefully to Murdoch's writings will we appreciate what is often passed over in critical studies of Sartre. Dialogue is more effective than the interior monologue and Murdoch's characters debate, each with the other, in the tradition of Plato and Socrates. Murdoch's novels bring us to our own inwardness in the active mode created by her adventurous plots. Her philosophy is her reflective education, her novels are her existential acts and her language is her moral compass.

NOTES

1. Murdoch, 1987, 84, 138. I will refer to the 1987 Chatto and Windus edition, as it contains the extensive introduction that Murdoch wrote for this edition. She dedicated the 1954 edition to Raymond Queneau (1903–1976); they met in 1946 and she was strongly influenced by his work — Conradi, 2001, 231–33. Sartre (Jean-Paul Sartre 1905–1980) had written the following major texts by the time she wrote *Sartre, Romantic Rationalist*: *Transcendence of the Ego* (1938); *Nausea* (1938); *Being and Nothingness* (1943); *The Roads to Freedom* trilogy (1945–49); *Baudelaire, Genet* (1952).
2. Murdoch, 2003, x–xv. Malcolm Bowie, in his introduction to the novel, exemplifies excessive use of adjectives etc.
3. Murdoch, 1987, *Sartre*, 79, 102.
4. Murdoch, 1953, 10.
5. Murdoch, 1987, *Sartre*, 111–12.
6. *Ibid.*, 14–21.
7. *Ibid.*, 15.
8. I draw upon her essays in *Existentialists and Mystics* e.g., 1950 "Sartre's The Emotions"; 1953 *Sartre, Romantic Rationalist*; 1957 "Hegel In Modern Dress"; 1959 "The Sublime and the Beautiful Revisited"; 1987 *Sartre, Romantic Rationalist* with extensive *Introduction* by Murdoch; and 1992 *Metaphysics as a Guide to Morals*.
9. Dosse, 1998; Murdoch, 1992, 112. Existentialism was a dominant part of the Continental philosophy scene until it was usurped by structuralism.
10. Scruton, 1994, 459.
11. Murdoch, 1987, *Sartre*, 25–38.
12. Another important reason for the underestimation is the subtlety of her approach; for example she is often considered to have been enthusiastic about Sartre early on and then to have become disenchanted (Conradi, 2001, 270–72). Conradi detects a more positive early view of Sartre in 1953, less so by 1957, even less so in 1987 and in 1992. Clearly this is partly true, yet I believe she had a nuanced view of Sartre from 1953 on, insisting upon her right to admire certain aspects of his work while criticizing others.
13. Conradi, 2001, 215–16.
14. *Ibid.*, 76–77.
15. Murdoch, 1997, Chatto, 122; Diamond in Antonaccio and Schweiker, 1996; Stephen Mulhall "Misplacing freedom, displacing the imagination: Cavell and Murdoch on the fact/value distinction" in O'Hare, 2000.
16. Paul Ricoeur (1913–2005), Alison Scott-Baumann, 2009, *Ricoeur and the Hermeneutics of Suspicion* (New York, London: Continuum). We know that Murdoch read at least two of Ricoeur's major texts and he taught courses on Sartre at the Sorbonne (1957–64). Conradi tells us that in 1964–65 Murdoch was teaching tutorials on Sartre, Marcel and others (Conradi, 2001, 472).
17. *La Métaphore Vive* (1975) and *The Conflict of Interpretations* (1974), both in the Murdoch Archives. Murdoch read and marked these, which are two of Ricoeur's most significant texts.
18. Ricoeur, 1967, 208.
19. Maurice Merleau Ponty (1980–1961).
20. Murdoch, 1992, Chatto, 463.
21. Whereas the world was seen as constantly in flux by Heraclitus, Parmenides proposed a totalizing vision; all is one and we cannot discuss what "is not." In fact it was Plotinus, as the leading Neo-Platonist, who exaggerated these differences between Heraclitus and Parmenides and then offered his own dialectical model that argued for both positions (Scott-Baumann, work in progress, on *Ricoeur and the Negation of Happiness*).
22. Murdoch, 1997, Chatto, 171–186.
23. Murdoch, 1992, Chatto, 154–55.

24. Murdoch, 1987, *Sartre*, 11; 1997, Chatto, 271.
25. Murdoch, 1987, *Sartre*, 132, 55.
26. Murdoch, 1997, Chatto, 104.
27. Gabriel Marcel (1889–1973), often called a Christian existentialist, a term he did not accept, although he was both Christian and existentialist. He influenced Ricoeur.
28. Murdoch, 1997, Chatto, 74.
29. *Ibid.*, 125–29. Marcel, 1950.
30. *Ibid.*, 127.
31. Conradi, 2001, 270.
32. Murdoch, 1987, *Sartre*, 60–61, 85.
33. Murdoch, 1997, Chatto, 136. Her approach resonates with that of Ricoeur and Marcel.
34. *Ibid.*, 136; 1987, *Sartre*, 84, 80.
35. Murdoch, 1997, Chatto, 136.
36. Paul Ricoeur addresses these tensions with gritty yet compassionate suspicion and Murdoch develops narrative devices using metaphor and parable to deal with the contrasts.
37. Murdoch, 1987, *Sartre*, 101.
38. Birchall, 2004, 7.
39. Murdoch, 1997, 130–145. This is a development of part of Kant's assertion that we perceive the world in ways that are peculiar to each one of us and not objective and Sartre sees this as a great contribution that Husserl develops. For Husserl, being at the centre of the perceptual world is neither narcissistic nor negative. Murdoch comments in *Sartre. Romantic Rationalist* how "the vision of the phenomenologist has something in common with that of the poet and painter," and that Sartre invites us to "rediscover our vision" and look more carefully (Murdoch 1987, *Sartre*, 47).
40. Conradi, 2001, 356. Others have written about these aspects of Murdoch the writer, e.g., Antonaccio, Byatt, Conradi, Nichol and Rowe.
41. Raymond Williams makes a similar comment about Sartre's version of Antigone in *Les Mouches*, which he describes as made more interesting as a sort of case study of how one can change the plot, rather than the drama having an intrinsic effect: "the legend is not so much a form as a case. The philosophical interest is indeed considerable, but the play is an example of a gain in interest at the expense of intensity" (Williams, 1964, 221; Murdoch, 1987, 60).
42. Murdoch, 1997, Chatto, 277.
43. *Ibid.*, 278.
44. Murdoch, 1987, *Sartre*, 81, 84, 86.
45. *Ibid.*, 57, 59, 60, 86.
46. Murdoch, 2002, *Under*.
47. Murdoch, 1987, *Sartre*, 88, 78.
48. Murdoch, 1997, Chatto, 153.
49. *Ibid.*, 280.
50. Murdoch, 1987, *Sartre*, 51.
51. *Ibid.*, 49. Murdoch tells us that this is only one interpretation of Sartre's gluey gunge. A.S. Byatt, 1994: Byatt analyzes Murdoch's "deliberate parallel" of Sartre's Roquentin through Jake.
52. *Ibid.*, 44. Sartre, *Nausea*, 1938, 252.
53. Conradi, 2001, 384. Murdoch (1997, 285) uses the term "contingent" to mean both that which may or may not take place, and that which happens to be so without there being any need for it. Both meanings have a dangerous free-playing quality of the unpredictable and the inexplicable, which she believes must be defended, for contingency "is the essence of personality."
54. Murdoch, 2002, *Under*, 275.
55. Murdoch, 1987, *Sartre*, 84.
56. Murdoch, 1997, Chatto, 27.
57. Byatt 1994, 63. Byatt provides a counter example, where Murdoch, in *The Flight from the Enchanter* shows Rosa's need to live in a complex and messy world that must include other people.
58. Murdoch, 1992, 154.
59. Murdoch, 1997, Chatto, 29.
60. *Ibid.*, 267.
61. *Ibid.*, 270.

62. *Ibid.*, 279.
63. Byatt, 1994, 268–69. Two of the other first person male narrated novels are *A Severed Head* and *A Word Child*. We, the readers, are invited to be this other, this male voice, and then to use this voice for discussing the other characters, so the othering takes an existentialist turn. The reader becomes another person discussing others, and we are then also made aware of the narrowness of our vision as this male voice. As A.S. Byatt shows us, both *Under the Net* and *The Black Prince* are narrated by the first person male voice and she argues that Murdoch uses this device when she is "particularly concerned with illusion, partial understanding and self-deception."
64. Murdoch, 1997, Chatto, 117–18.
65. Murdoch, 1987, *Sartre*, 54.
66. Dosse, 1997 Vol. 1, 383.
67. Murdoch, 1987, *Sartre*, 91ff; Sartre, 1943, 624ff; Murdoch, 1992, Chatto, 156.
68. Sartre, 1943, 626.
69. *Ibid.*, 626.
70. *Ibid.*, 627.
71. Ricoeur demonstrates how both Sartre and Ryle insist upon giving more emphasis to Kant's reproductive imagination, while avoiding the problem of productive imagination: Sartre wants us to think that he is telling us how it is when in fact he is *creating* certain irresistible images. See Ricoeur in Schilpp, 1977, 167–178.
72. Murdoch, 1987, *Sartre*, 93.
73. *Ibid.*, 93.
74. *Ibid.*, 107.
75. Murdoch, 1997, Chatto, 377.
76. T. Moi, 2002, 195; Article in *Le Monde* 18 April 1964, "En face d'un enfant qui meurt, La Nausée ne fait pas le poids"; Interview with Jacqueline Piatier entitled "Jean Paul Sartres' explique sur *Les Mots*."
77. Beauvoir, 1987, 378.
78. Moi, 2002, 183.
79. Cavell, 1996.
80. Murdoch, 1997, Chatto, 120–121.
81. Sartre, 1943, 644.
82. Murdoch, 1987, *Sartre*, 32.
83. *Ibid.*, 34.
84. Sartre, 2003, 325–26.
85. Ricoeur, 1986, 138.
86. Murdoch, 1987, *Sartre*, 135.
87. *Ibid.*, 136.
88. Murdoch, 1992, Chatto, 186.
89. Murdoch, 1997, Chatto, 283–84.
90. Conradi, 2001, 269–72.
91. Murdoch, 1997, Chatto, 285.
92. Murdoch, 1987, *Sartre*, 34.
93. Birchall, 2004.
94. Badiou, 2007.
95. Murdoch, 1992, Chatto, 362.
96. Conradi, 2001, 597.
97. Murdoch, 1992, Chatto, 266.
98. Murdoch, 1987, *Sartre*, 85.
99. *Ibid.*, 60–61, 85; 1992, 499.
100. *Ibid.*, 38.

9

Suffering and Contentment

Tony Milligan

We want to avoid suffering and try to avoid it. We want to be happy and try to be happy, even if this is not all that we want and try to secure, and even if our efforts are not always crowned with success. These familiar concerns with contentment radiate from Iris Murdoch's novels. They depict, with some regularity, the pointlessness of various forms of self-inflicted suffering. On this matter, there is an overlap between her two kinds of writing. She shows a concern to secure contentment in the philosophical texts just as she does in the novels.[1] This is how the philosophical texts *feel* as you read them. This is their overall *tone*.[2] They invite the reader to find ways out of the familiar rat-runs inside which egocentricity can trap us. They invite us to a better and, we may at least hope, more contented way of life.

However, there is a gap between this overall tone of the philosophical writings and their explicit normative force. They advocate a way of living (unselfing) within which contentment has no clearly defined role. In what follows, I will focus primarily upon the philosophical texts and more occasionally draw from the novels. Section one will set out the marginalization of contentment within the former and argue that Murdoch has the aspiration to place a commitment to contentment within her philosophical ethic but little scope to do so. Section two will suggest that this problem results, at least in part, from her conception of unselfing as a distinctive mode of suffering and not as a comprehensive way out of suffering. Section three will argue that making sense of unselfing in this way has a number of advantages. It is, for example, a corrective to any overemphasis upon Murdoch's proximity to Buddhism and it rules out any conception of unselfing as an exercise in escaping from familiar forms of human vulnerability. The concluding section will set out the way in which unselfing, understood as a mode of suffering that does not exclude a concern for contentment, allows us to give content to the concept of moral courage. (This is a virtue of some relevance to our times.)

The Marginalization of Contentment

Consider the following scenario drawn from Murdoch's novel *The Sandcastle*. Mor, a middle-aged teacher, is about to leave his family and run off with a young, attractive and talented artist called Rain Carter. He is diligently intercepted by the sympathetically-portrayed but puritanical art master Bledyard and the following exchange takes place. Bledyard points out that Mor is "deeply bound" to his wife and children, and "deeply rooted" in his own life. "Perhaps that life will hold you in spite of yourself. But if you break these bonds you destroy a part of the world." Mor, who is suddenly and uncharacteristically assertive, is ready to bite this particular bullet. "Possibly," he replies, "but I might then build another part." Murdoch credits Mor with enough sense to recognize that these are winged words. In the face of Bledyard's comments, they sound "empty and trivial" even to the speaker. But he is carried forward by his own momentum. "And how can you, an outsider, assess the value of these bonds, as you call them, in terms of happiness?" Bledyard is puzzled. He has mentioned nothing of the sort. "Happiness?" he replies. "What has happiness got to do with it? Do you imagine that you or anyone, has some sort of right to happiness? That idea is a poor guide."[3]

In this exchange, who speaks for Murdoch? It is not obvious that either character does. She does not use her novels as a direct means of instruction in moral philosophy. Instead, there is a sense in which these are the kinds of comments that characters like Mor and Bledyard would make in circumstances of just this sort. Simply because Bledyard is portrayed sympathetically, and allowed to state some home truths about Mor's blinkered vision gives us no reason to assume that Murdoch is on the side of the puritans.[4] What might, however, tempt us to align her more closely with Bledyard is the disturbingly tagged-on quality of the treatment given to contentment in Murdoch's philosophical texts. You will not find a concern for contentment explicitly written into *The Sovereignty of Good*. And even if we assume that the happiness of *others* is important, we may not obviously assume that the happiness of *self* has a similar standing. Amid repeated castigations of the oversized and relentless ego, the reader of the *Sovereignty* is given no direct guidance on this matter.

The desirability of contentment is not directly addressed in the philosophical texts until Murdoch takes steps, in the 1970s, to downplay and distance herself from what she regards as the more puritanical side of Plato. And even then, an explicit acknowledgement of the importance of being contented has to make its way in from the periphery of her texts. Her Platonic dialogue on "Art and Eros" ends with Plato announcing that he is "so happy" and Socrates (who is depicted as an anti-puritanical rod for Plato's back) reciprocates by announcing that he is "so glad." Similarly, at the conclusion of the companion dialogue, *Above the Gods*, the character Acastos abruptly resolves, "Anyway, let's be happy," but in doing so he identifies with a concern for happiness which puts into question its relation to what has gone before. Concern for happiness is introduced as something extraneous to and apparently separate from the main body of deliberations.[5]

It is not until her final work of synthesis, *Metaphysics as a Guide to Morals*, that Murdoch's concern for contentment is allowed to move at least some way in from the concluding margins. Yet even in the latter there is a continuing emphasis upon its separateness. The *Metaphysics* is the first of Murdoch's philosophical texts to provide a clear-cut statement of the kind of commitment that readers of her interviews may be all too familiar with. "Human beings love each other, in sex, in friendship, and love and cherish other beings, humans, animals, plants, stones. Imagination and art are in all of this, and the quest for happiness and the promotion of happiness."[6] Those who have plunged into the film *Iris* may recognize these words as an opening testament, the assumption of the film being that this solitary assertion is characteristic of her philosophical standpoint.[7] And in a sense it is, but it is not characteristic of the philosophical texts. Be that as it may, even in the *Metaphysics*, where contentment/happiness is clearly in evidence, it is still a separate concern, something that may lead us to say *anyway, remember that happiness is important*, or *don't lose sight of it*.

The way in which this is done in the *Metaphysics* is by giving happiness an *axiomatic* status. Axioms in this sense are principles that are not inferentially dependent upon other claims. A specification of some or other right would be one example of an axiom. A religious commandment would be another. We have a *prima facie* reason for acting upon them but they may clash with other axioms or with other non-axiomatic considerations. Under such circumstances they may be overruled. As such, they are independent but defeasible. This defeasibility is built into Murdoch's own examples of axioms: happiness, justice (as primarily retribution) and, more generally, rights. These are the kinds of independent considerations that we play off against each other and do not always expect to be simultaneously satisfied. The action that secures someone's rights may impact negatively upon another person's happiness, and vice versa. Similarly, justice is not always served by trying to please people, "we all understand the importance of happiness. It is *a*, not necessarily final, argument against doing something to someone, that it will reduce his happiness."[8] Such judgments about trading off justice, rights and happiness against each other may be taken to rely, as so much does in Murdoch, upon good moral vision, and often there will be no hard or fast rules about which consideration should triumph.

It is tempting to follow Peter Conradi and collapse the distinction between these kinds of axioms and duties but Murdoch does not do so. Perhaps miserable people make others miserable while contentment keeps us ticking over in a way that allows us to be of service to others, but Murdoch does *not* treat a concern for happiness in this dutiful way.[9] Nor does a duty of contentment look like the *dominant* form that our concern for happiness could take. That is not to say that there is no such duty. In some localized contexts, such as that of lone or professional careers (such as nurses), there may be a good case for saying that a career ought to look after their own needs and that they have a duty to do so.[10] In other contexts the idea of a duty of contentment seems at least more strained. It is not obvious that anyone should or could play golf or wear party hats primarily out of duty. Perhaps there are intermediate cases. Listening to jazz, or reading Shakespeare look like things that one might initially do out of duty (because one *ought* to cultivate certain special kinds of enjoyment) but acting out of such a duty looks suspiciously like a provisional step towards less strained forms of enjoyment.[11] Whatever role a duty of contentment might play in legitimating our human concern for, and pursuit of, happiness it is not obviously in a position to do all or even most of the work. The fact that an act is a likely source of contentment seems more like a stand-alone reason for certain kinds of actions that needs no appeal to a sense of duty.

For Murdoch, axiomatic concern for happiness is not the same as a duty of any sort. The *Metaphysics* acknowledges the obviousness of both axioms and duties but not their equivalence: "The idea of duty is almost as familiar to us as the idea of happiness. It is perhaps, after the pursuit of happiness, the most evident fact in human life."[12] In this comparison, Murdoch tries to give each separate concern its due.

What we can say about an axiomatic concern for happiness is that, from a Murdochian point of view, it must be a proper part of the moral domain. That is to say, it must fall within the bounds of what is morally worthwhile and cannot be extraneous to the moral life. It cannot be an additional, extra-moral or amoral concern because Murdoch does not allow for any partitioning between the moral domain and anything else. We do not get time off for amoral thought and deed.[13] "Morality is and ought to be connected with the whole of our being.... The moral life is not intermittent or specialised, it is not a peculiar separate area of our existence."[14] If Murdoch is concerned to locate a concern for happiness anywhere, she must locate it as an integral part of the moral life.

The moral life, as she conceives it, is *internally* partitioned into public concerns and private unselfing. The primary arena of moral effort is the private redemption of desire (*eros*) through the continuous effortful work of attention directed towards what is other. "What I have called Eros pictures probably a greater part of what we think of as 'the moral life'"; that is, most of our moral problems involve an orientation of our energy and our appetites."[15] However, if mistaken for the whole moral life, such an approach would justify a charge of spiritualized egocentricity. (This indicates a preoccupation with our own moral well-being rather than the well-being of the other.) Accordingly, the *Metaphysics* sets up a public sphere where moral conduct is limited by axiomatic concerns (happiness, justice, rights) and by duties which may cut across our preformed desires and which may require intermittent *efforts of will* (rather than ongoing *efforts of attention*).[16]

Political involvement, for example, is a legitimate public moral concern, sometimes even a duty, but *qua* public concern it is not governed by the same standards of perfectionism that govern private moral improvement (unselfing).[17] "Society, and so the state, *cannot* be perfected, although perfection is a proper ideal or magnet for the individual as moral agent. We set aside the idea of perfection in the one case, not in the other."[18] This multiply-partitioned moral domain is where Murdoch has to place contentment. There is nowhere else for it to go. What remains troubling is that even though this framework allows Murdoch to move a concern for contentment in from the margins, she does not explicitly move it into the arena of private moral improvement (unselfing).

> The right to be happy is both like and unlike the right to vote. In considering this kind of thinking and argument we are making a place for problems faced by individuals which, as it were "hang in the air" and are not easily assimilated into inwardness, into the continuous daily moral work of the soul fighting its way between appearance and reality and good and evil.[19]

Here, and at other points, Murdoch writes of happiness in terms of a *right* to be happy, in terms of considerations that guide conduct in the public sphere.[20]

More specifically, happiness is taken to be an objective of political life, the "natural and proper sphere for utilitarian values."[21] But happiness of this sort is morally unambitious. Even when it is not an overriding consideration, we are instructed "in legislation, always consider happiness."[22] And the kind of happiness at stake is not explicable in other terms or analytically equivalent to anything else. It is "*sui generis*" and not the same as "being virtuous."[23] It is protectively isolated from any joined-up, interconnected conception of virtue in which we can only have one virtue if we have all the others. "This lack of connection, characteristic of liberal political thinking, should be *contrasted* with the way in which private morality discovers the interconnection of the virtues."[24]

By introducing the claim that happiness is a "sui generis" liberal commitment, Murdoch helps to defuse a charge leveled at Plato, a charge that he is concerned with contentment of such a rarefied sort that he (1) downgrades any recognizable human concern and (2) opens the door to an authoritarian treatment of happiness as obedience to some politically-enforced moral norm. Any authoritarian state or nocturnal counsel that requires us to pursue the, perhaps somewhat ethereal, contentment that belongs only to the virtuous would not be a state to be admired. We do not want the citizenry to be informed, when the time is right, that by definition "the system which makes them orderly is also making them happy and good."[25] We do not want to say that in some favored state dissidents are necessarily confused, unbalanced or suffering from conceptual confusion.

Against this, Murdoch's axiomatic concern for everyday contentment of a morally unambitious sort seems well placed. "Axioms may not 'win' but must remain in consideration, a Benthamite utilitarian conception of happiness must not, as a frequently relevant feature, be eroded by high-minded considerations about quality of happiness or by theories which make happiness invisible, or of course by political objectives."[26] The state is not to make us happy by making us into virtuous individuals. "It is not the fundamental task of the state to make us good. It is the fundamental task of each person to make himself good."[27]

Subject only to the minimal constraint at the very bottom of the scale that "degraded or evil pleasure cannot count as simple or silly happiness," Murdoch's partitioning of the moral domain and assignment of a concern for unambitious happiness to the public domain helps to curtail any threat that ordinary contentment might be lost sight of or displaced by state moralism.[28] However, to accept that Murdoch's axiomatic public-sphere concern for contentment is well-placed is not to say that it is the *only* kind of concern for contentment that we can or should try to account for. Finding contentment in the right sort of things (at the right time, in the right way, and with all the usual qualifications) is surely bound up with the reconfiguration of our desires, which is largely constitutive of private moral progress.

So are there two kinds of Murdochian concern with contentment or, more plausibly, two kinds of happiness (the non-debased but morally undemanding and protected utilitarian sort and the sort secured through private virtue)? It is tempting to think so. After all, once she has put in place the protective measure of restricting political concern to morally-unambitious happiness why would she want to deny that there is also another kind of happiness that only the virtuous person secures? One consideration that might lead us to think that such a virtue-contentment nexus may be ruled out is that for Murdoch we are to be good "for nothing."[29] However, to see this as a problem may be to conflate reward and motivation. Happiness can be a reward that is recognizably desirable, but a reward that comes unsought in the pursuit of virtue.[30] To say that the virtuous person may have a special kind of contentment that is not available to others is not, automatically, to suggest that their motivation is egocentrically compromised. Although an awareness of reward may threaten to subvert proper other-centered motivation, this danger is consistent with the view that happiness of the best, fullest sort, can come unsought (and only unsought) as a by-product of other-centered concern.

Once we recognize that such a nexus between virtue and contentment need not conflict with the claim that we must be good "for nothing," there is little that can be said to decisively rule out the connection. Furthermore, there are at least occasional hints of sympathy with such a nexus as early as *The Sovereignty of Good*. When Murdoch writes about art as an analogue of the Good, and about nature as an object of attention she does so in terms of "delight," "enjoyment" and even, on one occasion of "pure delight." One of the things that art shows us is that just discernment can itself be a source of pleasure. Similarly, she writes of nature as a source of uncompromised pleasure. Brooding resentment may be lifted by encounters with other non-human creatures.[31] "It is so patently a good thing to take delight in flowers and animals that people who bring home potted plants and watch kestrels might even be surprised at the notion that these things have anything to do with virtue."[32] Although such enjoyment may be too flimsy and transitory to amount to contentment in any robust, durable sense, it is at least an indication that pleasure may be connected to effort, discernment and (explicitly) to virtue. That is to say, such pleasures are not excluded by the life of unselfing but may, perhaps, be an integral part of it.[33]

Unselfing as a Distinctive Mode of Suffering

In what follows I will not deny that it is a plausible Murdochian aspiration to retain some nexus between virtue and contentment. Indeed, I am inclined towards the view that Murdoch does see the need for some such linkage. I will aim only to draw attention to the way that she sets up unselfing in self-sacrificial terms to the exclusion of *explicit* concern for contentment. While the life of unselfing is guaranteed to be arduous, its standing as a happy life is precarious or otherwise vulnerable. Unselfish mothers of large families, saints, heroes, and hero-saints are Murdoch's preferred exemplars of moral virtue, and they are all individuals who *sacrifice* themselves for the sake of the other.[34] Indeed, sacrifice seems to be central to Murdoch's conception of the virtues in a way that separates it off from more easy going Aristotelian conceptions of virtues as necessarily rewarding. The lives of Murdoch's exemplars of virtue include denial and loss of a sort that is bound up with their goodness. The very terminology of "unselfing" may itself seem to point towards this demanding love of the other *at the expense of* the self.

At this point we need to exercise caution. The terminology of "unselfing" is drawn from Simone Weil, for whom the moral pilgrimage of a well-lived life *was* one of mystical suffering (more specifically "affliction"). We offer ourselves as hostage for the other, come to know the void and suffer in this knowledge. However, "unselfing" is a term that is hardly used by Murdoch. It occurs only once in the *Sovereignty*.[35] It does have a couple of companion occurrences in the *Metaphysics*, but this is a sparse allowance.[36] The use of "unselfing" is favored by commentators because it puts a simple tag onto Murdoch's complexities. Be that as it may, the use of this tag is not something that she sought actively to counteract and it does serve to differentiate Murdoch from Aristotelian conceptions of moral virtue. The overtones of "unselfing" are sacrificial while those of the Aristotelian "good life" are rewarding and hence more prone to subvert other-centered motivation. With this borne in mind, I will stick by the use of "unselfing" as a shorthand for Murdoch's preferred path for aspiring moral pilgrims. Yet this path is Murdoch's and not Weil's. She regards Weil as ultimately compromised by a romantic cult of suffering that is associated with Christianity. Both find redemptive suffering, and indeed suffering as such, altogether too attractive.[37] In terms that Murdoch deploys regularly, they are implicated in a form of sadomasochism.

In making this rather large charge Murdoch is not suggesting that Christianity is implicated in any *peculiar* self-punitive disorder. (Although Weil perhaps may be.)[38] The disorder that is present in Christianity is normal, even commonplace. In her novels Murdoch does, at times, play upon the Freudian account of sadomasochism as a special developmental failure.[39] But ultimately, she agrees with Sartre (on this matter if not others) that it is the ordinary and familiar human condition.[40] What Murdoch critiques is "our ubiquitous (romantic) sado-masochism," the "cult of suffering" and the "system to which the technical name of sado-masochism has been given."[41] It is peculiarly attractive and all too accessible, a dangerous simulacrum of unselfing. What is wrong with it is not the predilection for some special form of sexual gratification but rather the misdirection of attention and concealment of this misdirection. "It is the peculiar subtlety of this system that, while constantly leading attention and energy back into the self, it can produce, almost all the way as it were to the summit, plausible imitations of what is good."[42]

Awareness of sin is a real event. Our ordinary position is one of moral weakness and of recognizing this weakness. Guilt follows wrongdoing (real and imagined) but guilt is a self-directed emotion. When left to its own devices, without some special ordering, it can lead us back into a fascination with, and attention to, self.[43] "To buy back evil by suffering in the embrace of the good: what could be more satisfying, or as a romantic might say, more thrilling? Indeed the central image of Christianity lends itself [to] just this illegitimate transformation."[44] Murdoch's conception of sadomasochism in which "suffering, mercifully offers a route back into the ego" may raise concerns about the prospect of an inescapable self-enclosure.[45] But while she does not posit any absolute escape from our default sadomasochistic economy, she does at least agree with Freud that its influence can be significantly mitigated, although the exit route, the *way out* is unselfing and not therapy.

The singular ineffectiveness of therapy as a remedial treatment for our condition is a theme that surfaces in several of the novels, most notably *A Severed Head*, where a poised and self-controlled therapist turns out to have feet of clay and to be trapped in a sexual liaison with his sister. The theme reappears again in *The Sacred and Profane Love Machine* where another therapist has troubles of his own to worry about. The central character finds that his therapeutic discipline provides a story for his situation, a narrative explanation of why he carries on with a profane sadomasochistic relationship (complete with unspecified bedroom paraphernalia) while seeming to enjoy the pleasures of a well-ordered home life. But this therapeutic diagnosis comes with no remedy and promotes instead a sense of personal weakness and guilt, an awareness of fault from the character cannot extricate himself. The analysis is impotent, hence part of the problem.

Murdoch's overt hostility towards the commonplace cycle of suffering and occluded vision sets her apart from Simone Weil but it does *not* directly imply either (1) a positive attitude towards contentment or (2) a hostility towards suffering as such. It does not imply the former because it is perfectly intelligible to adopt an asymmetrical attitude towards suffering and contentment. Some of our relations with others often involve just such an asymmetry. There are situations, such as bereavement, where we are called upon to relieve the suffering of others to whatever degree this can be done, but not to make them happy. Murdoch's critique of sadomasochism does not imply (2) because it is perfectly intelligible that not all suffering is of this everyday, ubiquitous and sadomasochistic sort. Murdoch says only that suffering, mercifully, offers a route back into the ego. She does not insist that this is the road that those who suffer must take whenever it is available. That is to say, there is a danger of overgeneralizing Murdoch's hostility to suffering.

Consider two commentators on Murdoch's views about suffering: Stanley Hauerwas and Henry Jansen. Hauerwas claims that, for Murdoch, "when we try to use our suffering as a means of purification, we only increase our self-fascination. Although suffering always appears on the surface to be the giving of the self for the other, it is seldom ennobling."[46] Here, I want to focus upon this *seldom* and to suggest that Hauerwas is right to include it as a qualifying term. It sets up suffering as problematic but allows room for a mode of suffering that is involved in moral progress. Henry Jansen is slightly less cautious, claiming that "if any good emerges from suffering, it does so irrespective of the suffering and is not tied to it in any direct way."[47] Jansen is cautious enough to avoid stating that for Murdoch suffering *must* involve or lead to compromised moral vision; he does allow that suffering can be incidental to the quality of moral vision, but at best it can *only* be incidental.

In his defense (and given that Jansen's study of suffering and comedy is an interesting and useful one) his comment makes good sense as a generalization about Murdoch's view of the subject matter of novelistic comedy. We suffer in accidental, useless, often harmful ways, which we try to romanticize into something grander and personally redemptive. This is undesirable, comic and even ridiculous. However, even if we narrow our focus down to Murdoch's literary interest, she is not only concerned with the genre of comedy, she also views tragedy as a realistic medium and her own novels try to combine elements of both genres. "Contemplation of the suffering of the innocent can be redemptive when the spectator is moved by both guilt and love."[48] The problem is not the impossibility of learning from suffering, but the difficulty of the task. The temptation to romanticize our sufferings is often too great. "Yes, it is possible, but very often just too difficult, to 'learn' from deep despair."[49] It is part of the achievement of tragedy that it tackles this difficulty and illuminates through the spectacle of suffering. The chorus of the *Agamemnon* informs us that wisdom must be taught by pain, and it is this same chorus that Murdoch uses to set the opening context for her *Acastos* dialogues.[50]

What I want to suggest is that once we have overcome the romantic/sadomasochistic images of ourselves as individuals alone and bravely facing up to suffering, what is left is a difficult and enduring task which is best regarded as a quite different mode of suffering, the kind that may have no enraptured audience. It is hard going against the ego, resisting the consoling warmth of our preoccupation with self. "The exercise of overcoming one's self is indeed exhilarating. It is also, if we perform it properly which we hardly ever do, painful."[51] Murdoch even writes of cultivating "a kind of intellectual ability to perceive what is true, which is automatically at the same time a suppression of self."[52] Here, we might have qualms about this formulation. It may seem infelicitous, but the punitive overtones are clear. So too is the implication that unselfing requires some form of courage.

If I am right about this then the good Murdochian pilgrim, who has the courage to undergo the life of unselfing, will face non-accidental suffering, a suffering that is bound up with a tearing away from the unrelenting ego. Such suffering will involve the difficult and sustained task of forgoing and reconfiguring desires. The unselfing pilgrim will experience and learn not from the solitary guilt of the familiar sort involved in the Christian story of personal redemption but from what Murdoch refers to as the "clean pain" involved in the experience of the "void." This imagery of void is drawn from the punitive but ultimately rewarding personal progression described by mystics such as John of the Cross and Julian of Norwich. We move forwards, and ultimately into punitive life, through ordeal, suffering, and personal crisis. It is noteworthy, however, that Murdoch's *Metaphysics* progresses towards a final substantial chapter on the void before terminating with its brief attempted summary of what has gone before. There is no final rewarding unity that it projects, or at least none that we are capable of seeing without radical distortion. The suggestion is rather that, in the end, we lose everything.

Murdoch connects up this imagery of a pilgrimage into loss with an awareness of the reality of death and the courage to face it. Following Plato, Murdoch holds that the moral life is a certain kind of figurative death and that it is just *this* that Christianity has always found difficult to accept. Death, which is most successfully depicted not by Christianity but by tragedy, shows our ultimate contingency, our ultimate loss of everything in the end.[53] This is a painful reality that we cannot cope with in our default egocentricity and part of the reason *why* it is painful is precisely because of our egocentricity. Facing up to death is a criterion by which the suffering of unselfing and that of sadomasochism can be distinguished. In the *Sovereignty* it is the humble man who sees the difference between suffering and death.⁵⁴ In the *Metaphysics* the same theme is bound to the unique realism of tragedy. Alluding to Weil's term for unselfing (*"decreation"*) Murdoch remarks that

> the tragic image of death in art is a counterpart or reflection of selfless decreated being, it is contingent mortal existence held in a clear gaze. The philosopher, as religious man, practices dying; he may gradually internalise the conception of death or may be confronted with it face to face in extreme affliction. Absolute pain is absolute in that it realises the idea of death. There is no place here for personal histrionics, wry glances, black humour or sado-masochistic play.⁵⁵

The unselfing Murdochian pilgrim will undergo the particular form of affliction that Murdoch variously calls "a purified suffering," "Real *deathly* suffering," "deathly pain," and "absolutely deathly pain."⁵⁶ This is not the suffering of the rack or of the great saint who is observed by an admiring posterity, by his God, and ultimately by his awestruck self.⁵⁷ Instead, it requires a moral courage that resists the imposition of various readily-accessible forms of consolation even if it is not obvious that all consolation is excluded. Indeed, it is difficult to imagine that such a life could be bearable without significant and sustaining consolations of some sort. But even with these, such a life seems very far removed from the, at times almost hedonistic, life of most characters in Murdoch's novels. The gap between the latter and the life of unselfing may reinforce an impression that unselfing could only ever be a part of the moral life, and not its entirety.

Advantages of this Conception of Unselfing

There are a number of advantages to be gained by adopting this conception of unselfing as only a part of the moral life and as, perhaps, the most difficult part of it. Firstly, treating unselfing as a mode of suffering helps to make sense of Murdoch's difficulty in situating any explicit commitment to contentment *within* the sphere of the private cultivation of virtue. This does not amount to a denial of any nexus or connection between virtue and contentment. It is still possible to hold that the good moral pilgrim undergoes a process that is *both* a mode of suffering *and* a movement into a precarious or vulnerable contentment. However, such a dual conception involves at least a representational problem. Murdoch is concerned with the task of conveying the right overall impression at the level of how her texts *feel*. She is concerned with tone and not just with the literal force of assertion.⁵⁸ Although we might sometimes wish for a little more precision, or at least precision of a different sort, a writing strategy of repeatedly hedging claims about suffering with multiple qualifications about the possibility of contentment might easily fail to convey the right impression of the demanding nature of unselfing and the precariousness or vulnerability of suffering. A contrasting strong emphasis upon virtue as rewarding (after the style of Aristotelian "virtue ethics") might similarly understate the vulnerability of the contentment on offer. Alternatively, it might invite the unwelcome reading that contentment is to be given a strong motivational role.

What Murdoch adopts instead is a workable representational response to the dual nature of unselfing as both a mode of suffering and a movement towards vulnerable contentment. She does this by stressing the sacrificial nature of unselfing while leaving contentment, and the finding of contentment in such a life, as an open but unstated option. If her expectations about how unselfing is liable to unfold are correct, those who undertake it may be expected to discover the relevant connections between suffering, virtue and contentment for themselves.

Secondly, conceiving of unselfing as a particular mode of suffering provides a response to the charge of *escapism* that is often leveled against Platonism. The charge also takes the forms of *pursuing self-sufficiency* and/or *invulnerability*. The particular version that I will focus upon is set out by Martha Nussbaum, a commentator on Murdoch who does not sympathize with her Platonism but who avoids making outlandish claims about its content.[59] According to Nussbaum, one of the great insights of tragedy (and following tragedy, also of Aristotle) is that the pursuit of what is good involves commitment to goods that are fragile in the sense of being vulnerable to loss. The more complex our conception of a life filled with goods, the more vulnerable to loss we will become. (Insofar as the individual goods that make it up may elude us, conflict with each other, or be impossible to retain in the long run.) We are not, of course, in a hopeless situation, but we are in one that is precarious and part of what accounts for this precariousness is the orientation of our desires towards others.

Nussbaum argues that this troubling relation between aspiration and suffering is dealt with by Platonism through a simplification of the concept of Good (through the pursuit of a unitary Good rather than multiple and potentially-conflicting goods) and through a reorientation of desire towards invulnerable objects (the forms) that do not degrade over time.[60] Here we may wonder about the particular interpretation of Plato that is in play, but even so Nussbaum seems to have a point. Plato does claim (at *Republic* 387) that the good man is self-sufficient in the sense that he can do without others. However, there is a need here to take account of the context in which this claim occurs. Plato is trying to show that virtue is its own reward, but we may concede (I am inclined to concede), that such a formulation places the Platonic good man in danger of becoming disengaged from the erotic of worldly things and ending up with desires only for what lies beyond being. This is problematic because any sort of decent life must surely involve *not* doing without others and *not* directing our desires away from what is vulnerable.

The options for anyone who accepts such a critique of Platonism will be exhausted by some combination of the following: (1) we may question Murdoch's credentials as a committed Platonist; (2) we may accept Murdoch's Platonist credentials but qualify her Platonism to exclude any pursuit of invulnerability; and finally, (3) we may hold that Plato's tendency towards a pursuit of invulnerability *is* inherited by Murdoch. With a little equivocation, Nussbaum prefers the first option.[61] However, the difficulty of moral struggle, the impossibility of ultimate success, the displacement imagery of *eros* do look Platonic, albeit with a sense of relevance that owes something to both Neo-Platonism and (up to a point) Christianity. Accordingly, I am inclined towards option two. Against both, a case has been made by Michael Weston for the third option, a direct application of the critique to Murdoch.

For Weston's Murdoch "we are constituted as a desire for the good, which as transcendent can only be related to in giving up all projections of good upon the world" and thereby, "even the power of death is overcome."[62] The latter claim should immediately set off some alarms because of Murdoch's position on mortality. The good man is the one who faces death, real death and not a romanticized simulacrum. The figurative death of unselfing which Platonism involves is informed by an acceptance of real, annihilative death. This much is clear from the final essay in *The Sovereignty of Good*, indeed it is the closing theme of the book. Be that as it may, Weston's Murdoch also endorses a fairly traditional (heavily Christian influenced) view of the *separability* of the Good that we find in commentators such as Gregory Vlastos.[63] Good of this sort looks suspiciously like the God who is transcendent in the sense of existing in some other ideal place. In *The Fire and the Sun*, by contrast, Murdoch makes clear that she is reading the transcendence of Good in a less Christian and, less separatist way, as primarily moral rather than ontological. Good is something that is *beyond* us in the sense that we cannot acquire and assimilate it. We may speak of it, metaphorically as an abstract metaphysical entity, but this is only a metaphor, albeit an important one. We are far removed from Good, not in the geographical sense that one object is at a considerable distance from another, but in the sense that goodness takes time to cultivate and may ultimately be out of reach.[64]

It is in this way that Murdoch approves of Plato's *Timaeus* myth of a Demiurge, a divine creature who sees and copies the perfect Good into an imperfect physical medium. "In the early dialogues the spiritual world is so close that we seem to be God's children. In the *Timaeus* we are his grandchildren." What comes to separate us from perfection is ultimately an "astronomical distance."[65] The ultimate standard of perfection is too remote to be reached even slowly. This is a thesis about limitedness and acceptance of limitedness. It is not a claim that a form-thing exists *out there* literally beyond being in some other transcendent place. Yet Murdoch also grasps that such limitedness may perhaps best be grasped by retaining locational metaphors at the expense of ontological ambiguity when working with the concept of Good. When dealing with what is beyond expression, ambiguity is to be restricted but not comprehensively removed.

Using a far more separatist view of Platonic transcendence as a background assumption, Weston appeals to her novel *The Black Prince*, to show Murdoch's supposed escapist tendencies. By its close, the central character, Bradley Pearson has been falsely imprisoned for murder and has become (or believes himself to have become) rapturously released from attachment to finite, perishable goods. He tells the reader that the world is "perhaps ultimately to be defined as a place of suffering" in response to which we should "forswear the fruitless anxious pain which binds to present and future our miserable local arc of the great wheel of desire."[66] For Weston, 'this train of thought implies a motivation by fear of suffering which would make the "willing for nothing" an illusion. It would be (what one may suspect Pearson's willing is) a willing for the sake of avoiding suffering."[67]

And so it would, but this involves a reading of Murdoch that is not just problematic in this or that respect. Rather it is straightforwardly ruled out by a conception of unselfing as itself a mode of suffering. By definition, unselfing when understood in the latter sense involves embracing a certain kind of suffering and not pursuing invulnerability. The good pilgrim lives in and with a continual steady undramatic sacrifice of some (not all) desires and in a state of vulnerability to loss. Even if goodness does provide opportunities for contentment it also involves an ongoing sacrifice of fulfillment *in at least some respects*, sacrifice of a sort which means that inadvertently secured contentment can only ever be of a vulnerable sort. And even were we to reformulate the charge of an escapist pursuit of invulnerability, in some more careful way which did justice to the peculiarities of Murdoch's Platonism, it is not at all clear that this basic obstacle to the plausibility of the charge could be overcome. Any moral pilgrim who does not make the necessary sacrifices of self that are bound up with a love for the other, who does not expose themselves to loss and does not on at least some occasions actually experience it, is engaging in something other than Murdochian unselfing. For how other than through the actual experience of loss could we gain a sufficiently rich conception of what it involves?

A third and closely related advantage to conceiving of unselfing as a mode of suffering is the way that it allows us to clarify the limits of Murdoch's sympathies with Buddhism or at least with what we might call Buddhism *as it is understood from the outside*. By this I mean the usual cluster of practices and moral theory that place emphasis upon the four noble truths or (given reticence about following determinate principles) at least upon compassion and (more obscurely) upon emptiness. At the risk of oversimplification, the four noble truths are these: the reality of existence is one of suffering; desire is the origin and/or means of reproducing this suffering; there can be an end to suffering; and the way out of suffering is to be pictured as an elimination of desire.

The contrast here with Christianity may seem quite stark, and favorable to the popularity of Buddhism. Christianity may be seen as promoting a certain, unwelcome, kind of suffering and guilt (and this *is* how Murdoch sees it). Buddhism, instead, is about overcoming suffering. The contrast is neat and appealing. With this in mind, and given Murdoch's critique of Christianity, it is tempting to overstate her Buddhist sympathies. I will take it as an important desideratum that we should not do so. My reason for making this claim is that Murdoch attempts to construct a moral vision that is well-rooted in an appreciation of a spiritual conception of the world while not necessarily endorsing the detail or ontological commitments of any particular religion. However, her own spiritual past happens to be a Christian past rather than anything else. To make this point is not to question the depth of Buddhism or the wisdom of converts who are prepared to undertake its rigors. I question only the accessibility of such depth to those who approach it from the outside, Murdoch included.

Bearing this in mind, the key divergence between Murdoch and Buddhism (in the relevant limited sense) is over just this question of suffering and the elimination of desire.[68] Murdoch sets out unselfing as a *redirection* of desire and not its *elimination*. If desire involves us in a vulnerability to suffering it is a vulnerability that we must embrace and not seek to get away from. One of the reasons why egocentric fantasy is so powerful is precisely because it is "designed to protect the psyche from pain."[69] This is a protection that we cannot suddenly cast off but which should steadily be overcome and its overcoming will bring exposure to a potentially-painful reality. T.S. Eliot's claim that humans cannot bear too much reality is not far off the mark, particularly when the reality at issue is one that concerns ourselves and our self-images. From a Murdochian point of view, getting beyond fantasy involves such an exposure through a steady, gradual reconfiguring of our desires. Acceptance of exposure and vulnerability may even be a partial definition of love itself.[70]

This is not to say that *the practice* of Buddhism may not also be thought of as a rigorous way of accepting, facing up to, and not trying to escape from suffering. I am inclined to think of it in just such a demanding way. There are practices that aim to transform suffering into compassion. The Buddhist who suffers may encourage themselves with the hope that their own suffering is a proxy suffering that will save someone else from such pain. (A sacrificial theme with clear similarities to both Murdoch and Christianity.) Those with a deep grasp of its textual traditions may also point out that there is no radical disharmony here between Buddhist practice and doctrine. There are texts (particularly in the Mahayana tradition) in which the noble truths are downplayed in favor of compassion but where there is no end to suffering and no path out of it.[71] While Murdoch is perhaps close to Buddhism *of this sort*, it is not a proximity that involves any radical severing of her Christian roots. This is not Buddhism in the relevant restricted contra–Christian sense.

The significant divergence between Murdoch and Buddhism of the sort that seeks to comprehensively get away from suffering, works its way into the detail of texts like the *Metaphysics*. It can be seen in her view that justice should be thought of "primarily as retributive, making even."[72] By contrast, Buddhism (again in the restricted sense) assigns priority to compassion which takes the form of rehabilitation or even exile as a safeguard against further harm and as a protection of the offender from acts of retribution. However we try to make sense of the concept of suffering, the whole point of retribution is to make someone experience it.

Such advocacy of retribution by Murdoch may seem surprising given her Platonism and given that Plato's own view of justice broadly coincides with the Buddhist approach. Both view punishment in a primarily therapeutic manner and Plato even contrives to view capital punishment in this same way. Against this, we need to bear in mind Murdoch's liberal, un–Platonic concern to maintain a distinction between a public sphere, which is not to be governed by perfectionist therapeutic standards, and a private sphere, where unselfing takes place (and which is governed by perfectionism). It is not the job of the state to systematically grind rogues good by punishing them into contentment and virtue. Punishment is not to be thought of in this dangerous way, because a "weakening of the fabric of liberal political thinking occurs when, in relation to punishment, the concept of retributive justice is dropped or discredited in favour of (of course very important) utilitarian ideas of rehabilitation, of making the culprit 'better.'"[73] Murdoch's retributionism is, at least indirectly, an upshot of her liberalism.

She is also aware of the distance that this retributive conception of justice puts between herself and Buddhism even though compassion is also a liberal desideratum. This distance is not something that lurks in the background detail of her philosophical texts but it is played upon in *The Green Knight*. In the latter, the quasi–Buddhist Peter Mir (named with allusion to Peter Conradi) inflicts a symbolic and retributive wound upon the miscreant Lucas who had previously cracked Mir's skull in a public park. Mir recognizes this act of retribution as something of a "flaw" from his own Buddhist standpoint.[74] It is partly a symbol of the loss of purity, of the woundedness of *both* Lucas and Mir. Both are willing players of their respective roles. But the act is ultimately an act of justice as retribution and not just rehabilitation. The return of suffering is given the positive role of "making even" although such balancing-up takes place at the partial expense of compassion. And while it is true that here, and in Murdoch's general endorsement of retributivism, suffering plays a role outside of the private sphere of unselfing, it does parallel what I have argued for as the role of suffering within the latter. If Murdochian unselfing is itself a mode of suffering then in both the public and private spheres Murdoch's position is significantly at odds with any Buddhist hostility towards suffering *per se*.

Her position is one of openness to suffering as something to be worked with, responded to, experienced in a particular way but not ultimately and comprehensively overcome. This is part of the distinctiveness of Murdoch's approach towards the moral life. But such openness to a certain kind of suffering makes it difficult for Murdoch to explicitly situate contentment within the life of unselfing. The latter does open up the possibility of a vulnerable form of contentment but, at the risk of losing sight of such precarious contentment, Murdoch opts for a representation of unselfing which retains a formal similarity to Christian redemptive suffering while being deeply rooted in an appreciation of its limitations.

Moral Pilgrimage and Moral Courage

Every life involves suffering and vulnerability. What I have argued is that the life of unselfing or, perhaps less confusingly, of moral pilgrimage, involves embracing this uncomfortable reality and not trying to evade it but to live in and make progress through it. That is to say, the life of unselfing involves a way of facing up to suffering, or constitutes a particular mode of suffering. Insofar as this is Murdoch's position, I am inclined to say that her appreciation of the ubiquity of hardship may be deeper and more acute than that presented in the Aristotelian position which treats the suffering of good agents as a matter of the operations of bad moral luck.

Part of what is important about Murdoch's way of picturing the suffering which is integral to moral pilgrimage is the way in which it helps us to understand and to give content to a concept of courage. If the life of the good pilgrim unavoidably involves suffering and vulnerability to suffering, then it calls for the courage to endure, face up to and not run away from the relevant misfortunes. The best sort of contentment that virtue makes available to us will, accordingly, be of a sort that requires such courage to be one of the virtues that we possess. This is courage of a special sort. It clearly need not be physical courage, the courage to risk life and limb. We are not all, *qua* moral pilgrims, placed in situations of extreme physical danger. And it is a good thing that this is the case. We do not need warfare and strife to make us into better people. Moreover, the courage to face physical danger is something that liberal societies have good reasons to be cautious about. Physical courage is a favored characteristic of privileged agents within societies with masculinist, martial and excessively aristocratic leanings.

Our liberal suspicions about placing great weight upon the value of physical courage puts us in good company. Plato too, at least in the *Republic*, situates the physical courage of the guardian soldier as the kind of character trait that draws upon spirited self-assertion rather than wisdom.[75] Although it may, occasionally, be required, there is something better to be obtained although harder to understand. For convenience, I will refer to this something else as "moral courage." It may occasionally involve or require physical courage (in the sense that an individual action may be made sense of under both descriptions) but it is best understood or pictured in some other way.

A rudimentary (underdeveloped) form of such a conceptual distinction may be detected towards the end of *The Sovereignty of Good*. In the process of attacking the Kantian man favored by existentialists and analytic advocates of an equation of freedom with choice, Murdoch remarks that such a man "has the virtue which the age requires and admires, courage."[76] Similarly, from such a standpoint "the sovereign moral concept is freedom, or possibly courage in a sense which identifies it with freedom, will, power."[77]

Against this, Murdoch follows Plato's strategy of trying to articulate an account of moral courage as courage of the best sort. In the customary manner, she focuses upon the kind of courage that we need in order to face up to the most fearful things, especially death. Her treatment of courage and her treatment of accepting mortality go hand in hand. The good pilgrim accepts their own ultimate limitation and this allows them to love the other.

> Courage, which seemed at first to be something on its own, a sort of specialized daring of the spirit, is now seen to be a particular operation of wisdom and love. We come to distinguish a self-assertive ferocity from the kind of courage which would make a man coolly choose the labour camp rather than the easy compromise with the tyrant.[78]

Here, I want to suggest that the first part of this comment is more informative than the second, particularly given Murdoch's conception of the domain of the moral as inclusive of the whole of life. The second part remains focused upon something that equips us for extraordinary situations rather than the familiar moment-to-moment effort that is involved in moral pilgrimage of an undramatic sort. Moral pilgrims need not be called upon to make exceptional sacrifices and it is probably misleading to write about *anyone* coolly choosing the labor camp rather than moral compromise with tyrants.

Courage that is an operation of wisdom and love is a quite different matter. But here, we may wonder just what it looks like. As a first approximation, we may turn to Murdoch's roots in the Platonic account of moral progress. We get some notion of the rigors of progress from the allegory of the Cave. Able at last to look on reality, the good man's eyes would ache and he would wish to turn back to the undemanding and soothing shadow images that he has left behind. Coming to recognize that our consoling images, and particularly our consoling self-images and images of what it is a good thing to be, are in some respects false, is itself a painful experience, and Plato writes of it in just these terms.[79] In whatever way we think about Plato's endorsement of the view that virtue benefits its possessor, his account of moral pilgrimage remains intimately connected to an appreciation of its rigors and the moral courage that it requires. However, in Plato, suffering and moral courage may sometimes *seem* to be too intellectualized, as if he were concerned only with the kind of courage that is required to pursue a line of thought unflinchingly, wherever it may lead us. As a counterbalance to this danger we might think of moral courage and suffering in everyday contexts. Here, I want to suggest that the kind of suffering that the Murdochian moral pilgrim undergoes, and the courage required in the face of it, can be pictured in ways that are utterly familiar to us and do not require us to think of unselfing as an esoteric pursuit in which moral agents are assailed late at night by strange and unusual forces.

The following is a list of moral agents who suffer in the way that good pilgrims cannot avoid suffering. The person whose sense of self is bound up with their relationship to an other but who faces the loss of their partner and manages to go on; the person who accepts the decision of a daughter-in-law *not* to undergo a second round of chemotherapy; the person who remains able to trust others after many disappointments and does not retreat into a fantasy that all people are self-interested cynics. The person who allows someone they love to make a dreadful mistake.

These examples begin with the more dramatic, with the facing of what is most awful, i.e., death. But they become progressively more familiar, everyday and mundane. In line with this we might think of the suffering and courage of the person who learns to forgive themselves for some failing, or who at last accepts its commonplace character, rather than remaining locked into a false image that they are peculiarly interesting by virtue of their fault. Insofar as these are instances of suffering and involve confronting false images of the self, we can plausibly take them as exemplars of the kind of suffering that is partly constitutive of moral pilgrimage. What connects these exemplary cases as instances of the same type of courage is this corrective nature. Moral courage is a corrective against the consoling and false self-images that the good Murdochian pilgrim must face up to and reject, painful though the process must unavoidably be.

But if courage of the relevant sort is so commonplace, if it is there to be seen all the time, we might wonder about the demanding nature of moral pilgrimage and why the attainment of anything approximating to comprehensive moral goodness is so rare. Here, the difficulty is bound up with the way that goodness requires much more than courage. The possession and exercise of courage is itself inseparable from other core virtues, with practical wisdom, justice towards others and awareness of one's own limits (temperance or humility). Each involves holding the demands of self at bay and we may not have one without in some sense and to some degree having the others. But this makes courage continuously required for the possession and exercise of *any* of the core or cardinal virtues, and hence makes it a more saintly than heroic accomplishment. Even though moral courage itself may be utterly familiar, the ongoing rather than intermittent requirement for courage makes moral goodness strongly demanding. We are all, perhaps even in our default condition, capable of showing courage of the relevant sort on some occasion. What we conspicuously lack is an ability to sustain this from moment to moment and our best attempts to picture the contentment that would be available to us if we were able to do so is itself vulnerable to the operations of fantasy and the delusions of the self.

NOTES

    1. Here and below "contentment" will be used interchangeably with "happiness" in order to weaken the utilitarian overtones of the latter.
    2. Conradi, 2001, 71, 79, 85, 92–3. Conradi writes of a "pleasure principle" in the novels and suggests that it is also present in the philosophical texts, but no specific textual support is given.
    3. Murdoch, 2003 (1957), 215–16.
    4. This novel is contemporaneous with Murdoch's attack upon anti-puritan puritanism in "T.S. Eliot as a Moralist," reprinted in Murdoch, 1997, Chatto.
    5. Murdoch, 1987, *Acastos*, 66, 121.
    6. Murdoch, 1993, Chatto, 497.
    7. *Iris*, 2001, directed by Richard Eyre.
    8. Murdoch, 1993, Chatto, 365.
    9. Peter Conradi makes this claim that for Murdoch happiness is a "moral duty," 1986, but this is not the way that the two are related in the *Metaphysics*.
    10. See Sandra Haegert, 2004, for an illuminating treatment of Murdoch, Weil and care of the self in an applied context.
    11. Susan Wolf makes comparable comments on the limits of duty 1982, 79.
    12. Murdoch, 1993, Chatto, 493. For a further statement of the "obviousness" of happiness as a human value, see Murdoch, 1993, 360.
    13. Blum, 1986, 50.3; Diamond in Antonaccio and Schweiker, eds., 2000. By way of an objection to Murdoch's view of the moral domain, from an otherwise sympathetic commentator, see Mark Platts, 1991.
    14. Murdoch, 1993, Chatto, 495.
    15. *Ibid.*, 497.
    16. With the exception of her use of the formulation of "willed attention" in "The Darkness of Practical Reason" (reprinted in *Existentialists and Mystics*) Murdoch upholds Weil's contrast between gradualist efforts of attention and sudden efforts of Will.
    17. Murdoch, 1993, Chatto, Chapter 12 on "Morals and Politics" sets out the unambitious limits of the political sphere and comes appropriately, immediately before the chapter on perfection: "The Ontological Proof."
    18. *Ibid.*, 356.
    19. *Ibid.*, 355–56.
    20. *Ibid.*, 363.
    21. *Ibid.*, 369.
    22. *Ibid.*, 367.
    23. *Ibid.*, 363.
    24. *Ibid.*
    25. *Ibid.*
    26. *Ibid.*, 483.
    27. *Ibid.*, 362. I use the term "moralism" here to flag up moral judgment that is passed by an inappropriate authority.
    28. *Ibid.*, 483.
    29. Murdoch, 2001, *Sovereignty*, 69–70.
    30. For this separation of virtue as rewarding and motivation by the prospect of reward see Rosalind Hursthouse, 1999.
    31. Murdoch, 2001, *Sovereignty*, 82.

32. *Ibid.*, 83.
33. *Ibid.*
34. *Ibid.*, 51–52; Murdoch, 1993, Chatto, 120, 429.
35. Murdoch, 2001, *Sovereignty*, 82.
36. Murdoch, 1993, Chatto, 54, 245, 319.
37. *Ibid.*, 133.
38. Murdoch, 1997, Chatto, 160. Here, in her review of Weil's notebooks "Knowing the Void" she does suggest that Weil willed her own death.
39. The Freudian account of sadomasochism that I have in mind is the failure to integrate sexual desire and affection at the end of the latency phase of sexual development. Murdoch plays with this account of a debased and debasing desire/affection split in *The Sacred and Profane Love Machine*. For a more general account of sadomasochistic suffering in the novels see Margaret Scanlan, 1977.
40. Sartre, 1989, Part Three, Ch 3. Sections I and II.
41. Murdoch, 1993, Chatto, 121, 132–33; Murdoch, 2001, *Sovereignty*, 67.
42. Murdoch, 2001, *Sovereignty*, 66. For the concept of sadomasochism in Murdoch see especially *Metaphysics* Chapter 5. For a Sartrean-leaning treatment of this concept in Murdoch, see Backus, 1986.
43. Raymond Gaita (1991) stresses (perhaps overstates) this side of Murdoch's attitude towards guilt.
44. Murdoch, 2001, *Sovereignty*, 80.
45. Murdoch, 1993, Chatto, 130.
46. Hauerwas, 1981, 43.
47. Jansen, 2001, p. 71.
48. Murdoch, 1993, Chatto, 132.
49. *Ibid.*, 501–2.
50. Murdoch, 1987, *Acastos*, 64. The characters are, presumably, returning from a performance of Aeschylus.
51. Murdoch, 1997, Chatto, 216.
52. Murdoch, 2001, *Soveriegnty*, 64.
53. Milligan, 2007, "Iris Murdoch's Mortal Asymmetry."
54. Murdoch, 2001, *Sovereignty*, 80, 96 ff, 101. For an account of humility in Murdoch, see Milligan, 2007, 43.
55. Murdoch, 1993, Chatto, 140.
56. *Ibid.*, 500, 109, 130, 139.
57. *Ibid.*, 131.
58. Antonaccio, "Form and Contingency in Iris Murdoch's Ethics," in Antonaccio and Schweiker, 1996.
59. For a sympathetic treatment of Murdoch by Nussbaum, see "Love and Vision: Iris Murdoch on Eros and the Individual," in Antonaccio and Schweiker, 1996.
60. Nussbaum, 1986.
61. Nussbaum *The New Republic*, 31 December 2001 comes close to charging Murdoch with the vulnerability argument in her review of Conradi's biography of Murdoch, "When She was Good."
62. Weston, 2001, 76–77, 84.
63. Vlastos, 1973.
64. Iris Murdoch, 1978, 36. For direct comment on the concept of "separation" see Murdoch, 1992, Chatto, 399.
65. Murdoch 1978, 61, 62.
66. Cited in Weston, 2001 op cit. 81–82.
67. Weston, 2001, 82.
68. For a guarded alignment of Murdoch with Buddhism see Peter Conradi, 1986, xiv, 16–17, 86, 108; and his biography, 2001, 544–46.
69. Murdoch, 1992, Chatto, 77.
70. J. David Velleman, 1999, 365. Velleman's Murdochian-influenced account of love may go too far when he writes, "All that is essential to love, in my view, is that it disarms our emotional defences" but the love-vulnerability nexus *is explicitly there* in Murdoch at least in the novels. For

example, in *The Red and the Green* the republican revolutionary Pat Dumay views his love for his younger brother, Cathal, as his "Achilles heel," a truly dangerous weakness. It is the only thing that comes close to holding him back from his romantic participation in the 1916 Rising; Murdoch, 1965, 117, 133, 205.
71. Peter Conradi alludes to these in his short and popular *Going Buddhist* 2004, 125.
72. Murdoch, 1992, Chatto, 493.
73. Murdoch, 1992, Chatto, 359, see also 103–4, 131, 389, 493 for the primacy of retribution.
74. Murdoch, 1993, 319.
75. For a good recent treatment of this, see Rabieh, 2006.
76. Murdoch, 2001, *Sovereignty*, 78.
77. *Ibid.*, 79.
78. *Ibid.*, 93.
79. Notably, at *Republic*, 604c–d; *Gorgias* 479b–80d, 521d–22b; and *Sophist* 230d–e.

10

A Subterranean Dialogue with Nietzsche on the Demonic and Divine in *The Sea, the Sea*

PETER MATHEWS

> *What, if some day or night a demon were to steal after you in your loneliest loneliness and say to you: "This life as you now live it and have lived it, you will have to live once more and innumerable times more;" ... Would you not throw yourselves down and gnash your teeth? Or have you experienced a tremendous moment when you would have answered him: "You are a god and I have never heard anything more divine." If this thought gained possession of you, it would change you as you are or perhaps crush you.*
> — Friedrich Nietzsche, *The Gay Science* (Section 341)

Throughout her work, Iris Murdoch expresses a deep reserve about the philosophy of Friedrich Nietzsche. Her concerns are visible, for instance, in her reaction in *Metaphysics as a Guide to Morals* to Don Cupitt's Nietzschean vision: "As for Nietzsche and (late) Heidegger, roughly, I regard those great writers as essentially demonic."[1] In contrast to her work on Plato or Sartre, however, Murdoch rarely addresses her concerns about Nietzsche directly, choosing instead to allow these ideas to linger beneath the surface of her work, only breaking through at specific moments. Perhaps this reticence is a reflection of Nietzsche's description of himself in the 1886 preface to *Daybreak* as a "'subterranean man' at work, one who tunnels and mines and undermines."[2] Rather than a direct confrontation between Murdoch and Nietzsche, therefore, what occurs is an implicit dialogue between these two thinkers, one that begins in Murdoch's philosophical writings but carries over, in a move that has gone largely undetected by critics, into the realm of her fiction.

For Murdoch, the value of Nietzsche's thought derives from the refining flame it holds up to western philosophy, and it is in this unexpectedly *positive* sense that she labels him a "demonic" figure. In "The Existentialist Hero," for instance, Murdoch points to Nietzsche as a turning point in the history of modernity: "The values of the nineteenth century are gone. The destruction for which Nietzsche called has taken place."[3] Yet Murdoch is wary, like Nietzsche himself, of the nihilism that might engulf such a project. For this reason she takes care not only to undermine the hypocrisy of modern ideas, but also to reclaim their value by imbuing them with a new vitality. Murdoch's affirmation of Plato is a key example of this process, and her work provides the key model for this dual movement of criticism and redemption. She famously takes a stand against the modern tendency toward condemning Plato, restoring his preeminence as a key thinker in exploring the ongoing link, in western philosophy, between ethics and metaphysics:

> The moral life in the Platonic understanding of it is a slow shift of attachments wherein *looking* (concentrating, attending, attentive discipline) is a source of divine (purified) energy. This is a progressive redemption of desire: and sexual attachment in the ordinary sense can be one possible starting point for the overcoming of egoism. The movement is not, by an occasional leap, into an external (empty) space of freedom, but patiently and continuously a change of one's whole being in all its contingent detail, through a world of appearance toward a world of reality.[4]

Murdoch is not straightforwardly opposed to Nietzsche's project, therefore, but seeks instead to complement the "demonic" force of his thought by evoking a "divine" vitality that simultaneously purifies and revalues the object of its critique. This ambivalence toward Nietzsche may be interpreted as a reflection, in turn, of his own uncertain feelings about the Socratic tradition, which also go against the prevailing trends of his time. Nietzsche regards Socrates, the mouthpiece and teacher of Plato, with an extraordinary mixture of admiration and dismay, from his early work *The Birth of Tragedy*, in which the destruction of Greek tragedy is attributed to "an altogether newborn demon, called *Socrates*," to the opening chapter of *Twilight of the Idols*, where Nietzsche concludes that ultimately "Socrates was a misunderstanding" of the "divine" relationship between instinct and reason.[5]

Rather than providing a vast (and unavoidably impressionistic) survey of how these debates unfold across the span of Murdoch's writings, I have chosen instead to focus on *The Sea, the Sea*, a work that not only engages in a strategic evocation of Nietzsche's work at key moments, but which is also the text where Murdoch addresses most directly her concerns about nihilism and its relation to the "demonic." Her subterranean dialogue with Nietzsche has received only marginal attention from critics of her work. In his magisterial biography *Iris: The Life of Iris Murdoch*, for instance, Peter Conradi characterizes his subject, in passing, as a practitioner of Nietzschean "star friendship," but makes no other point of comparison between the two thinkers (Conradi xxiii). The key intertextual focus of *The Sea, the Sea*, as Lindsey Tucker points out, is Shakespeare's play *The Tempest*, and it is from this point of reference that the criticism surrounding the novel has largely derived.[6] Whereas the Shakespearean connection in the novel is easily visible from the novel's surface (the protagonist, Charles Arrowby, was born in Stratford-upon-Avon, Shakespeare is his entry-point into theater, and he makes numerous allusions to Prospero and other characters in *The Tempest*), the influence of Nietzsche in *The Sea, the Sea* is at once covert and ubiquitous. Murdoch never names Nietzsche directly in the novel, but she establishes a conversation with his work through a series of pointed references. The most obvious of these occurs in the Prehistory section, in which Arrowby talks about his "will to power," an allusion to one of Nietzsche's most famous concepts.[7] Murdoch also repeatedly borrows metaphors from Nietzsche's work. The final conversation between James and Arrowby, for instance, contains the comment: "You're a sea man. I'm a mountain man," an oppositional metaphor of high and low that Nietzsche employs many times in his writings.[8]

There are also important structural similarities between Murdoch's novel and Nietzsche's *Thus Spoke Zarathustra*. When the reader first encounters Zarathustra, he has just emerged from his cave in the mountains after ten years of solitude. Zarathustra proceeds to address the sun (the traditional symbol of reason, as established by Plato's myth of the cave) to announce that he is going down from the mountain to spread his wisdom among the people. Murdoch reverses this opening scenario: having been among the people for many years, Arrowby begins the novel by retiring to his house by the sea, "my cave."[9] Rather than addressing the sun directly, he describes its symbolic inaccessibility: "We are in the north, and the bright sunshine cannot penetrate the sea.... [T]he sky looks cold, even the sun looks cold."[10] There are other similarities: the invasion of Arrowby's house by multiple guests in the latter parts of the novel parallels the arrival of the Higher Men at Zarathustra's cave, for example, and both works conclude with the portentous arrival of a long-awaited animal: the lion for Zarathustra, the seals for Arrowby. Murdoch's reversal of Nietzsche's opening scene sets the pattern for her interaction with his ideas in this novel. She thus inverts the values expressed by Zarathustra the wise: Arrowby is his double, his shadow — his buffoon.

Despite these apparent differences, Murdoch and Nietzsche are nonetheless focused on exploring a common dilemma: the insidious paradoxes that arise when critical thought turns, demonically, against itself. Zarathustra, for instance, apprehends this problem at the end of the Prologue, when he realizes the vanity of amassing disciples from the herd: "I need living companions who follow me because they want to follow themselves — and who want to go where I want to go.... To lure away from the herd — that is why I have come.... The creator seeks companions, not corpses or herds or believers."[11] To instruct others to leave the herd opens a dangerous contradiction, for people who obey such a command blindly merely exchange one herd for another. Within the pages of *The Sea, the Sea*, it is James, Arrowby's cousin, who masters the subtleties of this philosophical distinction. Discussing the difficulty of achieving true spirituality, James contends: "All spirituality tends to degenerate into magic.... Demons used for good can hang around and make mischief afterwards."[12] Nietzsche and Murdoch, therefore, see in the demonic voice of skepticism an ambiguous function that is at once healthy, insofar as it makes one capable of thinking for oneself, but also potentially nihilistic if destruction is allowed to become an end in itself.

Woman and Performance

Arrowby's evolving status in the novel derives from his ability to combine within himself both ends of this problematic spectrum. Clearly he is a man of talent, and yet he repeatedly overreaches his capacities, a tendency that culminates in his relentless pursuit of Hartley. In other areas, too, he pushes things to the point of nihilistic absurdity, such as his apparent inability to draw a line between the drama of real life and that of the stage. When Arrowby's friends hear of his retirement, for instance, they universally proclaim that he will not be able to leave the theater behind him: "'You will never retire,' Wilfred told me. 'You will be *unable* to.'"[13] For Arrowby, acting is a mode of power, one that tacitly grants him the right to shape reality in accordance with his own narcissistic desires. Howard Moss writes: "Power intoxicates people.... What one wants seems so obviously what the world ought to provide that shaping it to a desired end strikes ... Charles as exactly what the world *does* want."[14] So while Arrowby does not literally return to acting, Murdoch makes it clear that, despite his outward renunciation of the world, he never, for a single moment, stops performing — for the reader, for his friends, and, most of all, for himself.

Murdoch draws this broader theme of inauthenticity from both Sartre and Nietzsche. *The Sea, the Sea* is littered with references to Sartre's work — the scene late in the book in which James and Arrowby are throwing stones into the sea, for instance, is an allusion to the opening section of *Nausea*. So too is Arrowby's desire to write, which stems not only from his compulsion to perform, but rather reflects Roquentin's need to ground reality in the written word as a way of purging his nausea and bad faith. In her study of Sartre, Murdoch writes:

> He [Roquentin] does not imagine that while writing his novel he will experience any sense of justification or escape from absurdity. Nor does he think that he can rest upon having written it — *being* an author.... It is rather that through the book he will be able to attain a conception of his own life as having the purity, the clarity and the necessity which the work of art created by him will possess.[15]

Despite her admiration for Sartre's work, however, Murdoch believes this process to be problematic: "Yet this is a very thin and unsatisfactory conclusion. A novel *may* be thought of as aspiring to the condition of a circle.... But how is Roquentin, the creator, to transfer these yearned-for properties to, even, his own past? ... Any such sense of necessity would be illusory, for reasons which Roquentin has been offering all through the book."[16] The idea of writing the past that closes *Nausea* thus provides the starting point for *The Sea, the Sea*, in the form of Arrowby's journal. Murdoch tests the ideas put forward by her philosophical influences by placing them in constant dialogue with each other. While Sartre and Nietzsche start with a similar ethical critique ("bad conscience" in Nietzsche, "bad faith" in Sartre) the novel asks the same question of each of them: what does it mean to perform?

Nietzsche frequently condemns actors for their general lack of honesty. He writes in *The Gay Science*: "In the theater one is honest only in the mass; as an individual one lies, one lies to oneself"—a principle that describes Charles Arrowby rather well.[17] But there is a qualification in Nietzsche's thought that complicates the relationship between performance and honesty. He does not, for instance, condemn acting in order to institute a system of bovine honesty, in which the truth must be told at all times. On the contrary, Nietzsche states elsewhere that his vision for an honest human being, an "animal with a good conscience," is someone who possesses a "delight in masks and the good conscience in using any kind of mask."[18] Dissimulation is beneficial, but only when it is used in a pragmatic way: the truly honest person performs as a means of either affirmation or protection, and thus retains the ability to be sincere. The actor, by contrast, is distinguished by the fact that—as in Arrowby's case—he is *incapable* of not acting. Because performance has become the primary mode in which he lives, Arrowby the actor has forgotten how to be truly sincere. Instead, he engages in a paradoxical substitution: rather than being truly honest, he *performs* honesty. This logic of simulation is Nietzsche's true target, and he repeatedly takes aim against those who resort to this strategy: the hermit, the martyr, the scholar—in general, the "man of renunciation," who makes a show of sacrificing himself with the ulterior motive of making himself visible, "to conceal from us his desire, his pride, his intention to soar *beyond* us."[19]

But while Nietzsche condemns actors in general, some of the most (in)famous passages in his work relate to what he sees as the theatrical character of women. In Section 361 of *The Gay Science*, titled "On the problem of the actor," Nietzsche concludes his analysis with the following observations:

> Finally, *women*. Reflect on the whole history of women: do they not *have* to be first of all and above all else actresses? Listen to physicians who have hypnotized women; finally, love them—let yourself be "hypnotized by them"! What is always the end result? That they "put on something" even when they take off everything.
> Woman is so artistic.[20]

Nietzsche's frequently unkind comments about women seem to be motivated by his repulsion for the role of actress that society gives women to play. By situating Charles Arrowby at the center of her narrative, Murdoch engages in an implicit dialogue with Nietzsche and his views on women. She does not dismiss his ideas out of hand — Hartley, for instance, could hardly be called a model for feminist liberation — but instead she engages in a subtle and effective evaluation of Nietzsche's remarks.

The battleground for these ideas is provided by one of the novel's central motifs: marriage. Arrowby has never married, and his ruminations on the subject provide a crucial insight into his character. Murdoch, following Sartre, teaches us to distrust language, to read between the lines: "Talk is *mauvaise foi*, choice reveals the man, and is the truth."[21] While the reader cannot trust her narrator, Murdoch counters this problem by building into the narrative a virtual continuum of values that makes it possible to measure Arrowby's views on acting, women, and marriage. Arrowby moves back and forth between the extremities of this continuum, shifting rapidly from solitude to marriage, from acting to honesty, from the moment to eternity. The basis for the continuum is provided by the opposing figures of Clement and Hartley. At the beginning of the novel, Arrowby's plan is to write about Clement Makin, the wise and pragmatic actress who initiated him simultaneously into life and the theater. By the end of the Prehistory section, however, Arrowby has forgotten his original intention and is instead "possessed," as it were, by his pursuit of the "innocence" and "purity" of Hartley, his childhood lover. The way in which Arrowby constructs these two opposing figures determines his prevailing attitude toward marriage and the theater. In his earliest attempt to discuss Clement at length, in a passage that precedes an extended discussion of the theater, Arrowby reflects on the character of women: "Of course women act all the time. It is easier to judge a man."[22] When he returns to the subject later in the chapter, he links this characterization to his views on marriage: "What suits me best is the drama of separation, of looking forward to assignations and rendezvous. I cannot prefer the awful eternal presence of marriage to the magic of meetings and partings."[23] As the first section of the novel unfolds, therefore, Arrowby has shifted his alliance from the robust health represented by Clement to the demonic pursuit of Hartley.

This switch induces the farcical comedy that unfolds throughout the novel. At the same time, it returns Arrowby to a dialectic made familiar by feminist criticism, which divides the position of woman into the two archetypal extremes famously illuminated by Sandra M. Gilbert and Susan Gubar: the whore and the angel.[24] Murdoch makes it clear that this pattern is a regression on Arrowby's part, especially because he realizes later in the novel that it was Clement who had stripped away the illusions surrounding his immature and self-indulgent desire to marry Hartley in the first place. Arrowby's point of view thus provides Murdoch not only with the opportunity to explore the general self-deluding tendencies of humanity, but also to engage in a subtle feminist critique of how Arrowby's bad faith feeds directly into the construction of his misogyny. As Katherine Weese writes: "Murdoch's self-consciousness about history, individual and societal, undermines the novel that Charles writes and critiques the ideology on which it is based."[25]

These ideas are intimately connected to the Nietzschean currents in the novel. Despite the surface misogyny of his views on women, Nietzsche provides the philosophical tools to pull apart the basic assumptions of Arrowby's perspective.[26] In his book *Spurs: Nietzsche's Styles*, for instance, Jacques Derrida goes beyond the usual dismissal of Nietzsche's views on women in order to demonstrate the philosophical ambivalence that motivates them. Derrida transposes into French a play on words that appears in Section 361 of *The Gay Science* (quoted above): "donner" (to give), "se donner" (to give oneself), and "se donner pour" (to dissimulate).[27] Derrida's careful reading sets out to interpret not only Nietzsche's direct comments about women (which are, for the most part, unfavorable) but also his evocation of the feminine (which, through symbolic figures such as Sophia (Wisdom) and Ariadne, is largely positive). Derrida argues that it "is impossible to dissociate the questions of art, style and truth from the question of the woman. Nevertheless the question 'what is woman?' is itself suspended by the simple formulation of their common problematic."[28] Nietzsche's views on women, in other words, are as complex as his views on truth or art. Woman cannot simply be dismissed as an actor: if we look carefully, Derrida suggests, there is a set of nuances that goes beyond the surface misogyny of Nietzsche's statements.

Parallel to the meanings provided by this play on words, Derrida contends that Nietzsche puts forward three intertwining visions of woman. The first two of these positions are immediately recognizable. First, there is woman as the demonic actor, "a figure or potentate of falsehood.... In the name of truth and metaphysics she is accused here by the credulous man."[29] This is the archetypal image of the "false woman," the "whore" (within Gilbert and Gubar's schema), and the Rosina of Murdoch's story.[30] The second perspective is the reverse of the first: Hartley, the "angel of the house," the pure woman who, "through her guile and naivety (and her guile is always contaminated by naivety), remains nonetheless within the economy of truth's system."[31] Arrowby's idealistic reconstruction of his love for Hartley narrows his vision to these two alternatives, but Derrida (via Nietzsche) and Murdoch offer a different perspective, one that challenges the "phallogocentric" economy that makes possible the first two positions. The crucial missing figure is Clement, who was meant to be the original focus of Arrowby's musings. Her rapid disappearance from his thoughts marks the beginning of his demonic madness. Clement thus provides the third vision of woman, in which

> woman is recognized and affirmed as an affirmative power, a dissimulatress, an artist, a dionysiac. She affirms herself, in and of herself, in man. Castration, here again, does not take place. And anti-feminism, which condemned woman only so long as she was, so long as she answered to man from the two reactive positions, is in its turn overthrown."[32]

It is the divine Clement who returns to Arrowby's thoughts at the end, promising to exorcise the demons stirred up by Hartley.

Eternal Return and the Promise of Friendship

Murdoch's critique of woman and acting thus lays the foundation for a revaluation of marriage in *The Sea, the Sea*. Once again, the framework of the novel demonstrates an unpromising surface negativity toward the subject. In *On the Genealogy of Morals*, in much the same vein, Nietzsche writes that "the philosopher loathes marriage along with all the arguments in its favor — marriage as obstacle and disaster on the path to the optimum. Which of the great philosophers up to now has been married? Heraclitus, Plato, Descartes, Spinoza, Leibniz, Kant, Schopenhauer — none of them married; further it is impossible even to *imagine* them married. A married philosopher belongs *in comedy*, such is my proposition: and that exception Socrates — the mischievous Socrates, it seems, got married *ironice*, expressly in order to prove this very proposition."[33] But if Murdoch seems to accord Arrowby's views with Nietzsche's position, since his own comments about marriage are almost universally negative, her keen sense of irony works to undermine every one of these ideas. Just as she speaks through Arrowby, the male hysteric, in order to pull apart the discourse of gender, so too Murdoch, as a married woman, uses both Nietzsche (who never married) and Arrowby to question and then redeem marriage from the grasp of demonic nihilism.

The motif of marriage in Murdoch's novel again points to *Thus Spoke Zarathustra*. One of the key themes in *The Sea, the Sea* is time: Murdoch offers a profound meditation on the interlacing of the past and present, as Arrowby struggles to come to terms with his personal history. But while the invasion of the past into the present dominates the action of the novel, this meditation is governed by Arrowby's views about the future. Marriage thus becomes an important signifier of this struggle, for matrimony is a promise, a statement about the future that unites both past and present. This conception of marriage is a central metaphor in the book, linking Murdoch's novel thematically to *Thus Spoke Zarathustra*. Not only does Nietzsche announce in that work his own theory of temporality, the eternal return, he also provides the prototype for Murdoch's metaphor when Zarathustra sighs: "Oh how should I not lust for eternity and for the wedding ring of rings — the Ring of Recurrence."[34]

As with Nietzsche's views on women, it is necessary to shun a facile interpretation of this crucial concept, to avoid characterizing it crudely as a philosophy of history in which all events repeat themselves in an endless cycle. Read from this point of view, Murdoch's critique in *The Sea, the Sea* would be justifiably scathing. Arrowby's attraction to his falsely constructed past with Hartley, and in particular his tragicomic attempts to win her back, would constitute a vain attempt to force the Wheel of time (another recurrent metaphor in the novel) in his favor. In *Nietzsche and Philosophy*, by contrast, Gilles Deleuze argues that the eternal return ought to be understood within the full context of Nietzsche's theory of will. For Deleuze, the eternal return is created by Nietzsche not as a philosophy of history in the tradition of Hegel or Marx but as a thought experiment, a way of measuring the value of our actions. When Zarathustra first conceives the idea, he is overcome by nausea: "The eternal return of the mean, small, reactive man not only makes the thought of the eternal return unbearable, it also makes the eternal return itself impossible; it puts contradiction into the eternal return."[35] The unhealthy side of Arrowby's character comes from the disjunction between his will (his misplaced desire to marry Hartley) and the impossibility of doing so.

The product of this reaction, to use Nietzsche's terminology, is *ressentiment*: Arrowby is attempting to reconstitute a past that had no possibility to begin with. For Nietzsche, this railing against reality, this effort to preserve what *ought* to have been in place of what is, goes to the heart of modernity's ethical problems. Humanity artificially conserves many things that do not deserve to survive, and does so, moreover, at the expense of true vitality. As a thought experiment, therefore, the task of the eternal return is to diagnose whether or not something is being preserved in this unethical fashion. "Only the eternal return can complete nihilism *because it makes negation a negation of reactive forces themselves*," writes Deleuze. "By and in the eternal return nihilism no longer expresses itself as the conservation and victory of the weak but as their destruction, their *self-destruction*."[36] Murdoch's evokes the eternal return in this sense, making it Arrowby's task throughout the novel to come to terms with this process of ethical selection. He must allow his desire to marry Hartley to die its natural death, to acknowledge that, within the refining fire of the eternal return, it has no right to continue to exist. It is not exorcised by external action, but by its own disintegration — that is, it self-destructs from its own lack of intrinsic force.

Arrowby's not so naïve idealism becomes the ultimate philosophical expression of *ressentiment*, railing simultaneously against what cannot (empirical) and should not (ethical) be. Murdoch thus rereads the idealist tradition, through Arrowby's character, as the expression of an underlying vein of resentment and denial that runs through western history. The novel is littered with such revisions: Arrowby channels his self-disgust through the example of Augustine, for instance, and creates melodramatic comparisons of his relationship with Hartley to the romances of Dante and Beatrice, Orpheus and Eurydice, and Adam and Eve.[37] Arrowby's repeated sense of himself as a chivalric knight, come to rescue his fair maiden in Hartley, is thus given a quixotic overtone that derives from the schizophrenia of bad faith. He wants to believe in the truth of his project but cannot, and it is this disjunction that makes his actions appear both ridiculous and unethical, like those of a man possessed.[38]

Murdoch does not, however, reject marriage altogether, although she does warn that it remains forever open to corruption. In one of the novel's subplots, for instance, the reader is given brief insights into the marriage of Rosemary and Sidney Ashe, friends of Arrowby's who are held up as an exemplary married couple throughout the book. Toward the end, however, Arrowby receives a letter from Rosemary with the news that the marriage is over, that Sidney has run away with a young actress. "So much for the ideal marriage," he concludes.[39] The novel is riddled with these epigrams about the nature of marriage, such as Arrowby's bewildered exclamation "Why do people ever marry?" and "It occurred to me: I could not conceive of married life."[40] The ideal set up by the Ashe family is paralleled by several other couples in the text: the contrast between Arrowby's lackluster parents and his aunt and uncle, for example, but also by the Arbelows (whose marriage Arrowby had broken up years before), Lizzie (whom Arrowby strings along, exploiting her never-ending hope that he will marry her), Hartley (with her own dysfunctional marriage), and Clement (who taught Arrowby not to take too seriously the idea of marriage in the first place).

But Murdoch is far more positive in her approach to marriage than these examples might suggest. Marriage is something that cannot be defined by an ideal, but must instead be submitted repeatedly to the pragmatic test of the eternal return in order to maintain its authenticity. The novel's most important example is provided by the comic situation of Peregrine Arbelow, who at first appears to rail against the institution of marriage:

> "Every persisting marriage is based on fear," said Peregrine. "Fear is fundamental, you dig down in human nature and what's at the bottom? Mean spiteful cruel self-regarding fear, whether it makes you put the boot in or whether it makes you cower. As for marriage, people simply settle into positions of domination and submission. Of course they sometimes 'grow together' or 'achieve a harmony,' since you have to deal rationally with a source of terror in your life. I suspect there are awfully few happy marriages really, only people conceal their misery and their disappointment. How many happy couples do we know? All right, Sid and Rosemary..."[41]

Armed with the knowledge given later in the book that the Ashes' (Sid and Rosemary's) marriage collapses, this discourse would seem to have reached the status of a universal truth. But Murdoch counterbalances this possibility through the startling restoration of the relationship between Peregrine and Rosina. Peregrine's speech is thus reframed by Murdoch: these are not his real thoughts, but instead turn out to be the product of his well-concealed resentment toward Arrowby for stealing his wife.

The authenticity of marriage is guaranteed, first and foremost, by possibilities that are defined by contingency, by the imperfections that make up the random texture of life. The symbiosis between acting and *ressentiment* derives, according to both Nietzsche and Murdoch, from a culture steeped in idealism and bad faith. In making this philosophical diagnosis, Murdoch foregrounds marriage because it is rooted in a promise of friendship. Nietzsche writes: "The breeding of an animal which is *entitled to make promises* — is this not the paradoxical task which nature has set itself with respect to man? Is this not the real problem which man not only poses but faces also?"[42] Murdoch places Arrowby before the reader and asks: is this a man entitled to make promises? Does he have the "virtue" (in the Aristotelian sense) that enables him to make an authentic commitment? His attachment to Titus, to take just one example, suggests otherwise, as Murdoch ironically juxtaposes Titus's imminent drowning with a "rainbow that joined the land and the sea"—the rainbow being the symbol that God chose as a symbol of his covenant with Noah that he would never again drown all of humanity.[43] A further example is Arrowby's broken commitment to Rosina. "You promised that if you ever married anybody," she reminds him, "you would marry me."[44] Over and over, Murdoch shows that Arrowby's outlook has rendered him incapable of making an authentic promise.

The notion of a promise must be grounded, after all, by a possible return in the future. But what is to be promised if, after Nietzsche and Murdoch, we cannot pledge an adherence to the ideal? Nietzsche's answer, in *The Gay Science*, is the pragmatism of "star friendship." He writes:

> We are two ships each of which has its goal and course.... But then the almighty force of our tasks drove us apart again into different seas and sunny zones ... our exposure to different seas and suns has changed us. That we have to become estranged is the law *above* us; by the same token we should become more venerable for each other — and the memory of our former friendship more sacred.... But our life is too short and our power of vision too small for us to be more than friends in the sense of this sublime possibility.— Let us then *believe* in our star friendship even if we should be compelled to be earth enemies."[45]

Nietzsche places "star friendship" in implicit opposition to the idealism of Kant's categorical imperative, which reflects "the starry heavens above me and the moral law within me."[46] For Nietzsche, friendship represents a promise for the future, but one that is left undefined, forever open to the test of the eternal return. If the friendship ends, so be it, it has passed its course and died a natural death.

So too, with the departure of Hartley, Arrowby comes to understand the importance of friendship — the friendship, that is, of Clement Makin, the woman who was originally to be the subject of his memoir. It is Clement, he gradually comes to realize, who first pulled him beyond his childish infatuation with Hartley into the adult world of experience. "Clement was the reality of my life, its bread and its wine. She made me, she invented me, she created me, she was my university, my partner, my teacher, my mother, later my child, my soul's mate, my absolute mistress. She, and not Hartley, was the reason why I never married."[47] Clement is the touchstone to which he eventually returns, the principle of experience that clears away the feigned "innocence" that Hartley represents. "What a queer gamble our existence is," muses Arrowby with regard to his decision not to marry. "We decide to do A instead of B and then the two roads diverge utterly and may lead in the end to heaven and to hell."[48] This allusion to William Blake (notably, to "The *Marriage* of Heaven and Hell") cements Murdoch's rejection of an idealistic return to innocence. Marriage is not an obligation but instead the open promise of friendship, a contingent "arrow of longing" that reflects the eternal chaos within our beings.[49]

Within the pages of her novel, therefore, Murdoch finds a way to "marry" the demonic force of critique (Will) and the divine process of salvation (Good). If Arrowby's redemptive journey through *The Sea, the Sea* is read in these triumphant terms, then it would seem that Murdoch has discovered a solution, where Nietzsche admitted he could not, to the "problem of Socrates" explored in *Twilight of the Idols*. Murdoch takes up the force that Nietzsche's denunciation of nihilism embodies, using it as a means for clearing a path toward the Good. Yet the end of the novel, far from assuring the reader that Arrowby is safely assured of his redemption, hints at a potential return of the demonic via the accidental toppling of the casket: "The lid has come off and whatever was inside it has certainly got out. Upon the demon-ridden pilgrimage of human life, what next I wonder?"[50] Driven by the refining processes of demonic critique and divine redemption, Murdoch traces an ethical path in which Arrowby, starting from the baseness of his desire for Hartley, engages in a "progressive redemption of desire."[51] This vision of the Good is not to be found in any moral act but instead comes into being through an opaque, subterranean process — mysterious and "unimaginable," as James states — so that even Arrowby, who makes so many mistakes, learns that he has fortuitously had a positive impact on the life of his chauffeur: "I might stride as a demon in the dreams of some, but in the mind of Freddie Arkwright I evidently figured, quite undeservedly, as a beneficent deity."[52] Despite her Platonic allegiances, therefore, Murdoch, like Nietzsche, comes to see the Good in a curiously pre–Socratic manner, in which the tragicomedy of "unselfing" rests firmly in the chaotic hands of the divine.

NOTES

1. Murdoch, 1992, Chatto, 456.
2. Nietzsche, 1982, 1.
3. Murdoch, 1997, Chatto, 109.
4. Murdoch, 1992, Chatto, 24–5.
5. Nietzsche, [1872] 1967, 82; [1888]1990, 44.
6. Tucker, 1986, 378–95.
7. Murdoch, 2001, *Sea*, 61.
8. *Ibid.*, 440.
9. *Ibid.*, 4.

10. *Ibid.*, 1.
11. Nietzsche, 1969, 51–52.
12. Murdoch, 2001, *Sea*, 441.
13. *Ibid.*, 3.
14. Moss, 1986, 228.
15. Murdoch, 1987, *Sartre*, 46.
16. *Ibid.*, 46–47.
17. Nietzsche, 1974, 325.
18. *Ibid.*, 132–33.
19. *Ibid.*, 100–1. It is in this respect that I find David J. Gordon's contention that Murdoch's "moral objective is not greater autonomy of the ego but its death or, better, its flaying" to be deeply problematic (Gordon, 1990, 120). Who is to undertake this process of "flaying" if not the ego itself?
20. Nietzsche, 1974, 317.
21. Murdoch, 1987, *Sartre*, 34.
22. Murdoch, 2001, *Sea*, 32.
23. *Ibid.*, 51.
24. Gilbert and Gubar, 1979.
25. Weese, 2001, 636.
26. Unlike the earlier discussion of acting, Nietzsche's views on women and marriage are subjected to critique but not to revaluation. This task, it seems, has been left to his commentators, and there has been a steady flow of critical discussion of Nietzsche's relation to the feminine, starting with Sarah Kofman's seminal essay "Baubô: Theological Perversion and Fetishism" and Jacques Derrida's *Spurs: Nietzsche's Styles*. The most notable of these texts is Luce Irigaray's *Marine Lover of Friedrich Nietzsche* and an essay collection titled *Nietzsche and the Feminine*.
27. Derrida, 1979, 70.
28. *Ibid.*, 71.
29. *Ibid.*, 97.
30. Murdoch, 2001, *Sea*, 104. Rosina even compares herself to a demon, threatening Arrowby that, should he ever get married, she will be "a demon in your life and her life."
31. Derrida 1979, 97.
32. *Ibid.*
33. Nietzsche, 1996, 86–87.
34. Nietzsche, 1969, 244.
35. Deleuze, 1983, 65.
36. *Ibid.*, 70.
37. Murdoch, 2001, *Sea*, 8, 369, 125, 83.
38. There is perhaps an underlying symbolism to the village's local hotel, The Black Raven — a reference, no doubt, to Poe's own Raven and its infamous "Nevermore!"
39. Murdoch, 2001, *Sea*, 458.
40. *Ibid.*, 70, 139.
41. *Ibid.*, 158.
42. Nietzsche, 1996, 39.
43. Murdoch, 2001, *Sea*, 371.
44. *Ibid.*, 102.
45. Nietzsche, 1974, 225–26.
46. Kant, 1993, 169.
47. Murdoch, 2001, *Sea*, 479.
48. *Ibid.*, 83.
49. Like Charles, we must "arrows be." The reference to the "arrow of longing" comes from *Thus Spoke Zarathustra*.
50. Murdoch, 2001, *Sea*, 495.
51. Murdoch, 1992, Chatto, 25.
52. *Ibid.*, 441, 454.

11

Naturalism and the Good

JOHN HACKER-WRIGHT

> "A post–Kantian theory of morals: survey all the facts, then use your reason. But, in the majority of cases, a survey of the facts will itself involve moral discrimination."
> —Iris Murdoch, *Metaphysics as a Guide to Morals*

Murdoch's attack on the divide between fact and value and her defense of the objectivity of value have rightly been taken to be central features of her work.[1] Cora Diamond points out that Murdoch's "Vision and Choice in Morality" is among the first twentieth century writings to challenge the idea that a fallacy is committed in the attempt to derive an evaluative conclusion from factual premises.[2] Yet, Murdoch's views on the Good have not received the same substantial treatment as her attack on the fact/value divide.

I take it that the reason that Murdoch's views on the Good have not received an adequate hearing is that they seem implausible from the perspective of contemporary scientific naturalism, by which I mean a metaphysical picture of the world that tends to dismiss as unreal anything that does not figure irreducibly in a natural scientific description of the world.[3] The divide between fact and value can be attacked without challenging scientific naturalism; there are various strategies for analyzing value in terms of scientific fact. But in asserting the existence of the Good, Murdoch is positing the existence of an entity that transcends any possible reduction to the vocabulary of the natural sciences, and for this reason, in the eyes of many, it is metaphysically suspect.

Yet, Murdoch does not just want to replace that scientific naturalism with an easily dismissible supernaturalism. I will argue here that her argument for the Good is part of an attempt to work out a more adequate naturalism, albeit a naturalism that contains some crucial elements that cannot be reduced to the vocabulary of the natural sciences. Murdoch relies on very general features of Freud's naturalistic account of the human psyche, an account that has at least some scientific credentials. In particular, Murdoch invokes Freud in her claim that the mind starts out attached primarily to itself; that is to say, we look at the world initially through the lens of our own needs and desires. Our attention is turned outward only by a difficult and often painful process of redirection toward other people and objects.[4] It is in the context of the difficult turn outward towards particular others that the notion of the Good has its home.

The Good is what we attend to as we attempt to uncover reality. Any object that is the focus of attention may be colored by private fantasy. The Good is an ideal of attending to individuals well, in light of recognizing that our views on others are influenced by our own interests. Since, on Murdoch's view, there is no turning outward without an effortful redirection of attention, we must either exert ourselves to attend to the world or have no grasp of the world as it is; the Good is a concept that overarches our moral-epistemological encounter with the world, an encounter which is presupposed by any scientific endeavor. The Good is a category that Murdoch believes to be essential to make room for the description of our moral experience of knowing the world, and it cannot, she thinks, be contained within a natural scientific account of the world.[5] Hence, scientific naturalism cannot, she thinks, account for its own conditions of possibility.

The critical element of Murdoch's challenge to scientific naturalism is her denial that the facts are just there to be discovered by a morally neutral investigation. She argues that access to the facts is a task involving moral discrimination. It is also, for Murdoch, an erotic task in the sense that it engages the will in transforming our desires and attachments.[6] Often, for her, access to the facts requires our overcoming our attachment to ourselves and directing our attention to a world that we know, at first, only through the lens of selfish attachments. Gradually, through a process Murdoch calls "unselfing," we come to grips with the world as it is independently of those selfish attachments. For Murdoch, this is a process without terminus; still, one can, she thinks, achieve a *morally better* view of the world. Such a view of the world is what she means by *reality*. "Moral realism" for Murdoch labels an appeal to us as agents to take the task of improving our view of the world seriously, as perhaps the most central part of our moral lives. As she declares, "Morality ... is a form of realism."[7]

It is within this context that Murdoch's most ambitious and least considered claim must be situated; that is, her claim that the Good exists, and exists necessarily. In what follows, I will try to show that Murdoch makes a significant, though underappreciated argument for the existence of the Good. First, I review her claims about the inadequacy of scientific naturalism. Then, I will map Murdoch's arguments for the existence of the Good together with the implications of that argument, both metaphysical and moral. Finally, I will show how Murdoch's affirmation of the Good results in a distinctive ethical naturalism (a view that grounds ethics in a substantive picture of human nature) that is a neglected option in contemporary philosophy.

Murdoch's Critique of Scientific Naturalism

In this section, I attempt to lay out Murdoch's core objections to scientific naturalism. On Murdoch's account, contemporary naturalism is laden with false psychological and moral assumptions. Specifically, she criticizes, in "Against Dryness," the naturalistic picture of the human being as a "bare naked will" in an easily comprehended world."[8] Murdoch challenges both the notions of the will and of the empirical world as found in contemporary naturalism, because they do not describe the conditions by which the world is knowable by us, and also because these notions artificially delimit the scope of our moral lives. Murdoch's criticism of scientific naturalism, then, has two interrelated branches. First, she holds that scientific naturalism belies the very conditions of generating knowledge, including scientific knowledge. Second, she believes that scientific naturalism fails to provide concepts adequate to describe our moral lives and that it thereby turns us toward defective moral ideals. I say that these are interrelated because, for Murdoch, possessing concepts adequate to describe our moral lives will include providing an understanding of how we can know the world accurately. Her position in the end is that the vocabulary of the natural sciences needs supplementation with a broader vocabulary that makes it possible to describe our moral experience of knowing the world; that vocabulary will include the concept of the Good. For Murdoch, our metaphysical description of the world must contain elements that allow us to describe the difficult journey from ourselves outward toward the world. It seems fairly clear that Murdoch did not aspire to change the practice of the sciences, or alter the theoretical vocabulary of scientists. Rather, she is challenging a worldview that places the natural sciences in the position of dictating the whole of our metaphysics.

The main reason that scientific naturalism belies the conditions of generating knowledge is that it supposes "an easily comprehensible world." Of course, Murdoch does not mean to suggest that the scientific naturalist necessarily denies the labor that goes into scientific research. The problem here is a denial of the *moral difficulty* of knowing the world. On one common story about scientific training, a scientist must learn how to put her preferences aside, and because she does that, she engages in science as a "value-neutral" endeavor. By contrast, one of Murdoch's central points in *The Sovereignty of Good* is that the mastery of a discipline is an instance of moral development. She writes, "In intellectual disciplines and in the enjoyment of art and nature we discover value in our ability to forget self, to be realistic, to perceive justly."[9] So, for Murdoch, the setting aside of individual preferences which is a prerequisite of engaging in science is not a matter of setting aside value, but of developing a different, better set of values. It involves developing the value of "perceiving justly," which is to say, the value of appreciating the specific features of individuals that I encounter.[10]

Now, the question for Murdoch is why scientific naturalism cannot accommodate this moral difficulty about knowing the world. The answer is that in order to see the difficulty of knowing the world as a genuine moral difficulty, it must be more than a mere psychological matter. Yet, it seems that if scientific naturalism is an adequate metaphysical view, then we must be able to exhaustively to describe our contact with the world in at least psychological terms.[11] No doubt the struggle to know the world is often in large part a psychological matter. But Murdoch contends that the moral element of the struggle cannot be captured from looking at it from the psychological perspective alone. Let us say that we aim to understand an artwork, say, Piero della Francesca's *Resurrection*. What, Murdoch would have us ask, does coming to understand such an artwork involve? In many cases, at least, the viewer might not possess an adequate conceptual apparatus needed to do justice to Piero's masterpiece (I am fairly sure that I do not). Probably, if I were to become able to describe it justly, the description would invoke concepts that I am already in some sense familiar with, but it would apply them in a way that I am not at present able to foresee. One can, for instance, come to see as "graceful" objects or persons one never would have thought would fall under that term. What occurs in such a case, then, is conceptual change. The conceptual change that Murdoch describes as a change of moral vision means realizing that an individual object or person merits being described with a particular concept because this is an instance where this concept *should* be applied, that is to say, because the individual *merits* it.[12] A purely psychological approach, Murdoch implies, might be able to describe the mechanics of such conceptual change, but could not capture what it means to say something or someone "merits being described as graceful." A psychological account might describe thoughts typical of a person in such a situation, predict her future behavior, even discriminate between healthy and neurotic behavior, but could not, it seems, make sense of "meriting" as anything more than an attitude of the agent. Yet, if such "meriting" is merely an agent's attitude, Murdoch holds, then we have no reason to believe that there is really justice being done in the description. In that case, the supposed "justice" being done would consist of a mere story the agent is telling herself about what she is doing. The moral difficulty of knowing the world is, for Murdoch, a matter of describing things and people as they merit being described, or seeing matters justly. So, we must be able to hold onto that sense of "meriting a description" as more than a psychological matter in order to hold onto the moral difficulty of knowing the world. Because a psychological approach cannot capture this idea of just perception, we can see that it cannot capture the moral difficulty of knowing the world.[13]

Now, the second branch of Murdoch's criticism of scientific naturalism follows closely from the first. On her view, it is precisely because scientific naturalism excludes the moral difficulty of knowing the world that it cannot furnish us with an adequate description of our moral lives. For if part of the moral work of our lives does not involve knowing the world, then it involves only making choices in view of facts that are already known. The result is the Kantian-existentialist morality Murdoch criticizes throughout her philosophical writings. On such a view, moral evaluation is focused on choices effectuated by the will of the agent acting in view of a world that is adequately known. However one fills out the substance of that evaluation, Murdoch thinks that the Kant-style morality will inevitably fall short. Her criticisms are moral: it will produce a "dangerous lack of curiosity about the world" and a "dream-like facility."[14] Now it is important, I think, to realize that Murdoch is *not* worried simply that the agent acting under a Kant-style view of the nature of morality will have perhaps overlooked some of the facts that she needs to have gathered in order to act rightly. That would be the "dream-like facility" of which she is critical. For this way of putting it misses the transformation that Murdoch believes must occur if the agent is to come to terms with reality. As I've just described, the agent might well have to undergo a change of concepts in order to be able to do justice to others; for Murdoch there is also an investment of attention (which I will describe more fully below) that is required to attain that transformation, and this investment has implications for one's desires and emotions. In the end of such a conceptual and psychological transformation, the agent may find herself *compelled* to act in some way just by the description another falls under (e.g., "I *had* to help, because he was suffering so much"). As Murdoch puts it, "If I attend properly I will have no choices and this is the ultimate condition to be aimed at."[15] For Murdoch, then, the *freedom* that features so prominently in Kant-style morality is a symptom of its failing to take seriously the moral task of knowing the world. Many of the "choices" the facing the Kant-style ideally rational agent on Murdoch's view stem from an inadequate appreciation of his situation.[16] Hence, freedom, for Murdoch is a flawed moral ideal; we should, if we are good, feel ourselves compelled to act, say, in the face of the suffering of others.

Murdoch therefore believes that scientific naturalism will lead us morally astray, because it does not have a place for the way that a description can move us to act. For the Kant-style morality that Murdoch sees as accompanying scientific naturalism, facts are always motivationally neutral; the agent's desires and will must enter to effectuate some action. On the Kantian account, the will comes into play in deciding how to act after having assessed the facts, and only then. The world, of course, may resist my will; it might foil my intention by putting insurmountable physical or psychological obstacles in the path to implementing my action. But provided that I have disposed my will properly, none of these obstacles detracts from the moral worth of my intention.[17] For Murdoch, by contrast, the will comes into play as it were much earlier than it does for Kant, in establishing our contact with the world. To be capable of acting with the discernment that Kant presupposes, Murdoch points out that I have undertaken a transformation that begins when I will myself to pay attention to the world around me. A significant effort over time is involved here. For Murdoch, the world does not only resist my will in producing obstacles to my action. It also resists the will in not being describable as I would like. In the end, I may just describe it how I want it to be, but not if I am a good person. I can be excused of these faults only if I am mentally disturbed. To be good, one must exert just or loving attention, and as Murdoch puts it, just or loving attention can change one's moral vision by making it apparent that a given concept has an application to a new case. Hence, my conception of reality changes and deepens as I pay attention to the world and my concepts become more adequate to the individuals I encounter there. My will is thus, for Murdoch, importantly involved in my discovery of the world, and my discovery of the world is an essential constituent of my moral life.

Now let us look at how it is that a description could motivate action. It is not the case that for Murdoch the facts *by themselves* can compel action. It is, after all, only those with good character who find themselves compelled to act in view of, say, someone left injured by a car accident. Hence, the will is involved in becoming the kind of person who feels compelled to act in those circumstances. But it is not the case that the agent is covertly choosing; that is, the agent is not choosing to feel compelled. Murdoch's point is that choice is displaced by the facts that confront someone with good character; the facts that confront the person with good character are not the same as those that confront the person with bad character. On Murdoch's account, then, there is a different range of facts available to one who has good character. Hence, the will is involved in determining what kinds of facts are available to an agent, on her account. The will affects the kinds of facts available to an agent via attention. The agent chooses to direct her attention to certain features, and, over time, this affects the kind of facts that are then available to her.

Let us examine how the will and attention bring about such a change. Murdoch proposes, I take it, an ethic of attention; this means that for Murdoch, paying attention is something we can do well or poorly, and the central task of our moral lives is to pay attention to others well. An ethic of attention is also an ethic of description. How we describe another person, for example, will depend on how we attend to her. This is what is happening in Murdoch's famous M and D example, where M is a mother-in-law who harbors unjust negative views of her daughter-in-law, D, because of a jealous attachment to her son.[18] In the example, M attends to D poorly at first, but then exerts herself to attend to D better, and thereby arrives at a different set of descriptions of her. What happens when M exerts herself to attend to D better? Murdoch is insufficiently explicit here, but I think a picture of what happens can be elaborated that follows quite clearly from Murdoch's views.

Description can be employed in a variety of ways. Often, description is deployed in service of the ego; for example, one might offer negative descriptions of others as a sort of punishment when one perceives that they have acted against one's interests. Murdoch suggests that this is the case in the pre-transformation M. M describes D punitively because D has encroached on her son. One can of course also offer positive descriptions as a sort of reward for actions perceived to advance one's interests. A person employing descriptions in such an egoistic economy is, however, living in a fantasy realm. Every other person or thing is described relative to her interests, not as they really are. One might object that someone could use descriptions in this way without necessarily buying into them, and surely this does sometimes happen. Yet if Murdoch is correct that it takes significant effort to come to terms with other people and particular things, then someone who is given over to this egoistic economy of descriptions has almost surely not invested the effort necessary to hold independent descriptions that are the product of such an effort. Further, one who has undertaken an effort to arrive at true descriptions would have necessarily overcome the focus on her own interests that underpins the egoistic economy of description, and so would not intentionally use egoistic descriptions. Murdoch suggests, then, that a quite different "economy" of description is possible. This alternative economy of description is a product of "unselfing," and involves, according to Murdoch, attending to others under the idea of the Good, in a sense I will explore below.

Before moving on to see how the notion of the Good functions in Murdoch's ethic of attention, let us complete the argument of this section by returning to the question of how a description can motivate action for Murdoch. When I attend to the world virtuously, for Murdoch, there are some beliefs it is not possible for me to have, and some ways it is not possible for me to act, given those beliefs. I can, to be sure, end up with mistaken beliefs even after having undertaken virtuous attention to the world. Yet there are at least some ways in which it is not possible for those mistaken beliefs to arise, if I am correctly described as virtuous. Let us modify Murdoch's M and D example to illustrate this: imagine that D does something plainly virtuous, in full view of M; in that instance, it would not be possible for a virtuous M to resist the belief that D is better than she had previously thought. To avoid that belief would require a refusal to acknowledge a plain fact that would demonstrate stubborn malignity and would overturn M's claim to virtue. Likewise, she must act consistently with that belief, to embrace D in her virtue, and, indeed, that motive must *silence* her inclination to snub D. If she stands back in a condition of freedom, even for a moment, contemplating whether it would be best to embrace D for her virtue or rather to work on some way of concealing D's virtues and pitting her son against D, she *ipso facto* demonstrates a lack of virtue. So, a belief can compel action and indeed being under the compulsion of a belief is often the mark of virtue, for Murdoch.

To review, Murdoch rejects scientific naturalism for its inability to accommodate the moral difficulty of knowing the world. Because it cannot accommodate this moral difficulty, it leaves out what she regards as the core of our moral lives, and in doing so has the danger to lead us astray morally. We are lead astray morally insofar as we are led to embrace an ideal of freedom that is inconsistent with genuine moral goodness. A good person does not regard herself as free to do ill.

The Existence of the Good

In the previous section I outlined the central arguments of Murdoch's critique of scientific naturalism. Now, I aim to show how her argument for the Good forms the core of her construction of an alternative to scientific naturalism. In order to construct such an alternative, she must show that there is real need to incorporate into our metaphysical picture elements that are in principle irreducible to the vocabulary of the natural sciences, and that we can do so in a way that is intellectually credible. I believe that she accomplished both of these goals in her argument for the existence of the Good, and will attempt to argue for this point presently. Then I will argue that the Good plays a central role in an ethic of attention.

First, why would admitting the existence of the Good require us to abandon scientific naturalism? Of course, there many are ways of spelling out the meaning of the word "good" that would not conflict with scientific naturalism. Non-cognitivists spell out the meaning of the word "good" in terms of an attitude of approval, which can easily be accommodated within scientific naturalism via psychology. One can even give cognitivist accounts of the meaning of the word "good" in terms of preference or desire satisfaction that does not involve introducing anything at odds with scientific naturalism. If (to take a simple version) whatever satisfies some desire of mine is good then it is either true or false that any given thing is good, and this fact does not require any additions to scientifically describable reality, assuming desire can be accommodated by psychology. But Murdoch's interest is not chiefly in providing an analysis of "good." Rather, she is interested in providing a framework within which the moral difficulty of knowing the world can be adequately accommodated. That means making sense of the notion of "meriting a description" that was explained in the previous section.

Recall that according to Murdoch, describing the world accurately requires that we overcome what I called an "egoistic economy of description," in which descriptions are offered as punishments or rewards in view of how other people and things fit with our interests. For Murdoch, the Good is essential to our ability to overcome this egoistic economy of description. Murdoch speaks of the Good as "a single perfect transcendent non-representable and necessarily real object of attention"[19]; she also says, "Good is the focus of attention when the intent to be virtuous coincides (as perhaps it almost always does) with some unclarity of vision."[20] What is noteworthy here is that the Good is an object, and something to which we can pay attention. Yet the Good can be neither defined nor experienced.[21] It is therefore not a property attributed of things that serve us well or persons who act well. For Murdoch the Good is what those who act well attend to. How, then, do we know that it exists, and indeed, that it exists necessarily?

Murdoch's answer is that great art gives us a proof of the necessary existence of the Good. In this argument, Murdoch connects the Good with striving for perfection in art. As she points out, whenever one participates in any complex product-oriented activity, such as the arts, one realizes that there are scales of excellence, and that nearly every product of that activity falls short of perfection in some way.[22] The awareness of everything's falling short brings to mind the idea of perfection, a goal that is magnetic, yet non-representable. That is, we have no idea of what the perfect painting would look like, and yet, every serious painter (that is, any painter who strives to paint well) in some sense strives after the perfect painting;[23] likewise, Murdoch claims, with conduct in general. Anyone who attempts to act well acknowledges scales of conduct and realizes a transcendent ideal of perfect conduct. The serious painter must learn to pay attention to things without "seizing them" by viewing them through the lens of his interests. Likewise, the virtuous agent must learn to pay attention to other persons and things as they are, attempting to overcome, so far as she can, the egoistic economy of descriptions. Hence, both the serious painter and the virtuous agent must learn detachment and engage in unselfing. For Murdoch, the Good is the ideal of perfection that pertains not to some individual art or discipline, but to the task of attending well in general. Just as the practice of an individual art, such as painting, implies an idea of perfection toward which one strives, so the effort of attending to the world well which underpins any such undertaking and good conduct in general, implies an overarching ideal, and this Murdoch names the Good. The serious painter and the virtuous agent are similar, then, in their common pursuit of the Good. Since the Good is a condition of attending perfectly well, and great art attests overwhelmingly to the possibility of paying attention well (i.e., under the guidance of the ideal of the Good), Murdoch holds that this evidence proves that the Good exists. Further, since the Good, as an ideal of perfection, is not the sort of thing that can cease to exist, that is, it is not a contingent being, it exists *necessarily*.

Now, Murdoch is at pains to show that what we are striving at is not merely a psychological construction of human agents. Why should we take this striving so seriously as to posit the reality, indeed, the necessary existence of the Good? After all, we could just say that a human agent needs to see the Good as real in order to be able to paint well or act well without admitting that the Good really exists. Great art, then, is a proof, not of the Good itself but of the power of the *idea* of transcendent perfection on the human mind.

The problem with that argument, however, is that it presupposes some viewpoint on human beings that is itself independent of the need for the Good. Can psychology or the other natural sciences do with a merely psychological notion of the goal they are striving after? It might seem that they could. Consider that it seemed to Kant impossible to have moral motivation without affirming the existence of God, an immortal soul, and free will; he thought that we need to affirm in the existence of God and the immortal soul as conditions of moral action even though the affirmation or denial of their existence surpasses the human understanding. He thought God and the immortal soul to be necessary to motivate us because we need to see justice being done; those who are worthy of happiness should attain it, and those who are not, should not. Without such a notion of justice, he thought, we would despair over the pervasive injustice of this world. For him, God and the immortal soul are affirmed as practical postulates, ideas we must affirm because we need to affirm them in order to act morally.[24] But, we might point out that the existence of moral atheists stands as a proof that Kant was merely mired in cultural values such that he (possibly) needed the idea of God, but we (or some of us) do not. Likewise, we would perhaps only need to imagine the possibility of committed scientific naturalist artists and virtuous agents to disprove Murdoch's claim that we need a necessarily existing Good. Yet there is a line of defense for both Kant and Murdoch. Essentially, they can claim that in spite of what the agent attests, he or she presupposes the existence of God or the Good in acting (or even, for Murdoch, in thinking).

For Kant, God, the soul, and freedom are implicitly affirmed by human rational agents when they are acting, in other words God and freedom exist "from a practical point of view." This might hold even if the agent is a materialistic atheist who denies free will.[25] As Thomas Hill puts the point in the case of freedom, "Rational agents, in deliberating and deciding what to do, necessarily see themselves as free, regardless of their standing convictions on the metaphysical status of determinism."[26] Now, whether or not Kant's notions can be successfully defended in this way, the same style of argument can be pursued by Murdoch, only it will be significantly more radical. After all, Murdoch is denying Kant's split between theoretical and practical reason. For her, knowing the world is itself a moral task; hence, she will assert, more radically than Kant, that the Good, which escapes human understanding, is presupposed whenever we so much as attempt to understand the world. Hence, there is no qualification on Murdoch's affirmation of the existence of the Good, as there is with Kant's notion of freedom; the Good does not exist merely "from the practical point of view." It exists, she thinks, necessarily, for anyone who so much as attempts to think about the world. The agent-knower need not put the point in that way, and may even openly disagree with Murdoch, but Murdoch's position can be defended by pointing out that the agent-knower is engaging in a kind of contradiction.

Now, let me attempt to fill this argument in. Why must anyone, from an experimental physicist or a psychologist to an artist or a philosopher, affirm the existence of the Good in their various attempts to know the world? Every technique of knowing the world to which we accord validity is, for us, a technique of getting at the truth. For Murdoch, unsurprisingly, truth is a moral ideal, it is something we strive after; it is connected with the suppression of ego involved in realizing that something is the way it is, regardless of one's preferences. When we apply a technique successfully, and get results, the technique compels our assent. Now, for Murdoch, the compulsion of assent is connected with the Good. As Murdoch has it:

> I would suggest that the authority of the Good seems to us something necessary because the realism (ability to perceive reality) required for goodness is a kind of intellectual ability to perceive what is true, which is automatically at the same time a suppression of self. *The necessity of the good is then an aspect of the kind of necessity involved in any technique for exhibiting fact.*[27]

Now, I take it that psychology has various techniques for exhibiting fact, and that practitioners of psychology credit these techniques as valid techniques for getting at truth. When they do credit their techniques as valid, the technique, when successfully applied, generates conviction over what it reveals, that is, it compels belief. Of course, people sometimes feel conviction over "truths" revealed by techniques that lack validity (e.g., astrology). Believers in astrology might experience the same sort of suppression of self when their technique reveals a "truth." Yet, one might think, the technique is not bringing the practitioner closer to reality because the technique itself is entirely flawed. It is true that in retrospect, we can say that the conviction of astrologers was "merely psychological" in the sense that we now see the conviction as unmerited by the technique. That is, in light of solid evidence that the stars exercise no influence over individual lives, we can no longer derive any conviction from the practice of astrology, and therefore do not take reports of such conviction, past or present, seriously. Still, for astrologers who preceded the production of such evidence, there is a sense in which the practice of astrology was connected to the Good. After all, the same sort of suppression of ego that is necessary to give oneself over genuinely to the results of even a flawed technique is also necessary to admit the force of the evidence showing that technique to be flawed. In short, the pursuit of truth presupposes a readiness to be compelled to believe something that is against one's desires or interests. To that end, we must engage in the techniques at our disposal and pursue unqualified excellence in practicing them, even to the suppression of our desires; that is, we must pursue the Good.

Now if, in the end, we decide that our conviction that something merits being described as some technique dictates is merely psychological, then we hold a belief that is inconsistent with a genuine conviction that we are getting at the truth, according to Murdoch. A psychological perspective on our pursuit of truth (via our pursuit of the Good) would, in other words, put us at a remove from that pursuit, and that remove is actually inconsistent with the pursuit of truth. Imagine a psychologist engaged in a psychological study. At the end of a research project, he performs some tedious operations (say, he verifies computations) against his inclination to merely send out his work for publication. He does this knowing it is essential to the integrity of the study. To his surprise he finds out that the results do not show what he initially thought, and indeed the results call into question a great deal of his previous research. Nevertheless, after repeated verification, the results come up the same. Now, can he consistently say that the ideal of scientific practice that leads him to affirm the disappointing results at which he has arrived is just a psychological construct that he carries around in order to do his job well? How is "doing one's job well" to be characterized here? The scientific naturalist would want to characterize it in some fashion that avoids positing something that is not in keeping with a possible scientific description. For example, "doing one's job well" might mean "in a way that I (the practitioner) approve of," or "in a way my community approves of," or "in a way that meets my preferences" or "in a way that meets our collective preferences." There are many ways of spelling out what that phrase might mean that do not involve anything metaphysically suspect from the scientific point of view. These would be ways of saying that in science, as in art, the Good is merely an idea that we carry around that motivates us to do well, i.e., that it is not real, but rather a motivating fiction. Yet none of these alternative interpretations of the psychologist's ideal has a connection with just perception, and so they are inconsistent with his aim to get the truth. After all, if, in engaging in his pursuit, the psychologist is really just trying to get the approval of his scientific community by applying techniques and methods that they see as admirable, then he is not really concerned with describing things as they are. Murdoch thinks that anyone who is seriously engaged in an intellectual discipline or art would necessarily be attempting to attain just perception, and that requires, on her view, positing a transcendent ideal of perfect attention to things as they are. No attempt at defining that ideal (the Good) in natural terms would capture it; for such a definition would inevitably say, "What you are *really* trying to do is x," where x is some effort other than getting an accurate and just description of things as they are. So, genuine pursuit of an intellectual endeavor requires the affirmation of the Good, Murdoch thinks; to deny the existence of the Good is to hold a belief that is in contradiction with one's intentions, if one is seriously engaging in the discipline.

Likewise, genuine suppression of the ego requires the affirmation of the Good. Suppression of the ego, we should note, is not good in itself for Murdoch. She is no ascetic. Yet, contact with individuals as they are does require suppression of the ego in the sense that it requires arriving at descriptions independent of our interests. Now let's say our psychologist insists that he performed his self-deflating actions, which he describes as "doing his job well" out of a concern for acting in a manner that would be approved of by his scientific community. Actions falling under that description can surely bring a suppression of the ego in some sense, but not in the sense that Murdoch has in mind. For if the psychologist presents himself sincerely as having an overriding interest in what his scientific community thinks of him, then he must possess a very strong desire to please that community. That desire may require him to override many other desires he has, but always under the guidance of a stronger desire to be pleasing to his scientific community. In the end, he desires to arrive at descriptions pleasing to his scientific community because those are descriptions most in keeping with his interests as defined by his strongest desires. Hence there is no real transcendence of his interests involved here. He can learn what sorts of things are pleasing to his scientific community, and manage his actions so as to bring about, predictably, the satisfaction of his desire to please that community. Now, we might imagine that the desire to describe things and persons justly operates in a similar manner; that is, we might imagine that in the good person, the desire to describe things as they are is overriding, so that suppression of self amounts only to suppression of one desire by another. Hence, the good person might not escape the egoism of which Murdoch is critical. But what is the desire for just perception? The desire for approval of one's community is quite concrete; one can imagine words of praise in print or from the mouths of specific people whom we admire, and, unless we are living in a world with highly erratic scientists, we can predictably bring about these results (provided also sufficient talent and some luck). The desire for just perception is neither so concrete nor so predictably produced; I may have no idea how another will be justly described. It may be said that what I really desire is the feeling of fittingness that I have when I think I've arrived at the just description. But in reality arriving at the just description may be quite unsatisfying and deflating as one would imagine the results to be in the psychologist's case I described above. It seems that there is such a thing as desire for the Good, but that such desire is open-ended, inviting more or less constant, unpredictable transformation of descriptions and the concepts employed in them. The desire to arrive at just descriptions is a desire to arrive at descriptions that are independent of my interests; hence, it is a genuine desire for transcendence.

Because the Good is necessary to the genuine transcendence required for arriving at just descriptions of individuals and it is apparently irreducible to any natural description, there is therefore intellectually credible motivation for affirming the Good as an object of attention that is irreducible to any natural description. Now I want to describe briefly how the Good, understood as the ideal that underpins any effort at attending well, generates a conception of morality at odds with the Kant-style morality described in the previous section. Murdoch's claim is that the Good, understood as the guiding ideal of attention, is the unitary source of all value. Every virtue rests on this ideal, and involves conscious attention to the Good (even if it is not put in such terms by the agent). For example, attending to another may require humility. For Murdoch, humility "is selfless respect for reality."[28] Humility is a virtue and partakes in the Good, for Murdoch, just insofar as it involves attending well to reality, that is, to the individual before one, whether a kestrel or another human being. So, for Murdoch, there are virtues of attending well, such as humility. But other traditional virtues also partake in the Good for Murdoch. As John McDowell points out, possessing the virtue of kindness requires knowing what circumstances call for kindness, versus, say, honesty.[29] Often, this requires very fine moral discrimination between slightly different circumstances. Because the operation of any virtue requires acute situational appropriateness, and that in turn requires awareness of the individuals involved in a given circumstance, the exercise of attention is required in any good conduct. The Good, again, is an ideal of perfect attention. Hence, even traditional virtues depend on the Good.

Now, one might think that the Good really gets us nowhere in ethics. After all, it seems to be the case that after getting at the reality of another person, say, one must still decide how to act in view of the facts. But this view of the relation between facts and the will is part of the Kantian-style morality Murdoch criticizes. For adherents to such a view, there are coolly contemplated facts, on the one hand, and acts of the will (choices), on the other. The central ethical moment on such a view would be the decision of the will. Murdoch's picture is quite different. Ethics is on the scene as soon as we begin to take in the world. My ability to know another human being, on her view, requires displacing my selfish desires and developing virtuous character traits. To the extent that I am able to grasp that there really are others, on Murdoch's view, certain ways of treating them are ruled out and others become *necessary*. As she puts it: "the more the separateness and differentness of other people is realized, and the fact seen that another man has needs and wishes as demanding as one's own, the harder it becomes to treat a person as a thing."[30] This passage emphasizes the negative aspect of the obligations that arise as a result of grasping the reality of another, namely, obligations not to treat a person merely as a thing, but there are also positive obligations. That is to say, insofar as I come into contact with the Good, it becomes necessary for me to act in certain ways. For example, the more that I become aware of another's hunger, on Murdoch's view, the less able I am to avoid feeding her. That is, I become less free to consider not feeding her. At the end of the day, a hungry mouth, for Murdoch, *is something to be fed*.

From the perspective of an adherent to the Kantian-style view of facts and values, there may appear to be something fishy about this view. It claims that someone who fails to act on another's hunger is less in touch with reality than someone who does. Counterexamples may come to mind, such as the idea of a villain whose in-depth knowledge of another's hunger helps the villain to extract greater suffering from his victim, perhaps allowing him to provide just enough food to keep the victim feeling excruciating hunger pangs. It would seem implausible to say that the villain is out of touch with the reality of the victim's needs. Murdoch may therefore seem to have defined "being in touch with reality" to suit her ethical needs. But that is not the case. The villain may indeed have knowledge of his victim's hunger, and may even have the detailed physiological knowledge needed for his purposes. Still, the villain hasn't realized the significance of the other's needs apart from his own interest in maintaining the victim in pain, even if, as in the case of a psychopath, he finds that pain intrinsically interesting. Thus, he is not aware of his victim as "separate and different." The other's condition is viewed only in light of his malicious project. One might be tempted to say that the ethical individual only appreciates someone else's discomfort from the perspective of her interest in being helpful. No doubt there are such people, but for Murdoch they would be less than fully virtuous. The morally mediocre individual, from Murdoch's perspective, will experience himself as having a choice whether to feed the hungry person, and may begrudge the intrusion of the other's hunger on his projects, or delight in the opportunity to appear good before others. Murdoch's ideal points us toward people who take in another's discomfort apart from their own interests. Her claim is that the motivational displacement necessary to do that is essentially linked to the motivation to act on the awareness of that discomfort. For gaining such awareness requires the deep interest in others for their own sakes that is found only in good people. Becoming aware of the independent reality of another's suffering is an instance of coming into contact with the Good, and it is necessarily motivating. This argument supports the conclusion that the Good is motivating to all that come into contact with it, and that it is indeed a unitary source of value that can explain a wide range of our moral lives in terms of an ethic of attention.

Murdoch and Ethical Naturalism

Above I claimed that Murdoch's introduction of the Good, although part of a critical response to scientific naturalism, is nevertheless part of an attempt to work out a more satisfactory naturalism. After presenting Murdoch's arguments, it may not be obvious any longer in what sense she can still be considered a naturalist. Murdoch's views are in fact a kind of ethical naturalism. Bernard Williams put the project of ethical naturalism succinctly and clearly as "the project of thinking out, from what human beings are like, how they might best and most appropriately live."[31] Of course, in some sense all moral views must take account of how human beings are, unless they make inhuman demands on us, but the ethical naturalist hopes that substantive ethical norms may be derived from human nature. Murdoch's own views rest on her claim,

"Objectivity and unselfishness are not natural to human beings."[32] In other words, she holds humans to be naturally fantasy-prone and selfish. And yet, in some sense, we *need* to attain objectivity and unselfishness. She traces her views about human nature back to Freud, who was attempting to work out a scientific conception of human psychology. The success of Murdoch's moral philosophy does not hang on the details of Freudian psychology but rather on his core picture of human nature. Still, her basic view of natural human selfishness or fantasy might be challenged scientifically, by psychologists. Though it seems implausible that any single experiment could falsify her moral philosophy, it might turn out that humans are less fantasy-prone, less naturally self-absorbed than she claims, and that would certainly make her view seem less attractive. I take it that it is a merit of her work that it might be so challenged. It shows that she has staked her moral philosophy on substantive claims about human nature. Yet I don't think this basic picture has been effectively challenged; it is therefore still quite plausible.

Ethical naturalism has been subject to larger philosophical objections, especially by Bernard Williams. Briefly, Williams' view is that ethical naturalists assume an antiquated, Aristotelian view of nature. Aristotle looked at nature as having purposes inscribed within it. These purposes support a conception of human beings as destined by nature to be ethical beings, for our purpose as rational animals requires developing moral virtues such as honesty. By contrast, our modern conception of human nature reveals no such purposes, and there is, in Williams' view, no sign that human beings are destined by nature to be ethical beings. After all, it is a plain fact that vicious people flourish on the "ethological standard of the bright eye and the gleaming coat."[33] And so, it may seem that being virtuous is neither necessary nor sufficient for flourishing as a human being.

Murdoch explicitly denies assuming a final end for human beings. Still, she does seem to be assuming that a good human being partially overcomes her natural selfishness and fantastical views of persons and things. She may not mean to suggest that this goodness is connected to human flourishing, but it would nevertheless pose a problem for her view if the good human by her measure were typically unhappy or unhealthy. Williams' objection may then be put to Murdoch: perhaps human beings flourish well under conditions of self-delusion and selfishness. Among other things, contemplating the suffering of others, which Murdoch's ethic of attention would require us to do, is extremely difficult and surely could lead to unhappiness, if not depression.[34]

In response, we should note that Murdoch's naturalism is not limited to the domain normally circumscribed as "moral" or "ethical." Many Aristotelian virtue ethicists do not challenge the Kantian division of intellect and will. Generally, they are concerned with moral virtues, but not with the moral effort required to know the world. Hence, one response to Williams's objection, open uniquely to Murdoch, would be to say that even answering it requires developing certain Murdochian virtues, that is, certain dispositions toward knowing reality; we must be able to look at ourselves and others unflinchingly. As I have noted, Murdoch draws support for the existence of the Good from the scales of excellence that are contained within our practical endeavors. To engage in an inquiry that would settle a dispute over human nature such as this would require excellent and selfless practice of psychology. It would be a difficult truth for many of us to learn that we would be unhappy being as good as we might like to be. Yet we may indeed find that there are general predictable limits to our psychological capacities relevant to morality; for example, it may prove psychologically harmful for us to contemplate the suffering of others for more than a certain length of time, at certain levels of intensity. Such a fact would only support the value of self-delusion, however, if to be happy we needed to be convinced that the suffering in the abstract did not exist. In all likelihood, our limitations are simply that we must periodically rest, and rest may involve play and play may involve fantasy. But the open-eyed periodic indulgence in fantasy is of course something other than giving up on the pursuit of reality altogether.

Still, settling any important issues about human nature requires Murdochian virtues. Assuming that Williams would agree that knowledge is a good that humans need to flourish, if he conceded that there is something like the moral difficulty in knowing the world that Murdoch identifies, he would have to admit that Murdochian virtues are indeed necessary for flourishing. The Good, then, is something we need because of the way that we are. Murdoch's is in some sense a naturalistic view; the Good is something we strive after in relating to each other and engaging in our practices. It is not a quality and is not sensible. No science will detect it, yet the existence of the sciences, as well as of the arts, supports its existence.

Murdoch convincingly defends the notion of the Good as a component of the world, even though it does not fit into the world as described by the natural sciences. In place of a picture of the world as composed of coolly contemplated facts in view of which we then make choices, Murdoch presents us with a picture of a world that is known only with a moral struggle that shapes our character so that we then respond to individuals that we encounter with unavoidable actions. Unlike many other ethicists, she acknowledges the moral struggle that is involved in coming to know the world at all. Her broad attack on the scientific naturalism gives her a unique perspective on the nature of value that I hope this paper will bring to fuller appreciation.[35]

NOTES

1. Putnam, 1981.
2. Antonaccio and Schweiker, 1996, 79.

3. This seems to be Murdoch's target of criticism when she speaks of "modern empiricism" (see, e.g., 1970, 57).
4. Murdoch, 1970, 50.
5. There are equal parts Plato and Kant in her view here. In tracing the conditions of possibility for our experience, she is in some sense making a transcendental argument, and so she is indebted to Kant. Less recognizably, but no less significantly, she is indebted to Plato, who claims of the Good that it "gives the power of knowing to the knower" (*Republic* 508e, trans. Shorey). I thank Matthew J.M. Martinuk for pointing out the transcendental structure of Murdoch's arguments in a fascinating forthcoming dissertation entitled "Being toward the Good: A Study in the Philosophical Anthropology of Charles Taylor and Iris Murdoch" (University of Guelph).
6. Murdoch, 1992, Chatto, 495.
7. Murdoch, 1970, 59.
8. Murdoch and Conradi, 1999, 290.
9. Murdoch 1970, 88.
10. Even with activities as apparently value neutral as logic and geometry, it would follow from Murdoch's position that there is some moral difficulty. We tend to take for granted the mastery of desires and outward orientation of attention that must be developed to engage in the intricate manipulation of symbols.
11. I say "at least" because for many scientific naturalists, it would be desirable to effect even further reductions of psychology to biology and that in turn to physics.
12. Wright, 2005, 375.
13. As I will describe below, Murdoch employs the concept of the Good together with a special understanding of attention to achieve a non-reductive account of "meriting a description."
14. Murdoch, 1997, Penguin, 293.
15. Murdoch, 1970, 38.
16. In an article on Kant and Murdoch, Nancy Schauber writes, "Since what is morally meritorious for Kant is premised on seeing others as they really are, Murdoch and Kant should be seen as allies with a common goal" (Schauber, 2001, 478). We can see that this claim is fundamentally mistaken, however. Kant just assumes access to others as they are. Knowing others as they are is not a goal for him, and the whole of morality is independent of knowing others as they are, for Kant. For Murdoch, the greater part of morality consists precisely of the attempt to know others, and there is very little, if anything to settle morally after that task is completed.
17. Kant, 1996 [1787], 8.
18. Murdoch, 1970, 17.
19. *Ibid.*, 54.
20. *Ibid.*, 68.
21. *Ibid.*, 58.
22. *Ibid.*, 60.
23. Note that this is perfectly compatible with acknowledging one's shortcomings. One need not be a self-punishing perfectionist. The simple effort to paint well implies this idea of perfection, as a formal goal one is approximating, however far from it one might be.
24. Kant, 1996, 740.
25. I find Kant's argument more convincing in the case of freedom than in the case of the existence of God, but I am not concerned to argue against Kant on this point here.
26. Hill, 1992, 117.
27. Murdoch, 1970, 64.
28. *Ibid.*, 93.
29. Murdoch, 1997, Penguin, 51.
30. Murdoch, 1970, 64.
31. Williams, 1995, 109.
32. Murdoch, 1970, 50.
33. Williams, 1985, 46.
34. Of course, we owe others our attention in any circumstance, including happy circumstances, but it is most challenging and demanding, arguably, to pay attention to others who are suffering.
35. I would like to thank the editors of this volume, as well as Peter Loptson, Matthew J.M. Martinuk, and Laura Hacker-Wright for their helpful comments on this paper.

12

Morality in a World Without God

MILES LEESON

> *I am a little worried about how far one should let the philosophy come in. I think that sometimes it comes into the centre of the plot, as it did in* The Time of the Angels[1]
> — Iris Murdoch, *A Tiny Corner in the House of Fiction*

Murdoch's earliest work is preoccupied with the relation of her fictional writing to the work of some of her greatest philosophical influences and can be neatly summarized as a philosophical discussion of language[2]: she admits as much. This is surprising when viewed against the polemic nature of *Against Dryness* and an interview of 1978: "I have definite philosophical views, but I don't want to promote them in my novels or to give the novel a kind of metaphysical background.... I don't want philosophy, as such, to intrude into the novel world at all."[3] This essay aims to not only assess the impact of Heidegger upon Murdoch's work, with specific regard to *The Time of the Angels*, but to discuss Murdoch's unpublished manuscript, "Heidegger: The Pursuit of Being," concerning Heidegger's *Sein und Zeit* and her rejection of Germanic existentialism. It is my firm belief that Murdoch's concern with Heideggerian philosophy—and existentialism in general—stretches for the length of her career and had a greater impact upon it than has been given attention before this point: indeed Peter Conradi, Elizabeth Dipple and Barbara Stevens Heusel either omit Heidegger from influencing "Murdochland" or mention him briefly in passing footnote. Thankfully the work of Stephen Mulhall and Justin Broakes is beginning to reassess his influence to some degree—although this is only a philosophical redress, not an interdisciplinary one as this essay will be. I should state at this point that I am not an expert on the intricacies of Heideggerian philosophy, so it should not be thought that this essay attempts a reductionist reading of it. I intend to explore Murdoch's engagement with Heidegger; it falls to others to assess the merits of her work *in toto*.

For Murdoch the trinity of Plato, G.E. Moore and Simone Weil were counter-balanced throughout her career by Kant, Sartre and Heidegger (and, to an extent Nietzsche): opposing forces from which her best fiction seemed to emanate. *The Time of the Angels* concerns the development of world secularization in relation to an enclosed community (of sorts) as well as the abuse of power and sexual domination. The central issue is this: can one be a theist without succumbing to the lure of a false idol or simplistic consolation within religious belief? Marcus Fischer, the figure of the "good," is in the early stage of planning a book concerned with (and titled) *Morality without God*. The main theme of his work is an attack upon those who believe that moral judgments are expressions of the will, or of choice, a concept which Murdoch argues against in her own philosophical writings. Her own creation, however, and a much later work, *Metaphysics as a guide to Morals*, seems to wish to achieve the same purpose, namely replacing god with "good" in much the same way that Fischer imagines but via a different route. Certainly, this is something which had been developing in Murdoch's own mind since the 1960s. The opposition to this view is taken by Marcus's brother Carel who marvels at his control over the inhabitants of his rectory:

> The author of the book of Job understood it. Job asks for sense and justice. Jehovah replies that there is none. There is only power and the marvel of power; there is only chance and the terror of chance.[4]

From this view amorality is justified; for the Nietzschean and the Heideggerian (not that the two are so parallel), will to power is everything. If there is no longer a valid moral choice does vision therefore become all? Is this perhaps the only option? Murdoch sees "vision" thus:

> What must here be clearly separated is the notion of inner or private psychological phenomena, open to introspection, and the notion of private or personal vision which may find expression overtly or inwardly ... morality is a choice, and moral language guides choice through factual specification.[5]

The vision could clearly be one in which God is placed at the center; but if there is no God, does it follow that there is no morality either? This is the main issue debated in the novel — the updated Hegelian notion (present within Dostoyevsky, another influence upon the novel) that "God is not only dead, everything is permissible," or, what morality might mean in a world without God:

> Suppose the truth were awful, suppose it was just a black pit, or like birds huddled in the dust in a dark cupboard? Suppose only evil were real, only it was not evil since it had lost even its name?[6]

It is Carel who speaks these words but his brother holds the same to be true:

> Suppose the truth about human life were just something terrible, something appalling which one would be destroyed by contemplating? You've taken away all the guarantees.[7]

Murdoch, although in conversation with these notions, does not hold any of them to be true. Her vision still holds Platonism to be the ultimate philosophical doctrine. This Platonism finds form within the novel in the philosophical writing of Marcus Fischer. As Mary Warnock argues, "She [Murdoch] holds that goodness has a real though abstract existence in the world. The actual existence of goodness is, in her view, the way it is now possible to understand the idea of God."[8] For herself, Murdoch says that "[o]ur general awareness of good, or goodness, is with us unreflectively all the time, as a sense of God's presence, or at least existence, used to be for all sorts of believers."[9] So, in the widest sense *The Time of the Angels* serves as a functional philosophical debate, quite unlike anything she had attempted in previous fiction; indeed, it would be true to say that Murdoch never did come to full knowledge of Heideggerian philosophy as she rejected her work on Heidegger and left it unpublished in 1993.[10] She allows the awfulness of her emotion toward his form of existentialism to find form within the novel when Pattie (literally) stumbles upon a copy of Heidegger's *Sein und Zeit*. Pattie exists to service Carel who refers to her as "Pattie beast" or his "black Madonna."

> In death, Dasein (being-there) has not been fulfilled nor has it simply disappeared; it has not become finished or is it wholly at one's disposal as something ready-to-hand.... Ending, as Being-towards-the-end, must be clarified ontologically in terms of Dasein's kind of being.... The existential clarification of Being-towards-the-end will also give us an adequate basis for defining what can be possibly be the meaning of our talk about a totality of Dasein, if indeed this totality is to be constituted by death as the end.[11]

Pattie recoils in horror at reading these words, not because she understands them but because they fill her with dread as "the words sounded senseless and awful, like the distant boom of some big catastrophe."[12] This shudder is how the words affect both Murdoch, who did not truly understand them herself and the vast majority of her readers:[13] death is the natural end but to dehumanize the language makes it an unimaginable act of "unbeing." Heidegger is arguably the most difficult philosopher to engage with securely as his focus on being and language can at times be impenetrable. One of Murdoch's later projects was to write a definitive account of his philosophy, but she abandoned it once the proofs were written: "Iris decided that this book, on which she had been working for six years, was no good and should be abandoned."[14] She had written in her journal several years previously that 'I am spending a lot of time at last trying to understand Heidegger — all his ideas, and his development. Wish I had thought of this earlier!'"[15] Gilbert Ryle first introduced her to Heidegger and she viewed both men as lacking a Platonic view of the world, which, if they were able to obtain, would greatly enhance their individual philosophies. Even so, she came to devote a great deal of time to Heidegger and became firm friends with Ryle.[16] It is clear that Murdoch uses a highly technical (and typical) quotation from Heidegger to bring the reader into the narrative from Pattie's perspective to elucidate Murdoch's rejection of his philosophy. As Conradi states: "Her foes are Nietzsche, Heidegger, Derrida and a collective hydra-headed monster she terms 'structuralism,' all hostile to transcendence."[17] A summary with which I agree entirely. She believes each of these philosophers to be actively engaged in separating the self from any concept of the transcendent other. Indeed her unpublished work on Heidegger was an attempt to fully integrate herself within his discourse — sadly a failure. As she mentions toward the end of her manuscript her judgment cannot be trusted when assessing Heidegger's philosophy which rather lends itself to the idea that if this work were to be published in its entirety her reputation as a philosopher of significant importance could be called into question. Although this may well be an ironic aside, it would be doubly so if it were to be the lasting impression of her later philosophical works, i.e., that she was no longer capable of forming a useful theory of her own. I believe that it is necessary to publish such a work not merely to stimulate discussion about Murdoch's relationship with Heideggerian theory but also for biographical reasons. I do not believe her reputation would be seriously called into question if it became apparent that she could not argue against a philosophy she did not truly understand. She certainly is a scholar by any definition, but this rather damning conclusion, and the subsequent rejection of this work by Murdoch herself, and later by Conradi's decision not to publish it, is certainly not to be taken lightly. Few readers of her fiction, unless engaged in philosophy, would be able to grasp the subtle relationship between Dasein's Being-at-an-end and the notion of Being-toward-the-end, which is why Heidegger engenders a feeling of the uncanny on first glance.

In order to understand this tension, the reader reads the text with Pattie and does not fully grasp the meaning of it even though they have understood all that has come before it in terms of language if nothing else. In doing so the reader's focus is firmly renewed upon the prose. Murdoch refocuses the attention of the reader via this literary device by suddenly coercing us to question what we have already read. Murdoch's use of language up to this point has been understandable to anyone with a standard education. Now she moves into another realm entirely, and this very conscious effort (on her part) is felt immediately.

Pattie is the innocent in these proceedings. She has only had a limited education and cannot comprehend the situation around her, until it is exposed to her by the discovery of Carel and Elizabeth entwined on Elizabeth's bedroom floor; Carel and Elizabeth being involved in an incestuous relationship of Carel's devising. Dipple has said that she finds the narrative progress here "very simple and natural,"[18] which seems a little odd given that it describes developments which are, by any normal idea unnatural to say the least. Pattie then reveals to Muriel that Elizabeth is in fact her sister, which is the catalyst for the end of the novel and the death of Carel; and with his death the rejection of the philosophy that he embodies. Muriel's negative action, the permitting of her father to die from an overdose, allows the novel to conclude on a Platonic overtone.

Murdoch came to believe that although Wittgenstein and Heidegger were the two most important philosophers of the twentieth century Heidegger was too convoluted and obscure, and she lamented the lack of contemporary philosophers and writers who were willing to engage with both of them. She believed that Heidegger's development of Kant, to produce a godless universe, made him "the devil himself" although a philosopher who could (twice) call for a demythologization of the New Testament and connect moral philosophy with religion.[19] She develops this in "Heidegger: The Pursuit of Being" when she says that Heidegger is abandoning the very center of religion insofar that he removes the notions of duty, goodness and love which enables the individual to connect with the "other" against nothingness. It is not the removal of a personal god that she objects to but the lack of these central concepts.

This demythologizing of religion, especially Christianity, is at the core of *The Time of the Angels*. I am thinking here specifically of abstract symbolism being reduced to actual influences upon human behavior. The symbolism used in the novel to achieve this is apparent from the beginning; first by the development of Carel as the priest of no parish and no god who uses the promise of salvation to seduce Pattie; secondly, by the use of the swirling fog around the rectory and the annihilation of surrounding London, and, thirdly, by the imprisonment of the rectory's inhabitants and the distance between Carel and the Bishop, the master no longer controls the servant through any sense of goodness. This enables Murdoch to criticize not only the hopelessness of a philosophy where the self is everything but also what she designates in "Against Dryness" as the "modern neurotic novel":

> We need to be able to think ... in a non-metaphysical, non-totalitarian and non-religious sense, the transcendence of reality.... We need to return from the self-centred concept of sincerity to the other-centred concept of truth. We are not isolated free choosers, monarchs of all we survey, but benighted creatures sunk in a reality whose nature we are constantly and overwhelmingly tempted to deform by fantasy.[20]

The Time of the Angels holds a mirror to the self-centeredness which Murdoch believes pervades modern society: a sure distinction between the Platonic and the Heideggerian. It is of course a development which has been taken to an extreme but it does, as *Under the Net* did with Sartrean values, expose the limitations of such a belief system. In that novel, she created a West London suburb which was the scene to an unfolding comedic drama concerning the development of the self toward a greater understanding of the other. In *The Time of the Angels* Murdoch's central character has progressed so far toward a complete infatuation with the self that it is only through his death that the other inhabitants of the novel are set free. How is it, then, that Carel actively promotes Heideggerian theory? I would argue that is through his action and development as Heideggerian-Man Murdoch sets up her most convincingly evil character since Mischa Fox in *The Flight from the Enchanter*. It falls then to Murdoch to set up an idea of transcendence within the novel which illuminates both the "fallenness" of believing in any Heideggerian notion of inner development toward the Platonic ideal of a vertical transcendental shift. For Murdoch transcendence is ultimately caught up with two separate propositions, perfection and certainty:

> Are we not certain that there is a "true direction" towards better conduct, that goodness "really matters," and does not that certainty about a standard suggest an idea of permanence which cannot be reduced to psychological or any other set of empirical terms?[21]

In broad terms then, Dasein(being), composed of its ontological and existential dimensions disclosed as Being-in-the-world (the self in relation to an 'other'), must be understood in the context of Selfhood, which we can relate to *The Time of the Angels*. Carel Fischer must have ownership over his household. It is he who wishes to remove the inauthenticity of the other and assert the total being of the self. Murdoch wishes show from the very beginning of her evaluation of Heidegger that his is ultimately a valueless philosophy: "I shall argue [that] Heidegger portrays it [Dasein] as curiously bereft of values,"[22] and therefore of little use to how she views the world. As mentioned earlier the lack of the transcendent in his philosophy is of grave concern to Murdoch; it is certainly possible that Heidegger's rejection of it may have led to her abandonment of her critical work on his "Dasein." Murdoch must surely have known that to tackle such a project was dangerous as Heidegger is set against any argument for "vertical transcendence," but it would appear that her confidence to try to argue against Heideggerian theory won through. Perhaps with hindsight, she would not have attempted such a challenge. It was certainly a brave attempt; perhaps if more philosophers and academics had access to her — so far unpublished — work, a more reasoned conclusion could be sought.

The major difference between the two is this: Murdoch is proscribing whereas Heidegger is describing. For Murdoch one must develop beyond language: she refutes Heidegger's view in *Sartre: Romantic Rationalist* and remains resolutely against existential thought:

> In his [Heidegger's] system, moral insight or inspiration is a later, or farther, or special, or specialised, narrowly defined achievement. Sartrean existentialism and the morality of Marxism also display this pattern.... Heidegger holds no theory of a transcendent systemised order of spiritual reality, or true knowledge, which it is man's proper destiny to realize.[23]

It is this lack of "spiritual reality" that immediately concerns Murdoch here. Heidegger expounds on another structural element in the ontological constitution of Dasein, that of "fallenness"; an interesting term implying some form of past transcendence that one would not normally associate with Heidegger.

Murdoch comments:

> His [Heidegger's] account, perpetually suggests that value, moral orientation, virtue exist only at a level markedly above that of the day. So it is not even worth examining the idea of *Gerede* [idle chatter], which Heidegger uses in a disparaging sense but also denies that he does.[24]

At this point, we must clarify the meaning of Dasein's falsehood, or, what Murdoch believes to be its failings with regard to transcendent reality. In his essay *On the Essence of Truth*, Heidegger explicates the Greeks' understanding of *aletheia* as disclosedness or unconcealment. Murdoch has this to say:

> As I have argued earlier, I think such theorising is important and welcome in philosophy. However, Heidegger's concepts and distinctions in this field seem to me too much influenced by an idea of phenomenology as a definite philosophical method, and also by Heidegger's final metaphysical aims, especially his prime desire to establish "the authentic" as against the "inauthentic." To put it crudely, Heidegger wants to exalt his "hero" to use a word which recurs at intervals in his writings.[25]

The Dasein who has fallen into falsehood closes itself off from authentically Being-in-the-world and even more significantly from Being-with and Being-toward itself. In psychoanalysis this might be given to the defense mechanism of denial, that is, people need to deny the ontological obligations of Dasein in the service of more primordial psychological needs or conflicts, such as psychodynamic motivations surrounding security, attachment, and as Heidegger points out, "tranquility."[26] Murdoch's relationship with psychoanalysis is one fraught with contradictions. Her novel *A Severed Head* is intimately connected with the idea that the development of Freud's ideas concerning the ego, and their application in psychoanalysis, lead us to consider not the form of the good, but rather an inward-looking ontology which does nothing to neither free us from the Platonic cave nor engender within us any concept of "attention." Even though she calls Freud "a self-styled modern disciple of Plato,"[27] it is clear that he dismisses the possibility that the ego may be tempered by art. This is "a problem [which I consider later], for Freud and those whom he inspires, whether such analyses can be devoid of radical value judgments."[28] It is the fantasy of Carel to control the household and the neurosis of Marcus which holds the narrative together, and these are not only Freudian but also Heideggerian — neither has realized the extent of their respective egos and Marcus only finds consolation in Carel's death as it frees him from his compulsion to save his brother. This is necessarily the same for Heidegger: his assumed value judgments concerning transcendence, the ego, and the nature of the self do damage, Murdoch believes, to understanding the internal struggle of the individual. The point is therefore quite a simple one: does Heidegger have any lingering understanding of a human's intuition for the transcendent? If we concern ourselves with Carel being a caricature of Murdoch's view of Heidegger's stance it is clear that she believes he does not and will not yield to any notion of a secondary "other," neither the realization of uniqueness amongst individuals nor the notion of a metaphysical "other." Carel's failure to comprehend the desires and needs of the rest of his household lead to its destruction, the absence of freedom within the novel is tangible: this is certainly not a house fit for free characters.

Perhaps Heidegger's Dasein is too concerned about the absence of freedom which it does not engender. This was also a concern of Murdoch's, as she believed that the individual must be conceived of as a whole: although one must aspire toward self-realization (for Murdoch) we must also not remove that which is propelling us toward it.[29] By using an existential critique of the false Dasein, it appears structured to actively promote fallenness. This is its ontological structure, and Heidegger is, in the broadest sense, an existentialist philosopher. Murdoch, being trained at Oxford in linguistic analysis, assessed this philosophical idea and used it to create Carel Fischer, who in turn inversely reveals Murdoch's vision that being-for-self is not a worthy state of being. It is only through being good-for-nothing that we can actively approach an idea of perfection; this is connected with "good" though not necessarily with god. Here, as in her earliest work, Murdoch approaches the domain formerly occupied philosophically by Simone Weil. This is reflected in her pronouncements on the need for moral change:

> Human beings are far more complicated and enigmatic and ambiguous than languages and mathematical concepts, and selfishness operates in a much more devious and frenzied manner in our relations with them.... Our attachments tend to be selfish and strong, and the transformation of our loves from selfishness to unselfishness is sometimes even hard to conceive of.[30]

Carel then is ultimately a selfish creation by any standard, no matter if he believes in the mantra that "God is dead — therefore all is permissible," a curious amalgam of Hegel, Nietzsche and Dostoyevsky. He is, for Murdoch, the antithesis of her moral vision. Carel's deceitfulness and lack of respect toward the other members of his household stems from his need to fill a void in his life: for example the seduction of his own daughter, the seduction and subsequent rejection of Pattie and his refusal to acknowledge Muriel as an individual. Murdoch implicitly creates Carel as an empty vessel into which she can pour what she sees as Heidegger's damaging rejection of what Simone Weil terms as "attention." The black void at the center of Carel is his lack of humanity toward those whom he has a duty to care for. He is not a "free character" in the Murdochian sense as he inhabits a role with defined parameters. Here we can return to the idea of the artificial (and superficial) notion of Dasein and relate it to psychoanalysis, in particular a psychoanalytic view of the morality of both *The Time of the Angels* and Carel Fischer. Here we should consider Murdoch's view of the perceived shift in the value of the united self; from a central concept to a peripheral vision in mainstream philosophy.

The rejection of the self stems, she believes, from the shift away from the religious. Although Murdoch is not theist, in any academic sense, a worldview of religion is central to her philosophy — whether it is to be rebelled against or not. Although Murdoch believes that this shift brought about the beginnings of the rejection of the self, and rightly brought about critical vision to theistic concepts which had gone unchallenged up until that point, she nevertheless was far from the view held by Richard Dawkins (in conversation with Garth Wood) that religion is one of the great evils of contemporary society "[being like] the smallpox virus, but harder to eradicate."[31] She challenges the almost automatic assumption that ethics are removed from and autonomous of religious claims and beliefs. Murdoch always held the religious life in great esteem: "Our general awareness of good, or goodness, is with us unreflectively all the time, as a sense of God's presence, or at least existence, used to be for all sorts of believers."[32] For Murdoch, then, the filling of the void left behind by the absence of god in general and the ideology of Christianity in particular is central to both *The Time of the Angels* and her moral philosophy. She believes that we must reject the current denial of the interior and establish a working concept of the self, one which is not fragmented or misaligned. Through the development of Marcus, the elder brother, whom she connects with paternal instincts (and has long since departed from reality as he and Carel have been estranged since Carel's departure from both his previous parish and Christianity), Murdoch fictionalizes the split between the two opposing sides in the debate; Carel as Kantian man and Marcus as a (albeit flawed) model of the Cartesian solitary knower."[33] This is not to say that Murdoch is at one with the Cartesian world view; Marcus is developed as somewhat weak and ineffectual. As we have seen earlier, she commends post–Cartesian thinkers for the proper assertion that "thinking is not a mental composition repeated aloud verbatim, spoken words do not have to have mental equivalents, words are not the names of things."[34] By rejecting the Cartesian picture of the self, one which places too much emphasis on the all-knowing knower, Murdoch places herself in a precarious position; she no longer seems to be on any side (which is not only Heidegger against Descartes) of the argument, merely waiting for the next move from the empiricists.

Hume is, for Murdoch, the beginning of the erosion of the concept of the self that was first formalized in philosophy. It was he who announced that self was an illusion of mind, fragmented memories and experiences held together by imagination and dreams. Heidegger maintains that some non-transcendent force must be at work in the development of Being. Encounters with others are individual acts which affect us at that specific moment, and this perception of an "other" forces development. Both, of course, hold that the other is vital but Heidegger refutes any totalizing system.

Murdoch believes this to be partly true — the notion of self as a series of interlocking units of the mind — as it closely resembled her own belief toward the foundation of a human's moral awareness.[35] Where she vehemently disagrees concerns the lack of a unity within consciousness, an area upon which Kant focused. Hume and Kant, Murdoch believed were the foundation for the negative opinions of the self held by Hampshire, Ayer and Ryle. We must also remember that she rejected structuralism with its closed language system and disregard of the referent, the real world. She believes that Kant was discontented with much of Hume's work as he was not prepared to rest scientific determinism upon a psychological association of ideas. Kant's model focused instead upon "discrete units of experience" which Murdoch interpreted as lacking in an approach to "moral experience, or moral consciousness as a 'morally coloured' awareness."[36] Consciousness and moral development in particular, are, for Kant, not an active individual experience at all but rather "an empty consciousness, a structure of intuition, understanding, reason, which is the same in every rational creature."[37]

Murdoch is wary of placing too much emphasis on psychoanalysis in general and Freudianism in particular, certainly regarding the construction of psychoanalysis as a "life philosophy" (derided in *A Severed Head*). Hence, she is again caught: Kantianism is too far removed from human experience; Freud makes too much of it. Heidegger for his part was apathetic toward psychoanalysis, but his philosophy affected it. Murdoch employs both Freudian analysis and Heidegger's philosophy to enable her narrative to function. Without the impact of these, occasionally opposing, factors *The Time of the Angels* would have little sense of purpose: the conversation between Carel and Muriel concerning the mental state of Elizabeth is useful here:

> "I think she's perfectly alright," said Muriel. She found that her hands were still gripping the desk, her fingers pointed toward Carel's fingers. She removed her hands and clasped them tensely together. "Of course she's all right Muriel, and she's going to go on being all right. Only we must take more care of her, extra-special care of her. We must protect her from shocks. She must be allowed her thoughts, her dreams. There must be no shocks and no intrusions. These could have the gravest consequences." ... "I don't agree. I think she needs to see people. She's just a bit bored ... all this loneliness makes her sleepy."[38]

It is important to take the entirety of the conversation in context and it is, unfortunately, beyond the scope to reproduce it here in its entirety. However it is important to note that Carel's insistence on the existence of a "dream world" precludes Elizabeth from realizing her predicament as slave to his will: to keep the unconscious to the fore. One must have actual experience of the real to enact any change and, whatever their differences, both Murdoch and Heidegger would agree on this point. Transcendence needs an active will and imagination.

While potential conceptual quandaries between the ontological discourse of Heideggerian theory and the ontological discourse of psychodynamic approaches exist, Heidegger's existential ontology has profound implications for understanding the ontology of the unconscious and the question of authenticity. So, Murdoch is therefore drawn to link both Heidegger's notion of the Being-for-itself and Freud's analysis of the self in the world, as she reveals this in her unpublished manuscript when discussing human moods:

> His [Heidegger's] theory of "moods," another philosophical way of characterising consciousness, is a more dubious and arbitrary matter. I like the idea of speaking, in philosophy, about moods. But what exactly is a mood? In reading novels we have no trouble with the concept ... here (it seems to me) Heidegger creates his primary (descriptive) concepts with a view to his later (evaluative) ends.[39]

Although psychology is not a true insight into ontology, some linkage between the two is apparent. Therefore reason is contingent on some prior form of consciousness that necessarily requires an underlying ontology. This for Murdoch is the key to Carel, and the reverse is true for Pattie. As Pattie plays the innocent, caught up in the terrible turn of events through no fault of her own (except perhaps her lack of self development) she becomes the antithesis of Carel. In this sense she is also the gateway through which the reader can begin to react to the novel; underlying Pattie's willingness to please is fear, "Fear, for instance, is a mode of state of mind,"[40] directly paralleling Heidegger's *Being and Time*; where he claims that fear is not a state of mind itself but engenders itself upon the mind, which she criticizes here in her unpublished work. If we enlarge on this concept of fear within *The Time of the Angels*, we begin to understand the enchantment Carel holds over the members of his household and those beyond it. It is an obvious echo from *The Flight from the Enchanter*, and it would not be unreasonable to find elements of Mischa Fox within Carel Fischer — the most ominous moments echoing Mischa's basement with Carel's study with the emphasis on the "blackness."[41] This notion of the "false self," and the uncertainty it creates within Murdoch's early fiction, is directly paralleled within the work of both Freud and Heidegger. Dasein's psychological structures, for example, become more lucid with the assistance of a psychoanalytic explication of the self, which in turn enhances Heideggerian philosophy. While Freud does not offer a systematic theory of the self, the notion of the self is implicit in his final tripartite-structural model of the mind; the self is the unity of the id, ego, and superego and must be so or psychological issues follow. So to be alienated from your true self would be disastrous for any sense of purpose within the individual. If we relate this back to the text, can we find any parallels with the major characters?

There is, quite plainly, the obsession with Canetti[42] in *The Flight from the Enchanter*, and his influence is to be found, albeit to a lesser extent within Honor Kline of *A Severed Head* and Gerald Scottow of *The Unicorn*. Carel however is a clearer cut creature who has no foil or ambiguity — he is a godless man who fears no one (a device borrowed from Nietzsche). Echoes of Canetti remain not least I suspect because *Crowds and Power* was still an influence on Murdoch's work and she was unable to shift him from her wider circle of friends. In *The Time of the Angels* myth and psychology come together to create Carel's enchantment of his household, but it is his relationship with Pattie which is the most central to the narrative:

> When Carel had said "Will you suffer for me, will you be crucified for me?" she had thought he had meant ordinary suffering of the kind she was familiar with. In all her imagination of what she might suffer for Carel she had not conceived of this.... After all there was no salvation, no one to call the lapsed soul or weep in the evening dew. The house had fallen down.... She would have to go, she would have to leave him at last ... she could not love him enough to save him, not that much, not with that suffering.[43]

Pattie is both a narrative device in her placement as a "black Madonna" and also as a sign of her innocence, honesty and ultimate salvation through the death of Carel. This then, is the outcome of the suffering to which Carel has subjected Pattie: she rejects him and with this comes his death. In some respects, *The Time of the Angels* is a tragedy, one replete with fear; fear for the future and the fear that the other characters feel for Carel. Murdoch explains this in greater depth in her unpublished work on Heidegger:

> Such an analysis [of states of mind] is seems to me, cannot but be arbitrary, and in this case are designed by Heidegger to offer primary support ... for his later theory of "authentic" being, which consists of higher and enlightened forms of whatever are already represented as fundamental structures. A good novelist can more accurately describe these fugitive aspects of the human condition, but of course that is not philosophy, and the novelist too has his formal purposes.[44]

If we return to the novel in question the links to Continental writing are apparent.

Murdoch's linking of *The Time of the Angels* to the Germanic mode of fiction is not limited to her use of philosophy.[45] She has referred to it as "a tight metaphysical object, which wishes it were a poem, and which attempts to convey, often in mythical form, some central truth about the human condition," in effect being "a novel like *The Stranger* of Camus, which is a small, compact, crystalline, self-contained myth about the human condition"[46] in the French existentialist style. Louis Martz goes on to refer to it as "Miss Murdoch's only truly 'philosophical novel'"; the allusions to Heidegger [he says] provide an "accurate clue to her theme and design."[47] However, Murdoch's attachment to the 'devilish' work of Heidegger is best appreciated by understanding the earlier works of Kant.

Murdoch believed that the existentialists, such as Heidegger, who claimed to be following Kant and developing his philosophy, clearly misunderstood his intent; hence the creation of Carel as Heideggerian-Man. Kant, as she understood him, did not hold that "the Good" was created by human reason; least of all that it was a creation of the individual will. Thus, she says that:

> Reason itself is for him [Kant] an ideal limit: indeed his term "Idea of Reason" expresses precisely that endless aspiration to perfection with its characteristic moral activity. His is not the "achieved" or "given" reason which belongs with "ordinary language" and convention, nor is his man on the other hand totally unguided and alone [existentialist]. There exists a moral reality, a real though infinitely distant standard: the difficulty of understanding and imitating remain.[48]

Murdoch would certainly, at this point in her career, point to both Kant and Plato as her two philosophical masters, although it was Plato whom she regarded as the greater and would return to later in her career.[49] It is probable that her early study of Plato directed her toward Kant rather than toward Aristotle, whom she actively disliked.[50] For Heidegger she says that the basis of his curse is theological in nature: if we are to get involved with what he terms "thinking the truth of being," which he never fully elucidates but rather leaves dormant in the text, we must ultimately experience a form of holiness. By being able to discover a form of "God" we can go on to discover new ways of thinking and, subsequently, being.

Although Murdoch warmly welcomed the shift away from religious doctrine, which in turn was part of the religious worldview of the time, because it brought with it useful criticism and debate concerning religious concepts, she was concerned with the movement away from not only "God" but "good." In this respect, Marcus Fischer most clearly characterizes Murdoch's philosophy; his own philosophical writings mirror her thoughts on Heidegger. In the novel, she writes that:

> Those who thought to rescue the idea of Good by attaching it to the concept of will intended chiefly to prevent the corruption of that sovereign value by any necessary connection with specific and 'too too human' faculties or institutions. Since a good conceived of as absolutely authoritative was deemed an insult to human freedom, the solution in terms of action was tempting.[51]

It has been suggested by Conradi that Murdoch is not averse to mocking her own philosophical point of view, portraying Marcus as weak and ineffective in both his relationship with Carel and his inability to create a publishable work of moral theory.[52] I think this is a relatively safe assumption, as it is a theme that she returns to in her later works (e.g., *The Philosopher's Pupil* and *The Book and the Brotherhood*) in which mystics and philosophers are consumed with existential doubt while writing philosophy. Indeed the latter presents itself as a book written by a philosophical novelist about a philosopher writing a large book of philosophy. What is central however is the evident concern that Murdoch had for not allowing her philosophy to impinge on her fiction. We should perhaps remind ourselves of her thoughts on this subject: "I am not a philosophical novelist in the way that Sartre or Simone de Beauvoir are."[53] This seems to be a fair assessment as it places her within the sphere of the French existentialists, but not close to them — being a philosophical novelist but not writing her fiction to promote an existential world view; however, it does not rule out the fact, inherent within the statement, that she is, and considers herself to an extent, a philosophical novelist, or, to further define or crystallize the notion, a novelist who deals with moral philosophy and realism. It appears that the end of her work on Heidegger mirrors that of her earlier essay "On 'God' and 'Good'" where she states:

> At this point someone might say, all this is very well, the only difficulty is that none of it is true ... what seems beyond doubt is that moral philosophy is daunted and confused, and in many quarters discredited and regarded as unnecessary. The vanishing of the philosophical self ... has lead in ethics to an inflated and yet empty conception of the will, and it is this that I have been chiefly attacking. The search for unity is deeply natural.[54]

This is precisely where Murdoch is in relation to Heidegger; and the cause of her discrediting and rejecting her own work concerning his philosophy. It is obvious that more work and development need to occur in this specific area of Murdoch studies as this essay has only just begun to comprehend the importance of her relationship to Heidegger in both her philosophy and her literature. What it has uncovered is that their relationship is not as straightforward as the major critics would have us believe. Of course, Murdoch has reservations about the "horizontal transcendence" that Heidegger promotes, but as she does not fully comprehend his thought and gets caught up in the minutiae of his language analysis (a difficult barrier to cross). In that morass, she fails to realize that perhaps the end product of transcendence is not dissimilar to her own writing. Her dismissal of her manuscript and its subsequent obscurity is a loss for both Murdoch studies and the wider philosophical community: it is my hope that it will one day be more widely available.

However, Murdoch is at her most consistent when her fictional work is matched by her philosophical preoccupation and her unpublished work on Martin Heidegger reveals that, even though it was never published or widely acknowledged, she was, to some extent, fascinated by his philosophy for a great deal of her career.

NOTES

1. Dooley ed., 1968, 21. Iris in informal conversation with W.K. Rose in 1968.
2. Murdoch, 1992, Chatto, 187.
3. Dooley, ed., 1968, 58.
4. Murdoch, 1966, 184.
5. Murdoch, 1992, Chatto, 78–79.
6. Murdoch, 1966, 170.
7. *Ibid.*, 103.
8. Warnock, 1996, 598.
9. Murdoch, 1992, Chatto, 509.
10. Conradi briefly discusses this in *Iris Murdoch: A Life*, p. 586.

11. Murdoch, 2002 (1966), 150.
12. *Ibid.*
13. She states on pp. 221–222 of the Heidegger Manuscript that she is not a scholar of Heidegger and it should not be assumed that she has any worthwhile insights—a statement I disagree with.
14. Conradi, 2001, 586. She had decided to discard this work in November 1993.
15. Iris Murdoch. From her personal journal 20 April 1987. From Peter Conradi, *Iris Murdoch: A Life*. The proofs of her attempts are now kept at Kingston University in the Murdoch archive.
16. Murdoch's manuscript is not likely to be published in full in the near future due to its unsuitability (it is a collection of thoughts and ideas rather than a fully-formed text). It can be viewed at Kingston University library and is around 300 pages in length, the scope being Murdoch's conflict with Heideggerian philosophy and her views on the transcendent nature of self. Peter Conradi confirmed to me in a private communication of 2005 that only a small section of the manuscript is soon to be made publicly available: The introduction to "Heidegger: The Pursuit of Being" is now to be published in an OUP book edited by Justin Broackes, in—I think—2006. He goes on to say that an introduction [in Broackes work] should explain why we want to publish this—and only this. The reason behind only publishing a small amount of the manuscript is made clear in an email between Stanley Rosen and Conradi from 2001: "I have read the excerpt from Iris's manuscript ... even though you [Conradi] have apparently decided not to publish, I feel it is a great obligation to formulate my opinion as carefully as possible [as Murdoch wished to dedicate a published version to Rosen]. On balance I think that you are right in your assessment." Conradi's assessment being that to publish the manuscript in full would be detrimental to Murdoch's legacy insofar as it would be of inferior quality than the work published in her lifetime which both men feel was of a far greater quality than her unpublished work. Broackes monograph, *Iris Murdoch, Philosopher* is due to publish from Oxford in late 2009, and will contain the first chapter of the manuscript. I have decided, therefore, to quote only from the first chapter in this essay: to do otherwise would be against the wishes of both Murdoch and John Bayley.
17. Conradi, 1986, 356.
18. Dipple, 1982, 75.
19. Dooley, ed., 1968, 209. Originally from an interview with Jonathan Miller, 3 April 1988.
20. Iris Murdoch, 1997, Chatto, 293.
21. *Ibid.*, 349
22. Murdoch, Heidegger, 7.
23. *Ibid.*, 6–7.
24. *Ibid.*, 10. The notion of *Gerede* is important here as Heidegger stresses the markedness between it and "correct" moral orientation. Murdoch suggests that *Gerede* is useful insomuch as it relates the individual to the subject.
25. *Ibid.*, 21
26. Heidegger, 1997, 265.
27. Iris Murdoch, 1992, Chatto, 20.
28. *Ibid.*, 23.
29. Murdoch, 1997, Chatto, 76.
30. *Ibid.*, 96.
31. Wood, 1999, 15.
32. Iris Murdoch, 1992, Chatto, 509.
33. *Ibid.*, 150.
34. *Ibid.*, 152.
35. *Ibid.*, 25–26.
36. *Ibid.*, 221.
37. *Ibid.*, 134.
38. Murdoch, 2002 (1966), 142.
39. Murdoch, Heidegger, 20. Murdoch also acknowledges the influence of Meister Eckhart on Heidegger in *Metaphysics as a Guide to Morals*.
40. *Ibid.*, 13.
41. A certain echo of Milton's *Paradise Lost*—"No light therein rather darkness visible."
42. Elias Canetti was a German sociologist and Nobel-prize winning author who was an early lover of Murdoch. It is his influence which is felt throughout her work when she develops the idea

of the "enchanter figure" and the demonic sage. For more on Canetti see Peter Conradi's *Iris Murdoch: A Life*.

43. Murdoch, 2002 (1966), 226–227.
44. Murdoch, Heidegger, 13.
45. I am thinking here of the development of Hegelian ideas in Heidegger. This should not be inferred to mean the totality of German philosophy, especially Kant.
46. Dooley, 1968, 54.
47. Martz in Bloom, ed., 1986, 52. The allusions to Heidegger he refers to are caught up in Murdoch's arguments for a Platonic vision of the self.
48. MacIntyre, 1982, 15–16.
49. Peter Conradi, 2001, 481. For her return to Plato one need only read her following novels *The Nice and the Good* (1968) and *Bruno's Dream* (1969).
50. Although this may have been connected with her dislike of linguistic philosophy and Alfred Ayer in particular who espoused Aristotle.
51. Murdoch, 2002 (1966), 116.
52. Conradi, 1986, 168.
53. Dooley, 1968, 58.
54. Murdoch, 1997, Chatto, 361–362.

Conclusion: A Meditation in Swerves

Luisa Muraro

In 1952, London was still scarred by the bombings of World War II. The city provides the main setting for the story *Under the Net*, published in 1954, the first of a long series of novels by Iris Murdoch. The narrative voice is Jake, a young man of barely thirty, the same age as the author. The novel tells of the events that lead this overtly neurotic character to find a new beginning in his life. A new beginning means on the one hand that he begins to see that people exist and that things are what they are (and not how he would like them to be); and on the other, that he decides to get a part-time job to support himself and get back to writing seriously.

Also in 1952, on June 9th at the Aristotelian Society in London, Iris Murdoch gave one of her first public lectures, the first for which we have the text. With a strange, evocative title, *Nostalgia for the Particular*, it argued for the opportunity to not exclude the notions of *experience*, *consciousness* and *inner life* from philosophical research; and thus it argued against certain exponents of the analytical philosophy of language, such as Ryle, the author of *The Concept of Mind*, and Ayer, the author of *Thinking and Meaning*.[1]

Murdoch argued against them with the Husserlian theory of a phenomenology of thought, as well as the existence, illustrated and corroborated with a quote by Rilke, of "symbolic experiences." These occur when the experience speaks itself, and we immediately grasp the significance of an occurrence or a work of art. This bold new idea had remarkable similarities with the "hermeneutic experience" which Hans Georg Gadamer was reflecting upon at the same time, completely independently.[2]

These were the beginnings of the career of an author whose oeuvre covered the two fronts of literature and philosophy. Her work has been recognized as being excellent on both fronts, but its philosophical originality is still to be discovered, as has rightly been pointed out.[3]

Generally speaking, what strikes one from an initial reading of these texts is that the remarkable vigor of Murdoch's philosophical prose is not matched with the wish to prove herself right, which readers of philosophical texts are used to. Iris Murdoch does not go back over what she has already said to rearrange or correct, develop and reiterate. This does not mean that her philosophical theories do not echo and interweave with each other, becoming amplified and stronger; but they do so in a fairly free way, with variations that, on certain themes, are almost a contradiction, and which allow space for unforeseen developments. She swerves. She does not seek to corroborate her ideas with the construction of a doctrine, as great thinkers are wont to do.

Although Murdoch avoids systematic construction, it is not in the name of an exclusive reference to the contingency of the human existence, which she does accept; nor is it in the name of some insurmountable problematic issue in human thought, which she does not accept. Indeed, she does not exclude the search for a metaphysical truth and the possibility of reaching it. Her position is anti–anti-metaphysical. An expression of her dissatisfaction with the anti-metaphysical decrees of modern philosophy and the thought of a spark of transcendence were to return over and over in her writings, often in these terms: "There is more than this." She describes this formula as "a metaphysical position but no metaphysical form."[4] When she dwells on the great metaphysical themes, her remarks have something in common with those of the mystics who speak of God and then add: what I've said is false. They undermined certainty in order to make a comparison between the inexhaustible wealth of the presence of their beloved, which they had understood through direct experience, and wanted to convey to others as their own devoted but incomplete knowing.[5] For her part, Murdoch establishes that she is taking a metaphysical stance without being able to give form to that stance. Her intent is to prevent philosophical thought, her own first and foremost, from taking that "authority" (her word) that is the province of reality as it presents itself to experience informed by love, whether in the moral life of good people or in the fruition of beautiful things.

This latter statement catapults us into the heart of Murdoch's philosophy and, it creates some problems; but that is inevitable for two reasons. First, because a discourse attempting to explain the thought of Murdoch comes up immediately and inevitably (later we shall see why) against ideas that claim citizenship in (her) philosophy, without having all the necessary requirements—ideas *sans papiers*, as the French would say. Secondly, because love is not a modern philosophical concept, as Murdoch notes, even though it is a "central concept in morals."[6] What's more, she gives it an unusual definition: "Love is the perception of individuals. Love is the extremely difficult realisation that something other than oneself is real."[7] It is knowing, and accepting that knowing as partial, even desiring that partiality. Perhaps in order to rectify the irregularity that is created in her philosophy with this *sans papiers* concept, some commentators emphatically refer to Murdoch's Platonism — as she herself does, for that matter. The reference is relevant yet secondary, in my opinion. It should be passed over for a more careful consideration of the unexpected which she admits to the realm of philosophy — that is, her following of swerves in the philosophical road.

For some time, I went on thinking about Murdoch with the feeling that there was some "secret" to be discovered. And it's true, as long as we recognize that the secret is before our very eyes: it is the typical mobility of her thought that prevents her mind from remaining stably on one point of focus, prevents her reasoning from moving along a single trajectory, and prevents her discourse from developing on the same level. There is no shortage of post-modern thinkers who theorize this mobility without practicing it; she does not theorize it but she practices it, and we, reading her, feel "caught off guard," as they say. As I will show, the swerves that characterize her thinking involve the two kinds of writing together, without undermining the mutual independence of philosophical essays and novels. I would like to use this to take a new approach to Murdoch's philosophy: I am not sure why but everything I have written about her so far takes the form of an introduction.

There has already been discussion about the relationship between the two types of writing found in Murdoch's work. Some have maintained that Murdoch's literary engagement was motivated by theory, and can therefore be considered a development of her philosophical oeuvre.[8] There is some truth in this thesis, although the opposite is also true, I think, in the sense of narration preceding speculation. As Peter Conradi's biography demonstrates, Murdoch had "always" written novels and never took leave of philosophy.[9] In Murdoch's life, there was not *one* change in activity; rather there were many, from one kind of writing to another, so in her work there are many *exchanges* between the two types of writing. For the reader, these exchanges between the novels and philosophy create an intriguing effect of resonance, which seems to derive from a symmetry without complementarity.

On the same question, we also have Murdoch's testimony, which is as precious as it might seem misleading. Bryan Magee interviewed Iris Murdoch in 1977 on the relationship between philosophy and literature, in general and in her own personal experience.[10] Her reply enlightens us on her concept of literature and its relations with philosophy, and helps us to better understand her novels and her thinking. For example, when she says that "though they are so different, philosophy and literature are both truth-seeking and truth-revealing activities" and that: "For better and worse art goes deeper than philosophy."[11] Her words raise a problem in an entirely different sense. Some literary critics considered her a writer of philosophical novels.[12] Perhaps Murdoch feared that, tipping this in the other direction, her philosophy would become a novelized philosophy? That did not happen. Her considerable fame as a novelist did not interfere with the renown of her philosophical writings, which followed its own independent course. As for the idea of a continuity and, perhaps, fear of confusion, between the two forms of output, she rebutted this with literary arguments that are convincing: artistic creation in itself does not answer to philosophical truth; the characters in a well-written novel do not embody general ideas. But the problem is that her depiction of the philosopher is not only unconvincing in general, but also risks being deceptive as far as she herself is concerned. Indeed, she claims that the philosopher avoids or seeks to avoid all rhetoric; does not seek to please the reader, and leaves the reader no space; writes for a small audience, and speaks with an impersonal voice, aiming to solve difficult technical problems. Whatever her intentions, nothing of what she says corresponds precisely with her own philosophical prose, of which she disregards some significant characteristics. Her swerves are local and general, leaving much room to the reader.

Firstly, her philosophical voice as she speaks (let us remember that many of her essays were originally lectures) sometimes interjects in the text either to declare her discontent ("I am not content") and disagreement with certain dominant ideas; or to signal the introduction of theories that are not adequately reasoned; or to help the listener (or reader) to keep up with her. Moreover, her style of writing features a restrained and effective rhetoric. This rhetoric, so specific to her, sometimes brings to mind the art of the tightrope-walker, balanced between the critical requirements of philosophical reasoning and the incontrovertible certainties that the philosopher shares with common people. The tightrope-walker cannot stop, he would lose his balance; and so would she, as her thoughts move to demonstrate something in order to show something beyond that. This is one of the many things that literature does: showing what the world is, offering a vision of reality by demonstrating less to show more.[13] At other times her philosophical writing makes one think of that move animals make when being pursued by a predator or a bullet, the *schivata* in Italian, *esquive* in French, *swerve* in English, when they jump suddenly from one path to another. She does the same, at times escaping from a theoretical construction which is totally closed to facts and objections; and at times fleeing the rightful demands of critical thought, which is forced to await the continuation of her discourse before it can be satisfied. Here is an example, from a passage at the end of a long zigzagging train of thought in "The Idea of Perfection": "What is real may be 'non-empirical' without being in the grand sense systematic. In particular situations, 'reality' as that which is revealed to the patient eye of love is an idea entirely comprehensible to the ordinary person."[14]

In actual fact, what Murdoch describes as the duty of the philosopher in the 1977 interview only corresponds to part of *her own* philosophical work. Among the two types of writing, the more creative kind and the more rational kind, there is a tension that each one reproduces within itself in different ways. The presence of philosophy in Murdoch's novels is a very significant theme, of which Antonia Byatt began a sound exploration many years ago.[15] The presence of fiction in her philosophical writings is what is occupying us here. That presence makes itself known in the fiction through the sudden mention of a name, Patroclus, Cordelia, Mr. Knightley, and in the way that characters discuss philosophy, or refer casually to its concepts. In the philosophy that symmetry shows up in use of an image, "somebody is hungry or somebody is crying"; or of an idea "if stories are told, virtue will be portrayed" and in the little narratives. The symmetry moves both ways, and at other times, it becomes the theme of an entire text, such as *The Sublime and the Beautiful Revisited*, which relates the moral and political problem of freedom to the art of the novel and the creation of free characters.

The most conspicuous and already much discussed example of that presence is the inclusion in a 1962 philosophical essay, "The Idea of Perfection," of a short story which tells how the relationship between a mother-in-law (M) and a daughter-in-law (D) has improved. In Murdoch's development, this short story is a decisive bond; in its context, it is no less important than the Platonic myths called upon to replace dialectic reasoning. Another case is the invention of the figure of "the objector" in that first lecture, mentioned above, held before a fairly intimidating audience for a young female thinker who does not agree with the prevailing ideas in the room: "We can speak of facts without speaking of experiences. But, *the objector* may argue, can we really?"[16] This figure returns several times before the end, sometimes taking the role of the "defender of the inner life" and so gives the lecture a dramatic structure.

This prompts the question: while it is clear that Iris Murdoch's novels are novels, what exactly does her philosophy resemble?

We have an answer from Mary Warnock, who was her fellow student and colleague. She maintains that despite Murdoch's many criticisms of Sartre, she herself is part of existentialism: "her immersion in the real world makes it not inappropriate so to describe her."[17] Her argument for her immersion in the real world is as evocative as it is vague; but Warnock most probably calls "immersion in the real world" Murdoch's philosophical commitment to saving the reality of the real world from the growing control of unreality, spectacle, simulacra (*fantasy*, in her language) which is affecting our civilization. It must be said that that commitment, which was also peculiar to existentialism, led to a certain rupture with philosophical tradition. Philosophy allows this: the task of *always starting from scratch* with the work of thinking. That of Murdoch was first class.

There is undoubtedly existentialism in Iris Murdoch's "always starting again from scratch." The thinking and example of the existentialist philosophers made her aware of a growing invasion of analytical techniques, both philosophical and scientific, assailing every demonstration of human subjectivity. That thinking and that example also taught her to stand against them. How? By recognizing and thematizing the emergence of the human subject, its uniqueness and contingency, compared to every totality, however it is interpreted (philosophically, religiously, ideologically) and however it is imposed (with the force of dictatorship or with democratic consensus).

Murdoch undoubtedly owed a lot to existentialism. But equally, a large distance separated her from it. Indeed, she immediately took a different path — further evidence being provided by her 1952 essay on Sartre. She distances herself from existentialism along with her entire philosophical path. To briefly give an idea of the extent to which the two paths separated, let us say that she does not agree with the intellectual *arrogance* (her word) of existentialism.[18] As a philosopher she does not intend to arrogate to herself the authority to decree the limits of human possibilities; because our possibilities (for freedom, for true knowledge, for happiness) become clear on their own account in forms over which the philosopher has no power of supervision. In her eyes, the analytical philosophy of Oxford and Cambridge (except Wittgenstein's thought) has an attitude no different to that of existentialism.

In her polemic with existentialism on the one hand, and the analytical philosophy of Oxford and Cambridge on the other, for Murdoch there is not just the inadequate or fallacious representation that those doctrines provide of human beings as moral agents — a representation that must be enriched or corrected by referring for example to the wealth and precision of language and representations of moral life in great classical novels. More radically, it is the problem of the philosophical construction as such, which prevents us from knowing if there is anything else and consequently, does not allow reality to be seen for itself. Discussing a certain position, Murdoch says that it does not satisfy her as "it ignores certain facts and at the same time imposes a single theory which admits of no communication with or escape into rival theories."[19] However, she will not take the path of so-called deconstructionism — a term which only appeared in the Seventies. Instead, she chose the path of accounting for the fact that the philosopher is a common man, and that philosophy is an activity that has things in common with other things: firstly that it cannot separate facts from judgments. According to Murdoch, philosophy must, from the inside out, account for something that essentially takes place outside it. That is the experience of the ordinary person (including the philosopher), who lives in relation to others, who is able to change for the better and sometimes manages to do so, thus putting him or herself in the position to see things as they are, and to know that other people really exist.

This takes us back to the symbolic experiences of the first lecture, and the moral change in the protagonist of Murdoch's first novel. Right from the beginning, a distinctive feature of Murdoch's philosophy is to appeal to experience just as human beings live it and interpret it. She sometimes does this with remarkable vivacity such as when, interrupting her exposition of the behavioral notion of inner life, she writes, "This is the point at which people may begin to protest and cry out and say that something has been taken from them."[20] Above all, right from the beginning she linked experience together with the possibility of richer meaning. And the very principle of morality lies in this possibility, unlike the theories of supposedly free choice. For instance, in "The Idea of Perfection," after having quoted Rilke's testimony, reflecting on symbolic experience, she writes that much of our experience is poor, but that every now and then it *happens* that it is rich and meaningful, richer than any verbal explanation could suggest. She ends by expressing her dissatisfaction when faced with the modern analytic techniques of philosophy which do not take into account such happenings: "It is such happenings ... that give to the idea of 'immediate experience' that inexhaustible richness the neglect of which prompts both resentment and vain investigation."[21] The speaker asks that philosophy realize the richness of experiences, and she asks it using words that speak of her experiences; she herself gives words to the feelings of common people who do not identify with philosophical theories.

The requirement to which she appeals against the "arrogance" of modern (and post-modern) philosophies in general, is not that of experience interpreted generically and emptily, but as it is lived and expressed in the contexts of practical life. Philosophy is called upon to account for human action that is not exclusive to philosophy and which, in fact, is best demonstrated in the conduct of good people and in the work of great artists. These two areas of the human being transcend the specific area of philosophy and have a task that has its place in an infinite horizon, that of perfection. In Murdoch, philosophy seems to be animated internally by reference to a perspective, towards perfection, that enriches it but that it cannot possess.

But from a philosophical point of view, what do "good person" and "great artist" mean relation to perfection? Not for the first time, my discourse finds itself trapped in the position of not being able to successfully account for itself, at the risk of ending up in a vicious circle. It is placed in this position by the very movement of Murdoch's thought, demonstrating less in order to show more, in a tension that is not merely dialectic as it is practically resolved, insofar as it requires a transformation in the observer. This transformation has the characteristics of a struggle (the word that Murdoch herself uses). The main battleground consists of the words of common language. Very soon in Murdoch's thinking there appears and is then consolidated the certainty that morality is not conformity to a norm nor obedience to an imperative; rather it is a guidance implicit in language, which is capable of acting within us and stably guiding us. "Words constitute the ultimate texture and stuff of our moral being ... words are where we live as human beings and as moral and spiritual agents."[22]

In the brilliant opening to "On 'God' and 'Good,'" we find this definition: "To do philosophy is to explore one's own temperament, and yet at the same time to attempt to discover the truth."[23] The two directions, which all too often we practice as though they were discordant or unrelated, proceed "at the same time," and are indeed the two sides of a single process that gives rise to the transformation of oneself in the world, and of the world in oneself; in this process words are, on each occasion, the discovery of what is possible and the report of what is real.

The words of this opening evoke the great wager of a lifetime. Everything points to the fact that Iris Murdoch's philosophy is always about Iris Murdoch as well. Murdoch chose (or was chosen by) her battleground, which is the work of a creative imagination in writing novels. I am not qualified to express my opinion as to the validity of her theory of literature, but it is crystal clear that this theory, in a sort of critically weighed up report, is based on her practice as a novelist. Literature, she states, "can give us a new vocabulary of experience, and a truer picture of freedom."[24] Two themes stand out in that which she theorizes: the struggle between fantasy and imagination, on which the value of the truth of art depends; and the creation of free characters which sets the standard of the art of the novel. When working at its best, the imagination invents, or rather discovers and creates, the real possibilities for good in this world, in the form of stories and characters. As is well-known, Murdoch prefers the realist variety of 19th century classical novels, and she presents herself as that sort of novelist, interested in the normative value of "the real" in the moral and literary field too. To invent a realistic story, such as *A Fairly Honourable Defeat*, in which good and evil confront each other (Murdoch energetically uses this language, perhaps inspired by Simone Weil) is for the artist, and potentially for us all, a chance for freedom and true knowledge. This is, this makes a masterpiece. To understand this point means to understand the philosophy of Murdoch.

In the past, when I harbored the idea of a "secret of Iris Murdoch," I spoke about an intuition that I claimed was the basis and origin of her philosophy, and attempted to voice it: the intuition that the mediation of experience is the work of thought, internally guided by a love of the good; this guidance being implicit in language itself and especially present in literature.[25] Now, were I to put this so-called intuition into words, I would describe it more simply as the *realism of goodness*. That goodness which helps us to gain freedom and, as our freedom grows, helps us to see that other people really exist and that things are what they are. But I now believe that talking of an "intuition" does not tally with certain features of her philosophical research. Firstly, the importance of words in experience and in the transformation of the self. Much better to take a cue from Murdoch herself and pay attention to her effort to say something that commonly exists but is weighed down by a sort of incredulity and indefensibility that pushes it towards illusion. With one of her telling swerves, in a parenthesis that explains what she is doing, she says, "Philosophy is often a matter of finding a suitable context in which to say the obvious."[26] Suddenly, mindful of Wittgenstein's lesson, she lays before us the secondariness of philosophy. Compared to what? To the "obvious" (a strange word that in some languages does not even exist). In other words, anything that has never claimed to give itself value with this or that argument, because it went without saying and did not need arguments; today perhaps it might need arguments, but this "something" (that love is central to the lives of many, that we have the duty to be good without ulterior motives, that other people really exist) is of such a nature that any argument would be too much, and so Murdoch seeks to give it not reasoning but "a suitable context."

Let it not be thought that the task of philosophy described thus is of little consequence. It is a case of making declarable and communicable the symbolic power of morality, so that Murdoch, with her language that has a talent for surprising us, talks of "fabric of being."[27] This metaphor appears in that example of M and D (mother and daughter in law) which provides a narrative link to a delicate theoretical passage. The idea is that there is no experience without words, and that the words that are able to enrich our experience makes us see what we could not see, and make us become that which we were not. In other words, we find ourselves faced with the symbolic process that Charles S. Peirce theorized by calling it semiosis; and, more specifically, with his great discovery of the nature of the sign, which he calls *thirdness*: in a word, symbolic activity.[28] We have seen that Murdoch defends experience as the place which gives rise to the formation of the subject which has the possibility to be free, and is therefore able to relate to the world through the mediation of words. To use a term which does not belong to Murdoch, she defends experience as the place in which semiosis originates. Those familiar with Peirce's semiotics know that his theory of the sign and of the efficiency of the sign leads into a theory on habits. For her part, Murdoch says we act in the right way, when the right time comes, "not out of strength of will but out of the quality of our usual attachments with the kind of energy and discernment which we have available."[29] These correspondences, although slight, encourage a further comparison of the two thinkers, from the normative conception of reality to the reference to Platonic eros. However, putting this promising investigation to one side, we are only referring to Peirce here in order to shed light on Murdoch's thinking with the concept of *thirdness*; this means conceptualizing that "fabric of being" that is enriched with the enrichment of experience and makes the stuff of the world within us/of us in the world.

Scholars have pointed out that Murdoch's imagination, both philosophical and literary, works well with pairs of concepts or of characters, and that this dual structure does not lead to a synthesis.[30] Any thirdness would appear to be excluded. However, upon closer consideration, I believe that we can talk of *a thirdness without synthesis* not just for Peirce's semiotics but also for Murdoch's philosophy. Indeed, let us consider how the lack of a unitary synthesis in Murdoch's vision and work does not condemn the subject to go to pieces nor to remain in an unresolved ambiguity. One example (or icon, as Peirce would say) of this is found in the plot of *Under the Net*. The neurotic Jake's personality is characterized by a rejection of that which has no reason and cannot be defined (which escapes the "net"). "I hate contingency," he says at the beginning of Chapter Two; and this puts him in contrast, without a solution but not without results, with Hugo, a successful industrialist who pursues the here and now of individual reality. These two could embody two philosophies; but they cannot be reduced to that, because Jake admires Hugo, and this admiration turns him into someone else, who is not the synthesis of the two.

Let us recall that at the very beginning of Murdoch's philosophical activity, she read Simone Weil's *Cahiers*, which influenced her profoundly and for a long time.[31] The French philosopher and the history of her century taught Murdoch that which Hegel neither saw nor predicted: that the will to overcome duality to reach synthesis catastrophically leads to the triumph of force and to unreality. Weilian thought places great importance on that duality which is not resolved in any synthesis. Simone Weil teaches that the simultaneous presence of opposites is lacerating yet insurmountable in this world, on pain of a simplification that distracts the soul from goodness. The suffering of the ripping in two is not at all sterile, if we learn from the practice of virtues that are incompatible with each other: *"L'existence simultanée des vertus incompatibles dans l'âme est la condition de la stabilité à travers les accidents de la vie sans invulnérabilité* [the simultaneous existence of incompatible virtues in the soul is the condition for stability through the accidents of life without invulnerability]," writes the French philosopher. She gives the counter-example of a communist who, in dedicating himself to serving justice, loses his love for justice.[32]

I think, and invite readers to think, that the duality that features in Murdoch's work overall, and which we find as a swerving structure in her imagination when working on philosophical research and in literary invention, introduces us to the thirdness without synthesis, just as Peirce conceives it, and spiritually bent by Simone Weil's Platonism. This means that it places the individual person, each of us in flesh and blood, in the place of the synthesis; us, willing to suffer and to change, to thus open up a passage to the reality of what is real, without having an overall vision. This has nothing to do with the immersion in the real world, described by Mary Warnock. On the contrary, it is the shift — a truly symbolic swerve — rather than perfected synthesis that allows us to gain a sense of reality by freeing us from a reactive, specular duality.

This thirdness which is not a synthesis offers us, on each occasion "if we seek for what is best," a double revelation; i.e., the understanding of the detail of the world, together with an intuition of unity.[33] There is no end to this process, just as there is no limit to semiosis: a process that is unlimited but guided from within. Peirce states that we are destined for truth, and explains how (this explanation being his pragmatism). Murdoch speaks of perfection, and her philosophy is the speculative context that explains the meaning of this word and this perspective to us. She has to be followed to the very end, I mean to say up to the point at which she translates this perspective into a new kind of utilitarianism, which would make the practice of virtue a basic necessity, on the same level as food, a home, a life without fear.[34] She says so in a context of political reflection, as an alternative to other points of view — that of the existentialists for whom freedom counts, that of the mystics who place value in the spirit—and to herself. Indeed, she speaks of "a kind of somersault" between existentialism and mysticism. "Reality is incomplete," states Murdoch in "Against Dryness." She specifies that it is on this terrain of "respect" for incompleteness and contingency that the imagination struggles with fantasy, to say the truth about that which is, about that which we are.[35]

At this juncture, we are helped once again by a short story, *Something Special*, confirming that Murdoch's philosophy is in some ways the speculative report of her work as a writer of fiction. This is the only short story that she published. It is a real gem, and is also remarkable for another reason: in it, unlike in her novels, the author is not omniscient and only knows her characters through what they show with their words, gestures and behavior. The main character is Yvonne, a young woman from a modest social background. She will not resign herself to living a mediocre life, courted by a young man who loves her and of whom her family approves, but who is no Prince Charming. She spends an evening with him during which certain not uninteresting things happen, none of which however seems able to turn the situation around. That night she returns home and, after remaining in the dark for fifteen minutes thinking we know not what, Yvonne informs her mother that yes, she will marry him, and she cries without letting anyone hear.[36] The result is clear but Yvonne's behavior is not, and the meaning of the story hangs in the balance. Why has she decided to marry Sam? Why is she crying? The key seems to lie in whatever she was thinking in those fifteen minutes ("She had never stood still for so long in her whole life"). We have a clue in the few words, "It's a sad thing," with which Yvonne answers her mother when she asks for an explanation, and which refer to a strange episode that evening. However, this is not enough to give us an exhaustive point of view that keeps us out of the story, and we risk falling into it, in the sense of wanting to complete it.

The recent Italian edition of the story, *Una cosa speciale*, includes two comments in the appendix.[37] One essentially says: Yvonne has found her path, she is crying from the pain of leaving behind her dream of love and facing up to reality. The other says: for Iris Murdoch love is the most dangerous of illusions, humanity is not free, we have moments of lucidity that cause us suffering, but we have to return to a life that needs illusions. The first comment saturates the incompleteness with a progressionist point of view, while the second saturates it with a nihilistic conclusion. The point is that neither of the two bears the pain of a soul divided in two, to use Simone Weil's words. On the other hand, it is impossible for someone who has read the story not to take a stance, the story itself demands it with its "incompleteness." Which is the incompleteness of reality itself, and the stance that we are asked to take is not to complete it; it is to encounter duality as tension, to put ourselves in flesh and blood, willing to suffer and to change, in the situation of the true possibilities for freedom and happiness that remain (or open up) to Yvonne.

Today, many currents of thought refer to Iris Murdoch, labeled as cognitivism, communitarianism, virtue ethics, rehabilitation of practical philosophy, literary turn of ethics. I can see the grounds for these references to her, but I can also see that there might be a temptation to "complete her." On the other hand, provided that we don't complete her wrongly, it is right and normal that we approach the work of Iris Murdoch on the paths along which we swerve in our own personal research. I myself, for example, see her as a thinker who worked at a deep level to give an adequate philosophical context to that obviousness that is "women exist and I am one of them," against the philosophical "arrogance" of post-modern thinking.[38] But in the same vein, I believe it is better still to read her without attempting to characterize her within the philosophy scene. In this way we can understand the radically new thing that, with her, happened in the history of philosophy: the ability to detach oneself from philosophy, thanks to philosophy, in order to obey reality.

Notes

1. Murdoch, 1997, Penguin, 43–58.
2. *Wahrheit und Methode*, the major work by the founder of philosophical hermeneutics, would be published in 1960. Iris Murdoch does not mention this thinker and was probably not aware of his existence. To my knowledge there are no studies on the relationship between the hermeneutical experience of Gadamer and the symbolic experience of Murdoch.
3. Bagnoli, 2002, 51–63.
4. Murdoch, 1997, Penguin, 359–60.
5. My main reference on this theme is *The Mirror of Simple Souls* by Marguerite Porete.
6. Murdoch, 1997, Penguin, 299.
7. *Ibid.*, 215.
8. "My point will be that Murdoch's change of activity should be seen as theoretically motivated, and was in fact a development of her philosophical work" (Ricciardi, 2002, 5).
9. Conradi, 2001.
10. Murdoch, 1997, Penguin, 3–30.
11. *Ibid.*, 11, 21.
12. Byatt, 1994, 207.
13. Murdoch, 1997, Penguin, 12.
14. *Ibid.*, 332.
15. Byatt, 1994, 207.
16. Murdoch, 1997, Penguin, 44 (my italics).
17. Warnock, 1996, xliii.
18. See Conradi's preface to *Existentialists and Mystics* which shows that Murdoch ascribes the same arrogance to structuralism, which she observed as it developed in English-speaking countries in the Seventies, with the name post-structuralism (Murdoch, 1997, Penguin, xxix).
19. Murdoch, 1997, Penguin, 299.
20. *Ibid.*, 309.
21. *Ibid.*, 58.
22. *Ibid.*, 243–42.
23. *Ibid.*, 337.
24. *Ibid.*, 295.
25. Muraro, 2006, 20.
26. Murdoch, 1997, Penguin, 326.
27. See pp. 316, 323, 326 of Murdoch (1997, Penguin).
28. Peirce is never quoted by Murdoch. In a letter to Lady Welby, Peirce explains that "Third-

ness is the triadic relation existing between a sign, its object, and the interpreting thought, itself a sign" and that the essential function of a sign (which is the quintessence of thirdness) is to make efficient relations that would otherwise be extinguished, but not in the sense of directly provoking action, not remaining in the reactive dimension, but in the sense of establishing "a habit or general rule whereby they will act on occasion" (Pierce, 1958, 389–90).

29. Murdoch, 1997, Penguin, 375.
30. Antonaccio, 2003, 22–24.
31. See Muraro, 2006, 18–19.
32. Weil, 2002, 68.
33. See Murdoch, 1997, Penguin, 379.
34. *Ibid.*, 230–33.
35. *Ibid.*, 294–95.
36. Murdoch, 1957.
37. Murdoch, 2006; the "progressionist" comment is by me, the "nihilist" comment by Joyce Carol Oates.
38. For the path that Murdoch opened up to me, I returned to philosophy, as I explained at the 11th Symposium of the International Association of Women Philosophers, IAPH, Rome 2006, turning my back on certain philosophical futilities about sex and gender (see Annarosa Buttarelli and Federica Giardini, edited by *Il pensiero dell'esperienza*, Baldini Castoldi Dalai, Milano 2007, in print).

Bibliography*

Aarne, Antti, and Stith Thompson. 1987. *The Types of Folktale: A Classification and Bibliography*. Helsinki: Academia Scientiarum Fennica.
Adamson, Jane, Richard Freadman, and David Parker, eds. 1998. *Renegotiating Ethics in Literature, Philosophy, and Theory*. Cambridge: Cambridge University Press.
Adorno, Theodor. 1967. "Essay on Cultural Criticism and Society." In *Prisims*. Trans. Samuel Weber and Shierry Weber. Cambridge, MA: MIT Press.
Altorf, Marije. 2007. "Reassessing Iris Murdoch in the Light of Feminist Philosophy: Michèle Le Doeuff and the Philosophical Imaginary." In *Iris Murdoch: A Reassessment*. Ed. Anne Rowe, 175–86. Hampshire: Palgrave Macmillan.
Anderson, William. 1990. *Green Man: The Archetype of Our Oneness with the Earth*. New York: Harper Collins.
Antonaccio, Maria, and William Schweiker. 1996. *Iris Murdoch and the Search for Human Goodness*. Chicago: University of Chicago Press.
——. 2003. *Picturing the Human: The Moral Thought of Iris Murdoch*. New York: Oxford University Press.
Arendt, Hannah. 1951. *Antisemitism, The Origins of Totalitarianism, Vol. 1*. San Diego, New York, London: Harcourt Brace Jovanovich.
——. 1958. *The Human Condition*. Chicago: University of Chicago Press.
——. 1958. *Rachel Varnhagen: The Life of a Jewess*. London: East-West Library.
——. 1965. *Eichmann in Jerusalem: A Report on the Banality of Evil*. 2d ed. 1963. New York: Viking.
——. 1966. *Love and St. Augustine*. Trans. Joanna Vecchiareilli Scott and Judith Chelius Stark. Ashton. Chicago: University of Chicago Press.
——. 1968. *Men in Dark Times*. New York: Harcourt Brace.
——. 1973. *Men in Dark Times*. London: Pelican.
——. 1978. *The Life of the Mind: Volume One, Thinking*. Ed. Mary McCarthy. London: Secker & Warburg.
——. 1978. *The Life of the Mind: Volume Two, Willing*. Ed. Mary McCarthy. London: Secker & Warburg.
——. 1978. "Martin Heidegger at Eighty." In *Heidegger and Modern Philosophy: Critical Essays*. Ed. Michael Murray, 293–303. New Haven: Yale University Press.
Backus, Guy. 1986. *The Novelist as Philosopher, the Philosopher as Novelist: The Unicorn as a Philosophical Novel*. European University Studies Series XIV: Anglo-Saxon Literature and Language. Berne: Peter Lang.
Badiou, Alain. 2007. *"De Quoi Sarkozy Est-Il le Nom?" Circonstances* 4. Paris: Nouvelles Editions Lignes.
——. 2007. *The Century*. Cambridge: Cambridge University Press.
Baehr, Peter, ed. 2000. *The Portable Hannah Arendt*. Harmondsworth: Penguin.
Bagnoli, Carla. 2002. "Realism as a Moral Achievement." *Nitizie di Politeia* 66, 18: 51–63.
Baird, Forrest, and Walter Kaufmann, eds.

---

*In the case of Murdoch's texts, our authors consulted many editions of both U.S. and British publication. Consequently, Murdoch's texts are listed alphabetically by title but with publication years first. In footnotes, texts are distinguished by year and title where necessary, or by year and publisher where necessary.

1994. *Philosophic Classics.* Englewood Cliffs, NJ: Prentice Hall.

Bayley, John. 1998. *Iris.* London: Duckworth.

Beauvoir, Simone de. 1987. *Force of Circumstance.* London: Penguin.

Bellamy, Michael. 1986. An interview with Iris Murdoch. *Contemporary Literature* 18, 2 (Spring): 129–140.

Berkeley, George. 1940. *A Treatise Concerning the Principles of Human Knowledge.* LaSalle, Il: Open Court.

Bettelheim, Bruno. 1976. *The Uses of Enchantment: The Meaning and Importance of Fairy Tales.* New York: Knopf.

Bhreatnach, Aoife. 2006. *Becoming Conspicuous: Irish Travelers, Society and the State 1922–70.* Dublin: University College Dublin Press, 2006.

Birchall, I. 2004. *Sartre Against Stalinism.* New York. Oxford: Berghahn Books.

Bloom, Harold, ed. 1986. *Iris Murdoch.* London: Chelsea House.

Blum, Lawrence. 1986. "Iris Murdoch and the Domain of the Moral." *Philosophical Studies* 50, 3: 343–67.

Bostridge, Mark. 2008. "Books: The Goddess and the Demon Prince." *The Independent.* 10 Nov. 2008.

Bove, Cheryl Browning. 1986. *A Character Index and Guide to the Fiction of Iris Murdoch.* New York: Garland.

_____. 1993. *Understanding Iris Murdoch.* Columbia: University of South Carolina Press.

Braidotti, Rosi. 1994. *Nomadic Subjects: Embodiment and Sexual Difference in Contemporary Feminist Theory.* Gender and Culture. Eds. Carolyn C. Heilbrun and Nancy K. Miller. New York: Columbia University Press.

Brenner, Rachel Feldhay. 1997. *Writing as Resistance: Four Women Confronting the Holocaust.* Philadelphia: Pennsylvania State University Press.

Bronzino. 1540–50 c. *An allegory of Venus, Folly and Time.* Held by the National Gallery, London.

Brooks, Peter. 1992. *Reading for the Plot: Design and Intention in Narrative.* Cambridge: Harvard University Press.

Burgard, Peter J., ed. 1994. *Nietzsche and the Feminine.* Charlottesville: University Press of Virginia.

Burke, Carolyn, Naomi Schor, Margaret Whitford, eds. 1994. *Engaging with Irigaray: Feminist Philosophy and Modern European Thought.* Gender and Culture Series. New York: Columbia University Press.

Burke, Edmond. Quotation. *Oxford Dictionary of Quotations.* 1999. Oxford: Oxford University Press.

Büttner, Gottfried. 1995. *The Lady and the Unicorn: The Development of the Human Soul as Pictured in the Cluny Tapestries.* Trans. Roland Everett. Stroud: Hawthorn.

Byatt, A.S. 1994. *Degrees of Freedom: The Early Novels of Iris Murdoch.* London: Vintage.

Canetti, Elias. 1962. *Crowds and Power.* Trans. Carol Stewart. London: Victor Gollancz.

_____. 2005. *Party in the Blitz.* Trans. Michael Hofmann. London: The Harvill Press.

Canovan, Margaret. 1974. *The Political Thought of Hannah Arendt.* London: J. M. Dent & Sons.

Cavell, S. 1996. *Contesting Tears: The Hollywood Melodrama of the Unknown Woman.* Chicago: University of Chicago Press.

Cemitile, Maria C., and Elaine P. Miller, eds. 2007. *Returning to Irigaray: Feminist Philosophy, Politics, and the Question of Unity.* SUNY Series in Gender Theory. Ed. Tina Chanter. Albany: SUNY Press.

Chevalier, Jean-Louis, ed. "Closing Debate." In *Renconcontres avec Iris Murdoch.*

Clendinnen, Inga. 1998. *Postmodernism and the Holocaust.* Eds. Alan Milchman and Alan Rosenberg. Amsterdam: Rodopi.

_____. 1999. *Reading the Holocaust.* Cambridge: Cambridge University Press.

Clement. Behind the Name. http://www.behindthename.com/clement.

Cojocariu, Marinela. 2008. "The Reception of Iris Murdoch by the Romanian Literary Criticism." *Studies of Science and Culture (Studii de Știință și Cultură)* 13: 57–62.

Conradi, Peter J. 1986. *The Saint and the Artist.* London: Harper Collins.

_____. 2001. *Iris Murdoch: A Life.* London: Harper Collins.

_____. 2004. *Going Buddhist.* London: Short Books.

_____. 2006. "'Divine though unfinished':

Letters to Roly Colchrane." *The Iris Murdoch Newsletter* 19 (August): 29–32.

Cowley, Jason. 1999. "A Divine Literary Intelligence." *New Statesman* 128.4423: 15.

Da Vinci, Leonardo. 1503–05. *La Gioconda (Mona Lisa)*. Held by the Louvre, Paris.

Deane, Seamus. 1979. "Mary Lavin." In *The Irish Short Story*. Ed. Patrick Rafroidi and Terence Brown, 237–47. Gerrards Cross: Colin Smythe.

Deleuze, Gilles. 1983. *Nietzsche and Philosophy*. Trans. Hugh Tomlinson. New York: Columbia University Press.

Derrida, Jacques. 1979. *Spurs: Nietzsche's Styles*. Trans. Barbara Harlow. Chicago: University of Chicago Press.

Deutscher, Penelope. 2002. *A Politics of Impossible Difference: The Later Work of Luce Irigaray*. Ithaca: Cornell University Press.

Dipple, Elizabeth. 1982. *Iris Murdoch: Work for the Spirit*. Chicago: University of Chicago Press.

Dooley, Gillian, ed. 2003. *From a Tiny Corner in the House of Fiction: Conversations with Iris Murdoch*. Columbia: University of South Carolina Press.

Dosse, F. 1998. *History of Structuralism*. Vol. 1 and 2. Trans. Deborah Glassman. Minneapolis: University of Minnesota Press.

Duddy, Thomas. 2006. "Iris Murdoch (1919–1999)." *Continuum Encyclopedia of British Philosophy*. Vol. 3. 2286–87.

Dunker, Patricia. 2000. Introduction to *Flight from the Enchanter*. Iris Murdoch. London: Vintage Classics.

Ellam, Julie. 2007. "Zadie Smith." Contemporary Writers. The British Counsel. http://www.contemporarywriters.com/authors/?p=auth257. (Accessed 1 Aug 2008).

Erlande-Brandenburg, Alain. 1997. *The Lady and the Unicorn*. Paris: RMN.

Ettinger, Elzbieta. 1995. *Hannah Arendt and Martin Heidegger*. New Haven: Yale University Press.

Fanon, Frantz. 1970. *Black Skin, White Masks*. Trans. Charles Lam Markmann. London: Paladin.

Farias, Victor. 1987. *Heidegger et le Nazisme*. Paris: Verdier.

Fetcher, John. 1985. "A Novelist's Plays: Iris Murdoch and the Theatre." *Essays in Theatre* 4, 1: 3–20.

Fiander, Lisa. 2004. *Fairy Tales and the Fiction of Iris Murdoch, Margaret Drabble, and A. S. Byatt*. New York: Peter Lang.

Fitz-Simon, Christopher. 1996. *New Plays from the Abbey Theatre 1993–1995*. Introduction. Eds. Fitz-Simon and Sanford Sternlicht, ix–xv. Syracuse: Syracuse University Press.

Flew, Anthony, ed. 1986. *Dictionary of Philosophy*. Oxford: Oxford University Press.

Francine, Thomas Florentin. 1624. *La Fontaine des Medici*. Held by Jardins de Luxembourg, Paris.

Frankova, Milada. 1995. "The Green Knight and the Myth of the Green Man." *Brno Studies in English* 21: 77–83.

Frazer, James George Sir. 1957. *The Golden Bough: A Study in Magic and Religion*. London: Macmillan.

Freeman, Margaret. 1976. *The Unicorn Tapestries*. New York: Metropolitan Museum of Art.

Freud, Sigmund. 1919. *Totem and Taboo: Some Points of Agreement between the Mental Lives of Savages and Neurotics*. Trans. A.A. Brill. New York: Moffat, Yard.

———. 1950. *Totem and Taboo*. Trans. James Stratchey. London: Routledge.

Frey, Northrop. 1976. *The Secular Scripture: A Study of the Structure of Romance*. Cambridge: Harvard University Press.

Gaita, Raymond. 1991. *A Common Humanity*. Hampshire, UK: Macmillan Press.

Gerstenberger, Donna. 1975. *Iris Murdoch*. Irish Writers Series. Lewisberg, PA: Bucknell University Press.

Gilbert, Sandra M., and Susan Gubar. 1979. *The Madwoman in the Attic*. New Haven: Yale University Press.

Gimbutas, Maria. 1991. *The Civilization of the Goddess: The World of Old Europe*. Ed. Joan Marler. San Francisco: Harper.

Gmelch, Sharon. 1986. *Nan: The Life of an Irish Travelling Woman*. London: Souvenir.

Gordon, David J. 1990. "Iris Murdoch's Comedies of Unselfing." *Twentieth Century Literature*. 36, 2 (Summer): 115–36.

Gornick, Vivian. 1999. "Hannah Arendt and Martin Heidegger." In *The End of the Novel of Love*. 103–12. London: Virago.

———. 2004. *Letters 1925–1975: Hannah Arendt and Martin Heidegger*. Ed. Ursual Ludz. Trans. Andrew Shields. Orlando: Harcourt.

Gregory, Richard. 1997. *Mirrors in Mind*. New York : W. H. Freeman/Spektrum.

Grestenberger, Donna. 1975. *Iris Murdoch*. London: Associated University Presses.

Grimshaw, Tammy. 2007. "Plato, Foucault, and Beyond: Ethics, Beauty and Bisexuality in *The Good Apprentice*." In *Iris Murdoch: A Reassessment*. Ed. Anne Rowe, 163–75. Hampshire, UK: Palgrave Macmillan.

Grosz, Elizabeth. 1994. *Volatile Bodies: Toward a Corporeal Feminism*. Bloomington: Indiana University Press.

Haegart, Sandra. 2004. "The Ethics of Self." *Nursing Ethics* 11.5: 434–43.

Haffner, Sebastian. 1978. *Ammerkungen zu Hitler*. Munich: Kindler.

Hals, Frans. 1624. *The Laughing Cavalier*. Held by the Wallace Collection, London.

Hartman, Geoffrey. 2002. *The Longest Shadow: In the Aftermath of the Holocaust*. New York: Palgrave Macmillan.

Hauerwas, Stanley. 1981. *Vision and Virtue*. Notre Dame, IN: University of Notre Dame Press.

Hegel, G.W. F. 1977. *Phenomenology of Spirit*. Trans. A.V. Miller. Oxford: Oxford University Press.

Heidegger, Martin. 1990. *Being and Time*. Trans. J. Macquarrie & E. Robinson. San Francisco: Harper and Row.

_____. 1977. "On the Essence of Truth." In *Martin Heidegger: Basic Writings*. Ed. D. F. Krell, 113–43. San Francisco: Harper Collins.

Hill, Susan. 1982. Interview. *Bookshelf*. BBC Radio 4. 30 April. MT40685, National Sound Archive. London. In *Iris Murdoch: A Descriptive Primary and Annotated Secondary Bibliography*. 1994. Eds. John Fletcher and Cheryl Bove. New York and London: Garland.

Hill, Thomas. 1992. "Kant's Argument for the Rationality of Moral Conduct." In *Dignity and Practical Reason in Kant's Moral Theory*. Ithaca: Cornell University Press.

Holcomb, Gary E., and Kimberly S. Holcomb. 2002. "'I Made Him': Sadomasochism in Kincaid's *The Autobiography of My Mother*." *Callaloo* 25, 3: 969–76.

Holistic qualities of gems. Fruits of the Sea. http://www.fruitsofthesea.com/gems.htm. (Accessed 10 August 2007.)

Hollywood, Amy. 2002. *Sensible Ecstasy: Mysticism, Sexual Difference, and the Demands of History*. Religion and Postmodernity Series. Ed. Mark C. Taylor. Chicago: University of Chicago Press.

Holman, C. Hugh, and William Harmon. 1986. *A Handbook to Literature*. 5th Ed. New York: Macmillan.

Holt, Madeline. 1999. "Literary World Mourns Dame Iris Murdoch." BBC News Online. 19 Feb. http://news.bbc.co.uk/2/low/uk_news/275552.stm.

Homer. 1973 (c.720 b.c.e.). *Iliad*. Trans. E. V. Rieu. London: Penguin.

Honig, Bonnie, ed. 1995. *Feminist Interpretation of Hannah Arendt*. University Park: Pennsylvania State University Press.

Howard, Jacqueline. 1994. *Reading Gothic Fiction: A Bakhtinian Approach*. Oxford: Clarendon Press.

Humm, Maggie. 1995. *The Dictionary of Feminist Theory*. Columbus: Ohio State University Press.

Hursthouse, Rosalind. 1999. *On Virtue Ethics*. Oxford: Oxford University Press.

Ignatieff, Michael. 2003. "Arendt's Example." Hannah Arendt Prize Ceremony. Bremen, Germay. November 28. PDF, 9. http://www.harvard.edu/Cchrp/pdf/arendt.24.11.03.pdf.

Irigaray, Luce. 2002. *Between East and West: From Singularity to Community*. Trans. Stephen Pluhácek. New York: Columbia University Press.

_____. 1993. *An Ethics of Sexual Difference*. Trans. Carolyn Burke and Gillian C. Gill. Ithaca: Cornell University Press.

_____. 1999. *The Forgetting of Air in Martin Heidegger*. Trans. Mary Beth Mader. Austin: The University of Texas Press.

_____. 1993. *Je, Tu, Nous: Toward a Culture of Difference*. New York: Routledge.

_____. 1996. *I Love to You: Sketch for a Possible Felicity in History*. Trans. Alison Martin. New York: Routledge.

_____. 2004. *Luce Irigaray: Key Writings*. Ed. Luce Irigaray. London: Continuum.

_____. 1991. *Marine Lover of Friedrich Nietzsche*. Trans. Gillian C. Gill. New York: Columbia University Press.

_____. 2001. *To Be Two*. Trans. Monique M. Rhodes and Marco F. Cocito-Monoc. New York: Routledge.

_____. 2002. *To Speak Is Never Neutral*.

Trans. Gail Schwab. New York: Routledge.
———. 2002. *The Way of Love*. Trans. Heidi Bostic and Stephen Pluhácek. London: Continuum.
———. 2000. *Why Different? A Culture of Two Subjects*. New York: Semiotext(e).
Janson, Henry. 2001. *Laughter Among the Ruins: Postmodern Comic Approaches to Suffering*. Frankfurt: Peter Lang.
Johnson, Deborah. 1987. *Iris Murdoch*. Key Women Writers Series. Ed. Sue Roe. Sussex: The Harvester Press.
Joy, Morny. 2006. *Divine Love: Women, Gender, and Religion*. Manchester Studies in Religion, Culture and Gender. Ed. Grace M. Jantzen. Manchester, UK: Manchester University Press.
Kane, Richard C. 1988. *Iris Murdoch, Muriel Spark, and John Fowles: Didactic Demons in Modern Fiction*. Rutherford, NJ: Fairleigh Dickinson University Press.
Kant, Immanuel. 1993. *Critique of Practical Reason*. Trans. Lewis White Beck. Upper Saddle River, NJ: Prentice Hall.
———. 1996. *Critique of Pure Reason*. Trans. Werner S. Pluhar. Indianapolis: Hackett.
———. 1991. *Observations on the Feeling of the Beautiful and the Sublime*. Trans. John T. Goldthwait. 1960. Berkeley and Oxford: University of California Press California Library Reprint Series Edition. Berkeley: University of California Press.
Kearney, Richard. 2001. *On Stories*. New York: Routledge.
Kilgour, Maggie. 1995. *The Rise of the Gothic Novel*. New York: Routledge.
King, Magda. 1964. *Heidegger's Philosophy: A Guide to his Basic Thought*. Oxford: Basil Blackwell.
King, Nicola. 2000. *Memory, Narrative, Identity: Remembering the Self*. Edinburgh: Edinburgh University Press.
Kofman, Sarah. 1988. "Baubô: Theological Perversion and Fetishism." In *Nietzsche's New Seas: Explorations in Philosophy, Aesthetics, and Politics*. Ed. Michael Allen Gillespie and Tracy B. Strong, 175–202. Chicago: University of Chicago Press.
LaCapra, Dominick. 2001. *Writing History: Writing Trauma*. Baltimore: Johns Hopkins University Press.
Leach, Maria, and Jerome Fried, eds. 1984. *Funk and Wagnall's StandardDdictionary of Folklore, Mythology, and Legend*. San Francisco: Harper and Row.
Leeney, Cathy. 2004. "Ireland's 'Exiled' Women Playwrights." In *The Cambridge Companion to Twentieth-Century Irish Drama*. Ed. Shaun Richards, 150–63. Cambridge, UK: Cambridge University Press.
Lesser, Wendy. 1985. "Interview with Iris Murdoch." *Threepenny Review* 19: 13–15.
Levi, Neil, and Michael Rothberg, eds. 2003. *The Holocaust: Theoretical Readings*. Edinburgh: Edinburgh University Press.
Lindberg, David C. 1976. *Theories of Vision from al-Kindi to Kepler*. Chicago and London: The University of Chicago Press.
Ludz, Ursula, ed. 2004. *Letters 1925–1975: Hannah Arendt and Martin Heidegger*. Trans. Andrew Shields. Orlando: Harcourt.
Luprecht, Mark. 2006. "A Most Uncritical Critique: Looking at Murdoch'sTtextual Notes for Elias Canetti's *Crowds and power*." *Iris Murdoch News Letter* 19 Autumn: 33–5.
MacIntyre, Alisdaire. 1982. Review of *Iris Murdoch: Work for the Spirit*, by Elizabeth Dipple. *London Review of Books*, 15–16. 3–16 June.
Macquarrie, John. 1973. *Existentialism*. New York: Penguin.
Magee, Bryan. 1978. *Men of ideas*. London: BBC.
Maher, Sean. 1972. *The Road to God Knows Where*. Dublin: Talbot.
Marcel G. 1950. *The Mystery of Being. Vol. 1: Reflection and Mystery*. London: Harvill Press.
Massé, Michelle A. 1992. *In the Name of Love*. Ithaca: Cornell University Press.
May, Derwent. 1986. *Hannah Arendt*. Lives of Modern Women Series. Ed. Emma Tennet. Harmondsworth, UK: Penguin.
McCarthy, Mary, ed. 1978. *Hannah Arendt, The Life of the Mind: Volume One, Thinking*. London: Secker & Warburg.
———. 1978. *Hannah Arendt, The Life of the Mind: Volume Two, Willing*. London: Secker & Warburg.
McDowell, John. 1998. *Mind, Value, and Reality*. Cambridge: Harvard University Press.
Midgley, Mary. 2005. *The Owl of Minerva: A Memoir*. London: Routledge.

Milchman, Alan, and Alan Rosenberg, eds. 1988. *Postmodernism and the Holocaust.* Amsterdam and Atlanta: Rodopi.

Milligan, Tony. 2007. "Iris Murdoch's Mortal Asymmetry." *Philosophical Investigations* 30.2: 156–71.

———. 2007. "Murdochian Humility." *Religious Studies*, 43: 217–28.

Miyares, Ruben Valdes. 2002. "Sir Gawain and the Great Goddess." *English Studies* 83.3 (June): 185–206.

Moi, T. 2002. *Sexual/Textual Politics.* 2d ed. London: Routledge.

Morley, Elaine. 2008. "The Monster and the Maiden—An Unfinished Portrait? Towards a Re-assessment of Murdoch's and Canetti's Relationship." The 4th International Iris Murdoch Conference. Kingston University, London UK.

Moss, Howard. 1986. "Narrow Escapes: Iris Murdoch." *Grand Street* 6 (Autumn): 228–240.

Muraro, Luisa. 2006. "Introduzione." In *Esistenzialisti e Mistici: Scritti di Filosophia e Letteratura.* Ed. Peter Conradi. Preface Gorge Steiner. Trans. Egle Costantino, Monica Fiorini, Fabrizio Elefante. Milan: Il Saggiatore.

Murdoch, Iris. 1987. "Acastos." In *Two Platonic Dialogues.* London: Penguin.

———. 2003 (1971). *The Accidental Man.* London: Vintage.

———. 1999 (1973). *The Black Prince.* London: Vintage.

———. 2003 (1987). *The Book and the Brotherhood.* London: Vintage.

———. 1997. *Existentialists and Mystics: Writing on Philosophy and Literature.* Ed. Peter Conradi. London: Chatto & Windus.

———. 1997. *Existentialists and Mystics: Writing on Philosophy and Literature.* Ed. Peter Conradi. New York: Penguin.

———. 2002 (1970). *A Fairly Honourable Defeat.* London: Vintage.

———. 1978. *The Fire and the Sun.* Oxford: Oxford University Press.

———. 2000 (1956). *The Flight from the Enchanter.* London: Vintage.

———. 2000 (1985). *The Good Apprentice.* London: Vintage.

———. 1993. *The Green Knight.* New York: Penguin.

———. 1995. *Jackson's Dilemma.* London: Chatto & Windus.

———. ND. *Heidegger: The Pursuit of Being.* Unpublished. Iris Murdoch Archive Kingston University Library Special Collections. KUAS/6 Peter Conradi Research Collection. Copyright John Bayley.

———. 1992. *Metaphysics as a Guide to Morals.* London: Chatto & Windus.

———. 1993. *Metaphysics as a Guide to Morals.* New York: Penguin.

———. 2000 (1968). *The Nice and the Good.* London: Vintage Classics.

———. 2001 (1980). *Nuns and Soldiers.* New York: Vintage.

———. 1995. *The One Alone.* London: Colophon. Broadcast, 1987.

———. 1965. *The Red and the Green.* London: Vintage.

———. 1988. *The Red and the Green.* London: Penguin.

———. 2000. *The Red and the Green.* London: Vintage.

———. 2003 (1957). *The Sandcastle.* London: Vintage.

———. 1953. *Sartre: Romantic Rationalist.* London: Collin, Fontana.

———. 1987. *Sartre: Romantic Rationalist.* With a new introduction by the author. London: Chatto & Windus.

———. 2001 (1978). *The Sea, the Sea.* Harmondsworth: Penguin.

———. 1989 (1970). "The Servants and the Snow." In *Three plays.* London: Chatto & Windus.

———. 1976 (1961). *A Severed Head.* London: Penguin.

———. 1957. *Something Special.* London: Chatto & Windus.

———. 1966. *The Sovereignty of the Good Over Other Concepts.* Cambridge: Cambridge University Press.

———. 1970. *Sovereignty of the Good.* London: Routledge & K. Paul.

———. 1989. *The Sovereignty of the Good.* London: ARK.

———. 2001. *The Sovereignty of the Good Over Other Concepts.* London: Routledge.

———. 2003. *The Sovereignty of the Good.* London: Routledge.

———. 2002 (1966). *The Time of the Angles.* London: Vintage.

———. 2006. *Una Cosa Speciale.* Trans. Elena Dal Pra. Rome: Nottetempo.

———. 2002 (1954). *Under the Net.* London: Vintage.

———. 1996 (1963). *The Unicorn*. Harmondsworth, UK: Penguin.
Nicol, Bran. 2007. "The Curse of *The Bell*: The Ethics and Aesthetics of Narrative." In *Iris Murdoch: A Reassessment*. Ed. Anne Rowe. Basingstoke: Palgrave.
———. 2007. *Iris Murdoch: The Retrospective Fiction*. Basingstoke: Palgrave.
———. 1999. *Iris Murdoch: The Retrospective Fiction*. London: Macmillan.
Nietzsche, Friedrich. 1990 (1886). *Beyond Good and Evil*. Trans. R.J. Hollingdale. Harmondsworth: Penguin.
———. 1967 (1872). *The Birth of Tragedy: The Case of Wagner*. Trans. Walter Kaufmann. New York: Vintage.
———. 1982 (1881). *Daybreak*. Trans. R.J. Hollingdale. Cambridge: Cambridge University Press.
———. 1974 (1882). *The Gay Science*. Trans. Walter Kaufmann. New York: Vintage.
———. 1996 (1887). *On the Genealogy of Morals*. Trans. Douglas Smith. Oxford: Oxford University Press.
———. 1969 (1883). *Thus Spoke Zarathustra*. Trans. R.J. Hollingdale. Harmondsworth: Penguin.
———. 1990 (1889). *Twilight of the Idols: The Anti-Christ*. Trans. R.J. Hollingdale. Harmondsworth: Penguin.
Nussbaum, Martha. 1986. *The Fragility of Goodness*. Cambridge: Cambridge University Press.
———. 2001. "When She Was Good: Rev. of *Iris Murdoch: A Life*." *The New Republic* 31: 28+.
Obituary. 1999. Iris Murdoch. BBC News. http://new.bbc.co.uk/2/low/uk_news/275552.stm.
O' Hare, Anthony. 2000. *Philosophy, the Good, the True and the Beautiful*. Cambridge: Cambridge University Press.
Parekh, Bhikhu. 1981. *Hannah Arendt and the Search for a New Political Philosophy*. London: MacMillan.
Pater, Walter. 1986. *The Renaissance: Studies in Art and Poetry*. Oxford: Oxford University Press.
Perrin, J. M., and G. Thibon. 1953. *Simone Weil as We Knew Her*. Trans. J. P. Little. London: Routledge.
Peirce, Charles S. 1958. *Selected Writings: Values in a Universe of Chance*. Ed. Philip P. Wiener. New York: Dover.

Plato. 1973. *Phaedrus and the Seventh and Eighth Letters*. Trans. Walter Hamilton. London: Penguin.
———. 2003. *The Republic*. Trans. Desmond Lee. London: Penguin.
Platts, Mark. 1991. *Moral Realities*. London: Routledge.
de Pue, Stephanie. 2008. "Meeting the Enchantress: Unpublished Interview with Iris Murdoch." *IMR* 1, 7–13.
Putnam, Hilary. 1981. *Reason, Truth, and History*. Cambridge: Cambridge University Press.
Rabieh, Linda. 2006. *Plato and the Virtue of Courage*. Baltimore: Johns Hopkins University Press.
Raffel, Burton, trans and intro. 1970. *Sir Gawain and the Green Knight*. Afterword Neil D. Isaacs. New York: American Library.
Ramanathan, Suguna. 2007. "Iris Murdoch's Destructive Theology." In *Iris Murdoch: A Reassessment*. Ed. Anne Rowe, 35–44. Basingstoke, UK: Palgrave Macmillan.
Rembrandt (Harmenszoon van Rijn). 1632. *Dr. Nicolaes Tulp Demonstrating the Anatomy of the Arm*. Held by Mauritshuis, The Hague.
———. 1654. *Hendrickje Bathing*. Held by the National Gallery, London.
———. 1658. *Jacob Wrestling the Angels*. Held by the Gemaeldegalerie, Berlin.
———. 1662. *The Sampling Officials of the Draper's Guild*. Held: Rijksmuseum, Amsterdam.
———. 1660. *Self Portrait*. Held by the Louvre, Paris.
Ricciardi, Mario. 2002. "Philosophy, Literature, and Life." *Notizie di Politeia* 66, 18.
Ricoeur, Paul. 1974. *The Conflict of Interpretations*. Trans. D. Ihde. Evanston: Northwestern University Press.
———. 1986 (1960/65). *Fallible Man: Revised*. Trans. C.A. Kelbley. New York: Fordham University Press.
———. 1967. *Husserl: An Analysis of His Phenomenology*. Trans. E.G. Ballard and L.E. Embree. Evanston: Northwestern University Press.
———. 1975. *La Métaphore Vive*. Paris: Seuil.
Roberts, Simone M. F. 2005. "Burn the Panopticon: Irigaray's Ethics, Difference,

Poetics." *Reconstructions* (Spring): http://www.reconstruction.ws/o51/robertsintro.shtml.

———. 2004. "Irigaray's eastern turn: Tantra and *An Ethics of Sexual Difference*." *Rhizomes* 9 (Fall): http://www.rhizomes.net/issue9/roberts.htm.

Robinson, Hilary. 2006. *Reading Art, Reading Irigaray: The Politics of Art by Women*. New York: I. B. Tauris.

Rowe, Anne. 2002. "Painting, Literature and Form." In *The Visual Arts and the Novels of Iris Murdoch*. Lampeter: Edwin Mellen Press.

———. 2007. "'Policemen in a Search Team': Iris Murdoch's *The Black Prince* and Ian McEwan's *Atonement*." In *Iris Murdoch: A Reassessment*. Ed. Anne Rowe. Basingstoke, UK: Palgrave Macmillan.

———, and Arvil Horner, eds. 2010. *Iris Murdoch and Morality*. Basingstoke, UK: Palgrave Macmillan.

Rowe, Margaret Moan. 2005. "Dame Iris Murdoch." In *A Companion to the British and Irish Novel 1945–2000*. Ed. Brian W. Schaffer. Malden, MA: Blackwell.

———. 2005. Review of *From a Tiny Corner in the House of Fiction: Conversations with Iris Murdoch*. *Studies in the Novel* 37, 3 (Fall): 351–2.

Safranski, Rüdiger. 1998. *Martin Heidegger: Between Good and Evil*. Trans. Ewald Osers. Cambridge: Harvard University Press.

Sagare, S. B. 2001. An Interview with Iris Murdoch. *Modern Fiction Studies* 47, 3 (Fall): 696–714.

Sage, Lorna. 1977. "The Pursuit of Imperfection." *Critical Quarterly* 19, 2: 57–87.

Sage, Victor, ed. 1990. *The Gothic Novel*. London: Macmillan.

Sartre, Jean-Paul. 1989 (1943). *Being and Nothingness*. Trans. Hazel Barnes. London: Routledge.

———. 2004 (1960). *Critique of Dialectical Reason*. Vol. 1. Trans. Alan Sheridan-Smith. New York, London: Verso.

———. 2002 (1960). *Critique of Dialectical Reason*. Vol. 2. Trans. Quintin Hoare. New York, London: Verso.

———. 2002 (1949). *Iron in the Soul*. London: Penguin.

———. 1965 (1938). *Nausea*. Trans. Robert Baldick. Harmondsworth: Penguin.

———. 2001 (1945). *The Roads to Freedom: The Age of Reason* London: Penguin.

———. 2001 (1941). *The Reprieve*. London: Penguin.

Scanlan, Margaret. 1977. "The Machinery of Pain: Romantic Suffering in Three Works of Iris Murdoch." *Renascence* 29.2.

Schama, Simon. "Dutch Courage." *The Guardian* 23 June 2007. http://www.guardian.co.uk/books/2007/jun/23/art. (Accessed 1 August 2008).

Scott-Baumann, Alison. 2009. *Ricoeur and the Hermeneutics of Suspicion*. New York, London: Continuum.

Shakespeare, William. 2002. (c. 1610). *The Tempest*. Ed. Gerald Graff and James Phelan. Boston & New York: Bedford/St. Martin's.

Schauber, N. 2001. "Murdoch's Morality: Vision, Will, and Rules." *The Journal of Value Inquiry* 35, 4 (December): 447–91.

Schipp, P. A., ed. 1981. *The Philosophy of Jean-Paul Sartre*. La Salle, IL: Open Court.

Scholes, Robert. 1979. *Fabulation in Metafiction*. Urbana: University of Illinois Press.

Schreiber, Gerhard. 1988. *Hitler Interpretationen, 1923–83*. 2d ed. Darmstadt: Wissenshaftliche Bruchgesellschaft.

Scott, Joanna Vecchiarelli, and Judith Chelius Stark, eds. 1966. *Love and St. Augustine*. Trans. E. B. Ashton. Chicago: University of Chicago Press.

Scruton, Roger. 1994. *Modern Philosophy: An Introduction and Survey*. London: Sinclair-Stevenson.

Sekyi-out, Ato. 1996. *Fanon's Dialectic of Experience*. Cambridge: Harvard University Press.

Sheehan, Thomas. 1988. "Heidegger and the Nazis." *The New York Review of Books* 16 June, 38–47.

Shklovsky, Viktor. 1990. *Theory of Prose*. Trans. Benjamin Sher. Normal, IL: Dalkey Archive Press.

Skoller, Elanore Honig. 1993. *The In-Between of Writing: Experience and Experiment in Drabble, Duras, and Arendt*. Ann Arbor: University of Michigan Press.

Slaymaker, William. Nd. "Aesthetics of Freedom in Murdoch's Fiction." *PLL* 116–80. inc.

Smith, Zadie. 2009. *Fail Better: The Morality of the Novel*. London: Hamish Hamilton.

———. 2003. "Love Actually." *The Guardian Review* (1 November): 4–6.

———. 2005. *On Beauty*. London: Hamish Hamilton.

———. 2008. "Zadie, Take Three." The Atlantic.com. http://www.theatlantic.com/doc/200509u/zadie-smith-interview. accessed 1 August 2008.

Steiner, George. 1978. *Heidegger*. Sussex: The Harvester Press.

Stoller, Robert J. 1991. *Pain and Passion: A Psychoanalyst Explores the World of S&M*. New York: Plenum.

Thompson, Stith. 1955. *Motif-Index of Folk-Literature: A Classification of Narrative Elements in Folktales, Ballads, Myths, Fables, Medieval Romances, Expempla, Fabliaux, Jest-Books, and Local Legends*. Rev. and enlarged ed. Six Volumes. Bloomington: Indiana University Press.

Todd, Richard. 1984. *Contemporary British Writers: Iris Murdoch*. London: Methuen.

Todorov, Tzvetan. 1975. *The Fantastic: A Structural Approach to a Literary Genre*. Trans. Richard Howard. Ithaca: Cornell University Press.

Tougas, Cecile T., and Sara Ebenreck, 2000. eds. *Presenting Women Philosophers*. Philadelphia: Temple University Press.

Tucker, Lindsey. 1986. "Released from Bands: Iris Murdoch's Two Prosperos in *The Sea, the Sea*." *Contemporary Literature* 27: 378–95.

Vallar, Marcus. 1989. *The Message to the Planet*. London: Chatto & Windus.

Velleman, J. David. 1999. "Love as a Moral Emotion." *Ethics* 109 (January): 338–74.

Vlastos, Gregory. 1973. *Platonic Studies*. Princeton, NJ: Princeton University Press.

Von Franz, Marie-Louise. 1970. *An Introduction to the Interpretation of Fairy Tales*. Dallas: Spring.

———. 1972. *Problems of the Feminine in Fairy Tales*. Irving, TX: Spring.

Walker, Barbara G. 1983. *The Woman's Encyclopedia of Myths and Secrets*. San Francisco: Harper and Row.

Warnock, Mary, ed. 1996. *Women Philosophers*. London: Dent.

Weese, Katherine. 2001. "Feminist Uses of the Fantastic in Iris Murdoch's *The Sea, the Sea*." *Modern Fiction Studies* 47 (Fall): 630–56.

Weil, Simone. 1974. *The Gateway to God*. Ed. David Raper. Glasgow: Collins.

———. 2002. *Œuvres Complètes*, Tome VI, *Cahiers (Février-Juin 1942)*. Paris: Gallimard.

Wells, Orson, dir. 1949. *The Third Man*.

Weston, Michael. 2001. *Philosophy, Literature and the Human Good*. London: Routledge.

White, Frances. 2005. Letter from John Bayley. February. 10 March.

———. 2009. "*Jackson's Dilemma* and 'The Responsible Life of the Imagination.'" In *Murdoch and Morality*. Eds. Anne Rowe and Avril Horner. New York: Palgrave Macmillan.

Williams, Bernard Arthur Owen. 1985. *Ethics and the Limits of Philosophy*. London: Fontana.

———. 1995. *Making Sense of Humanity and other Philosophical Papers, 1982–1993*. Cambridge: Cambridge University Press.

Williams, R. 1964. *Drama from Ibsen to Eliot*. London: Penguin.

Williamson, John. 1986. *The Oak King, the Holly King and the Unicorn: The Myths and Symbolism of the Unicorn Tapestries*. New York and London: Harper & Row.

Wilson, A. N. 2003. *Iris Murdoch as I Knew Her*. London: Hutchinson.

Wilson, Sharon R. 1993. *Margaret Atwood's Fairy-Tale Sexual Politics*. Toronto: Ecw Press.

———. 2008. *Myths and Fairy Tales in Contemporary Women's Fiction*. New York: Palgrave.

———. 1976. "The Self-Conscious Narrator and His Many Faces." Diss. Ann Arbor: University Microfilms. 293 pgs.

Wolf, Susan. 1982. "Moral Saints." *The Journal of Philosophy* 79, 8 (August): 419–39.

Wood, David, ed. 1991. *On Paul Ricoeur: Narrative and Interpretation*. New York: Routledge.

Wood, Garth. 1999. "The 'Final' Death of God." *The Ottawa Citizen* (March 3):15.

Wright, John R. 2005. "Transcendence without Reality." *Philosophy* 80, 3 (July): 361–84.

Young-Bruehl, Elizabeth. 2004. (1982) *For Love of the World*. 2d ed. New Haven: Yale University Press.

———. 2006. *Why Arendt Matters*. New Haven: Yale University Press.

Young, James E. 1993. *Holocaust Memorials and Meaning*. New Haven: Yale University Press.

_____. 2006. *Hannah Arendt: For Love of the World*. New Haven: Yale University Press.

Zipes, Jack, trans. 1987. *The Complete Fairy Tales of the Brothers Grimm*. Illus. John B. Gruelle. Toronto: Bantam.

_____, trans and ed. 1989. *Beauties, Beasts, and Enchantment: Classic French Fairy Tales*. New York: New American Library.

About the Contributors

John Hacker-Wright is an assistant professor of philosophy at the University of Guelph in Ontario, Canada. He is interested in virtue ethics, the philosophy of action, and the metaphysics of value. He is at work on a book length study of ethical naturalism tentatively titled *Human Nature and the Virtues*, from which two articles have appeared: "Human Nature, Personhood, and Ethical Naturalism" in *Philosophy* and "What Is Natural about Foot's Ethical Naturalism" in *Ratio*.

Wei H. Kao, who received his doctorate from the University of Kent, England, now lectures at National Taiwan University. His articles on Irish women novelists and dramatists have appeared in *Moving Worlds: A Journal of Transcultural Writings*, *Journal of Beckett Studies*, *Essays on Modern Irish Literature* (2007), among others. His monograph *The Formation of an Irish Literary Canon in the Mid-Twentieth Century* (2007) was published by ibidem-Verlag.

Miles Leeson is a part-time lecturer in English at the University of Portsmouth. He studied for his DPhil at the University of Sussex and his dissertation was published (Continuum 2010) with the title *Iris Murdoch: Philosophical Novelist*. He is currently developing his second monograph, which has the working title *Beings in Time: The Twentieth Century Philosophical Novelist*, which will examine the writings of Kafka, Sartre, Camus and Kundera.

Peter Mathews is an assistant professor of English at Centenary College of New Jersey in Hackettstown. He holds a PhD in comparative literature and cultural studies from Monash University. Exploring the intersection between ethics and literature in his work, he has published numerous articles on twentieth-century and contemporary fiction. He is working on a monograph examining the theme of friendship in the work of British novelist Iain Pears.

Tony Milligan has published in various leading philosophy journals such as *Philosophical Investigations*, *Ratio*, *Philosophy*, and the *Journal of Applied Philosophy*. He is an honorary research fellow with the School of Divinity, History and Philosophy at Aberdeen and is completing a book on animals and ethics.

Luisa Muraro is a philosopher living in Milan where she contributed to the founding and support of the Library of Women of Milan. She has taught for many years at the University of Verona, and helped found Diotima, the feminine philosophic community, in 1984. From 2005 to 2006, she taught sexual difference in a master's program with the University of Barcelona, offered by Duoda. Her publications include *The Symbolic Order of the Mother* (1994) and *Guillerma and Maifreda* in Catalán, as well as many articles in the journal *Duoda*. She published *The Days of Women* (2003). Her latest book is *Al Mercato della Felicità* (Mondadori).

M. F. Simone Roberts is a poet and independent scholar of poetics and feminist philosophy. She is an assistant editor at large for the humanities journal *Common Knowledge*. Her monograph, *A Poetics of Being Two*, a study of ethics and sexual difference in the poetries of Saint-John Perse, Yves Bonnefoy, and Jorie Graham is forthcoming from Lexington Books in 2010. Her scholarly work resides in *Reconstruction*, *Rhizomes*, *Common Knowledge*, *Enculturation*, poetry in *Arabesques* and a few other journals.

Anne Rowe is director of the Centre of Iris Murdoch Studies at Kingston University, London. She is the author of *The Visual Arts and the Novels of Iris Murdoch* (2002), editor of *Iris Murdoch: A Reassessment* (2006) and co-author with Cheryl Bove of *Sacred Space, Beloved City: Iris Murdoch's London* (2008). She was editor of the *Iris Murdoch News Letter*, 1993–2007, and is now lead editor of the *Iris Murdoch Review*. She is currently working on *Iris Murdoch and Morality* with Avril Horner and *Literary Lives: Iris Murdoch* with Priscilla Martin, both for publication by Palgrave in 2009/2010.

Alison Scott-Baumann is a reader emeritus at the University of Gloucestershire, England, Representative for the Ricoeur Foundation in Paris, and member of the Conseil Scientifique. Her monograph *Ricoeur and the Hermeneutics of Suspicion* was published by Continuum in 2009, and she is currently working on *Ricoeur and the Negation of Happiness*. Her major recent interests lie in archival research on Ricoeur in Paris and in the application of philosophy to social justice projects, including a recent invitation from the British government to review Muslim faith leader training in Britain, especially that of women.

Amy Smith, assistant professor of English and modern languages, Lamar University, Beaumont, Texas, was issue editor for *Crossings* (8), and is completing a manuscript on Virginia Woolf's political uses of myth.

Judit Varga is a PhD candidate at the University of Bristol. Her thesis is entitled *Specularity and Self-Reflection in Twentieth-Century Life-Writing: A Study of Vladimir Nabokov, Virginia Woolf and Jean Rhys*. She recently presented a paper that rethinks "The Mirror-Metaphor and the Enigma of Autobiography" and published an essay on Johannes Gummp's *Triple Self-Portrait*.

Frances White is a research student at Kingston University, London, writing a thesis on "Remorse in the Philosophy and Fiction of Iris Murdoch." She is assistant editor of *The Iris Murdoch Review* and assistant director of the Centre for Iris Murdoch Studies.

Sharon R. Wilson is professor of English and women's studies and teaches twentieth-century literature and other classes at the University of Northern Colorado in Greeley. She is the author of *Margaret Atwood's Fairy-Tale Sexual Politics* and *Myths and Fairy Tales in Contemporary Women's Fiction*, and editor of *Margaret Atwood's Textual Assassinations* and, with Friedman and Hengen, *Approaches to Teaching Atwood's The Handmaid's Tale and Other Works*.

Index

Abbey Theatre 253
Above the Gods 169
Acastos 69, 170, 177, 256; *see also* Plato
Accidental Man 1, 123, 164
Adorno, Theodor 23, 26
aesthetics 6, 77, 78, 88, 122, 257
"Against Dryness" 35–38, 205, 220, 225, 247
Agamemnon 177
Aleph/Sefton 98, 99, 100–104; valkyries 96; *see also* aletheia
aletheia (truth) 69, 227
Al-kadir 96
allegory 22, 57, 58, 59, 60, 130, 134; Plato 65, 66, 185
An Allegory of Venus, Bronzino, Agnolo 81, 90, 252
allusion 77–79, 83, 85; myth 35, 40, 41, 47, 49, 92
Altorf, Marije 33n116, 251
ambiguity 120, 122, 127, 161, 169, 181, 231, 239, 253
ambivalence 1, 128, 132, 137, 191, 196
Amis, Martin 77
analytical philosophy 3, 149, 237, 242
anamnesis 50
Andromache 95, 100
Anglo-Irish 127–146
anti-Semitism 20, 251; Mill, J.S. 38; philo- 21; *see also* Arendt, Hannah
Antonaccio, Maria 1, 38, 149
Aphrodite 45, 46
Apollo 49, 95
Arendt, Hannah 4, 13–33; *Metaphysics as a Guide to Morals* 13
Aristotle 75, 116, 179, 218, 233
Armstrong, Katie 81, 85
Arrowby, Charles 78, 192, 194
Art and Eros 170
art, visual 5, 6, 74–91, 211, 262; *see also* artists
Artemis 46
artists 112, 123, 243
ascesis, Platonic narrative of 53, 57, 64–68, *see also* Plato; Platonic allegory
Até 66
Athena 46

attachment 9, 87, 204, 228, 245; *see also* Plato
attention 9, 22, 42, 83, 117, 172, 175, 208; Heidegger, Martin 224, 227; Irigaray, Luce 108, 112–115, 129; the Good 210–211, 214–216; loving 6, 25, 47, 108–12; Weil, Simone 39–40, 228
Atwood, Margaret 93–94
Austen, Jane 74
authority 60, 67, 132; feudal 132, 136; intellectual 16, 242; realist 213, 238; spiritual 18
axioms 24, 170–173
Ayer, A. J. 230, 237

Backus, Guy 70n1
Baehr, Peter 33n90
Balogh, Thomas 30n17
Barlow, Anthea 43–49
Basil 7, 127–146
Baudrillard, Jean 5, 19
Bayley, John 16, 18, 20, 21
Beauty and the Beast 95, 97, 99–101
Being and Time (Sein und Zeit) 10, 231
The Bell 81, 104
Bellamy 97, 99, 100, 103, 104
Benet 13, 18
Bentham, Jeremy 35, 135, 173
Bergonzi, Bernard 39
Berlin, Isaiah 20
Bhreatnach, Aoife 145n11
Biranne, Richard 26
birth, rebirth 92–106; *see also* Nietzsche, Friedrich
The Black Prince 40, 78, 181
Blücher, Heinrich 29n9
"Blue Beard" 95, 102
Blythe, Ernest 144n7
body 113–121, 135, 150, 162; *see also* Irigaray, Luce
The Book and the Brotherhood 23, 158, 233; *see also* Marx, Karl
Booker Prize 1, 8, 75
Botticelli, Sandro 79
Bove, Cheryl K. Browning 1, 57–58; *see also* *Understanding Iris Murdoch*

263

Bowen, Elizabeth 129; *The Last September* 144*n*10
Brecht, Bertolt 20, 47
"Briar Rose" (Sleeping Beauty) 95, 99, 101, 102
Broakes, Justin: *Iris Murdoch, Philosopher* 221
Bronzino, Agnolo *see An Allegory of Venus*
Brooks, Peter 56
Bruno's Dream 158
Buddhism 9, 168, 181–183; Mahayana 183
Büttner, Gottfried 71*n*28
Byatt, Antonia 240–241

Camus, Albert 37, 97, 155, 158, 232
Canetti, Elias 4, 14–18, 21, 22; Venetiana (Veza) 30*n*16
Canovan, Margaret 30*n*13
Carpaccio 95, 99
Carter, Angela 93
Cartesian 150, 158, 162, 229
Césaire, Aimé: *Discourse on Colonialism* 145*n*17
Cézanne, Paul 77
Chevalier, Jean-Louis 33*n*112
choice 40, 76, 111–112, 114, 203, 207–8, 216–219, 222, 242; as aspect of freedom 146*n*62; philosophy 149, 185; Sartre, Jean-Paul 148, 195; Weil, Simone 175
Christ 19, 82, 95, 97
Christianity 93; failed 142; *see also* religion
"Cinderella" 95, 101–104
Circe 95, 100, 102
Clergy, role in oppression 142
Cluny Tapestries 58, 252
comedy 176, 195, 197
communism 150, 157, 163–4; Communist Party 1, 14, 22, 148, 149, 163; Stalinist 149
Conradi, Peter 1, 17, 18, 21, 149, 152, 187; on Murdoch's "Heidegger" manuscript 224; on Murdoch's Sartre, Jean-Paul 54, 157, 160, 163, 164
contingency 38–39, 109, 158, 159, 163; in myth 42, 47–48
Cooper, Effingham 53–67, 94, 99
Crean-Smith, Hannah 5, 53–54, 60, 61
Crean-Smith, Peter 60
Crowds and Power 231, 252, 255

Daphne and Apollo 95
Dasein 223, 224, 226–228, 231; *see also* Heidegger, Martin
Dawkins, Richard 229
Deane, Seamus 143
death 24, 178, 180; in *The Green Knight* 97, 99; Irigaray, Luce 109; in *The Nice and The Good* 26; Plato 178, 180; Sartre, Jean-Paul 161; in *The Sea, The Sea* 198, 200; in *The Servants and the Snow* 132, 135, 140; in *The Time of the Angels* 45, 46, 224–225, 227, 232; in *The Unicorn* 63, 67, 68

De Beaumont, Jeanne-Marie Le Prince 100
De Beauvoir, Simone 37, 233
decreation 178; *see also* Weil, Simone
Della Francesca, Piero 206
Delphic Priestess 95, 100
Demeter 46
demonic 9, 41, 43–44, 123, 163, 190–202; *see also* Nietzsche, Friedrich
Derrida, Jacques 196, 224
Descartes, René *see* Cartesian
description 9, 40–41, 95, 147, 157; egoistic economy of 208–211; the Good 210–215; Irigaray, Luce 109–116; moral 157, 203–215
desire 77–83, 170–182, 201, 204, the Good 204–216; Kant, Immanuel 117; for power 132–140; redemption of 171, 191, 201; *The Sea, the Sea* 190–202; selfish 216
detachment 112, 211; *see also* suppression of ego; unselfing
dialectic 150; Hegel, G.F.W. 8; Irigaray, Luce 112; master-slave 131, 135, 150; Sartre, Jean-Paul 151, 161, 162
Diamond, Cora 203
Dickens, Charles 74, 93
Dinesen, Isak 27
Dionysus 5, 41, 49, 96
Diotima 112
Dipple, Elizabeth 34, 92, 221, 225
Dr. Nicolaes Tulp Demonstrating the Anatomy of the Arm 82; *see also* Rembrandt (van Rijn)
domination 127–146; of female bodies 135–136, 222
Dosse, François 159
Dostoyevsky, Fyodor 222, 228
droit de seigneur 130–142
duality 246–247
DuBois, Blanche 145*n*38
Ducane, John 26
Dunker, Patricia 253

Easter Rising (1916) 23, 127, 128
Edgeworth, Maria 129; *Castle Rackrent* 145*n*10
ego 2, 7–9, 23, 26, 37, 74, 77, 79, 119, 121, 182; Freud, Sigmund 227, 231; in the Good 213–214; Plato 191; suffering 175–177; unselfing 87
Eichmann, Adolf 21, 25–26, 32*n*62, 251; *see also* Arendt, Hannah
Eliot, George 74, 155
enchantment 92–106, 231–232
equality 134–135
Erlande-Brandenburg, Alain 71*n*27, 71*n*28, 253
eros 16–18, 66, 97, 101, 139, 169, 171, 180, 254
eternity 100, 195; Nietzsche, Friedrich 197
ethics 3–5, 10, 29, 34–52, 88, 114, 248; in *The Darkness of Practical Reason* 107; the Good 191, 204, 216, 234; Irigarian 114, 121, 124

Ettinger, Elzbieta 16
evil, banality of 13, 25
existentialism 221, 241–242, 247; European 3, 10, 149–152; Heidegger, Martin 221; Sartre, Jean-Paul 8, 148, 149–152, 155, 158, 162–164, 226, 241–242; in *The Servants in the Snow* 129

A Fairly Honourable Defeat 21, 40, 162, 164, 244, 256
fairytale 62, 92–106
faith 99, 102, 122–123, 142; bad faith 151, 153, 157, 159, 193–195, 198, 200
fallenness 226, 228; see also Heidegger, Martin
Fanon, Frantz 144
fantasy 36–42, 54, 57, 107–115, 123; "Against Dryness" 225, 247; art 74–80, 244; egocentric 182, 186, 187, 218; gothic 59–61; Plato 65–67
Fates 43, 46
Father Ambrose 142–143
femininity 41, 43–46, 49; Derrida, Jacques, and Nietzsche, Friedrich 195–196; Irigaray, Luce 107–108, 113–118
feminism 28, 92, 99, 100, 195; second wave 135
femme fatale 54, 55, 58
Fetcher, John: "A Novelist's Plays: Iris Murdoch and the Theater" 254
Fiander, Lisa 93, 95, 102, 103
fiction 18–27, 34–52, 75–77, 81, 88, 93, 190, 215, 221–224, 229; false self 231
The Fire and the Sun 180
Fischer, Carel 43, 44, 226
Fischer Elizabeth 43–44, 46, 224, 230–231
Fischer, Marcus 43–46, 222–223, 227, 229, 233
"Fitcher's Bird" 95, 101–104
Fitz-Simon, Christopher 144*n*7
The Flight from the Enchanter 21, 23, 43, 80, 226, 231
flourishing 107–126, 218–219; Irigaray, Luce 115, 122–124
Fontaine de Médicis 81, 82, 85
form, in novel 11, 34–35, 37, 74, 84, 157
Forster, E. M. 74, 76, 83
Four African Heads 78; see also Rembrandt (van Rijn)
Fox, Mischa 21, 226, 231
Fraenkel, Eduard 17, 29
Frankova, Mileda 95
Frazer, James George 253
Frederic 133, 134, 141
freedom 28, 93, 110–112, 185, 242–244; absence of 155, 228, 233; Anglo-Irish context 7, 135–141; Hegel, G.F.W. 110, 130, 150–151; Irigaray, Luce 114; Kant, Immanuel 110, 120, 207, 212–213; Sartre, Jean-Paul 152, 157, 160–163

Freud, Sigmund 36, 161, 203–204, 218; Anglo-Irish 7, 132, 136; sadomasochism 175; *A Severed Head* 227, 230–231
Frey, Northrop 253

Gadamer, Hans Georg 237
Gaze Castle 53–70
gender, reversal 94
General Klein 141, 143
genocide 4, 21, 24
Gerstenberger, Donna 127
Gifford Lectures 4, 14
La Giocanda (Mona Lisa) 79
Gmelch, Sharon 145*n*11, 253
Goddess 41, 45, 46, 87; myths 95–100, 104
The Good 168–189, 203–220; Good and evil 4, 18, 153, 172, 244; Good Man 86, 87, 162, 179, 180, 185; Irigaray, Luce 108; moral 8, 9, 24, 93, 122, 124, 163, 180, 186; *The Nice and the Good* 22, 26, 81; Plato 65, 179; "On 'God' and 'Good'" 37, 234; "The Sovereignty of Good" 24, 28, 173, 180, 185; "The Sublime and the Good" 40, 88, 110, 118; "The Sublime and the Good Revisited" 110
The Good Apprentice 27
Gordon, David 39, 43, 44
Gornick, Vivian 16
gothic 5, 53–73, 95; nightmare 61
The Gothic Novel 59
grail 95, 97, 98
The Green Knight 6, 92–106, 183
Green Man 95–106, 253
Grimshaw, Tammy 33*n*116, 254
Grüber, Propst Heinrich 33*n*91
Grundig 130, 134, 140
guilt 54–55, 175–177, 182
gypsy 21, 129, 138–140; Tinker 130, 135–142

Haffner, Sebastian 251
Hampshire Stuart 230
Hans Joseph 130, 139
"Hansel and Gretel" 95, 101–103
happiness 93, 157, 164, 169, 218–219; *Acastos* 169; contentment 89, 168–189; fairy tales 101–104; Irigaray, Luce 116–119; *Metaphysics as a Guide to Morals* 17–174
Harrison, Jane 46, 47, 49
Hauerwas, Stanley 176
Hegel, G.F.W. 110–111, 150, 151, 246; dialectic 150; Irigaray, Luce 116; Kant, Immanuel 38, 79, 108, 148, 155, 164; master-slave dialectic 128–140, 153; negation 150, 161; Nietzsche, Friedrich 198, 228; Sartre, Jean-Paul 79, 108, 110, 147–167; *The Time of the Angels* 222
Heidegger, Martin 13–33, 221–236; Arendt, Hannah 13–33; *Being and Time (Sein und Zeit)* 228, 231; Dasein (being) 224, 226–

228, 231; "Heidegger: The Pursuit of Being" 4, 10, 190–202; Jackson's Dilemma 13; "Martin Heidegger at Eighty" 251; National Socialism 18; *The Time of the Angels* 221–236
Hendrickje Bathing 85; see also Rembrandt (van Rijn)
Hera 45, 46, 47
Heusel, Barbara Stevens 34, 221
Hitler, Adolf 15, 19, 21, 25, 26, 100, 147
Hobbes, John 35
Holcomb, Gary E. 139
Holocaust 18, 22, 26, 27; Arendt, Hannah 15, 26
Homer, *Iliad* 73n67
honesty 194–195, 216, 218, 232
Howard, Jacqueline 59, 60
The Human Condition 19–22, 24, 175, 232; Arendt, Hannah 19, 22, 24
Hume, David 35, 229–230
The Hunt of the Unicorn 57, 59
Husserl, Edmund 3, 149, 162, 166, 237

"The Idea of Perfection" 36, 39, 240, 241, 243
Ignatieff, Michael 31n61
illusion 93, 247, self 229–230; in *The Unicorn* 56, 66
Industrial Revolution 129
intertextuality 6, 7, 94–97, 104
invulnerability 179–182, 246
Irigaray, Luce 7, 107–126

Jackson's Dilemma 13, 18, 27
Jacob Wrestling with the Angel 86; see also Rembrandt (van Rijn)
James, Henry 1, 74, 76
Jansen, Henry 176
Jaspers, Karl 7
Jewish people 15–32
Job 222
John of the Cross 177
Johnson, Deborah 255
Judaism see Jewish people; see also Arendt, Hannah
Julian of Norwich 177
justice 86, 98, 101, 107, 142, 170–172, 183, 208, 222

Kane, Richard C. 70n1, 70n6, 255
Kant, Immanuel 110, 118, 212, 216, 218, 232; antinomies 8, 152–153, 163–164; Descartes, René 150; Hegel, G.F.W. 148–150; Heidegger, Martin 222, 225, 232; Hume, David 230; Nietzsche, Friedrich 200; Sartre, Jean-Paul 148–150, 156, 157–160, 207
Keane, Molly 129
Kearney, Richard 27
Kierkegaard, Søren 3, 23, 150
Kilgour, Maggie 60
King, Julius 21, 40, 155, 164; Jewish 21

Klein, Honor 42, 46
Kore (Persephone) 45, 46
Kost, Willy 21

The Lady and the Unicorn 58–59, 67
landlords 127–146
Laughing Cavalier 77, 79
Lavin, Mary 127
Lazarus 95, 97
Leda and the Swan 95, 99
The Legend of the Fisher King 5, 63–64, 68
The Legend of the Unicorn 5, 53, 58
Lejour, Max 53–73
Lejour, Pip 54, 65
Leonardo da Vinci 79
Liberalism 23, 38, 108, 149, 183
Lichtenberg, Dompropst Bernard 33n91
"Life of the Mind: Thinking," "Life of the Mind: Willing" 14, 17; Arendt, Hannah 17
Lilith 5, 54, 55, 58
Lindberg, David C. 72n61
literature 6, 34, 37, 38–40, 50, 75–76, 83, 88, 155, 236, 244; Heidegger, Martin's philosophy 221–236; Sartre, Jean-Paul 148, 160, 164
Lochinvar 95, 98
Lucas 94–106
Luprecht, Mark 31n33

M and D parable 28, 208–209, 244
MacKinnon, Donald 17
Magee, Bryan 239
magic 6, 16, 24, 41, 131, 193–195; see also spell
magical realism 94, 100
Maher, Sean: *The Road to God Knows Where* 145n11, 255
Manuscript on Heidegger, Martin (unpublished) 123, 221–236
Marina 132–143
marriage 14, 15, 60–61, 101–102, 104, 129, 134–135, 195–201
Marxism 78, 147–148, 153, 162, 164, 226; in *The Book and the Brotherhood* 23; in *Metaphysics as a Guide to Morals* 23; Murdoch's 1, 14, 23, 135, 149, 163; in *The Servants and the Snow* 133–136
Massé, Michelle A. 60
master-slave see Hegel, G.F.W.
Mathias, William 128
Maxim 134, 136, 138, 142, 143
May, Derwent 32n62
McDowell, John 216
Medusa 5, 41, 42, 46, 48, 49
Meister Eckhart 235n39
Memmi, Albert: *The Colonizer and the Colonized* 145n17
Men in Dark Times 13; Arendt, Hannah 27, 29
Mephistopheles 95, 97, 98

Merleau-Ponty, Maurice 150, 162
mess 2, 5, 6, 7, 34, 37, 48, 50, 57, 107–126
The Message to the Planet 27; *see also* Holocaust
metafiction 53, 56–59, 68, 70, 94
metamorphosis 28, 67, 95
metaphysics 47, 111, 134, 148, 153, 161, 180, 203–206, 210, 238; "Against Dryness" 225; Heidegger, Martin 227–228, 232
Metaphysics as a Guide to Morals vi, 13, 26; Gifford Lecture 14, 23; God 222; happiness 170; Kant, Immanuel 203; Sartre, Jean-Paul 159, 160; stories 26
Mill, John Stewart 35, 38
mimesis, of sublimity 49
Minotaur 95, 97
mirrors 55–56
misogyny 79, 195–196
Moira 95, 96, 99
Momigliano, Arnoldo 30*n*17
Mona Lisa (*La Giocanda*) 8, 79
Mor 23
moral agent 110, 112, 157, 172, 186, 203–220, 242; artist, critic 112; Irigaray, Luce 113; Kant, Immanuel 110; Sartre, Jean-Paul 157; unselfing 186
Moore, G. E. 10, 222
moral courage 9, 168, 178, 184–186
morality 74–91, 112, 171–172, 221–236; art and literature 39, 75–78, 82, 112, 149, 162, 164, 204, 222; Kant, Immanuel 117, 207, 215–216; "Morals and Politics" 23; Sartre, Jean-Paul 147, 162, 226
Morgan le Fay 96
Morrison, Toni 93
mortality 82, 85, 180
Most, Daniel *see* The Message to the Planet
Mother Goddess 46
Mulhall, Stephen 149, 221
Murdoch Archive 3, 29*n*4, 32*n*62, 165*n*17, 235*n*15
Muriel 44, 224, 228, 230
mystery 53–68, 122
mystics 177, 233, 238, 246; *Existentialists and Mystics* 210; Irigaray, Luce 109
myth, use of 34, 47–51, 58, 79, 110; "The Existentialist Political Myth" 153; Greek 35, 40, 48, 54, 66, 181, 192, 241; *The Green Knight* 92–106; "Heidegger: The Pursuit of Being" 225; related to form 35–38, 40–46, 83–84; Sartre, Jean-Paul 148–163; *A Severed Head* 40–41, 48; *The Time of the Angels* 232
The Myth of Sisyphus 97

narrative 5, 6, 27–28, 42, 53–74, 94, 239; E. M. Forster 74, 83; first person narrative 42, 81–83, 87, 94, 154–155, 158, 237, layering 6; philosophy 194–195, 223, 228–232; Smith, Zadie 79, 83, 87; *The Unicorn* 94

naturalism 9–10, 203–220; ethical 218–220; scientific 215–210
nature: Freud, Sigmund 218–219; human 10, 22–23, 48, 199, 204
Nausea 8–9, 97, 109, 147–167, 193–194
negation/negativity 7–8, 35–38, 147–165; Deleuze 198; myth 47–50, 65; religion 142; Sartre, Jean-Paul 147–165
neuroticism 42, 109, 154–155; narcissistic 118; *A Severed Head* 42
New Testament 225
The Nice and the Good 22, 26, 81
Nicol, Bran 34, 38, 39, 48, 49–50, 53; *Iris Murdoch: The Retrospective Fiction* 24
Nietzsche, Friedrich 8–10, 150, 190–202, 231; on acting 194–195; Derrida, Jacques 196; Irigaray, Luce 123; *see also* marriage
Nolan, Denis 54, 69
"Nostalgia for the Particular" 237
Nuns and Soldiers 23
Nussbaum, Martha 88, 179–180

Oakeshott, Michael 30*n*17
Odysseus 45, 95, 97
Oedipal romance 48
Oedipus complex 136, 139
On Beauty 6, 74–91
On the Essence of Truth 227
ontology 237–231; gender 107; of the unconscious 231
oppression 7, 128–139, 153, 161
Oriane 130–143
Osiris 96
otherness 6, 8, 67, 76, 83, 109, 110, 115, 155; Hegel, G.F.W. 118; Irigaray, Luce 115; Kant, Immanuel 120

The Painter's Daughters Chasing a Butterfly 81
paintings 6, 74–91, 96, 112, 211; *see also* Rembrandt (van Rijn)
Parekh, Bhikhu 15
Pater, Walter 79
Patrice 7, 129–144
Pattie 44, 223–232
Pearson, Bradley 40, 78, 155, 181
Peirce, Charles S. 245–246
perception 8, 109, 111; Arendt, Hannah 25–27; Hegel, G.F.W. 150; Heidegger, Martin 229; Irigaray, Luce 111–117, 121; Merleau-Ponty, Maurice 150; Plato 48, 65, 79; Sartre, Jean-Paul 151, 157–158, 164
perfection 24, 172, 212; the Good 211; "The Idea of Perfection" 36, 39, 241–243; Kantian 233; Plato 180–183
Persephone *see* Kore
Perseus 96, 100
Peter Jack 132–143
Phaedrus 65

phenomenology 3; Gabriel Marcel 152; Heidegger, Martin 227; Husserl, Edmund 3, 237
Philoctetes 95, 98
Philo-Semitic 20
The Philosopher's Pupil 233
Plato 10, 37, 65–68, 150, 173, 179, 222–233, 246–247; allegory of the cave 37–38, 48, 185, 192; "Art and Eros" 169; Irigaray, Luce 112; language 51, 78, 155; neo-Platonism 34–35, 150, 156; Nietzsche, Friedrich 190–202; Platonic narrative/plot 53–54, 64–66; simile of the sun 65, 66, 192; *see also* ascesis; negation
pleasure 23, 26, 75; E. M. Forster 83; the Good 173; pleasure principle 60; *The Servants and the Snow* 135–140; unselfing 174
The Polish Rider 96, 100
politics 6, 23, 29; Arendt, Hannah 13, 22; colonial 131–136, 140, 143; gender 136; Irigaray, Luce 121; sexual 103–104
postcolonial thought 92, 131–133
postmodernity 6, 7, 48, 75, 92–97
poststructuralism 107–108
power 10, 46, 99, 124–146, 156, 242, 245; art 81–83, 88; character 38, 43–44, 48, 96–97, 103; description 94, 147–149, 161; female 19, 43–44, 46, 87, 104; Nietzsche, Friedrich 192–200, 222; "The Sovereignty of Good" 164, 185; *The Time of the Angels* 43–49
princess 100–104; princess lointaine 60, 64
psyche 36, 48–49, 107, 182; Freud, Sigmund 203; Irigaray, Luce 113
psychoanalysis 121, 150–151, 227–230
psychology 49, 213, 219, 231; Freud, Sigmund 218; the Good 11–12; with myth 232

quest 56, 59, 94, 96–97, 100, 101, 170

race 76–77
Radeechy, Joseph 26
"Rapunzel" 95, 99–101
rational agent 24, 36, 207, 212 *see also* rationalism
rationalism 35, 49; critique of 35, 48, 51; irrationalist 38, 48–49, 74, 83, 111; Rationalist, Romantic 157–167; resistance 48–49; *see also* Sartre, Jean-Paul
Reading Gothic Fiction 59, 254
realism 5, 40, 42, 77, 92, 108, 213; literary 38, 47–48; magical 94, 99; in *Metaphysics as a Guide to Morals* 178; moral 9, 204, 234, 244; nineteenth-century 38
The Red and the Green 23, 127, 153
redemption 9, 19, 171, 177, 191, 201–202
relationships 2, 4, 15, 17, 245; incestuous 44, 46, 224; master-slave 129, 132, 138–140; with God 162
religion 182, 229; Buddhist 98; chthonic 49; demythologizing 225; Father Ambrose 142;
Greek 46; Irigaray, Luce 111; *see also* Buddhism; Christianity
Rembrandt (van Rijn) 74–91; *see also Dr. Nicolaes Tulp Demonstrating the Anatomy of the Arm*; *Four African Heads*; *Hendrickje Bathing*; *Jacob Wrestling with the Angel*; *Seated Nude*; *The Shipbuilder and His Wife*; *Der Staalmeesters*
Renoir, Pierre-Auguste 79
repression 161, 127–146; sexual 139, 161
resentment 132–142, 174, 200, 243
resistance 127–146
respect 4, 17, 88; *Achtung* 120; the Beast 100; contingency 37–38; Kant, Immanuel 118; men and women 119; the other 100, 114, 122
responsibility 103, 108; Holocaust 25; Sartre, Jean-Paul 160, 164; "The Sovereignty of Good" 24
Resurrection 96
revolution 129, 153, 157; Arendt, Hannah 22
rhetoric 5, 137, 240
Ricoeur, Paul 149; existentialism 150; Marcel 152
Riders Castle 64
Rilke, Rainer Maria 77, 237, 243
riot 128, 131–133, 136
romance 5; chivalric 53–64; gothic 61
Rosalind 27
Rubens, Peter Paul 78
Rushdie, Salman 76
Russell, Bertrand 35
Ryle, Gilbert 152, 223, 230, 237

The Sacred and Profane Love Machine 175
sacrifice 131, 133, 142, 173; for the other 174, 181, 185
sadomasochism 8, 139–140, 175–178
Safranski, Rüdiger 29n8, 198
Sage, Lorna 49
Sage, Victor 59
St. Augustine 22
Saint George and the Dragon 95, 99–100
Sampson, Frederic 20
The Sandcastle 23, 78–79, 162, 164, 169
Sartre, Jean-Paul 1, 3, 7–8, 10, 35, 38, 79, 147–167; *Critique of Dialectical Reason* 167; existentialism 151, 241–242; Kant, Immanuel, and Hegel, G.F.W. 8, 148, 153; *Nausea* 97, 147, 150, 154–160, 193–194; negation 148–149, 153–154, 161–163; *Sartre, Jean-Paul: Romantic Rationalist* 147, 154–167, 226; *The Sea, the Sea* 194–201; *The Sublime and the Good* 110; *The Sublime and the Good Revisited* 110; Totalitarian Man 111, 113, 117; *Under the Net* 5, 7, 10, 23, 74–87, 225, 237, 245
Scharansky, Anatoly (Nantan) 32n87
Schauber, Nancy 220n16
Scholes, Robert 53, 54, 60
Schreiber, Gerhard 258

Scottow, Gerald 53–94, 232
The Sea, the Sea 1, 9, 190–202
Seated Nude 81; *see also* Rembrandt (van Rijn)
Sefton *see* Aleph
Sein und Zeit (*Being and Time*) *see* Heidegger, Martin, Martin
self 10, 19, 22, 36, 76, 77, 110, 112, 116, 175, 206; art 77, 80, 84, 123; false 186, 231; Hegel, G.F.W. 130; Heidegger, Martin 228–234; identity 41; Irigaray, Luce 113–117; Plato 176–177, 185–187; realization 111, 228; Sartre, Jean-Paul 155–160
selfishness 104, 218, 228; self-reflexivity 58–59; *see also* ego; unselfing
semiosis 245–246
The Servants, libretto 128
The Servants and the Snow 7, 124–144
A Severed Head 40–43, 46–48, 49, 54, 78, 80, 227, 231, 256; psychoanalysis 175, 230
Sheehan, Thomas 30n27
The Shipbuilder and His Wife 87; *see also* Rembrandt (van Rijn)
Shklovsky, Viktor 258
Sibyls 95
Silkies, as selkies 95, 99
"Sir Gawain and the Green Knight" 95, 96, 103, 257
Sirens 43, 45, 46
Slaymaker, William 93
"Sleeping Beauty" 95, 98, 99, 102
Smith, Zadie 5, 74–91
socialism 22, 133, 146–154, 163–164; National 18
Socrates 155, 164, 169, 197, 201; Plato 191; Nietzsche, Friedrich 191
solipsism 24, 28, 150
"The Sovereignty of the Good" 24, 28, 156, 164, 169, 173, 174, 177, 179, 185, 205
spell 6, 46, 62, 95, 98, 102; *see also* magic
Sphinx 43, 46
spirituality 65, 193
Der Staalmeesters 83; *see also* Rembrandt (van Rijn)
Steiner, Franz 17, 20
Steiner, George 18
Stern, Günther 29n9
structuralism 108, 224, 230; Dosse, Francois 159
subjectivity 139, 241; Irigaray, Luce 112, 114–115, 119, 121, 123
sublime 5–7, 34–52, 121–124, 107–126, 241; aesthetic of 38–39; Kant, Immanuel 36, 110; Sartre, Jean-Paul 157, 164; "The Sublime and the Beautiful Revisited" 165
"The Sublime and the Good" 110; Kant, Immanuel 119, 120; love 40, 88, 118, 120
suffering 8, 15, 19–21, 45, 56, 66–69, 140, 168–189; non-accidental 178; unselfing as a mode of 178, 181
swerve 237–250

symbol 5, 6, 18, 46, 53–73, 79–95, 97–104, 108–121, 128, 159, 183–200, 225, 243–245
Symbolists 110–111
Synge, J. M. 145n11
synthesis 11, 150, 170, 246; thirdness without synthesis 245

Taylor, Marian 53–69
therapy 176–186; *see also* psychoanalysis
The Third Reich 14, 19
thirdness 11, 245–246; third sense 5, 24–52
Timaeus 180
The Time of the Angels 10, 43, 49, 164, 221–236
Todd, Lefty 23
Todorov, Tzvetan 62
Tolstoy, Leo 93, 155, 157
tragedy 60, 92, 177; European 128, 149; Hegel, G.F.W. 136; Marx, Karl 136; *Metaphysics as a Guide to Morals* 178; Nietzsche, Friedrich 191; "The Sublime and the Good" 118; suffering 177; *The Time of the Angels* 232
transcendence 113, 117, 224, 226, 230; "Against Dryness" 226; Heidegger, Martin 226, 227, 230; horizontal 234; Irigaray, Luce 115; metaphysical 238; Murdoch's writing 234; Plato 180–181
transformation 6, 92–106; descriptions 216; illegitimate 175; magical 69; of observer 78; of self 42, 61, 67, 93, 95, 97, 103
Travelers 129; *see also* Gypsies
truth 50, 88, 93–100, 196, 199, 213, 219, 222, 232, 238, 239; "Against Dryness" 225, 247; Buddhist 181–182; the Good 214; Hegel, G.F.W. 130; Heidegger, Martin 227, 233; in art 6, 74–78; 82–85, 239–240, 244; Irigaray, Luce 107–108; of marriage 195–200; Nietzsche, Friedrich 194, 196; Peirce, Charles S. 246; psychological 213–214; Sartrean 151, 154–156, 160–162; Smith, Zadie 77; truthfulness 74, 76, 77; *The Unicorn* 63–69
Tuan 27, 142, 185–186
tyrant 23, 142, 185

Under the Net see Sartre, Jean-Paul
Understanding Iris Murdoch 57
The Unicorn 5, 53–73
An Unofficial Rose 47
UNRRA 15
unselfing 7, 8, 163, 169, 174, 179–184, 201, 204, 209, 211; dual nature of 171, 179; Irigaray, Luce 109–111, 118–122, negation of the self 67, 162; suffering as 8, 9, 174–178, 182–184; Weil, Simone 116, 174
utilitarianism 172–173, 246; Bentham, Jeremy 173; punishment 183

Valkyries 95, 96
Vallar, Marcus 31n50

Vernant, Jean-Pierre 45
victim 216–217; Arendt, Hannah 25; Frantz Fanon 144; gratuitous loser 157; Jewish 19–21; sacrificial 100
villain 25, 60, 61, 216–217
virtue 96–101, 174, 178–179, 203–220, 274; Arendt, Hannah 24; ethics of 248; Heidegger, Martin 227; in stories 241; Weil, Simone 246; Williams, Bernard 218–220
vision 1, 2, 40, 42, 97, 176, 222; Nietzschean 190; Platonist 223; *The Unicorn* 59–64; "Vision and Choice in Morality" 203; Weil, Simone 176, 240
visual arts 5–6, 74–91
Vlastos, Gregory 181
voice 23; Irish tinkers 141; male 158; Quentin, Anna 79
vulnerability 4–5, 78, 111, 139, 174, 198

Walker, Barbara 259
Wallenberg, Raoul 32*n*87

Weese, Katherine 195–196
Weil, Simone 10, 39, 158, 162, 222, 228; *Cahiers* 246; suffering 175–178; unselfing 116
Williams, Bernard 217–219
Williams, Tennessee 146*n*38
Williamson, John 72*n*28
wisdom 18, 154, 177, 182, 185, 196; Plato 65; practical 186
Wise Woman 102
Wittgenstein, Ludwig 35, 50, 85, 158, 162–163, 225, 242, 245
Wollstonecraft, Mary 145*n*41
Wood, Garth 229
World War II, influence of 15, 148, 150, 162, 164

Yeats, William Butler 99
Young-Bruehl, Elisabeth 16

Zipes, Jack 106*n*63, 260

www.ingramcontent.com/pod-product-compliance
Lightning Source LLC
Chambersburg PA
CBHW051213300426
44116CB00006B/550